Dorothea Lieven

Dorothea Lieven

A Russian Princess in London and Paris, 1785–1857

JUDITH LISSAUER CROMWELL

McFarland & Company, Inc., Publishers

Jefferson, North Carolina, and London

Library of Congress Cataloguing-in-Publication Data

Cromwell, Judith Lissauer, 1935–
Dorothea Lieven : a Russian princess in London and
Paris, 1785–1857 / Judith Lissauer Cromwell.
    p.   cm.
Includes bibliographical references and index.

ISBN-13: 978-0-7864-2651-5
ISBN-10: 0-7864-2651-9
(softcover : 50# alkaline paper) ∞

1. Lieven, Dorothea, Princess, 1785–1856.
2. Ambassadors' spouses—Russia—Biography.
3. Russia—Foreign relations—Europe.
4. Europe—Foreign relations—Russia.   I. Title.
DK190.6.L5C76   2007   947'.072092—dc22   2006031820
[B]

British Library cataloguing data are available

Cover painting: Lawrence Thomas (1769-1830), *Princess Lieven 1812-1820,*
©Tate Gallery, London/Art Resource, NY

Manufactured in the United States of America

*McFarland & Company, Inc., Publishers
Box 611, Jefferson, North Carolina 28640
www.mcfarlandpub.com*

To the past: My parents, John and Charlotte Lissauer

To the present: My children, John, Wendy, Laura, and Tom

To the future: My grandchildren, Sarah,
Zachary, Annabel, and Theodore

Acknowledgments

Princess Lieven has fascinated me since my undergraduate days at Smith College. But not until I successfully completed a corporate career in the international world of Wall Street could I focus fully on her. During ten years of researching and writing Dorothea Lieven's story, I accumulated a debt of gratitude to many people.

I particularly want to acknowledge those institutions that have generously allowed me to quote from their archives: Bibliotheca Nationalis Hungariae; Broadlands Archive Trust (University of Southampton); Estonian Historical Archives; National Archive (Prague); State Archive of the Russian Federation; The British Library; The National Archives of the UK; University College London, Library Services.

. My especial thanks to those who have kindly let me quote from sources still under copyright: from *The Private Letters of Princess Lieven to Prince Metternich*, Sir Peter Quennell editor and translator, reproduced with permission of Curtis Brown Group Ltd., London, on behalf of the Estate of Peter Quennell, copyright © Peter Quennell 1948, and with permission of Ivor Powell, copyright holder for co-translator Dilys Powell; from *A Selection from the Private Correspondence of the First Duke of Wellington*, edited by the seventh duke, published by kind permission of the Trustees of the Duke of Wellington; from the *Unpublished Diary and Political Sketches of Princess Lieven*, Harold W.V. Temperley, editor and translator, with permission of Professor Neville Temperley. Every possible effort has been made to contact the copyright holder for Lionel G. Robinson, translator and editor of *Letters of Dorothea, Princess Lieven during her Residence in London (1812–1834)* (London: Longmans, Green, 1902).

I appreciate the consideration of those institutions that have let me use items in their holdings as illustrations: Estonian Historical Archives; Hardwick Hall, The Devonshire Collection (The National Trust); Photographic Survey, Courtauld Institute of Art; National Portrait Gallery, London; Slavic and Baltic Division, The New York Public Library; Astor, Lenox and Tilden Foundations; Tate, London, 2005; The Faringdon Collection; The Trustees of the British Museum.

My recognition of their efforts on my behalf goes to librarians at Columbia University; staff at the British Library and librarians in its manuscript reading room; librarians in the Costume Institute at the Metropolitan Museum of Art; the Frick Art Reference Library; the Archives Nationales microfilm reading room; and the New

York Public Library, with especial thanks to Mr. Edward Kasinec and the staff of the Slavic and Baltic Division.

My gratitude to Mme. Catherine Coste for kindly allowing me to quote from the unpublished Guizot-Lieven correspondence; to the late Mr. Lewis Moss and Mrs. Vivian Lissauer Moss for providing a "home away from home" during the many weeks I spent examining fifty-nine volumes of Dorothea Lieven's mostly unpublished letters in the British Library; and to Professor Marc Raeff for his consistent encouragement, as well as his meticulous review of the manuscript. And to my family and friends for their patience, help, and support.

Contents

Key Events in
Dorothea Lieven's Life

1785	December 28, birth of Dorothea Benckendorff.
1789	French Revolution.
1791	Grand Duke Paul banishes Juliana Benckendorff and her daughter Dorothea.
1794	Dorothea and her mother return to Riga.
1796	Accession of Tsar Paul I.
1797	March, death of Dorothea's mother. June, Dorothea enters St. Petersburg's Smolny Convent Institute.
1800	February 24, Dorothea Benckendorff marries Count Christopher Lieven.
1801	March 11, assassination of Tsar Paul I; accession of Tsar Alexander I.
1804	Birth of Marie Lieven.
1805	Napoleon defeats the Austro-Russian army at Austerlitz. Birth of Paul Lieven.
1806	Death of Marie Lieven. Birth of Alexander Lieven.
1807	Napoleon defeats the Russians at Eylau and Friedland. Napoleon and Tsar Alexander I negotiate the Peace of Tilsit. Birth of Constantine Lieven.
1809	December 31, Count Lieven is appointed Minister to Prussia.
1812	Napoleon invades Russia. Count Lieven is appointed ambassador to Great Britain. December 10, the Lievens arrive in England.
1813	The Allies defeat Napoleon at Leipzig.
1814	June, Tsar Alexander visits London.
1814–1815	The Congress of Vienna.
1815	June 18, Battle of Waterloo.

1818   October, Congress of Aix-la-Chapelle. The Lieven-Metternich liaison begins.

1819   October, birth of George Lieven.

1822   August, death of Lord Castlereagh (Londonderry); George Canning becomes foreign secretary.
Autumn, Congress of Verona.

1823   Summer, death of General Christopher Benckendorff.

1825   February, birth of Arthur Lieven.
Summer, Countess Lieven's diplomatic mission to St. Petersburg.
November, death of Tsar Alexander I.
December, Tsar Nicholas I ascends the throne.

1826   April 4, St. Petersburg Protocol.

1827   July 6, Treaty of London.
August, death of George Canning.

1828   January, the Duke of Wellington becomes prime minister.
April, Russo-Turkish War breaks out.
September, death of General Constantine Benckendorff.

1829   September 14, Treaty of Adrianople ends the Russo-Turkish War and guarantees an independent Greece.

1830   July, revolution in France.
September, revolution in Belgium.
November, Lord Grey becomes prime minister.
December, revolution in Poland.

1834   May 20, Tsar Nicholas I recalls Prince Lieven.

1835   March, death of George Lieven.
April, death of Arthur Lieven.
October, Princess Lieven arrives in Paris.

1837   June 15, beginning of Dorothea Lieven and François Guizot's liaison.

1838   June, death of Constantine Lieven.

1839   January 10, death of Prince Christopher Lieven.

1840   August 30, Dorothea Lieven and François Guizot's "union" ceremony.
October 29, Guizot becomes foreign minister and de facto prime minister.

1845   October, death of General Count Alexander Benckendorff.

1848   February, revolution in France.

1854   March 28, Crimean War.

1856   March, Peace of Paris.

1857   January 26, death of Dorothea Lieven.

PART I

Russia, 1785–1812

Prologue

Born in 1785, into an exhilarating world of power and privilege at Riga, capital of the Russian Empire's Baltic provinces, Dorothea Lieven evolved from an unfulfilled young wife into a lover, confidante, and independent stateswoman operating in Europe's aristocratic socio-political milieu during a spectacular period in Western history.

"A tall, thin, erect woman who, although she did not lack lovers, never had any remarkable beauty," Dorothea "produced the effect of it, and one easily overlooked the details, because they resulted in their whole in such charm, and incomparable attraction."[1] Beneath "falsity as well as pettiness—genuine to the point of naiveté for the things that happened to her personally—which earned her the reproach of egoism, due up to a certain point," hers meant merely "surface egoism, which did not disturb her good nature and her loyal and true friendships."[2] A devoted mother, dutiful wife—in her fashion—a "person of the greatest intelligence and of a noble and upright character,"[3] Princess Lieven also commanded universal respect for her political authority.

"I am a woman and very much of a woman. I want things passionately and I believe them readily."[4] Married at age fourteen, Dorothea longed to play a prominent part in the exciting political events swirling about her. Her husband's appointment as ambassador to politically vibrant England gave his brilliant, magnetic wife a chance to satisfy her burning ambition. In 1825 Tsar Alexander I entrusted Dorothea with a crucial but secret diplomatic overture to the British government. This coup initiated her participation in a series of dramatic events that culminated in the birth of modern Greece. Dorothea Lieven's subsequent influence in the creation of Belgium established her status.

She "succeeded in inspiring a confidence" with prominent men "until now unknown in the annals of England,"[5] the circumspect Russian foreign minister enthused. Princess Lieven enchanted men's hearts and engaged their political thinking. Her friendships with them opened avenues of power. Dorothea's devotees included monarchs—Great Britain's George IV—and ministers of state—Metternich, Wellington, Canning, Nesselrode, Talleyrand, and Guizot. She exerted authority in the diplomatic councils of Great Britain, France, and Russia. And a mesmerizing blend of passion and political machination marked her love affairs with Metternich and Guizot.

By the time she reached middle age, Dorothea Lieven stood at the apogee of power, only to lose everything. After suffering agonizing tragedy, to say nothing of waging a severe struggle to resolve the central conflict in her life—to achieve a satisfying combination of passion and politics—Princess Lieven then succeeded in reinventing herself. She died peacefully in 1857, at her home in Paris.

"She is a stateswoman and a great lady in all the vicissitudes of life."[6] Throughout history women have wielded power through their husbands and lovers, as the princess did during her remarkable career. But only Dorothea Lieven created a position for herself as an independent diplomat within nineteenth century Europe's extremely select political fraternity.

"Oh yes! Wasn't she the one who tarted her way around Europe?" my English historian friend asked with a knowing smile, when I told him I planned to write a biography of Princess Lieven. Posterity has trivialized, defamed, discounted, derided, and damned Dorothea Lieven with faint praise, let alone largely ignored her profoundly stirring personal story. Now is the time to do justice to this complex woman.

1

From Riga to St. Petersburg

> She did all that she did, she became all that she was, while staying what
> her birth and her family made her, while pursuing with regular step the
> path she had entered in her youth.[1]
> —François Guizot, Dorothea's third great love

On a frigid February day, in St. Petersburg's Imperial Winter Palace, a man and
a young girl stood before the Lutheran pastor and solemnly exchanged their marriage vows. Tall, slender, proudly erect, always distinguished but never beautiful, the
bride had large, dark eyes sparkling with vitality and incomparable charisma. Miss
Dorothea de Benckendorff, now Countess Lieven, was fourteen years old.

&0C&

Her world began in the Russian capital, the magnificent westward-facing city of
startling contrasts between riches and poverty, comfort and filth, plenty and hunger
that, less than one hundred years before Dorothea's marriage, Tsar Peter the Great
had forced onto the dreary Baltic marshes surrounding the Gulf of Finland.
Approaching St. Petersburg from the open sea, one's eye met an infinite vista of
steadily sinking flat and colorless countryside, a low, sultry land strewn with skimpy
birch trees.

Majestic, gilded, the white and green Winter Palace dominated the city center.
Its riches, gems, and treasures rivaled "the fancied contents of those described in the
Arabian Nights."[2] Empress Catherine II enlarged the palace to house Peter the Great's
fabulous collection of paintings and precious objects, not to mention her own outstanding acquisitions. Massive crystal chandeliers lit the succession of huge formal
rooms, each opening into the next, each embellished with grand marble columns and
elegantly furnished with the finest imported furniture; magnificent malachite, lapis
lazuli, and rhodonite vases, jars, and consoles; carved and inlaid chests; porphyry
and gilded bronze candelabra; parquet floors intricately inlaid with rare woods; and
doors and tables inlaid with tortoiseshell, semi-precious stones, and colored marbles
all either imported from Europe or exquisitely created in Russia by native craftsmen
trained in the West.

Romanov rulers meant this splendid profusion to overwhelm, to impress both
Russians and Westerners with the empire's refinement, riches, and power. On the

empress's birthday Peterhof, the summer palace, showed "all its magic splendor." The sparkling cobalt sea, hundreds of graceful fountains and waterfalls, fine black pine trees, and the "ancient gilded palace crowning the slopes—all this, and the brilliant Court, truly makes a most resplendent show."[3] In the evening Peterhof's gardens glowed with two hundred thousand colored lamps tended by two thousand menservants.

Nonetheless, abysmal sewage, rotting garbage, and the main means of transport—horses—let alone the regrettable fact that most Russian houses lacked indoor plumbing, made the streets of St. Petersburg stink. Summer heat intensified the penetrating reek. And when winter's accumulated filth and two-foot-thick ice began to thaw, "immense holes, which threaten to upset the carriage every moment,"[4] filled the streets.

Each noble house kept servants, but usually clad in shabby liveries. Grand palaces stood next to grungy shops offering shoddy goods. The city's "general appearance of dirt and untidiness" distressed "an eye accustomed to English neatness and cleanliness."[5]

And the climate! During the interminable winter, temperatures often fell further than sixty degrees below zero. This intense cold mixed with the extreme humidity of the marshes to freeze one's breath. "At the end of May, when the days are so long (it is quite light till past 10 o'clock P.M.) and the sun is powerful, one does look for something more genial than frost and snow, particularly after having had them uninterruptedly for seven months!"[6] Dorothea Lieven judged October the cruelest month for although hardly any yellow showed among the green leaves, deep snow covered the ground.

Summer's stifling heat combined with the swampy damp and lack of basic sanitation to breed disease. Typhoid fever and cholera vied for the most victims; not even the wealthy proved immune to influenza.

On Dorothea's wedding-day a bone chilling cold gripped St. Petersburg, but inside warmth prevailed (at least for the wealthy) thanks to double doors and plenty of cheap firewood. In a corner of every room stood a tiled, floor-to-ceiling stove "constructed upon a system which so thoroughly condenses the heat, that it is sufficient to make up a good fire once in the day constantly to maintain a very high temperature."[7] But Dorothea thought, not without reason, that the excessive indoor heat added yet another unhealthy element to St. Petersburg's atmosphere.

The entire Russian empire, stretching from Poland to the Pacific, revolved around this city, at once so beautiful and so harsh. At its core stood the magnificent court of the Romanovs, the nucleus of tsarist might. That court nurtured the future Princess Lieven.

ഇൡ

Somewhat to St. Petersburg's southwest a Teutonic crusader castle sits squarely on the Daugava river bank a few miles inland from the cold, gray Baltic Sea. The castle guards the rich old city of Riga and the river route into the Russian heartland. Today Riga castle's warm-tiled roofs, circular white tower, and yellow walls house the official residence of independent Latvia's president; in the eighteenth century the castle served as official residence for Riga's military governor.[8]

General Christopher von Benckendorff brought his bride Juliana[9] to Riga castle in 1780; and within a few years their two sons and two daughters frolicked on its flat, green lawns. The eldest, Alexander, would become the influential chief of his tsar's dreaded secret police. The older girl and third child, Dorothea, born at Riga Castle[10] on December 28, 1785, would play a brilliant part in the Great World of entrenched power and privilege, the world that Riga castle embodied. She evolved into the confidante and lover of Europe's most distinguished statesmen, the only female admitted into the cosmopolitan fraternity of monarchs and ministers who strutted so self-assuredly across the world[11] stage during the eventful decades following the Congress of Vienna (1815).

ಖಿಲ

The future Princess Lieven inherited her flair for politics, to say nothing of a potentially powerful position, from her mother. Baroness Juliana Schilling von Cannstadt, daughter of ancient south German nobility, grew up at the urbane court of Württemberg's Grand Duchy. Small, snug, and tastefully set in beautiful pleasure gardens, it had the added distinction of breathing the heady air of Europe's great intellectual movement, the Enlightenment. Baroness Schilling stood as best friend and lady-in-waiting to young Princess Dorothea Sophia of Württemberg who in 1776 went to Russia to marry the tsarevitch, Grand Duke Paul. Her parents chose Juliana Schilling to help their politically naive daughter make a difficult transition: from her benign, cultured home to the grandiose hub of Romanov power where treacherous courtiers routinely hatched vicious political intrigues. Extremely discreet, Baroness Schilling had keen powers of observation. She showed her young friend, now baptized Maria in the Russian Orthodox faith, how to navigate the shark-infested waters of her new home.

As senior lady-in-waiting to Grand Duchess Maria, Baroness Schilling mingled with the elite group of officers surrounding the tsarevitch. One in particular caught her fancy and she, his.

Christopher von Benckendorff belonged to a small but potent and unique nobility.[12] Descended from German crusading knights who had marched north to Christianize and colonize the fertile, densely forested country bordering the choppy Baltic, these proud nobles prospered.[13] And despite centuries of conquest the close-knit Baltic Barons clung tenaciously to their German culture and Lutheran religion, to their right to self-government and their own administration. When Peter the Great wrested the rich, well run Baltic provinces from Sweden, he, too, let the Baltic Germans keep their privileges. In return, the conservative, disciplined barons served the Romanov dynasty with fervent loyalty. True to her typically Teutonic heritage Dorothea von Benckendorff, as well, had the essence of politics—the judicious exchange of favors—in her genes.

Like his forbears, Dorothea's father joined the army; like them he distinguished himself. Popular and respected, he rose to the rank of general and adjutant to the Tsarevitch Paul. Empress Catherine liked Christopher Benckendorff; she remembered his mother—her favorite lady-in-waiting. Catherine appointed Christopher military governor of Riga.

"Goodbye dear angel, I embrace you I re-embrace you and I love you more than my life,"[14] Juliana later wrote her husband. These unusually tender words indicate a love marriage, one that would have affected their daughter Dorothea's expectations.

Christopher's marriage infuriated the Empress Catherine. Marriages among the nobility were almost always made for convenience and Catherine may well have had another match in mind for Benckendorff. As long as Empress Catherine lived, Christopher Benckendorff prudently avoided court.

Unwilling to surrender her privileged position as the Grand Duchess Maria's intimate, however, the politically adept and ambitious Juliana spent several months of every year at court. Not only that, she began to groom her promising daughter Dorothea for a place in the Great World of power and privilege by bringing the child with her to St. Petersburg.

As the little girl did morning lessons with her governess, Juliana burst into their quiet, airy room. Visibly upset, Dorothea's mother ordered the governess to pack at once. Tomorrow they must leave St. Petersburg. Grand Duke Paul had intercepted a letter from his wife to Juliana. Dorothea's unpublished memoirs reveal that the letter centered on Maria and Paul's rocky marital relations. (He had fallen under the spell of another woman which, not unnaturally, caused bitter quarrels between the royal couple.) Empress Catherine advised her son to ignore the letter but Paul, "who had never even considered a lackey without the Empress's permission now, committed a most illegal and arbitrary act. He banished not only from the Court but also from the capital two important people of the first rank."[15]

Dorothea was six years old. She and her mother did not return to Riga, nor were they sent to Siberia or any other punishing place in Russia; their banishment extended to all of the empire. Luckily, Juliana Benckendorff had kept up her close connections with several German courts; she chose to spend her exile with the King of Württemberg at Stuttgart.

How "his little Dorothea" missed her doting father. And even if she quarreled with her brothers and sister, as siblings do, she missed them as well—her ambitious brothers still in Riga with their tutor under General Benckendorff's watchful eye until they were old enough to board at Russia's premier military academy: Alexander, often bossy and later censorious but always Dorothea's protective big brother and Constantine, closest to her in age and interests. Indeed, she had a strong bond with both brothers, in childhood constant playmates, later sharing her appetite for politics. And Dorothea's sweet younger sister Marie, always a kind friend despite their having little in common, also stayed at Riga.

Juliana Benckendorff and her daughter Dorothea lived as exiles for a formative part of the child's life—age six to nine. This shared experience forged a close bond between them, made Dorothea feel extra special, gave her confidence.

And her residence at a prominent court strengthened Dorothea's sense of her place in the Great World. Conscientious and very bright, she had lessons with an older child, the Württemberg princess, and became "familiar with using the French language,"[16] the "language in which I first learned to talk, but now I mastered much more of it."[17] Several French émigrés enlivened the Württemberg court. Enchanting young Dorothea inspired one to compose a play in which she played the leading role.

Dorothea and her mother had already returned to Riga when, as the sun rose on November 10, 1796, a government courier galloped into the castle courtyard. Before dismounting from his sweating horse, he demanded to see General Benckendorff. Empress Catherine had died on the 6th. Tsar Paul I reigned. He "confirmed [Dorothea's] father as governor-general of the Baltic provinces and invited him to

Petersburg to pay his respects, an act of great honor accompanied by a gift of 3000 peasants in one of the Empire's richest provinces. This is how the Tsar redeemed the sanction of the Grand Duke."[18]

ༀ

The previous summer Juliana Benckendorff had taken her daughters with her to Reval,[19] a Baltic seaside resort. Captive of his military duties, Dorothea's adoring father suggested that she keep a journal. Its closely written pages disclose that rather than consigning Dorothea and her sister Marie completely to the care of governesses, Juliana personally groomed them for their future role as courtiers by including them in her social life. And when their mother dined with the governor the girls went to a party afterwards, with "lots of people, games and dancing."[20]

Juliana hoped Reval's invigorating sea air and salt water baths would relieve her rheumatism. When her right arm gave particular pain, she relied on the gifted daughter who had shared her exile. Nine-year-old Dorothea strove to live up to her mother's expectations; her best formal hand-writing spared Juliana the need to answer each of her many letters. And in this way Juliana passed on worldly knowledge: how to manage among the high and mighty, the importance of observing, of providing pertinent information. Dorothea did that with particular pleasure for the first man in her life: "my dear Papa."

Two years later Juliana fell

First letters—"My dear Papa, I did my lesson very well. I embrace you. Dacha"; and "I greet you most respectfully my dear Papa & I affirm to you that I love you, and that I want to see you soon, I am sending you some games to amuse you, think of me, and always love your little Dorothea." Courtesy of the Estonian Historical Archives.

gravely ill. Suddenly, "she had ten or twelve bowel movements with black and twisted blood clots in her stools, her pulse fell." Either her womb had ruptured or a blood vessel had hemorrhaged, her doctor reported to the Empress Maria. "Afflicted to the bottom of my soul, if God takes her from this world I would lose the friend of my childhood, the most worthy of women," lamented Maria. "She loves me as her child, and on my side also, how attached I am to her."[21]

Juliana Benckendorff died with "serenity, and showing exemplary resignation."[22] Dorothea was eleven years old.

In stark contrast to clearly expressed grief over her father's death some twenty-five years later, Dorothea wrote nothing about her first traumatic loss. The young girl's anguish over such a terrible shock as her mother's death struck too deep, her feelings were too strong to articulate, her emotions then and for ever after too raw to expose. "There are some names I can never say, not even write.... I bottle up all that," Dorothea confessed many years after. "I fear myself, the sound of my voice."[23]

Immensely upset at her friend's death, Empress Maria instantly wrote Dorothea. "She would adopt my sister and me as her children."[24] Feeling so bereft, and at such a vulnerable age, too, Dorothea gratefully grasped at this mother substitute, this protector. She saw Maria's guardianship as her mother's bequest, another facet of maternal care. The young girl loved Maria "as a child loves a tender mother." Indeed, all her life Dorothea spoke of how much she owed the tsaritsa, of "the motherly kindness with which she treated me," and "of the relations of extreme intimacy that existed between us."[25]

Besides surrogate maternal love, Juliana Benckendorff's legacy left her talented daughter a potentially powerful political position, a particular proximity to the Imperial family, to the empress, to her husband the tsar, to their sons—future tsars, and daughters—future consorts at Continental courts. "I am the only lady in the Empire who can be counted as living in close association with the Tsar and Tsaritsa. I belong to the family."[26]

This grieving young girl craved maternal love; she also burned with ambition. A girl as perceptive as Dorothea, a girl who already had some familiarity with courts, knew that if she wanted to shine in the world—among the brilliant aristocrats who ruled the drawing-rooms and directed the destinies of Europe—she could only do so through a close connection at the tsarist court. Hence, Dorothea transferred daughterly devotion from mother to empress.

୫୨୦୧୫

Rather than have his daughters continue their education at home, General Benckendorff now consented to the tsaritsa placing them in the exclusive Smolny Convent Institute. So shortly after Juliana's death, one of her friends brought Dorothea and her sister to St. Petersburg.

The palatial blue-and-white Smolny Convent complex, nestled in a bend of the broad Neva river, is still one of St. Petersburg's most impressive sights. Commissioned by Peter the Great's daughter, who in early life wanted to become a nun, the buildings look, from the outside, much as they did when Dorothea de Benckendorff boarded there as a special status student. The magnificent baroque Cathedral of the Resurrection dominates the center; two-story buildings surround it. Trees, shrubs, and brightly-colored flowers abound.

Empress Catherine converted Smolny from a convent into Russia's first government-sponsored school for noble girls. She wanted a generation of cultured females to enhance Russian society, and engaged Western Europe's finest teachers to instruct them.

Three hundred girls attended Smolny; five- to nine-year-olds were in the brown class; nine to fourteen in the blue; fourteen to sixteen in the white. Every class had one head teacher; four others each supervised twenty-five pupils. The three classes had their own study rooms and dining-rooms; the girls occupied four dormitories each with twenty-five beds. The teacher-in-charge slept in a separate room, but kept a weather eye on her pupils by leaving open her door to the dormitory. As the empress's foster children, Dorothea and her sister (together with their governess) lived in their own apartment where the girls also had their lessons—

Пис. Ritt — Peint par Ritt

Императрица Марія Ѳеодоровна, | L'Impératrice Marie Féodorowna,
1759-1828 | *1759-1828*

Empress Maria Federovna. Born Princess Dorothea Sophia of Württemberg, she married Grand Duke Paul, later Tsar Paul I. The best friend of Dorothea Lieven's mother, on the early death of her friend the empress adopted Dorothea. Artist: Augustin Ritt. Used by permission of the Slavic and Baltic Division, The New York Public Library, Astor, Lenox and Tilden Foundations.

four hours of study in the morning and four in the evening that focused on European (French and German) culture. They dined with the headmistress, and only came in contact with the other students during dancing classes. Empress Maria visited every week. "She reviewed all our notebooks and heard reports from all our teachers, she entered into the smallest intrinsic details; a mother could not have done better."[27]

During her three years at Smolny Dorothea improved her French, German, and Russian; as well, she studied history, geography, geometry, logic, physics, music, drawing, and dancing. This diligent girl showed an outstanding mind. "Finesse, grace, and the flexibility one only finds among women" tempered "male intelligence, serious and logical which one rarely finds in a woman."[28]

Smolny taught Dorothea how to carry herself with grace and to become familiar with the formalities and intricacies of court etiquette, so that by the time she reached young womanhood her natural dignity and distinguished manners were an integral part of Dorothea's make-up. She learned to play the piano exquisitely. "It goes fairly well with the music,"[29] eight-year-old Dorothea had written her father. She promised to practice, particularly the marches he sent her because, Dorothea lovingly flattered, since practicing "gives you pleasure that motive must be one for me to follow."[30]

At Smolny, Dorothea now discovered in herself an abiding passion for music. "How it intoxicates me! How it pleases me ... I listen to it, I feel it."[31]

Dorothea learned to converse, and began to develop this valuable skill into a fine art. She spoke "with vivacity, an almost epigrammatic precision, without the affectation of an epigram, in concise and clear language, brief and succinct; but at the same time easy, gracious, pungent—sometimes light-hearted, always proper—always the right word."[32] And not only speaking. Dorothea soon discerned that someone who felt understood would be sympathetic towards the person who understood him. She cultivated the ability to listen.

Conversation and letter-writing were the major communications media of the day. During her terminal illness it was to Dorothea that Juliana Benckendorff dictated her letters to the empress, thus continuing, up to the end, to pass on to her gifted daughter the political skills necessary for survival at court. Attached to her mother, identifying with her, determined to meet her mother's expectations, Dorothea took Juliana's lessons to heart. "My mother had a very pleasant and easy style. I formed mine on this first model."[33]

Later, one book continually nourished Dorothea: the *Letters of Madame de Sévigné*.[34] She read it repeatedly.

> To the constant study of these unrivaled letters she was no doubt considerably indebted for her own epistolary eminence, and for her admirable style of writing. Dorothea's letters lacked "the variety, the abundance ... the *abandon* of the great Frenchwoman but she was more terse and epigrammatic, and she had the same graphic power and faculty of conveying much matter in few words."[35]

෩෨

At age thirteen Dorothea decided it was high time to leave Smolny and make her debut at court. Her father and foster-mother dashed that design. Empress Maria asked General Benckendorff to explain that success in the world depended, for his ambitious daughter, on a constant mentor, a mother to guide her. Sadly, Dorothea's mother had died, so she had best stay at Smolny and apply herself to her studies. But as a special favor, every two weeks during the winter season the empress sent a luxuriously appointed carriage to bring the Benckendorff sisters to a performance at the tsar's private Hermitage theater. This gave Dorothea a chance to get used to the court circle before making her debut.

Besides this small victory Dorothea took comfort in another compensation.

While still living with her parents at Riga, she had attracted an admirer. Urbane Count Eugene Elmpt, temporarily banished from his prestigious court position for striking a member of the imperial family, took refuge in the city of his birth. Elmpt met the governor's elder daughter at one of those social occasions that her mother deemed appropriate. Dorothea's ebullient charm and expressive dark eyes at once enraptured the dashing count. "There is no real feeling at age eleven but I did not think so and I was in love with love. On his side there was no doubt." Elmpt's assiduous attention to her sexually charismatic daughter "did not displease my mother, and in spite of my young age she let me attach myself to" him; indeed, "in the hours before her death she sent for Count Eugene" and "from her bed blessed us."[36]

General Benckendorff did not share his wife's opinion, which could well have prompted his readiness to send his daughter to boarding school after her mother's death.

Nonetheless a clandestine correspondence, carried on with the connivance of Dorothea's governess, kept the relationship from dying a natural death. And adolescent rebellion, absence, and "a life with little amusement in it and then only occasionally, ended in inspiring in me something that resembled love for Count Elmpt."[37]

Dorothea had been at Smolny for some months when Tsaritsa Maria , whose numerous progeny had doubtless endowed her with extra keen maternal intuition, descended on her ward's room "like a whirlwind and demanded that my governess give her the letters I received from Count Eugene."[38] Then two police dragoons deposited the hapless governess across the frontier.

That evening the tsaritsa sent a carriage to Smolny, but not to convey Miss Benckendorff to the Hermitage theater. The carriage drew up in front of the Winter Palace; a solemn major-domo ushered an apprehensive girl into Empress Maria's delicately appointed white and gold private sitting-room. Ordered to stand under the sparkling crystal chandelier, Dorothea faced the insistent questioning of her furious foster-mother. "I told all, the Empress interrupted often, especially when I expressed how my mother had favored Count Elmpt. Regrettably my father did not like him, besides he was not there to listen to the accuracy of my feelings."[39] Elmpt's secret correspondence with such a young girl certainly validated General Benckendorff's judgment. And the empress, thinking her ward could do better for herself, ordered Dorothea to forget Elmpt. An extremely strict governess took over. She immediately deprived Dorothea "of all means of communication; I went on crying; but, as nobody took any notice of me, I recovered."[40]

⁸⓪⓷

In Dorothea's day aristocratic girls rarely married for love. Arranged marriages, especially in Russia, served a family's economic, political, or social interests. Youth was essential. Russian nobles judged an unmarried eighteen-year-old as practically beyond prayers. So it scarcely came as a surprise that shortly after the Elmpt episode, the tsaritsa sought a suitable match for her lively, sexually magnetic thirteen-year-old ward.

After what would have been a disastrous choice had not fate intervened,[41] Empress Maria's eye fell on the scion of a prominent Baltic Baron family that traced its roots to those Knights. Teutonic Knights who had colonized the Baltic provinces in the tenth century and who, in the eighteenth, furnished the Tsar's army with several distinguished officers. Still, Count Christopher Andreievitch Lieven owed his advancement to his mother.

Born into an old Baltic Baron family, widow of an artillery general, simple and unpretentious, Charlotte Lieven lived unassumingly in Riga with her children until an emissary from court utterly surprised her. Empress Catherine sought a modest, worthy Baltic German to fill the prestigious position of governess[42] to Tsarevitch Paul's younger children.

Sincerely religious and strictly moral, Baroness Lieven strongly disapproved of the rampant licentiousness that had the dubious distinction of characterizing Catherine's court; she shrank from involving herself, much less her children, in Catherine's way of life. But the empress's personal assurance that the baroness need see nothing of that life-style, let alone the chance to further her children's interests, convinced Charlotte Lieven to accept Catherine's offer.

Baroness Lieven lavished affection on her charges who, in turn, treasured her. She became a trusted friend of both their grandmother Catherine, and their mother Maria. Russia's rulers showered Charlotte Lieven with honors and riches, mostly in the form of valuable estates which her sons eventually inherited.

The second son, Christopher, came into the world twelve years before his intended bride. Above average height, slim, with curly dark hair framing a handsome face that featured a straight nose, deep blue eyes set under thick brows, and a dimpled chin, Lieven, in Sir Thomas Lawrence's portrait, looks at the world with a pleasantly proud expression. Dignified, with polished but cold manners and little, if any, sense of humor, Lieven spoke briefly but to the point. Straight-laced like his mother, a typical Baltic Baron, conscientious, diligent, and loyal, Lieven performed his courtly duties to perfection. Later a capable, but hardly what one could call a brilliant, diplomat, his average intelligence paled in comparison to his wife's superior talents.

At age fifteen Lieven followed his late father into the tsar's artillery. After he had seen active service the Empress Catherine, doubtless due to Charlotte Lieven's forceful efforts, chose the young officer to escort the Comte d'Artois, France's future King Charles X, to London. There Lieven spent a valuable year before crossing the Channel to enhance his military experience in Austria's army, then fighting against France. Christopher Lieven subsequently wended his way back to St. Petersburg.

Having re-joined his regiment to take part in Russia's expedition against Persia, Lieven, despite any conspicuous military ability, became a lieutenant-colonel. His mother's untiring labors as surely caused that promotion as they caused Tsar Paul to appoint Lieven his aide-de-camp, one year later at age twenty-four a major general, and then his minister of war. Custom now demanded that this eligible young man marry.

During the summer of Dorothea's last year at Smolny, Empress Maria arranged that her ward meet Count Lieven. At the same time Dorothea made her longed-for debut. She was formally presented to Tsar Paul I, and appointed lady-of-honor to the empress with an annual allowance of two thousand rubles.[43]

"There is no real feeling at age eleven," Dorothea had claimed in recording the Elmpt episode. Now she felt a strong sexual attraction for Lieven, and fell in love with the idea of being married. Concomitantly, Dorothea recognized her mental superiority. About to make the most important decision in her life, this young girl, barely three years before bereft of the guidance and protection that only a mother can give, now sought a substitute. A husband. No matter how fond, Dorothea's father had his duties in far off Riga; no matter how caring, the empress had other responsibilities. Nonetheless, Dorothea did confide her qualms to Maria, who found her ward's words "not precise enough."[44]★

"You tell me you have an inclination for Monsieur de Lieven, that he pleased you the first time you saw him but ... before determining your choice," your happiness demands that "the person whose fate it would be to guide you should know the World."[45] This last phrase, not unnaturally, somewhat confused the empress.

How difficult for Dorothea to know the world at age fourteen,

> difficult to find oneself there because with an honest and truly pure heart one is still capable of much imprudence. If God had deigned to preserve your mother, she would have been your guide and directed your choice, but without this pleasure I ask you, dear Dascha,[46] if you have enough wisdom ... [to] decide your choice for yourself and ability to distinguish in the World's turmoil a loyal and true man who would suit you and make you happy.
>
> I do not think this to be the case, my dear Dascha. To put your heart to this very test could be dangerous.... Reflect then and tell me in clear and definite terms if you wish to accept Monsieur de Lieven's hand? Or if you do not want him?
>
> All I wish to tell you about him is that he seems to be very sensible, reasonable, he is discreet and he has the great quality of being a good son which guarantees that he will be a good husband. I ask you for a reply without any ambiguity. Goodbye my child.[47]

In Dorothea's day marriage constituted the only possible career for a noblewoman. Marriage conferred status. Marriage offered a chance to exert influence through one's husband. Marriage meant a modicum of freedom from the social constraints girdling single females. And an ambitious woman, especially one determined to play a part in the world, must marry suitably. Worldly wise Maria had advised her adolescent ward to think with her head as well as with her heart. Christopher Lieven may not have embodied Dorothea's romantic ideal but he definitely qualified as suitable. In this first major manifestation of the strong practical streak permeating her character, Dorothea decided to cast aside her misgivings, and to follow her foster-mother's advice. She convinced herself that she could, even that she did, love Lieven or at least what he represented for her. Basically, however, Dorothea made a marriage of convenience.

৪৩৫৪

All the gilded youth and beauty of St. Petersburg gathered at a glittering ball held in the regal splendor of the Imperial Winter Palace. Dorothea eagerly anticipated this, her first court soirée. The empress patronized the Paris mode so her intensely fashion-conscious ward rejoiced at Maria's selecting the latest style, a high-waisted ball gown of sheer pastel muslin worn over a matching satin slip. The slim skirt and modestly square-cut bodice embroidered with silk flowers in a darker shade, short sleeves of patterned gauze, and three-quarter-length train showed Dorothea's willowy figure to advantage.

As the orchestra played dance music lately imported from France, Dorothea acquitted herself with charm and grace although her sober fiancé made an awkward, if punctilious, partner. Bubbling over with excitement about being at court, elated at the idea of being married, even intoxicated with the power of her own allure, the

★*Regrettably, this letter does not survive.*

vivacious bride-to-be, lacking a mother to curb her youthful exuberance, flirted with some handsome young men. Shocked, Lieven suggested Dorothea sit with his mother among the dowagers who cast the cloak of their chaperonage over the gaily swirling dancers. Dorothea refused.

"I do not want to reproach you any more for your indelicate conduct towards me, nor to complain of the torment you caused me, all that would be useless. But my honor dictates my speaking to you frankly," wrote Lieven, once his inamorata had been safely confined to her convent. Recently so happy, so much looking forward to his marriage, Lieven, alas, saw

> all my hope, all my joy change into black sorrow. The moment you appeared at Court animatedly, brilliantly you forgot, you humiliated at the same time a man entirely devoted to you, with only your happiness in view. You have found in this world many men preferable to me, who match you better: that does not surprise me! I have many faults and would not be suitable for a woman devoted to the great World; my position and my nature dictate my leading a retired life and when you said you cannot renounce the great World, I saw that our union, in many respects, would absolutely cause us misery.[48]

"I no longer love him," Dorothea told her schoolmates. One of them informed Lieven that Dorothea vowed "never to stop flirting," that "she only is marrying you to get away from the convent, and if she had known the Empress did not intend to leave her there, would not have wanted you." She "also made fun of your not writing to her anymore, and if Mme. P.[49] ordered her to write to you, she would do so as if to an enemy."[50]

Lieven always paid exaggerated heed to what people said. Still, his attention to this gratuitous account of an immature outburst (he quoted it to Dorothea) showed a singular lack of subtlety in a supposedly mature officer and experienced courtier. Indeed, he never completely understood his clever, captivating Dorothea although he did recognize—and soon came to resent—her talents. Until his dying day that realization made him the more determined doggedly, but usually quite ineffectually, to exert over his lively spouse the moral authority that traditionally belonged to a husband. She continued to flirt—and much more—all her life, and she certainly played an exceptional part in the Great World.

Flirting, however, did not necessarily represent the best way for a debutante to make her mark on the world. Although Maria cast a maternal mantle over Dorothea, this spat would not do for the empress's ears. So Dorothea's caring father asked the Smolny headmistress to explain a wife's duties to Dorothea, to show the defiant adolescent that she was wrong; and the headmistress tactfully asked Lieven to excuse his fiancée's youthful vivacity. Not for nothing did fourteen-year-old Dorothea descend from a distinguished military family; she beat a strategic retreat. "After the gravest reflection" she asked Lieven "to look at me not as most recently," but to "see me as that Dorothea you loved," ready "to sacrifice her life for your happiness, to prove her love, make you forget her faults. I need not tell you how impatiently I await your reply."[51]

This episode marked the first, but far from the last, time Dorothea quailed before Lieven's jealous temper. She suffered from it—in all fairness she often provoked it—all his life. Now, his reply made Dorothea very happy, "very ready at once to do everything to erase the damaging impression I made.... Be from now on the guide of my conduct, I swear to follow all your advice. I will submit to everything you explain to me."[52] Note the word "submit." It would create friction between brilliant, lively Dorothea and mundane, serious Lieven until his death ended their marriage, and would inform Dorothea's relationship with the man of her choice until her death.

General Benckendorff promised to come to the capital for his best-loved child's wedding and, meanwhile, gave her a generous dowry.

> I am deprived for some time of news from you, my dear Papa, and I assure you this worries me; I suppose you already have my last letter where I told you about the resumption of my marriage the day of which is not yet firm although I think I can assure you it will be at the start of next month.[53]

Dorothea had seen neither the empress nor Lieven for some days because the "little curse who reigns at our place stops anyone from Court from coming to our Convent but she does not bother me in the least. I am asking dear Lieven to forward this letter, he gives me his news regularly and you can imagine the joy this brings me." From now on Dorothea would focus on making Lieven happy. "He deserves to be because of all his good qualities the one I appreciate the most is the affection he has for you." Bestowing her special blend of love and flattery on the first man in her life as she would on all the others, Dorothea thought that seemed "natural to me for to know you is to love you; there could be nothing better my good dear Papa your daughter loves you always."[54]

ଚ୍ଚଠଔ

The nineteenth century had barely begun when Dorothea de Benckendorff took the most significant step of her life. On February 24, 1800,

> How joyfully I left my convent.... [How] delighted I was with my beautiful clothes, how well my wedding dress suited me. How pleased I was with my success when the Empress put some of her diamonds on me and took me in to the Emperor Paul and he led me into his drawing room to show me to his Court! I should have liked to get married every day, and I thought about everything except that I was taking a husband.[55]

2

The Romanov Court

I was fifteen years old, with a happy disposition, loving episodes, and viewing any catastrophe very lightly, so long as it made a change in the routine of the town.[1]

—Dorothea Lieven

Dorothea delighted in marriage. Her first love satisfied his sensual young bride physically and emotionally, if not mentally. "You know my husband (I give him this name with such pleasure!)," she burbled to her beloved elder brother Alexander soon after her wedding, "so you must know how much I love him, how happy I am."[2] Dorothea could not begin to describe her bliss, her profuse love. And her enhanced status at the imperial court elated the young countess.

Slender and above average height, the adolescent bride carried herself with the dignity she had inherited from her mother and enhanced under Smolny Convent's skilled tutelage. Distinguished rather than beautiful, Dorothea had a pointed nose, large ears, and long slender neck. A mass of dark curls framed her face with its decided chin, full and firm-lipped, sensual mouth, and large, dark gray eyes sparkling with vitality. Sir Thomas Lawrence painted her with a distinctly challenging expression.

The newly-weds had an apartment in one of the military buildings that lined the cobblestone street next to the Imperial Winter Palace, and overlooking the wide Neva river. Having gratefully shed Smolny's boring uniform, Dorothea now arrayed herself in the latest Paris mode. In glacial winter she wrapped herself in a three-quarter-length, thick, fur-trimmed pelisse, firmly settled a matching hat decorated with curled upstanding feathers over her head and ears, and buried her hands in an enormous muff. With her day dress of scallop-edged silk trimmed at the hem with appliquéd satin, silver sequins, and chenille, she wore a richly embroidered cashmere shawl that Russian fashion decreed must be three times as long as its wearer; Dorothea twisted one end of this chic accessory around her arm for drapery, while the other end fell in graceful folds to the ground; an embroidered velvet reticule and silk snood fastened at the front with a large bow completed this stylish toilette. In summer only a lace veil covered Dorothea's head, her dresses were of light silk or cotton muslin flowing to the ground, and she draped a modish silk shawl over her shoulders.

Daily, the young countess ordered her coachman to drive her to the Imperial

Winter Palace to pay her respects to her mother-in-law. In Charlotte Lieven's drawing-room Dorothea met contemporaries—the elder countess's charges—Tsar Paul's children. And among the many court notables who visited that authoritative lady, Dorothea had plenty of opportunity to refine her powers of observation, not to mention improving her mastery of a crucial skill: conversation. As well, the ambitious young countess continued to draw conclusions about listening: if, by listening to the speaker, she made him feel understood, he would be attracted to her.

Her married state gave Dorothea freedom to enjoy her brothers' company. She and Alexander grew much closer when he moved into the Lievens' apartment while he completed his military training. Dorothea saw Constantine, like her musical and adept at languages, whenever he could take time off from his studies as a budding diplomat.

Count, later prince, Christopher Lieven. Dorothea's husband and first great love. Artist: Sir Thomas Lawrence. Used by permission of the Slavic and Baltic Division, The New York Public Library, Astor, Lenox and Tilden Foundations.

But to her great disappointment Lieven's demanding duties as the tsar's minister of war prevented him from going into society, so his eager young wife could not go either. Court obligations as lady-in-waiting to the Empress Maria turned out to be tedious. Since Dorothea's duties were not such as to occupy either her day or her mind, and because her formal education ended with her departure from Smolny, the enterprising young countess engaged a private teacher to give her lessons in history and literature. However, a seminal event in Russian history taught this fifteen-year-old her first, never-to-be-forgotten lesson in practical politics.

෫෨ඓ

Tsar Paul I ruled autocratically over the vast Russian Empire during Dorothea Lieven's adolescence. Her diary described him as small and ugly; his eyes, if not suffused with rage, conveyed great kindness. When angry, Paul's expression terrified.

In public, every eye focused on him; in private, people concentrated their thoughts on him. The tsar's favor meant everything.

Courtiers hung on each word that fell from the imperial lips. Waiting to speak to Paul, an ambassador, "vexed at seeing him continually address one of his favorites, said, 'Sire, that is apparently some great man of your Empire?' 'Know,' replied the

Tsar, 'there is no great man but he to whom I speak, and that only as long as I speak to him!'"[3]

All Russia revolved around the "red sun,"[4] the ruler, the father of the whole nation. Love, fear, and intense deference coalesced into quasi-deification of the monarch.

To reinforce their power, Russia's rulers used sumptuous court spectacles, a policy Tsar Paul's wife, the Empress Maria, carried out to the hilt. A combination of frugal German *hausfrau* and educated Enlightenment sophisticate, Dorothea Lieven's foster-mother presided over the court. Still beautiful, imposing and fair and, after bearing several children, inclined to plumpness, she loved her rank and readily cultivated the pomp that constituted court life—the strict etiquette, the traditional "routine of the courtiers, frivolous things which have their serious side in a monarchical country,"[5] Dorothea's diary explained.

When young Countess Lieven attended the empress at official court functions, she entered a veritable vortex of gaiety and luxury—private theatricals, gala receptions, sleigh parties and skating parties, illuminations, fireworks, processions with wild animals from all over the world; parades on land, and on sea, such as "a vessel of 120 cannons launched on the Neva in the presence of the court reinforced by the entire city."[6] Only in Russia did thousands sit down to a four-hour banquet, with liveried servants handing around sixty different dishes including, in the middle of winter, fat purple grapes and tender young asparagus spears from the host's hot-houses or, in torrid summer, slabs of luscious, ice-cold watermelon. And each guest might easily receive a valuable jewel.

Such extravaganzas demanded European luxuries. Horse-drawn sleds brought them overland when the long, frigid winter froze access to the open sea. Dorothea attended a great palace ball where fifteen hundred boxes of the rarest flowers formed a fragrant grove. At one end of the ballroom, in the thickest part of a copse of exotic plants, a fountain spurted fresh, clear water. Clusters of candles lit these jets, making their water shine like a diamond spray; it cooled the air "kept in motion by enormous palm branches and banana plants, glistening with dew."[7]

Maria's official reception-room combined gorgeous magnificence with perfect taste. The windows consisted of a single pane, the walls of dazzling white scagliola[8] painted with the brightest flowers; there were splendid jasper columns, gilded doors, lapis lazuli vases, and malachite tables. In the middle stood the empress, "her dignified, graceful figure resting on a malachite jardinière filled with flowers, her whole person one blaze of jewels but all arranged with such perfect taste that their brilliancy struck you more than their weight." Her daughters the "Grand Duchesses were grouped behind her and the ladies entered one by one, first the two hundred maids of honor"; then the ladies of honor, young Countess Lieven among them, in full court dresses of silver embroidered with diamonds. Their "order was admirable— no pushing or squeezing or jostling; everyone knew his or her place."[9]

Their participation in these sumptuous displays let court nobles share in reflected glory. But Dorothea began to resent having to act like a marionette. The life she had so eagerly anticipated at Smolny, such a brief time ago, bored her. The court's fixation on details, "the importance attached to nothings, that entirely Russian way of hurrying too much in order to wait a long time: this désoeuvrement[10] which has the air of a toil, of a duty," did little to stimulate her brain. And she chafed at the "abdication of dignity by each person in order to incarnate it in the sovereign."[11]

Daughter of loyal, diligent Baltic Barons, Dorothea, nonetheless, punctiliously did her duty. Besides, she knew about the perils in store for those who dared to cross the omnipotent tsar; at age six she had shared her mother's exile. Still, this perceptive adolescent felt considerable chagrin at having to submit her vivacious charm and vaulting ambition to the court's stultifying etiquette, let alone the strictures of her sedate spouse.

Noblemen had authority over their wives, with one exception. Russian women fully controlled their property, which gave them remarkable freedom vis-à-vis their husbands. Indeed, a woman's power to dispose of her wealth checked any inclination her husband might have to oppress her. Hence, their financial autonomy made Russian ladies "appear prodigious independent in the midst of a despotic government!"[12]

Dorothea's father had given her a dowry; Empress Maria bestowed one as well. Her allowance as lady-in-waiting, a bequest from Maria, and accumulated interest made up Dorothea's Russian assets. When, later, she lived abroad Dorothea depended on her elder brother to act for her. "The two notes for fifty thousand rubles each[13] were deposited by your order at Meyer and Bruxner for which I send you the receipt. They told me you want the sum of the interest and the capital remitted to the bank and the bond on it"[14] also. Since Dorothea's money did not support her, and lay in a perfectly secure bank, Alexander recommended that she protect her capital by having the bonds either sent to her, or entrusting them to a family member like her mother-in-law. Later still, Dorothea invested approximately £5,500 in English funds.[15]

౪ᏣᏩ౫

Sitting sadly in solitude at the snowbound capital where "the steam-boats do not run any longer for the frost cuts us off now from the outer world,"[16] Dorothea Lieven, much later, scrupulously recorded a defining moment in Russian history, a moment vividly etched in her mind. Her memoir provides posterity with its most reliable account.

During the first year of Dorothea's marriage a miasma hovered menacingly over St. Petersburg's mixture of glitter and grunge, over the court's combination of elegance and ennui. Mystery shrouded Tsar Paul I. Was he mad, unbalanced, or merely eccentric? No positive proof existed, but since childhood the "fiery and sometimes cruel fits of wrath to which he gave way, justified the suspicion of a certain weakness of organization in a mind and heart naturally upright and good."[17]

Dorothea Lieven faulted his mother. Catherine the Great saw her son as a threat to her throne. She excluded him from court and on the rare occasions when she did bring herself to admit Paul, received him with marked coldness. Catherine's sycophantic courtiers followed her lead, even going so far as to treat Paul with patent rudeness. And as if that were not enough Catherine seldom let her son see his children; Russia's all-powerful ruler insisted that they live in a separate establishment. "To such a life, without being shown consideration, without mingling with men in business, without occupation and without pleasures, was condemned for thirty-five years a prince who would ascend the throne."[18]

Obsessed with fear of assassination, for which he can hardly be blamed considering his father's fate (Catherine had connived with a group of guards officers to rid herself and Russia of her unsatisfactory spouse, Tsar Peter III), Paul had secret stairs and concealed passages added to Gatchina Palace, where he held his court. And when he rose to ultimate power Paul instantly ordered all material and men diverted to build, in the center of St. Petersburg, a fortified, moated castle complete with gun emplacements and drawbridges. If nothing else, the Michael Palace stood out as unique.

"Omnipotence, that disease of the strongest heads, finished by developing sad germs" in this tsar. He became "the object of universal terror and hatred throughout his Empire."[19] Paul set spies on everyone; government officials, army officers, and court nobles rose to and fell from favor with startling speed.

Amidst this maelstrom, Dorothea observed the daily ebb and flow of politics, saw how her mother-in-law managed to keep her office and her honors, and how her husband maintained his portfolio as minister of war. The young countess learned the importance of discretion, the need to be wary of expressing decided opinions.

Paul's sudden and capricious fancies caused every courtier, and that included fifteen-year-old Dorothea, to live in a state of continual dread. New, important, rapidly issued regulations often contradicted each other. An unusually daring wit caricatured Paul holding a regulation in each hand; "order" was written on one, "counter-order" on the other; the Tsar's forehead displayed "disorder." But this was no laughing matter. Many were thrown into the grim Peter and Paul Fortress, sometimes for wearing their hair too long or their coats too short. One imperial decree established the allowable height of a gentleman's collar, and of hat style. Another forbad vehicles to be painted blue and coachmen to wear red liveries, because those colors connoted the French Revolution. The tsar banned waistcoats because they had made the revolution. A police regulation compelled his subjects, on meeting Paul, at once to stop their carriages. Coachman and footman must bare their heads; the occupants must alight, regardless of the execrable condition of the streets, to make a deep bow. Even women were imprisoned for not having descended from their carriages quickly enough on meeting Paul, "or for not having made a sufficiently low bow to him."[20] So between noon and one, the tsar's hour of promenade, Dorothea Lieven, like most nobles, stayed indoors.

The tsar dreaded lest his courtiers show inadequate homage—in view of the fashion in which his mother's court treated him, that is not hard to fathom—so the grand master of ceremonies had to instruct and rehearse the thousands of courtiers who daily thronged the palace. Each must wear prescribed dress, depending on his rank; each must conduct herself according to rank. No one must ever turn his back to Paul. On entering the tsar's presence courtiers must bow to the ground, go down on one knee, audibly kiss the tsar's hand, and receive his kiss on the cheek. Like flowers blowing in the wind, ladies sank into a deep curtsy before giving and getting their kiss.

Paul's idiosyncrasies exasperated everyone. Midnight arrests and deportations to Siberia multiplied. Over a hundred officers of the prestigious Imperial Guard were thrown into prison. To Dorothea's intense indignation her "husband was unfortunate enough to be the instrument of these iniquitous sentences."[21]

Then Count Lieven fell ill. His sickness confined him at home for several weeks. To his bride's delight Lieven's friend, Count Peter Pahlen, a Baltic Baron and St. Petersburg's military governor, visited him each evening. "The image of rectitude, carelessness, and of joy,"[22] Pahlen liked to amuse his lively young hostess. And Dorothea Lieven loved to laugh.

But when the men turned to politics they dismissed her. Deeply disappointed yet already "a little curious,"[23] Dorothea recorded with what can only be called gross understatement, she always got her sober spouse to divulge what he and Pahlen discussed.

Pahlen believed that the tsar planned to confine his wife to a convent and incarcerate his two eldest sons. Others whispered that Paul meant to marry a French actress.

> Did the conspirators invent these calumnies in order to enroll partisans and to press for action? Or did these extravagant thoughts indeed pass through the Emperor's head? However that may be, it was all repeated and believed. Consternation and terror were in every mind.[24]

Although completely recovered meanwhile, Lieven "willingly prolonged his convalescence, owing to the disgust which his duties had for some time inspired in him."[25] This taught his observant young wife how to manipulate one's health to serve a larger purpose; so did the fact that despite Tsar Paul's order to his physician to visit Lieven daily, the doctor "looked after the interests of"[26] Count Lieven.

"'Your indisposition has lasted too long,'" the tsar eventually told his minister of war. "'As business cannot depend on your intestines you will have to send back your portfolio.'" This left Lieven with no illusions. His "favor with the Emperor had reached its term. He went to bed disturbed in mind."[27]

At midnight on March 23, 1801,[28] absolute silence reigned in the recently completed, fortress-like Michael Palace.

> Owing to that deplorable mental aberration that made him suspect everyone, the Emperor Paul had some distrust even of the Empress, the most devoted and most respectable of wives, who had not ceased passionately to love her husband despite his notorious infidelities. He had shot the bolt and barricaded the door communicating with his wife's apartment.[29]

So when Peter Pahlen and some guards officers arrived at the tsar's bedroom door at half after midnight, Paul had already flung away his last chance of survival. The conspirators burst into their sovereign's room and stabbed him repeatedly through his bed linens; then they finished off Paul by strangling him to death with a silk scarf.

Dorothea and her husband slept soundly in their apartment near the Winter Palace. Suddenly, their *valet-de-chambre* irrupted into the bedroom with a startling announcement: the tsar had sent a courier with orders to speak to Lieven at once. The count turned to his bride. "'It is a bad message. Perhaps it means the fortress.'" In a moment, without giving my husband time to get up," the courier entered. "'The Emperor commands you to come at once to his cabinet in the Winter Palace.'"[30] But the tsar now lived at the Michael Palace. What could this message mean?

Count Lieven did not know what to do. But he did know that the wrong move could cause imprisonment, or worse. "My husband made me get up, and asked me to observe anything passing in the street and to tell him of it"[31] while he went to his adjacent dressing-room (which overlooked the courtyard) and slowly began to put on his clothes.

"Behold me on duty!"[32] Shrugging herself into her warm dressing-gown, Dorothea pushed aside the heavy velvet curtain hanging across their bedroom window, which faced the Imperial Guard barracks and the street leading directly to the Winter Palace.

"Ice, snow, not a passer-by, the sentry withdrawn and snowed up in his shelter, not a light at any of the barrack-windows, not the least noise."

"What do you see?" Lieven called from the other room.

"Nothing at all."[33]

The minutes crawled by; Dorothea "got bored seeing nothing. I had some desire to go to sleep. Finally I heard a noise, still very faint." Carriage sledge runners squeaked on the frozen snow. "I announced this great news by loud cries, but the carriage had gone by before my husband had time to run in."[34] Dorothea had little time to notice much about that carriage, but one fact did strike her. Although two servants rode on the outside, they were obviously officers in disguise. And in the glare of the headlamps Dorothea thought she recognized one of them as the tsar's aide-de-camp general. "My husband hesitated no longer. He flung himself into his carriage and went to the Winter Palace."[35]

"My part is finished. I learned all that follows," Dorothea recorded with typically scrupulous accuracy, "from the accounts of my husband and of my mother-in-law."[36]

So omnipotent stood the personal nature of tsarist power that Paul's assassination must produce momentous results. As Dorothea's politically attuned mind grappled with that thought, she pondered its immediate practical effect: "At what palace was I to pay my visit to my mother-in-law" whom "I visited every day? That was my greatest anxiety."[37]

Pahlen now confided to Lieven that he meant to include him in the plot but did not, because Lieven's health prevented active participation. That left a vivid impression on the fifteen-year-old countess. If Pahlen had divulged his dangerous secret, Lieven would have faced a terrible dilemma: to join in the plot, or do his duty to save the tsar, to deliver Russia's brightest and best to Paul's most severe vengeance—execution, exile, or prison. "And after? A regime more terrible than that under which Russia groaned." Had Pahlen spoken, Lieven "had only one part to play—to blow out his brains."[38]

༄༅

A "superb sun broke over this great and terrible day." St. Petersburg seemed intoxicated. Its citizens acclaimed the end of "four years of despotism, sinking often into folly, and sometimes into cruelty."[39] Shouts of relief and joy filled the air; people streamed into the streets, kissing each other. By noon they crowded into the immense parade ground in front of the Winter Palace to watch all civil and military officers, the entire court, assemble for a solemn ceremony: to swear allegiance to their new tsar. Everyone idolized him. His handsome face and fine figure radiating youth and serenity, Alexander appeared on the balcony, his beautiful young wife at his side. The throngs bowed to the stunning imperial couple "and surrounded them with an almost passionate love."[40]

Tsar Alexander I knew something of the plot but not its details; he thought the conspirators planned only to depose and imprison. Horrified at his father's murder, the guilt-ridden new tsar left the entire management of the court to his mother, even giving Maria great "influence in all that did not relate to the most serious affairs of the State."[41]

Yet, Alexander could not yield to the grieving widow's insistence that Paul's assassins be brought to justice; St. Petersburg's awesome joy, let alone the plotters' rank and number, precluded that. So rather than concealing his crime each conspirator boasted of it. Dorothea Lieven remembered Pahlen's story verbatim.

> "The evening of his death the Emperor Paul asked me, while looking me straight between the eyes, whether I knew that people were conspiring against him, that the plot was a vast one, and that people very close to him formed part of it.... [The tsar's stare] was penetrating, full of suspicion and terrible; the blood froze in my veins. I felt the saliva dry in my mouth for a moment so that I could not speak. I did not change countenance, however, and began to laugh and said to the Emperor: 'But, Sire, if there is a conspiracy I must be in it. I hold the threads of everything too much for anything to escape my knowledge. Keep calm. No conspiracy is possible without me, I answer for it on my head.' The Emperor took me affectionately by the arm and said to me: 'I trust in you.' I breathed again."

"This tale made me shudder,"[42] noted Dorothea Lieven.

Daily in her mother-in-law's drawing-room, the adolescent countess listened as one or two timid voices ventured to speak against the dreadful crime. "'Would you then go back to the Emperor Paul? Would you see the Imperial Family in the fortress and yourself in Siberia?'"[43] the majority loudly chorused.

Dorothea Lieven never forgot this, her first chilling lesson in "realpolitik." "Thirty-eight years ago today Tsar Paul died. How all of that is present in my mind. What frenzy at Petersburg! And how right to love and expect everything of the Emperor Alexander."[44]

∞

A tsar's assassination, to say nothing of the bizarre circumstances leading up to it, certainly qualified as a "change in the routine of the town." Nonetheless, little changed for Dorothea. That essence of discretion, that exemplar of courtly compliance, that epitome of duty, Christopher Lieven, knew, like his mother, how to transcend the treacheries of court life. True, the new tsar did not restore Lieven to his position as minister of war, but Alexander did make the count a trusted member of his inner military circle. And Countess Charlotte Lieven remained governess to the new tsar's siblings, as well as the intimate confidante of powerful empress-mother Maria.

Maria, in turn, carried on the grand court traditions, the formal etiquette, the sumptuous spectacles, all that young Dorothea Lieven now deplored as numbing routine. Romanov tsardom continued to insist that its courtiers resign their self-respect in order to invest it in the ruler. So it is not idle to speculate that this proud, ambitious, increasingly worldly-wise young wife already felt the first stirrings of rebellion against tsarist Russia's autocracy, its absolute control of mind and movement against which, ultimately, she would wage a monumental struggle for freedom.

3

Peace and War

I never liked to be taken as a young wife. I aspired to more than that.... I had a vague wish not to be like other women. The life I led in Petersburg did not please me.... I only saw the World at Court, that truly served to mould my manners, but my mind gained nothing from it.[1]
—Dorothea Lieven

What utter frustration to sit on the sidelines as her husband and brothers took part in the cataclysm rocking Europe in the wake of the French Revolution. Their professions got them out of gossip-riddled St. Petersburg, freed them from the constraints of court, challenged them mentally, and gave them a chance to satisfy their ambition. Dorothea Lieven knew she had at least as many talents as they did, but she was a woman.

After Tsar Paul's assassination (1801) Count Lieven often traveled, either on active service with his regiment or on Tsar Alexander I's business. In the capital he worked long hours, sometimes, to his wife's disgust, not even coming home for dinner. Early in 1803 Dorothea's adored elder brother Alexander, having completed his military training, moved out of the Lievens' apartment to join his regiment in the Caucasus. The foreign ministry posted her closest sibling in age and interests, her favorite brother Constantine, to Naples.

⁂

Young Countess Lieven, too, had a profession. Like all aristocratic wives she relied on a multitude of servants, and viewed the maids and footmen who cleaned her apartment, the cook and his minions who prepared her food, and the coachmen and grooms who provided transportation as mere cogs in her well-oiled household machinery. When Dorothea woke each morning, her personal maid brought a cup of steaming coffee and heated the huge porcelain stove that stood in one corner of her bedroom, so that when her mistress got up the room would be warm. After her maid helped her to dress, Dorothea breakfasted, gave her orders for the day to her butler, and reviewed the menus with her cook. Aside from her daily visit to her mother-in-law and her court duties, the rest of Dorothea's time belonged to her.

She redecorated Alexander's former rooms for their father, recently appointed a privy councilor, and expected in St. Petersburg to attend the court. "The small room used as a library upstairs, will be his study; it has new and very beautiful French upholstery, a Persian-style couch, and antique curtains and on the staircase, an English carpet."[2]

Living amidst loving family, with financial security and a devoted, highly-placed husband, the young countess seemed fortunate indeed. Yet, Lieven's demanding duties still precluded his taking Dorothea into society. Not only that, the count's jealousy cast a damper on his wife's effervescent charm. She had been walking in front of her house when a male friend came along and spoke to her. Judging this chance meeting "scandalous," someone "very high up" at court forbade any more such walks. Furious, Lieven favored his out-going young wife with a lecture on propriety. And to set the seal on her discontent, the glittering summit of her adolescent ambition, the glamorous center of Romanov power, turned out to be nothing but empty, boring ritual.

Dorothea could scarcely confide her frustration to her family, certainly not to her straight-laced mother-in-law, let alone to her caring foster-mother, now the powerful

Граф Александр Христофорович Бенкендорф, 1783–1844 | *Le Comte Alexandre Khristoforo... Benkendorff, 1783–1844*

General Count Alexander Benckendorff. A brave officer and talented military administrator, Dorothea Lieven's elder brother carried out his duties as head of the Tsar's secret police with tact and moderation. Artist: P. F. Sokoloff. Used by permission of the Slavic and Baltic Division, The New York Public Library, Astor, Lenox and Tilden Foundations.

upholder of court traditions. Her elder brother Alexander, always tending towards criticism, expected his gifted sister's ambition to focus on being an accomplished courtier. Indeed, their younger sister Marie felt perfectly happy as a lady-in-waiting to the empress. Dorothea's brother Constantine, even her father, might sympathize, but they were far away. No, Dorothea must look to her husband for guidance, for the innate sympathy she had lost when her mother died, for the kind of relationship her parents' love match had led her to expect. But Lieven's limited intellect and conventional outlook assumed that the male strutted while the female hovered modestly in the background. And in any case, an expression of Dorothea's growing dissatisfaction with the life she had chosen would be frowned on as dangerously rebellious in tsarist Russia.

So in her mother-in-law's drawing-room, not to mention her own, the charming young countess continued to polish her social skills. "In the evenings only serious men came to our house, they took infinite pleasure in my company. I liked old men. There were some intelligent ones among them, and their attentions flattered me."[3]

And Dorothea continued her private history and literature lessons. Her instructor introduced Dorothea to the famous letter writer, Madame de Sévigné, so the young countess refined the writing style she had first modeled on her mother's "agreeable and simple form." Dorothea "wrote in French in a charming manner; her style was varied, original and always natural,"[4] noted Prince Talleyrand.

In their day the major communications media were the spoken and the written word. Dorothea Lieven poured time, energy, and skill into her letters. They allowed her to create her own domain within the confines of her marriage, gave her scope for freedom from St. Petersburg's strictures, and some escape from the growing boredom of her life.

With Lieven away and Alexander too, Dorothea's mornings seemed tediously long. So she sharpened the nib of her quill pen, dipped it into ink, and prepared to cover the crackling sheet of paper before her with lively tidbits about the fulcrum of power—the imperial court. Dorothea derived pleasure from the thought of her letters amusing Alexander "a little and that is a good reason for me to write to you often, aside from the personal satisfaction it gives me."[5]

Brother and sister had always been, would always be, close and much alike. Tall, dark, and thin like Dorothea, with the same distinctive nose, ears, and swan-like neck, Alexander, too, had a sense of humor and could hold his listeners spell-bound. An animated talker, he enjoyed the social whirl, had exquisite manners and, clad in all the glory of his splendid green and scarlet dress uniform, graced grand soirées with impeccable dancing.

In 1804 Dorothea's brother participated in Russia's occupation of Corfu. En route from the Caucasus he visited the Ottoman capital. Dorothea would have been less than human if no pangs of envy mingled with fascination at reading the awed young officer's descriptions of Constantinople's extraordinary and gorgeous sights, of Turkey's astounding beauty, and "the variety of all the objects that here affect the traveler's sight."[6]

At the same time, March 1804, Dorothea gave birth to her first child. Baby Marie absorbed her mother. "She is so attractive. Such a dear little creature, and just made to charm you. How I wish she could talk now!"[7] Like her own mother, Dorothea involved herself in every detail of her daughter's upbringing, shielding her from St. Petersburg's unhealthy climate and protecting her with the latest medical advance— smallpox vaccination. All to no avail. Before she could talk, the little girl's weak chest succumbed to Russia's rigorous weather.

To lose her child is the most dreadful bereavement a mother can suffer, a loss with which many never come to terms. As with her mother's death not so many years before, Dorothea wrote nothing about the loss of this child. Again, she experienced such terrible grief that rather than expose her emotions, she locked them up. Yet, throughout her life Dorothea Lieven would yearn for a daughter, a link to her mother and to the generations of women who had gone before, a link to those who would come after.

Before little Marie died Dorothea had presented her husband with their first son, Paul. Her next pregnancy miscarried but soon afterwards Alexander, then Constantine came along. The young mother played with her sons; she laughed with them, cried with them, nursed them through their childhood illnesses, pardoned their peccadilloes, and interceded with their stern father, "for although you love them surely as much as I do, you perhaps do not know them so well & that is natural; & I want you to have all the good opinion of them that I myself do."[8] Her sons adored Dorothea and she them. Nevertheless, with the bitter wisdom of hindsight Dorothea, much later, felt she had been "too young to appreciate these gifts of God with the recognition and welcome they deserved."[9]

Meanwhile, her brother chafed on Corfu. Anything would be better than his enforced inaction. Alexander wanted to visit the British fleet wintering at Naples under Admiral Lord Nelson's command, to inspect the military installations at Malta and, above all, "I furiously feel like making war furiously on the French," the ambitious young officer wrote his sympathetic sister. "I beg you to plead my cause with your husband who is competent on this subject."[10]

"'My husband asked and obtained for you the Tsar's permission to go where it will seem good to you.'"[11]

☙❧

Increasingly frustrated at not finding fulfillment in her marriage, desperately seeking to relieve the tedium of her life, it is scarcely surprising that a woman with Dorothea Lieven's passionate nature and sexual charisma sought distraction in love affairs.

At the Romanov court love affairs were too commonplace to cause comment. Indeed, Europe's aristocracy condoned extra-marital intrigue so long as the woman played by the rules: to be discreet; respect the sanctity of the family; bear her husband sons.

Young, dashing Prince Peter Dolgorouki stood high in the tsar's favor. Among the thousands thronging court gaieties, he and Dorothea would not have been the only ones to slip away unnoticed (especially when Lieven traveled on the tsar's business) for an amorous interlude in one of the Winter Palace's many secluded rooms. Too much vodka prompted Prince Peter to pick a quarrel with another gentleman. A duel ensued. His opponent's bullet hit Dolgorouki in the knee, too close to a main artery for the surgeons to remove, and within a short time the hapless prince died. In regaling her brother Alexander with this item, Dorothea also confided that although Prince Peter's death ought to upset her, it did not. The duel had created a diversion!

Since her affair with Dolgorouki did not engage the young countess's emotions, neither guilt nor feelings of disloyalty to her husband disturbed Dorothea. Indeed, she probably thought a light liaison belonged to growing up.

Dorothea's next love affair scarcely surpassed the superficiality of this first, especially as many courtiers thought dalliance with a member of the imperial family added to one's consequence. Countess Lieven had known Grand Duke Constantine, heir to the throne, all her life. Named and raised with the idea of one day sitting on the throne of Constantinople, the would-be emperor of Byzantium had, according to Dorothea's diary, little height and less good-looks. A martinet "fanatical to the point of absurdity" about drilling his troops, Constantine loved parades but not war "(he said it spoilt the soldiers)."[12]

At age sixteen he distinguished himself by striking an officer; his grandmother the Empress Catherine had Constantine thrown in jail; he cursed her in monstrous language; she again had him imprisoned. Unable to endure Constantine's shocking conduct and savage temper, his wife left him or, to quote Dorothea: "Her husband neglected her; she consoled herself, and the consequence of her consolation forced her to leave Russia"[13] forever. Constantine consoled himself by plunging into the dissipated life of his country's capital.

Given Dorothea Lieven's insatiable ambition, Constantine's proximity to the throne must have added luster to a brief and shallow distraction; for although she tells us Constantine always behaved to her in an "amiable, spiritual, *gallant*"[14] manner "worthy of confidence,"[15] Dorothea could hardly otherwise have considered him attractive.

৪৩৫৪

Meanwhile, the aftershocks of the French Revolution gripped Europe. Count Lieven fought with his regiment at the battle of Austerlitz (1805) and at the bloody battle of Eylau two years later. At Friedland (1807) Napoleon again bested Russia. To gain a badly-needed breather, Tsar Alexander sued for peace.

Unwilling to cede the slightest diplomatic advantage to the other, the tsar of all the Russias and the emperor of France met privately on neutral territory—a raft in the middle of the Niemen river, the frontier between Russia and Prussia. Napoleon charmed his erstwhile foe into acceptance of French hegemony in Western Europe, and participation in an anti–British alliance. The tsar got control in the East, and convinced Napoleon to leave to his ally the king of Prussia, a rump of his former territory.

Already showing the political acumen which would earn her the diplomatic fraternity's enduring respect, young Countess Lieven at once saw that the Peace of Tilsit merely confirmed the power Napoleon's military prowess had brought France, to say nothing of embroiling her country in a pointless conflict with Great Britain that Russia could ill afford. Tilsit deeply humiliated Dorothea.

Her strong patriotic pride had nothing to do with any intrinsic "Russianness." Daughter of a German mother, born and married in the Baltic Barons' distinctive Teutonic culture, Dorothea Lieven grew up at an insulated court that purposefully styled itself as Western. Indeed, nothing of Muscovite Russia obtruded upon the resolutely Western architecture and decor of the imposing palaces and noble houses in Russia's westward facing capital. Dorothea knew only the "Russia" of the Baltic provinces, and the direct westerly route from St. Petersburg. Tsarist power politics, the Romanov family, ultimately the tsar, focus of the Baltic Barons' intense loyalty, meant patriotic pride in Russia to Dorothea Lieven.

Tilsit at least stimulated as much political discussion as Russia allowed. Starting to think independently, to challenge the conventional "superior male wisdom" embodied in her husband, Dorothea argued about Tilsit with everyone, all day long, particularly with her "husband, though without prejudice to conjugal devotion. In fact, I must argue in order to hide my bad temper, which I cannot overcome."[16] To avoid participating in the lavish peace festivities meant to disguise Russia's shame, she took her children to Tsarskoe Selo palace, outside St. Petersburg. "I am staying here alone because my mind is totally removed from such pleasures. And I am settled here despite my husband's return, and am content to see him for a few hours once a week."[17]

৪৩৫৪

History's great events engrossed her husband and brothers; Dorothea chafed at her lot. She knew she had exceptional talents, and she burned to achieve a worthy place in the world. Only one means existed: her husband. When not engaged at the front, Count Lieven often traveled on the tsar's business. Hence, Dorothea brought all her powers of persuasion—direct and indirect, logical and emotional, her artful blend of love and flattery, let alone her tenacity—to bear. After eight years of marriage, she cajoled her cautious spouse into taking her along on a business trip. Their journey to Berlin and Vienna gave Dorothea her first exposure to diplomacy.

As the Lievens' well-sprung carriage conveyed them comfortably homeward over Germany's rutted roads and Russia's even shoddier ones, Dorothea subtly planted in her husband's mind the seeds of her potential usefulness to him in a diplomatic career; besides, as a diplomat's wife she would live abroad, would escape the tedium of court, not to mention the capital's miserable climate which she blamed for killing her daughter and which, moreover, aggravated her tendency to severe chest colds. Foreign travel gave Dorothea "a taste for diplomacy and from that moment I applied myself to inspire it in my husband."[18]

That year, 1808, the count resigned his commission in the army and joined the ministry of foreign affairs. Senior officers often switched between the two services, but the timing of this move demands attention. Although Tilsit had imposed an uneasy peace on Europe, it virtually assured another war, a war that, like all wars, would give an ambitious officer ample scope to advance. Yet, one year after Tilsit, Count Lieven left the army.

Having familiarized himself with the protocols of his country's foreign service Count Christopher Lieven, on December 31, 1809, became envoy extraordinary and minister plenipotentiary to the king of Prussia.

Dorothea's unique relationship with the powerful empress-mother, to say nothing of forceful Countess Charlotte Lieven's important position, facilitated Lieven's career. Furthermore, both ladies recognized how greatly the gifted and driven Dorothea could help her husband. "Perhaps her government intended that her talents, her tact, and her savoir-faire would supplement the meager intelligence of M. de Lieven."[19]

"Perhaps." Count Lieven "had perfect worldly manners, much elegance and good taste, reserve, calm, essential qualities in diplomacy." Yet, "his entry into the army at age fifteen had cut short his formal education," so Lieven "completely lacked learning and even had great difficulty in composing" a letter, Dorothea's unpublished memoirs reveal. "From his debut in Berlin it was I who wrote all his private" correspondence. "I knew about everything; later at London I always wrote the private dispatches, my husband copied them, then they went to the Chancellery."[20]

Of course, helping her husband in his career constituted part of Dorothea's wifely duty, but this sort of assistance went beyond the usual and could not help but cause strain between husband and wife. Dorothea had instantly recognized her mental advantage over Lieven; now, her husband's acceptance of her writing his dispatches confirmed his admission of his wife's greater talents. Yet, custom conferred superior wisdom on the man; besides, Lieven, twelve years Dorothea's senior, had more worldly experience as well. So convention and practice combined to give Lieven the role of guide and support which, since their engagement quarrel, justified his insistence on Dorothea's submission to his better judgment; now, she guided and supported her husband's career. Before, Dorothea's abilities may have merely irked

Lieven; his current dependence on them surely rubbed raw the jealous count's tender ego. And Dorothea could scarcely be expected to rest content with staying demurely in the background while, partly thanks to her, Count Lieven wielded power on the world stage, the summit of her ambition.

Prussia's small, provincial capital disappointed Countess Lieven. And the stiff militarism of its court had little, if anything, to commend it. "I walk in the park with my children, I eat, I sleep, and these are the pleasures of Berlin," she grumbled after three months. "It is terrifying to think of living this stupid life perhaps for several more years. My health is bad, I am plain and dull, there is nothing to be attractive for."[21] Certainly not for deadly Berlin society. The fashion-conscious countess found German ladies disappointingly dowdy. Indeed, "the women have not much agreeable about them: the men are only so when one gives them a dinner, and as my house is scarcely fitted up for entertaining, I cannot judge of the effect that my cuisine is likely to produce on their tempers."[22]

Dorothea's caring father did his best to divert his "dear Dascha, this dear child."[23] Empress-mother Maria had arranged that General Benckendorff escort visiting royalty to Karlsruhe so that he could visit his children and take the waters. As he wended his way through the Germanies, the general regaled his daughter with droll society anecdotes as well as lively descriptions of noted cities, and of the elegant spas where Europe's aristocracy sought cures for sundry ailments—real, like rheumatism and eczema—or imagined, any ills they believed the waters might alleviate. And although the general dutifully followed Karlsruhe's regimen, he continued to have "trouble in writing my good Dascha but the pleasure of writing to you makes immaterial the pain I suffer in my arms."[24]

Dorothea always found comfort in her correspondence. She naturally wanted to keep in touch with her family; she also wanted to be well-informed so that she could hold her own among the diplomats. Her mother-in-law's affectionate weekly letters brought all the court news; her gentle sister Marie, happy with her lot as wife of a general and lady-in-waiting to the empress, augmented it. Currently military attaché at the Paris embassy, Alexander regaled his sister with news from Napoleon's capital. Politics began to pepper the letters between Dorothea and Constantine, her diplomat brother at Naples.

So Countess Lieven groomed herself for the role she deemed worthy of her talents because, despite Berlin's drawbacks, she did recognize the huge opportunities her husband's position offered. Dorothea confined herself to socializing only with the leaders of Berlin society and "a few foreigners, among them the French and Austrian ministers, the only persons here that are in the least distingué."[25] In this way, the countess created an exclusive circle that enhanced the status of her husband's embassy. And besides writing Lieven's dispatches, she watched how the diplomats conducted themselves. "I got into the habit of being very discreet and in gaining great experience in this profession which gave me enough assurance to become very useful to my husband in the whole path of his career."[26]

The Lievens had lived in Berlin for less than two years when Napoleon began to pull Prussia into his ill-starred plan to invade Russia. The tsar recalled Count Lieven.

Dorothea could hardly have rejoiced at the prospect of returning to St. Petersburg for Berlin had, at least, removed her from the imperial capital's debilitating climate. Nonetheless, in autumn 1811 she took her three sturdy boys back to Russia. At empress-mother Maria's insistence the young countess proudly presented them at court, taking particular pleasure in the favor shown to Paul, her eldest.

Spring found Dorothea, disconsolate, still in St. Petersburg. She had no idea where Lieven, on a temporary mission outside the capital, would be posted next. Fed up with this uncertainty, which even prevented her from ordering her household properly, Dorothea made up her mind to one thing: she would not see ice on the Neva next winter. If she could not meet her "husband again under a foreign sky, I will go to find a warmer one in Russia. I very much fancy the Crimea and Constantine has decided to go with me."[27]

ɢↃↃ

Before, when Napoleon's power stood at its peak, the tsar had withdrawn his long-time ambassador to Great Britain because it did not suit him to have an Anglophile representative in London, a sentiment Tilsit could scarcely be expected to change. With Napoleon now preparing to march his Grand Army across the Russian frontier, the tsar needed an ambassador, a man he could trust a loyal, diligent Baltic Baron who had the added advantage of already having spent some time in England.

In autumn, 1812, Tsar Alexander promoted Count Lieven to the top rank of his country's foreign service. "I have been given the most brilliant, the most important, and the most agreeable post to which I could possibly have aspired," Lieven exulted on his appointment as ambassador to the Court of St. James. "The present moment gives it not only importance, but the greatest relief." Elated, let alone thankful to "the Tsar at this outstanding display of his goodness and the extent of his confidence in me," Lieven wrote his brother-in-law Alexander Benckendorff that Dorothea wholeheartedly joined in his "happiness—how could she possibly wish for anything better?"[28]

PART II

England, 1812–1834

4

Heady Surroundings

How important personal deportment is, good demeanor, great demeanor, good house or great house depending on who profits in society, half a diplomat's success hinges on his hospitality and his grand manners. You dominate where you please, and you do not truly please unless you know how to spend.[1]

—Dorothea Lieven

On December 10, 1812, Countess Lieven stepped onto a brilliant stage. Instead of having to perform like a puppet at the tyrannical Romanov court, the ambitious countess could operate her remarkable blend of talents in an atmosphere of freedom, not to mention of constant mental stimulation. "What a good time," the "best time in my life."[2]

The countess made her London debut with suitable éclat. Russia and Great Britain had concluded a treaty against Napoleon. To impress his new ally, let alone the world's premier naval power, Tsar Alexander sent the Imperial Baltic and White Sea Fleet to visit English ports. So Count Lieven, his countess, and their three sons sailed across the Baltic to Sweden where the Russian fleet and its British escort of six warships awaited them. Comfortably quartered on the Russian admiral's flagship, the Lievens arrived in England at the head of this flotilla.

As their carriage bowled along the well-paved road to London, no industrial revolution yet scarred Dorothea's vista of a green and undulating landscape, of fertile fields bounded by hedgerows, or low stone walls. She admired the flourishing farms, placidly grazing cattle and clean, rosy-cheeked children playing near picturesque cottages. By this time the Russians had driven Napoleon from Moscow and were systematically annihilating his Grand Army; shouts "of 'Russia forever' welcomed us everywhere."[3]

The Lievens' arrival created a colossal sensation. Thanks to Napoleon having forced every continental cabinet either in reality or only in appearance to cut official ties with the island kingdom, London had not had a single important embassy for years. So the prince regent, the court, the aristocracy, in fact all England received the tsar's representatives with immense enthusiasm.

ฺ๏ฝ

Britain dominated the nineteenth century as France had dominated the eighteenth. Unlike Russia's single-minded focus on the tsar, which infused conversation and controlled thought, the small island nation with the worldwide empire embodied classical nineteenth century Liberalism. A constitutional monarch governed through a cabinet formed from the majority party in the "Mother of Parliaments" where Whigs (liberals) and Tories (conservatives) predominated. Inside and outside Parliament all classes took lively political debate as a matter of course. Indeed, in the drawing room and around the dinner table Dorothea Lieven now heard politics fully and frankly discussed.

Parliamentary elections astonished her. Candidates turned everything

> to account, women and children too; there is a whole method of attack, defense and defeat; there is systematic bribery and, in the midst of it all, a regular saturnalia. The proud aristocrat shakes the butcher by the hand, gives sweets to his children, bonnets to his wife, and ribbons to the whole family, ... [even to] dead animals for the butcher is careful to decorate his meat with pink ribbons.[4]

Cheers greeted wearers of the pink rosettes. Others got

> mud and boos and these mingle with the applause and confuse themselves in the oddest way. What a strange country! What a bizarre and beautiful thing its Constitution is! What a mixture of abuse and justice. What contrasts by all and for all here! And what beautiful harmony results from all these contrasts![5]

In contrast to St. Petersburg, which Peter the Great had ruthlessly imposed on the bleak Baltic marshes against all common sense, not to mention economic and political hurdles, Europe's oldest capital flourished as a vibrant trading center before the Roman conquest. Nineteen centuries later this rich metropolis had become the world's financial center. London's grand shops eclipsed any St. Petersburg offered because, unlike Russia, Britain boasted a thriving middle class that could well afford to buy. Parisian shops might be more elegant but London's were vastly better stocked, and with every conceivable luxury. "Drapers, stationers, confectioners, pastry-cooks, seal-cutters, silversmiths, booksellers, print-sellers, hosiers, fruiterers, china-sellers" jostled each other "without intermission, a shop to every house, street after street, and mile after mile."[6]

Street noise and commotion even carried a completely distinct character: "the tumult and clamor of business."[7] No extraordinary event occasioned the astonishing crowds—only the usual course of commerce. And the speed at which Londoners "moved was as remarkable as their numbers." Everyone "was in haste, yet no one was in a hurry."[8]

From the top of St. Paul's Cathedral one could see so many roofs, their chimneys shaping "so many turrets; towers and steeples; the trees and gardens of the inns of court and the distant squares forming so many green spots in the map"; Westminster Abbey, the Tower and a forest of ships behind it; and the Thames River "with its three bridges and all its boats and barges; the streets immediately within view blackened with moving swarms of men, and lines of carriages." In every direction "the lines of houses ran out as far as the eye could follow them." London was "the single spot whereon were crowded" more "wealth, more splendor, more ingenuity than on any other spot in the whole habitable earth."[9]

ഇ൝ങ

England's assured, affluent aristocrats had participated in government since the Middle Ages. They believed in ordered liberty; they opposed despotism and democracy.[10] Many British lords sat in Parliament, and several held state offices; their sons might serve at an embassy, or as officers in the armed forces. Educated in the Classics first at home, then at Eton or Harrow, afterwards at Oxford or Cambridge, young gentlemen then went on a two-year Continental tour to gain social polish in cosmopolitan society and to learn French, for, despite the wars raging on the Continent, Europe had, since the eighteenth century, adopted French as its language of culture. Governesses taught young ladies at home.

Lords devoted half the year to supervising the management of their vast acres; they also administered local justice, to say nothing of lavishly entertaining a steady stream of guests in their splendid country houses. Uniquely British, the country house symbolized national culture, confident taste, comfortable family fortune, and the clear connection between land-ownership and deep-rooted political power. Countess Lieven judged the duke of Devonshire's seat worthy of an emperor. And when she recalled Russia's country houses, not to mention its winters, Dorothea pitied her recently widowed sister Marie for finding it necessary to retire to the country.

The countess thought her English hosts harbored so much cordiality and common sense beneath their somewhat gauche and uninviting exteriors, that one "must sometimes shift the compliment and acknowledge" oneself "very gauche for having passed judgment on them." Indeed, had her brother Alexander been able to break away from his military duties to visit country houses with her, he "might gladly consent to be gauche at the price of the happiness"[11] the English enjoyed and spread around them.

England's aristocracy did not count sexual chastity among its sterling virtues. Unmarried women sometimes had lovers. Unmarried men openly kept mistresses. Extra-marital affairs were common; society condoned them as long as the partners kept a facade of propriety. One must, at all costs, avoid scandal. One must, at all costs, keep the sanctity of the family. A wife must obey her husband, even bring up his illegitimate children; husbands acknowledged their wives' bastards. Indeed, the aristocracy's easy-going sex life resulted in colossal hereditary complexities, but those involved took them as a matter of course. "Prudery is not my style or my taste; but there are liberties of manner and language, crude admiration of beauty and physical prowess that impress me quite unpleasantly," a startled French ambassador wrote during his first days in London. "Abandon is charming when it is the privilege and secret of intimacy, when passion inspires and in some sort stimulates it." But there was "no delicacy in thinking and saying out loud and at any hour what one feels and says in those moments that are the lightening flash of life."[12]

This dynamic, self-confident aristocracy combined in itself political power and social domination. Society meant everything. Society intertwined inextricably with politics. Politics invigorated society, gave it special distinction.

৪০৫৪

Unique, exclusive London society got its first glimpse of the tsar's new representatives when, in the chill December dusk, Dorothea and her husband descended the shallow stone steps of Russia's embassy at 36 Harley Street to enter their carriage and drive to prime minister Lord Liverpool's house for their first ministerial dinner.

A dignified butler announced His Excellency Count Lieven and Countess Lieven. Two dozen curious pairs of eyes took in a tall, slender woman, distinguished rather than beautiful, with strikingly proud bearing. Every female present instantly recognized that her deceptively simple silk gown with its low, square cut bodice, high waist, tiny puffed sleeves, and long slim skirt had been fashioned by the first modiste. The countess had draped an exquisite and extremely expensive shawl very correctly across her elbows. Her superbly cut dark brown hair, brushed until it shone, styled close to her head in a top-knot of curls, and ringlets over her forehead and ears, betrayed the hand of a master coiffeur. And a magnificent double strand of perfectly matched pearls hung almost to Dorothea's waist.

Cosmopolitan London society thought her "excessively clever, and when she chooses brilliantly agreeable. She is beyond all people fastidious. She is equally conscious of her own superiority and the inferiority of other people." Her "manners are very dignified and graceful, and she is extremely accomplished." Nevertheless, Dorothea Lieven's self-respect, her pride in having a uniquely close relationship to the imperial family, caused society to judge her "too chillingly haughty."[13]

Since the countess intended to benefit from her Berlin experience—to establish social ascendancy as the first, the essential step in creating a successful embassy— she soon became "famous for civility and empressements[14] to everybody; her manner very much softened."[15] Still, Dorothea failed to please society in general.

She did not seek popularity. Dorothea Lieven sought power. And if St. Petersburg had taught her nothing else, it impressed on her that power carries a particular brand of popularity. Both men and women flock to it as moths to a flame.

No longer confined by an autocratic court, no longer required to renounce her self-esteem in order to embody it in the tsar, Dorothea now basked in freedom, freedom to deploy her brilliant combination of talents. While continuing to hone her diplomatic skills, Dorothea applied her ability to listen, and her capacity to observe. The English were much more subtle than she at first thought, indeed "singularly vigilant and inquisitive, while at the same time seeming to notice nothing."[16]

Within three years of Countess Lieven's arrival in London, she was able to say, "it is not fashionable where I am not."[17]

⁝

She led the fashion. The tight, high-waisted bodice and slender, unstructured skirt of the Empire style admirably suited Dorothea's willowy figure and graceful movements. When Lord Granville became an ambassador his ungainly wife studied appearances to ascertain what she would need as ambassadress. "I advised her," the duke of Wellington regaled his friend Countess Lieven, "to beg you for a list of your wardrobe and to try to adopt some of your grand air, and above all to develop the habit of holding herself as if there were no means in the human form of bending either the neck or the back!"[18]

Countess Lieven's ability to converse in English, French, German, or Russian captivated society. Granted, critics thought her conversation sought less to please than to dominate, to satisfy her curiosity; that her pungency rested on her questions, rather than her answers. But no one doubted the animation, the precision, the clarity, and the grace of Dorothea Lieven's conversation; light-hearted or serious, she always found the right word.

And her wit! Wit meant more than quick repartee; wit included vivacity and social graces. At a grand ball the countess came across a man she detested; he reciprocated in kind. "You want to make me ridiculous, Madame," he charged. "No, my lord," Countess Lieven retorted; "You have no need of anyone to do that for you."[19]

Confiding her interest in a particular man, Emily Cowper asked her friend Dorothea Lieven if she saw "anything wrong in it, if I liked him too much?" A great deal, Dorothea replied. "You would have so much less amiability to spare for the rest of us."[20]

Her long neck earned Dorothea the nick-name "swan" or, less kind, "giraffe." Society said another lady of similar stature also resembled a giraffe; hence, she and Dorothea were "animals of the same species." But "it is not the same category," Dorothea countered. "The one eats the other and would have nothing but a bad meal."[21]

When telling a story Countess Lieven could reduce her audience to fits of laughter. At country house parties, where hosts expected their guests to join in providing diversion, Dorothea's wit assured the success of a favorite pastime: charades. Everyone admired her piano playing. "Invariably gay and brilliantly agreeable"[22] during the entire week of a country house party, Dorothea, after striking her last chord, rose from the piano stool and confided to the only male listener that very few men in England liked music. Next morning, as their host guided his guests around his admirably-stocked stables, Dorothea "slipped from under his arm to come and say, 'I have just as much pleasure in looking at these horses as you Englishmen have in hearing music.'"[23]

Society's upper crust elected Countess Lieven (the first foreigner so honored) a patroness of its holy of holies: Almack's—London's most exclusive social club, which held a weekly ball and supper during "the season." Seven exacting patronesses could arbitrarily blackball anyone they thought would lower Almack's august tone; so "many diplomatic arts, much finesse, and a host of intrigues, were set in motion to get an invitation."[24]

The club's strict rules allowed only sedate English country-dances and Scottish reels at its balls. Then Lady Jersey, a patroness with whom Countess Lieven consorted on terms of cold truce, brought the quadrille from Paris. Not to be outdone, the countess took advantage of Tsar Alexander's visit to London to introduce the waltz. Originally a German country-dance, the waltz first became fashionable at Napoleon's court; from there it spread to Vienna and St. Petersburg, but not for decades had London society been treated to the sight of a man clasping his partner closely around the waist—in public! The spectacle of Countess Lieven whirling gracefully around the dance floor with her handsome tsar caused huge excitement and, after some initial wavering, enthusiastic emulation.

"Why are you not here, my dear Alexander?" Astoundingly soon after she had complained about boring Berlin, Dorothea found herself fully enjoying London's social whirl, and even "amusing the English and amusing myself at the same time."[25] She danced, stayed out late, and found this new life "excellent for my pleasure and not even bad for my health. I see a number of people at home on fixed days, and without vanity" can "say that my *soirées* and those of Lady Jersey are the most agreeable and the most brilliant."[26]

☙ CB

Many years later Dorothea Lieven's close friend Lord Aberdeen reminded her that foreigners found it "no easy matter" to "cultivate an intimacy"[27] with a native of England.

Harriet, Countess Granville, figured as one of society's wittiest and most intelligent women. Born into its crème de la crème, the duke of Devonshire's daughter had such high social standing that she could leave the king's side if she found him boring—which she often did. Harriet preferred to sit in "the most obscure corner of a drawing-room, equipped with her lorgnettes, so that she can see how ridiculous all the surrounding faces are, and accompanied by someone she can laugh with."[28]

Someone like Dorothea Lieven. Harriet's mordant wit instantly found a kindred spirit in what she called Dorothea's "funeste franchise."[29] "I have had a most amiable entertaining letter from Mme. de Lieven," Harriet wrote her sister. "She says: 'Your sister had the goodness to come to see me. She has become as thin as her daughters have become fat.'"[30] Harriet, in turn, made Dorothea "die laughing. She is the best possible woman." Her "intelligence sweeps up all kinds, and she makes you walk with her, in all directions."[31] Harriet's brother, the bachelor duke of Devon-

shire, hosted a small dinner. It "went off very well, though my brother, Mr. Burrell, Granville, Monsieur de Lieven, and Miss Mercer scarcely uttered.... Madame de Lieven, Mrs. Burrell, and I were so talkative and the first so droll that I brought Granville to confess it was a very agreeable to hear us."[32]

Initially, Harriet disparaged Dorothea for her lack of "gentleness, sweetness, cheerfulness, kindness, abnégation de soi.[33] There is a great deal of decorum and propriety and I cannot believe in any very ardent feelings under it."[34] She grew to understand and love Dorothea for her innate warmth, her loyalty, and her upright character, "the good and the weak side of which no person who knows her but little can measure."[35]

Besides their shared sense of humor and intellectual brilliance these life-long intimates had both married merely competent diplomats twelve years their senior. Plain Harriet, however, had been in love with

Lady Harriet Cavendish, Countess Granville (1785–1862). Dorothea Lieven's life-long, close friend. Artist: Thomas Barber. Courtesy of Hardwick Hall, The Devonshire Collection (The National Trust). Photograph: Photographic Survey, Courtauld Institute of Art.

the romantically handsome Granville for years before he brought himself to propose. The marriage resulted in Granville giving up his numerous "gallantries" but not his gambling, a sacrifice his adoring spouse undoubtedly saw as the lesser evil. She brought up his two children, whom Granville had fathered with Harriet's aunt, with the same devotion as her own.

Harriet Granville had little interest in politics. And she would not, could not enter into her friend's extra-marital intrigues.

Pretty, flirtatious Emily, Lady Cowper, did. Born into a prominent Whig family, Emily, like Dorothea, had made a marriage of convenience. Intelligent, worldly-wise, and generally considered the most approachable of Almack's patronesses, so kind-hearted that she had difficulty in saying no, Emily enjoyed many love affairs. The Corsican Count Pozzo di Borgo,[36] who fled to England after breaking with Napoleon, probably fathered one of her children, Lord Palmerston another.

The Lieven family traditionally spent Christmas at the Cowpers' country seat, castellated Panshanger, which Emily had made a center of fashion. Guests easily differentiated Dorothea's dry and definite voice from Emily's deep

LADY PALMERSTON.
From the original painting by Lawrence, in the possession of Lady Edith Ashley.

Emily, Countess Cowper, later Viscountess Palmerston. For over forty years Dorothea Lieven's intimate friend. Artist: After Sir Thomas Lawrence. © Copyright the Trustees of the British Museum. Used by permission.

drawl. Her sons, like Dorothea's, attended boarding school. At Harrow the Lieven boys learned "nothing but Latin and Greek, Greek and Latin; and then they are up to all sorts of pranks. They all vie with one another in playing tricks on their companions or on their masters; and I fancy," Dorothea said of her eldest, "Paul is good at that."[37] Indeed, when the Lievens leased a house in the country, the owner complained that the three impish Russian boys drove her steward to distraction.

At Panshanger, and at other country houses, Dorothea and Emily met in their rooms after dinner. How they laughed over their indiscreet comments on fellow guests; the two intimate friends shared "such events and situations,"[38] probably including at least one lover: the politically promising Lord Palmerston, whom society dubbed Lord Cupid.

Disappointed in the two superficial love affairs she had at St. Petersburg, Dorothea now sought emotional fulfillment by plunging into the easy-going sex life of the English aristocracy. Country house parties offered an excellent opportunity.

Business often kept the conscientious count in London, so a considerate country house hostess would assign Dorothea and her lover adjacent bedrooms. Nor would one more interlude of dalliance be especially noticed during the glittering balls at grand London mansions. The countess's love affairs (real or rumored) caused considerable gossip, which sometimes made straight-laced Queen Charlotte irritated at the need to receive Countess Lieven with apt distinction. But the haughty countess knew what was due her consequence, and "would not have endured the smallest negligence in this respect."[39]

As for jealous-natured Lieven, he looked "black occasionally but prend sur lui[40] and behaves very well."[41] At other times Dorothea's husband looked miserable and "more jealous than anything I ever saw."[42]

His wife's superior talents had already made Lieven feel emasculated to the point of putting serious strains on their marriage; now, although her love affairs failed to touch Dorothea's heart, they provoked Lieven's jealous temper. Mutual frustration rocked the Lieven household with acrimonious quarrels as Lieven insisted on asserting his moral authority over his increasingly independent-minded wife.

She had to negotiate with Lieven for permission to attend a particular party. "I believe he wants to perpetuate the illusion of youth for me in treating me" as "he did at 14.... I detest arguing and especially moving him from habits that completely disorient him such as his invariably seeing me at a certain time reclining on my couchette and reading." Harriet Granville's witticisms almost made Dorothea forget "that *pouting* is in my husband's dictionary and on his face"; still, she did "remember and was in my bed at midnight."[43]

೫೦ಣಚ

When the Lievens arrived in London its politically permeated society had, thanks to the French emperor, been starved of the excitement of a major embassy. "No foreigners, perhaps, ever before gained such an influential footing in our best English society" as did the Lievens, because of their important political position and their wealth. To live in appropriate style at expensive London, luxuriating in the world's highest standard of living, an ambassador needed at least £17,000[44] a year. The tsar granted Lieven over twice that amount. "The Count's gentlemanlike manners" together with his wife's "talents and grand manner" made "their house, not only the resort of the most distinguished society, but the rival of our own most magnificent establishments."[45]

The ambassador, and his wife if she felt so inclined, epitomized his country, for monarchs and ministers rarely went abroad. Since disorder characterized international mail, embassies used their own couriers. Nevertheless, a government courier could take two weeks to go from London to St. Petersburg, and he had to summon his last ounce of finesse to get his diplomatic pouch past the host country's secret police, because in contrast to the postal service, if service one could call it, government intelligence activities were as extensive as they were efficient. Of course Lieven got general instructions from St. Petersburg but his interaction with other diplomats and with his host government assumed vastly more importance than it would today. Concomitantly, Dorothea Lieven's particular abilities became priceless.

The haughty countess dominated London's diplomatic corps as she did society. Still, the arrival of Austrian ambassador Prince Paul Esterhazy's wife caused the countess some concern. Austria stood as England's closest ally and the prince regent had always favored Esterhazy. His bride boasted youth and beauty; as well, her "plump figure seemed to emphasize the hopeless thinness of her rival."[46] And to Dorothea's disgust Princess Esterhazy, princess by birth (she was a great-niece of England's queen) as well as by marriage, delighted in flaunting her superior rank in Countess Lieven's face. To society's amusement, and especially the delectation of a diarist who detested Dorothea, the two ambassadresses hated "each other like poison with all the affectations of great fondness."[47] Dorothea, however, made sure that her rival's rank gave Princess Esterhazy "no sort of precedence here, as she is regarded as belonging to the corps diplomatique."[48]

Countess Lieven had an entrée everywhere. Although Lord Liverpool led a Tory government, Dorothea regularly attended Whig soirées, like those held at famous Holland House where the Whig elder statesman, Lord Holland, and his wife attracted an exalted circle. The center of Whig society and one of Europe's great cosmopolitan salons, Holland House gave its guests lavish gourmet meals in luxurious surroundings; brilliant conversation ranged over all subjects. Count Lieven never went there; he felt "he ought not to be seen in this nest of sedition." His wife agreed. "It is different for a woman."[49]

The countess combined her listening, questioning, and observational skills with her unparalleled place in English society to gather pertinent information. And in Britain's liberal atmosphere she discovered in herself a flair for politics. Since her drafting of Lieven's dispatches put her in a position to know all about his business,★ the exceptionally intelligent Dorothea could separate the wheat from the chaff of what she picked up, thereby contributing materially to the success of her husband's mission.

Dorothea once recapped Lieven's lengthy effort, and addressed it to the Russian foreign minister. "I have had quite an affectionate letter" from Count Nesselrode, she crowed. Some

> lines from me served him as a résumé of my husband's voluminous report; and he is enchanted to have found someone who can tell him so briefly what he wants to know. That sounds rather lazy; or, to put it more respectfully, it sounds like a man who knows the value of time. He asks me for a couple of lines of the same sort by each post, and I shall send them.[50]

In Dorothea's day, letters had tremendous importance. Dorothea dedicated hours to her correspondence with family, friends, social and political luminaries all over Europe. And ample evidence points to the extraordinary pains she took to be scrupulously accurate. Hence, powerful men realized that they could rely on Countess Lieven's information. She, in turn, realized that her appraisal of the facts which her social ascendancy put her in a commanding position to gather, gave her power to influence the decision-makers. Countess Lieven had started to develop her persona as a diplomat in her own right.

★*Lieven's unpublished papers contain dispatches, dating from 1813, with corrections of Lieven's drafts in Dorothea's distinctive handwriting; sometimes she drafted the full dispatch.*

5

Exalted Company

Her enemies accused her of base flattery. They alleged that she threw herself at the heads of people in power, and turned her back on them when they were there no longer. That is true.... To have good relations with Princes and Ministers, to sustain intimacy with those who are in power, was with her neither meanness nor falsity, nor feminine vanity—but quite simply the duty of her profession.[1]
—Countess Lieven's friend Lady Holland

Hard on the heels of her landing in London, Countess Lieven set out to captivate England's monarch. Since King George III had, by this time, deteriorated into his final madness, Parliament transferred the king's prerogatives to his eldest son. George, Prince of Wales, ruled Great Britain as regent. Because his dissolute personal life disgusted many in society, they shunned him. As a budding diplomat, Dorothea Lieven could not afford the luxury of scorning men in power. So she made a virtue of necessity.

The countess tells us that this prince loved luxury and laziness. He had spent an excessively wild youth, conspicuous for its lack of morals. Yet, the regent knew how to be gracious and kind, carried himself regally, and showed the world a sovereign mien. Still, Dorothea Lieven thought he lacked fairness and nobility, not to mention integrity. And she confided to her diary that he could very well prove to be perfidious.

A blatant libertine and compulsive gambler, the prince had secretly married a Catholic and a commoner (Mrs. Fitzherbert), under English law an illegal union. With gaming debts in the millions, Prince George yielded to parental pressure for a legitimate heir in exchange for financial relief. His marriage to his first cousin, the German Princess Caroline of Brunswick, had little, if any, chance to succeed. Prince George intended to be faithful—in his fashion—to Mrs. Fitzherbert. Not only that, despite her pretty face, Princess Caroline's obvious reluctance to practice the basics of personal hygiene gave her finicky spouse, hardly an eager husband in the first place, a rude shock. His wife's strong body odor repelled him. And her behavior on their wedding-night convinced him that she had not been a virgin. He is said to have visited her bed only three times. It sufficed. Within three months of their daughter's birth the prince coolly dismissed his wife and arranged their formal separation.

The scandal of this rupture did nothing to improve Prince George's popularity. People knew the circumstances of his marriage, knew he had returned to his mistress, knew he had encouraged, even abetted, his wife's taking a lover, had bribed witnesses and spies, and finally forced his wife into starting proceedings in which the popular and then still healthy King George III had openly sided with his daughter-in-law, a move his subjects loudly endorsed. And when the straight-laced queen snubbed her, the public vented its outrage in the street and in the press. Yet, as Dorothea Lieven realized, all that did not alter the fact that Prince George reigned as Britain's de facto monarch and, constitutional curbs notwithstanding, exercised considerable power.[2]

☙❧

Having cut her courtier's teeth at St. Petersburg, Countess Lieven easily charmed the vain, susceptible "Prince of Pleasure." Her conversation in English, French, or German (the regent had a German mother) could entertain England's de facto ruler for hours. Passionately fond of music, the prince kept a private orchestra and hired London's best musicians to entertain at his parties, often tapping his foot in accompaniment; the countess played the piano exquisitely. Foreign gossip amused him, foreign policy interested him; Dorothea knew all the juicy tidbits through her correspondence with luminaries in every European capital, and she knew diplomatic developments through her husband. A man of discriminating artistic taste, and a dandy despite his ample girth, the regent reveled in the flattering attention of an acknowledged leader of society, let alone the best dressed woman in London.

Of course Dorothea also got on good terms with the regent's heir, Frederick, duke of York. Each week that portly prince did himself the honor of paying her a private visit. At least he had brains and figured prominently in the House of Lords, but his brother, the gluttonous duke of Clarence (later King William IV), sported manners as vulgar as his conversation. "A good enough fellow with little intelligence, or, rather, none at all," Clarence often visited the Russian embassy for "the privilege of dining at it."[3]

Shortly after their arrival in England Prince George invited the Lievens to Brighton, the exclusive resort on Britain's south coast that his patronage had brought into fashion. Here the prince held a continuous house party in his brilliantly illuminated, centrally heated, lavishly decorated pavilion. Daily, thirty or forty people gathered for consistently excellent dinners; as many came afterwards. Around midnight they sipped iced champagne punch or lemonade, and nibbled on sandwiches.

Daily the Lievens came to lunch, walked, and dined with the regent. Then Dorothea, as usual, retired early. Since her husband did not, she returned to their house alone. One evening the burly duke of Clarence escorted the countess to her carriage.

Roughly pushing aside her footman, Clarence got into the carriage and ordered Countess Lieven's coachman to drive on.

> All this was done so quickly that I had no time to stop it, but I felt very ill at ease. Hardly was he in the carriage when he said: "Are you cold, Madame?" "No, Monseigneur." "Are you warm, Madame?" "No, Monseigneur." (His conversation always began like that.) "Permit me to take your hand." (This was an extra.) "It is needless, Monseigneur!" But this did not prevent him from taking my hand. Fear seized me, for he was evidently drunk. With the other hand I hastened to lower the carriage window as a precautionary measure.

How could Dorothea distract Clarence's attention? He had no interest in anything. She racked her brains. Hanover.* His one mania. "Do you know, Monseigneur, that my husband has had a courier from Vienna[4] to-day?" Dorothea asked in her dry, emphatic manner. "It is something that they have decided the question of Hanover." Clarence's bulging blue eyes almost popped out of his pear-shaped head.

> "What! Hanover? You don't mean that." He let go my hand for a moment. It was good, but he had to be distracted for four or five minutes. Madame Lieven: "Hanover is given to Prussia. (He leaped out of his seat) ... they are indemnifying you on the side of Westphalia and of Saxony."

Clarence's florid face turned almost purple: "God Damn! Does my brother know this?" Madame Lieven: "I don't think so yet." He "swore and got carried away, and forgot me completely amid a torrent of great words. At this moment the carriage came to my door, I got down slowly, planted my Prince in it, and said 'Good Evening' to him."[5]

Immediately on her husband's return Dorothea told him the whole story. "'What trouble you have caused me, I shall have to explain to the Regent ... how can I explain to him?'" exploded the humorless count, as "furious with the end as with the beginning of the interview." Dorothea "found it a little comic that he was not more willing to change the geography of Europe."[6]

Early next morning, unbeknownst to her sober spouse, the countess requested a brief audience with Prince George. Describing exactly what happened the previous evening, she begged his pardon for having disposed of Hanover in so cavalier a fashion. Dorothea's story lost nothing in the telling for the regent "laughed like a madman. I had never seen him so diverted. He had not seen his brother." Prince George thus accepted "Westphalia and the day was very much enlivened by this exchange of territory so readily conceded by the chief of the House of Hanover." That evening the regent escorted Countess Lieven to her carriage, "and he did this regularly till the last day of our visit to Brighton."[7]

Dorothea clinched her conquest of the regent by gaining great influence over him. Indeed, several years later when the Lievens stayed with George, now king, at his "cottage" in Windsor Forest, he confessed to Dorothea that he had been in love with her from the day they met, but had never dared tell her; he entertained the fond hope that she would discern it herself. "Today, an inner voice told him that I alone could guide him. Our minds are alike; our views agree; my tastes will be his: 'In a word, Heaven made us for each other.'" This astounding revelation, and the amorous looks that accompanied it, rather embarrassed Dorothea. Sure the elderly roué lied, she nevertheless tactfully replied that she, too, had always felt that they were almost as close as cousins.

"'You are satisfied too exclusively with the spiritual side; I can't be content with that—I am really and truly in love with you, very much in love,'" claimed the king.

> "That, Sir, does not seem to me to be written in Heaven; so I will leave you to think it over. You might regret having destroyed an old friendship; and you know that, as a friend, I love you dearly." I rose; he opened his bedroom door and asked me to look at the portrait facing his bed. It was a sketch of me.[8]

When, in the early eighteenth century, the Elector (King) of Hanover became George I of England, he kept Hanover, whose kingship descended to his successors.

Dorothea's rooms faced a dark, tree-shaded walk; the windows reached the ground and opened on a level with the garden. As the company got ready for an outing, George slipped behind a tree.

> I opened the window, and asked him if they were waiting for me. He put his finger to his lips and, with gestures and passionate looks, begged to be allowed to come into my room. It is so rude to laugh that I restrained myself; but I turned away, called to my maid aloud, and asked her for my hat.

On seeing the maid approach, the corpulent king "took fright, gave up his plan, and fled so hurriedly that he nearly fell, with the result that I had time to go back quickly to the drawing-room before he got there himself." All day the king "feigned exaggerated respect; but in the end we parted good friends."[9]

Friends. Not lovers. George "never failed to treat me with the greatest kindness; he believed in me and my friendship. He said to me more than once, 'You will be the only one to regret me.' He was right, both about others and myself."[10]

⟡⟡⟡

Meanwhile, by spring 1813 Tsar Alexander's armies had hounded the French out of Russia. Resolved to push Napoleon behind the borders of pre-revolutionary France, the tsar led his forces westward. With predictable patriotic pride Dorothea Lieven judged this war truly noble, one "worthy of Russians only." She ardently wished every success to Russia's brave army, and "its heroes who belong to me."[11]

Her beloved little brother Constantine had temporarily forsaken diplomacy for the battlefield. In Russia's first victory over the French he commanded a small force that carried out a daring rescue of some civilians. Promoted to brigade general, Constantine participated conspicuously in several battles, most notably the capture of Amsterdam. His intrepid older brother Alexander's exploits were, to his sister's intense satisfaction, mentioned in all the newspapers, especially his capture of Holland's strategic Breda with a small troop of Cossacks pretending to be the advance guard of a large army. Dorothea glowed with delight when, at a Russian embassy dinner, her husband read Alexander's letter from Breda to the entire English cabinet.

After the Allies (Austria, Great Britain, Prussia, Russia, and Sweden) had defeated Napoleon decisively at Leipzig they prepared to cross the Rhine into France. Tsar Alexander I, the "all-powerful, though unassuming chief of the great coalition of Kings and peoples," led them into Paris, notes Dorothea's diary. "Men knew what they had come to destroy, but not yet what should be built up. All was uncertainty."[12]

The Allied diplomats met at Châtillon. British foreign secretary Lord Castlereagh circulated a note; it proposed that the Allies agree to abstain from intervening in France's internal affairs. Austria and Prussia did not demur but the tsar, before replying, gave Castlereagh's note to his close advisor Count Pozzo di Borgo.

Concomitantly, Britain's regent decided to stop Castlereagh from coordinating any compromise that would keep Napoleon on the throne. Having openly scorned Britain's constitution for years, Prince George had no qualms about violating it. Without consulting any of his ministers, he asked Count Lieven to propose to the tsar that the Bourbons be restored to the French throne. In his youth the Russian ambassador had escorted Bourbon Louis XVIII's brother across Europe, and now kept in close touch with the entire royal family living in exile at London. Lieven and his wife knew the Bourbons favored a conservative regime for France; their tsar showed dangerous tendencies towards liberalism—except, that is, when it applied to Russia—and might well agree that Napoleon continue to sit on his throne. So Lieven eagerly complied with the regent's request.[13]

Meanwhile, Dorothea Lieven had charmed Prince George into confiding his secret opposition to Castlereagh's views and his wish that the tsar resist them. Prince George now arranged "that Count Münster* be sent to Châtillon under the pretext of Hanoverian business," and Dorothea gave Münster "a letter to give to Count Pozzo."[14] Pozzo, as Dorothea very well knew, wanted nothing more than to ruin Napoleon and re-establish the Bourbons. His comments on Castlereagh's proposal convinced the tsar to refuse it.

This diplomatic intrigue marked the first of many that would bring Dorothea Lieven fame. It is not idle to speculate that she and Prince George between them contrived or, more to the point, that Dorothea subtly sowed in the susceptible regent's mind the idea of sending Count Münster to Châtillon; indeed, this stroke smacks of Dorothea's modus operandi: always to follow-up a diplomatic move. Regardless, she used her knowledge of Pozzo's views to plant an influential seed where it mattered most.

౸○౧

The Powers did, in fact, decide on a Bourbon restoration, so the regent and Tsar Alexander had, in a fashion, conspired together and successfully, too. Their former reciprocal cordiality turned into warm friendship, and since a personal tie now strengthened state ties Prince George, eager to meet the tsar, repeatedly invited him to London.

Meanwhile the liberal-leaning tsar, European in culture and outlook, speaking better French than Russian, found the restored king of France less grateful than he thought he had a right to expect. Moreover, Louis XVIII's reactionary ideas displeased the tsar, so much so that Austria's Prince Metternich and Britain's Lord Castlereagh had to restrain the urges of what Countess Lieven's diary tactfully termed Alexander's "somewhat too lively imagination."[15] The tsar's liberalism also disappointed the anti-liberal regent. His zeal for his brother sovereign began to wane precisely when the tsar prepared to cross the Channel. Having successfully operated behind the scenes to strengthen the bond between the sovereigns, Dorothea Lieven viewed this development with no little dismay.

The tsar's recently widowed sister, Grand Duchess Catherine, preceded her brother to London. Despite the best efforts of her strait-laced governess, Charlotte Lieven, Catherine turned out to be "very seductive in glance and manners." And she exerted great influence over her brother the tsar, at least "real enough in private relations."[16] (Dorothea's memoirs here gave credence to the claim that Alexander and Catherine were lovers.) Intelligent and charming, the grand duchess also had a disproportionate thirst for power and an extremely high opinion of herself, which Dorothea thought somewhat unjustified; indeed, she had never seen a woman so bent on coming to the fore and effacing others.

The Lievens installed their grand duchess in the most modern and luxurious of

---

*A German diplomat reporting to the regent in his capacity as ruler of Hanover.

London's several superior hotels. At once the regent went to Piccadilly's Pulteney House to welcome her officially, but as luck would have it Catherine had not yet finished her toilette. In her hurry to greet Prince George, the grand duchess failed to allow her maid enough time to finish arranging her beautiful hair. Upset, Catherine's annoyance affected her reception of the regent. At dinner their antipathy became apparent. Dressed in mourning for her husband, Catherine rather readily spoke of her grief; to Dorothea's shock, to say nothing of dismay, the normally tactful prince remarked frankly on his guest's sorrow, proved even bold enough to predict that she would console herself.

The imperious grand duchess now seized every opening to displease her host. She embraced the liberal Whig opposition, froze the conservative Tory ministers, and favored the regent's mistress with conspicuous rudeness. She cultivated a friendship with the regent's daughter, Princess Charlotte, who stood on poor terms with her father, and saved her charm for those most openly hostile to Prince George. Catherine's final challenge consisted of a wish to meet the regent's estranged wife, the princess of Wales; this would mean a complete break with Prince George. Lieven had to resort to threatening the grand duchess with his resignation (and giving the tsar his reason) if she persisted. So Catherine reluctantly gave way, but avenged herself on her country's ambassador by excusing him from waiting on her. Hence, the ambassador's wife became the sole link between Russia's embassy and its grand duchess.

The Lievens introduced her to society at a series of dinners. Catherine controlled the invitation lists. She demanded the exclusion of people about court and rarely allowed cabinet ministers. Every dinner led to a small dispute.

Dorothea Lieven later claimed that those dinners taught her the nuances of diplomatic negotiation. She challenged "the invitations step by step; sometimes I gained the day, for the Duchess allowed discussion, and I often managed to exclude favorites, and get people put in whom she greatly disliked."[17]

Besides her diplomatic skills, Dorothea held another ace. Catherine insisted on knowing about the excitements that packed the spring of 1814, for not a day passed without some stirring news from France. Lieven told his wife, her diary recorded with becoming modesty, what she could repeat to Catherine; that gave the grand duchess ample reason to stay on good terms with the countess.

∞

At last Tsar Alexander and the king of Prussia arrived. And in their wake came an unprecedented assemblage: the rulers of the several German states, the leaders of the allied armies, the allied prime ministers, Prince Metternich, as well as many other dignitaries.

The regent had ordered apartments to be prepared in St. James' Palace, but the tsar preferred to stay with his sister. An immense throng massed outside the Pulteney House hotel. Cheering erupted. When Alexander appeared on the balcony the crowd roared its approval. The tsar's handsome face and winning smile, his benevolent and mild expression, his aura of general goodwill and purity captivated one's heart. Alexander's tall, imposing figure and noble bearing, the crown of glory that his victories over Napoleon had brought him, evoked such enthusiasm that during his stay Dorothea did not exaggerate in claiming there were never less than ten thousand people watching the street where he lived. Years of dissipation had, on the other hand, destroyed the regent's good looks and ruined his figure. Forced to take elaborate precautions to evade the crowd, Prince George drew jeers from his subjects when they did see him, and as often as not they threw mud, even stones.

As soon as he got word of the tsar's arrival in Piccadilly, Prince George announced his intention to come. The minutes slipped by. Alexander began to get impatient; his sister smilingly watched him. Dorothea and her husband knew this first clumsy move would put Grand Duchess Catherine in the right. Already she had planted in her brother's mind the negative impressions she had greedily collected about the regent, "and that with all the exaggeration her own malevolence could swell it with."[18] Alexander's equerry presented his master with a note; hostile crowds prevented Prince George from venturing forth to greet his guest.

Alexander got into his ambassador's carriage and away they went to Carlton House, Prince George's pillastered palace on Pall Mall. The tsar spent half an hour alone with his host. "What a poor Prince," the tsar pronounced at the end of this, his first and last private meeting with his host.

The two sovereigns now vented their mutual aversion; Alexander's open court of the liberal Whigs especially annoyed his conservative host, to say nothing of the tsar's flagrant attempt to flirt with the regent's mistress. And, as usual, their courtiers went one better. The Lievens failed to find a solution to this constant contest of pinpricks, for the grand duchess completely ruled her brother.

Angry he might be, but Prince George spared no pains to entertain the exalted visitors. After all, the war that had gripped Europe for twenty years had ended. So spectacular fireworks and brilliant illuminations burst into the night sky, Hyde Park held an elaborate and festive fair, on the Thames frigates fired ceremonial rounds of cannon, there were state visits to London's many theaters, to the opera, and to that ancient seat of learning, Oxford University; and of course countless elegant balls, banquets, receptions, masquerades, and dinners vied to outdo one another. The City dinners were for men only, but Grand Duchess Catherine insisted on attending. This rather shocked her hosts.

London's lord mayor held a sumptuous dinner at the Guildhall. The first course included four different soups, brook trout, turbot in lobster sauce, and a mammoth eel; then, ham roasted on a spit, chickens, a fillet of veal, roast ducklings, larded sweetbreads, and a meat pie all accompanied by delectable sauces and garnishes. The second course offered green goose with a variety of vegetables, quails, pheasants, lobster, fillet of young rabbit, and countless jellies, creams, and pastries. And a generous variety of fine French wines, which England's affluent had continued to imbibe despite the wars raging on the Continent.

Like all City dinners, this one featured national songs. The grand duchess disliked music; and since becoming a widow suffered from frequent nervous attacks. Scarcely had the musicians struck their first note when Catherine signaled her distress: "If that continues I shall be ill," she confided to Dorothea in Russian. Acutely embarrassed, Dorothea had no choice but to tell the regent. He announced in a loud voice: "Grand Duchess Catherine wishes the music to stop." It did.

Nonetheless, people kept coming to the royal table to speak to the prince. "This won't do in England," he told Dorothea. After a while George asked her if the grand duchess would allow "God Save the King."* Catherine haughtily answered, "As if that were not music!" Prince George gave in. But a dull murmur began to make itself manifest. At the royal table all eyes turned to Countess Lieven as if in warning. She got an anonymous note in English: "If your Duchess does not allow the music, we won't answer for the royal table." Dorothea immediately passed this note to Catherine who said: "Well, let them bawl, then!"[19] The company duly sang "God Save the King."

"When folks don't know how to behave they would do better to stay at home, and your Duchess has chosen against all usage to go to men's dinners,"[20] prime minister Lord Liverpool confided to the countess.

Mortified, she had to multiply her efforts to win the confidence of England's statesmen. Catherine and her brother's scorn for convention, their rudeness to the regent, not to mention their tactless enthusiasm for the opposition Whigs, had shocked government circles. So instead of cementing Anglo-Russian relations with a personal link between sovereigns, Alexander's visit aggravated British distrust of Russia. Dorothea Lieven heaved a sigh of relief when her tsar took himself off to the Congress of Vienna.

⁖Cγ

While the diplomats re-drew the map of Europe by day and reveled in Vienna's brilliant social life by night, Napoleon Bonaparte escaped from his island exile off the north Italian coast. From Elba he made his way to Paris, and raised an army.

The Allied forces assembled outside Brussels under the duke of Wellington's command. Tsar Alexander offered himself as commander-in-chief. Wellington declined. He wanted to test his mettle against the military genius who, until his ill-starred Russian campaign, had systematically crushed Continental armies. Hence, Russia failed to participate in the great Allied victory at Waterloo (June 18, 1815).

Countess Lieven genuinely liked Arthur, duke of Wellington, but, naturally, the glory enveloping Europe's greatest hero attracted her as well. A close friendship ensued. Dorothea and the duke relished gossip; they delighted in music—Wellington preferred Handel and Mozart to "moderns" like Rossini. And the lively countess loved to laugh and make others laugh. "Really I have no more pleasure in Society," lamented the duke when Dorothea went out of town. "I have no one in whom to confide what strikes me as ridiculous in our best of all possible worlds."[21]

Like Dorothea, staunchly conservative, Wellington sat in Parliament and joined the Tory cabinet.

> The only one who laughs at everything, and, above all, talks of everything ... charming, agreeable, and accommodating in the highest degree; he is a most excellent resource for us, and is quite happy if one will pet him. The truth is that London bores him, and that he is never so much at ease as in our house.[22]

Society nicknamed him "Beau"—and not because of his looks. Hardly known for holding the marriage tie in any especial degree of sanctity, the duke, having made a loveless match, paid only cursory attention to his duchess.

Dorothea's intimate friend Harriet Granville and her husband hosted an

Despite his madness and total retirement from public life, King George III remained immensely popular.

extremely select shooting party at their congenial country house. "Nothing could do better than our Grandeurs," Harriet exulted. Dorothea Lieven, her only female guest, delighted the company by playing enchanting waltzes on the piano. Wellington, life and soul of the party, happily accompanied the countess on the triangle; two other male guests sang. Outraged that this exclusive group had deserted her for the Granvilles, especially "indignant at the Duke leaving" on the pretext of cabinet business, a rival hostess wrote: "Dear Duke,—for Cabinet read boudoir."[23]

Meanwhile Count and Countess Lieven showed the world that they stood on the best of terms. "Whether walking or driving in the town, in the country or in society" they were invariably together. Nevertheless, "no one believed that this harmony was sincere."[24]

Married to an inferior partner whom by now she outstripped emotionally as well as mentally, living in the days when only men could shine on the world stage, Dorothea, despite her brilliant social position and promising political influence, felt increasingly frustrated. Forced to acknowledge his wife's superior talents, at least within the confines of their marriage, aware of her love affairs, the jealous count sought to assert his masculine superiority by flexing his moral muscle. Bitter quarrels erupted. "Hardly had you left my good dear Dachou," than "I was ready to run after you to throw myself at your feet to ask pardon for my inexcusable conduct and for the wrong I did," wrote a remorseful Lieven. In a reversal of their engagement spat he begged his wife, with heavy heart, for a brief note of forgiveness. Should he follow her?[25] "I promise never to cause you any anger ... you are more dear to me than anyone in the world."[26] Lieven impatiently awaited Dorothea's letter; she did not leave him in doubt for long. Surface harmony prevailed.

Society nick-named him "Vraiment"[27]—the word Lieven preferred to conversation. An honest, conscientious Baltic Baron, a competent ambassador who loyally represented his country's interests, but neither a brilliant nor a particularly perceptive diplomat, Lieven cut a fine social figure, "a man of most distinguished manners, speaking little, but to the point; cold but polite."[28] Some saw him "as a man of great depth, but the majority as a man of great emptiness." Society agreed that "the undisputed superiority of his wife" eclipsed Count Lieven; she, "however, pretended to attribute her position to his influence."[29]

In 1815 Great Britain was the world's mightiest nation, Russia the Continent's strongest power. So much of the well-being of a troubled Europe depended on good relations between them. "With such an important mission, with his abilities and next to such a limited associate, it is not to be wondered at that she developed a taste for politics and the habit of participating in high diplomacy at such a young age."[30]

By the time she had reached her thirtieth birthday Dorothea Lieven's expanding political influence over prominent public men gave her an excellent opportunity to satisfy her ambition. Yet, she also yearned for emotional fulfillment. She adored her sons, but Dorothea no longer loved her husband; and her love affairs had merely made her despair of ever finding the great, all-consuming love she sought. "I was desperately depressed.... I could think of no reason for going on living."[31]

6

Love in a Diplomatic Climate

*I am a woman and very much of a woman. I want things passionately and
I believe them readily.*[1]

—Dorothea Lieven

In summer 1818, Count Lieven took his wife to fashionable Brighton to see whether
a few weeks of warm sun and salt-tanged sea breezes would lift Dorothea's depression.
She loved the sound and motion of the waves and, thus, often sat on a rocky point dry
at low tide, but entirely submerged at high. The romantic poet Lord Byron had just
published the third Canto of his "Childe Harold." "Byron says terrible and sublime
things about death by drowning, and I had always thought that passage particularly
fine," Dorothea recalled. "I was reading it one day on the rock; and I felt that nothing
could be simpler than to stay on the point until the sea had covered it. I conceived the
idea quite dispassionately. I cannot help believing" that "we all have a certain tendency
to madness, which only the right circumstances are needed to bring out. Evidently, my
hour of madness had come.... I waited on the rock a good half-hour, my mind made
up; but the tide did not rise. When at last it did, my madness ebbed as the water
advanced." At that "moment, nothing seemed so delightful as the small details of life."[2]

A few weeks later fate took an unforeseen hand in the flow of Dorothea's life.
To the Lievens' utter surprise, Tsar Alexander commanded their presence at the first
all–European congress since Vienna.

A glittering galaxy gathered at the charming spa town of Aix-la-Chapelle.
Renowned since Roman times for its thermal springs, Aix-la-Chapelle stands on the
borders of France, Germany, and Holland amidst the gentle pastures and densely
wooded slopes of the Ardennes forest. Dorothea scarcely expected this placid place
to produce the one vital element her life so far lacked.

Having soon resolved outstanding issues, the diplomats turned their attention
to the amusements arranged by their host, the king of Prussia. World famous orches-
tras performed from early afternoon until late at night; a four-year-old prodigy
astounded on the bass viol; after haggling for an extortionate fee Catalani, the greatest soprano of the day, sang like an angel; two amazing female aerial acrobats daily
dazzled onlookers. And the distinguished delegations gave dazzling balls, gala receptions, sophisticated soirées, and grand dinners, and arranged delightful excursions
into the scenic surroundings.

An impressive retinue traveled in Tsar Alexander's wake. It included his official hostess, his mother the Empress Maria and her traveling companion, Countess Charlotte Lieven. Maria had not seen her foster-daughter for six years, nor had Charlotte Lieven seen her children and grand-children since they left St. Petersburg, so the two senior ladies surely had something to do with the Lieven family's presence.

"My dear, my good sister!" "[Your precious letter] is between my hands and you can judge how it pleases me, above all the news that brings me the delight of seeing you again,"[3] rejoiced Dorothea's brother Constantine, a member of the tsar's entourage.

"What delight you must have had in again seeing your dear brother, how joyful and content you must have been to find yourself with your mother-in-law and present the delightful grand-sons," Dorothea's fond father wrote wistfully from far-off Riga. "Could you ever imagine how happy this would make her?"[4]

Ecstatic at again seeing the entire Russian court, Dorothea "thought it most accommodating in coming from so far to meet me."[5]

Russia's contingent naturally included her foreign minister. Neither a strong leader like his British colleague Lord Castlereagh, nor later a puissant chancellor like his friend and fellow conservative Prince Metternich, Count Carl Robert Nesselrode precisely suited the rulers he served with self-effacing loyalty for five decades. And if this Baltic Baron's stewardship of tsarist diplomacy did not assure him immortality, his sweet tooth did. The cream pie filled with rum soaked candied fruits and topped with shaved dark chocolate that Nesselrode had favored at the Congress of Vienna and his "bombe à la Nesselrode" (a ball of ice-cream with a hot chocolate center) preserve his name for posterity. Imperious Marya Nesselrode, ugly but wealthy and well-connected, could be counted on to strike terror into the hearts of her husband's juniors. She might be a dangerous enemy, but she could also be a loyal ally: "a courageous person full of good qualities and large faults,"[6] according to her long-time friend Dorothea Lieven.

Prince Clement von Metternich. "Coachman of Europe" and chancellor of the Austrian Empire. Dorothea Lieven's second great love. Artist: William Say. National Portrait Gallery, London.

ജ്ഞ

Countess Lieven's friends, foreign secretary Lord Castlereagh and the duke of Wellington, cabinet member and commander of the Allied army of occupation in France, led Great Britain's delegation. But among all the powerful statesmen at Aix-la-Chapelle, the chancellor of the Austrian Empire[7] stood out.

Prince Clement Lothar Wenzel von Metternich-Winneburg, scion of an ancient German family that had served the Holy Roman Empire with consistent distinction and concomitant reward, was a cultured, cosmopolitan aristocrat. Metternich had studied law at Strasbourg and Mainz universities, and contracted a politic marriage at age twenty-one. His wife's connections, not to mention Metternich's superior diplomatic talents, landed him a leading position at court. Promoted ambassador to the Emperor Napoleon he made it his business to fully understand "a nation that placed itself above all nations," as well as "one of the most extraordinary men that has ever appeared on the world's stage," a man "who placed himself above all men."[8] After Napoleon's ruinous invasion of Russia, Metternich, now chancellor, joined with Castlereagh to organize Europe against him. Napoleon's fall made Metternich, at age forty-two, the Continent's premier statesman.

Witty and charming, above average height, slim and graceful, "the Adonis of the Drawing-Room" had fair hair, an aquiline nose, a well-shaped mouth, a high forehead, and piercing blue eyes; Sir Thomas Lawrence painted him contemplating his fellow creatures with his habitually impassive expression. It masked a daunting, politically focused intellect that also cared intensely for beauty. Classical Rome cast Metternich into ecstasies of admiration. Nature inspired him to paint, as well as to describe some favorite countryside as having "huge mountains, delightful valleys; liquid and abundant waters; a greenness that braves the sun's ardor."[9] In bad weather "the pines seem like great ghosts & it is rare if their peaks are never touched by some rays of sun that are hidden by the vales."[10] Metternich's many admirable qualities did not, however, include conjugal fidelity. He had already had several well-noted love affairs with prominent women.

Of course Prince Metternich and Countess Lieven were bound to bump into each other socially. They disliked one another on sight. The countess found Metternich cold, intimidating, and far too self-important. She hit the mark, for this monumental egotist believed himself "a man apart from most of my fellow men,"[11] and liked nothing better than to expiate, often at exhausting and exhaustive length, on his favorite subject: himself. Dismissing Dorothea as merely one more Russian lady traveling in the tsar's wake, Metternich forgot having met her during Alexander's visit to London four years before, and treated Countess Lieven with complete indifference.

The haughty countess hardly considered herself merely another Russian lady. She had always "aspired to more than that." Cavalier treatment would not do for the empress-mother's foster-daughter, let alone a leader of London society and a woman who had won the confidence of England's premier statesmen. Countess Lieven commented to foreign minister Nesselrode that she found Prince Metternich disagreeable.

Dorothea Lieven's singular position at the tsarist court could scarcely fail to impress Count Nesselrode. And he noted with approval that this ambitious, charismatic, and talented woman had already captivated England's leading statesmen, to say nothing of the prince regent. So the Russian foreign minister called on his friend and colleague, and diplomatically hinted that his coldness towards Countess Lieven had caused comment.

On October 22 an extremely select company sat down to dinner. Wax candles in wrought silver holders shed a golden light on damask napery, shining cutlery, and wine in sparkling crystal decanters. Wooden-faced footmen neatly clad in handsome livery, white gloves, and powdered wigs handed a succession of succulent dishes created by the artist reigning over the Nesselrodes' kitchen. Prince Metternich found himself seated next to Countess Lieven.

Gracefully blending flattery with tact, she drew him out on his favorite subject: Napoleon. He "served us as intermediary. I confess not to have thought he had this merit. At least it proves that he served me better from his rock than from his throne"; as the poet Horace said, "*Utile miscuit dulci.*"★[12]

Prince Metternich spoke wittily and well. Aside from the occasional astute comment, Countess Lieven confined herself to listening. To listen well was "a trick worth learning. A man who feels that he is understood immediately becomes well disposed towards the person who understands him."[13]

That conversation began the last, most famous of Metternich's extra-marital affairs, the most notorious of Dorothea's.

They had plenty to talk about. Both belonged to Europe's cosmopolitan aristocracy, had been groomed to take their places in the world, and were basically German. In extreme youth each had made a convenient marriage that now united them to inadequate partners.

They disliked rising early in the morning, disliked cold weather, disliked the same people. They liked the same paintings, furnishings, and books. Open Shakespeare's "works at hazard. Wherever you look, you are sure to find genius," Dorothea wrote. "After him, everything seems stupid." What "disorder, and what truth!"[14] Yes, Shakespeare knew that a man who loved, loved a lot, agreed Metternich. The poet gave Juliet "the beautiful verses you quoted to me; there is still a man and he only has the heart of a man. He searched in his own depths while writing those verses that make you cry, and cry because of me!"[15]

Dorothea met the witty author of a new novel. *The Pirate* revealed

> the same talent, the same power of imagination, and a subtlety of observation, a fidelity in characterization that no novelist before Scott has ever achieved. It is asking a great deal to expect you to read a three-volume novel in a language you do not know very well; but it is a pity you do not read Walter Scott—it is not a waste of time as it is with the others.[16]

Metternich sent Dorothea the *Autobiography of Benvenuto Cellini*. She read it conscientiously. The famous Florentine's vanity surprised her more than his artistic talent. And she thanked heaven for not living in the sixteenth century, since Cellini's all too ready dagger would have made her extremely uneasy.

Like Dorothea, Metternich adored his children; like her he delighted in the frailty of his fellows. Clement had "an inexhaustible fund of gaiety—you are the most *good-humored* man I have ever met; and I am fond of laughing."[17]

Dorothea's description of the prince regent's pride and joy, the Royal Pavilion at Brighton, kept Clement in stitches. Long and low with colonnaded portico, crenellated turrets, and a large onion dome, the roof of this blend of Kremlin and mosque supported a succession of small, green domes and tall, slender minarets. Inside, the

---

★*"Usefulness mixes with sweetness."*

fashion for chinoiserie prevailed in a profusion of oriental opulence. Dorothea found it rather disgusting to spend the evening reclining on cushions under dazzling lights as servants plied one with liqueurs, and music filled the perfumed air.

> You cannot imagine how astonished the Duke of Wellington is. He had not been here before, and I thoroughly enjoy noting the kind of remark and the kind of surprise that the whole household evokes in a newcomer. I do not believe that, since the days of Heliogabalus,[18] there has been such magnificence and such luxury.[19]

Meanwhile, in Europe's music capital Clement collected all the waltzes he could get hold of "at the risk of hearing myself blather, for I want you to listen to what I hear for hours at a time. Music also speaks."[20] It moved Metternich to the core; music ranked as the best thing in the world after love. He sent works lately written by his favorite composer (Rossini) so Dorothea could take pleasure in the same music as he did. Metternich's daughter played Rossini "very well, but she does not play like you."[21]

Dorothea played the organ for the first time in her life. Prince George ordered all nine handsome crystal chandeliers that hung from the hexagonal ceiling of the Royal Pavilion's grand music room fully illuminated for the occasion. "At the start, I was as bad as can be. I made sudden movements and deafened everybody, beginning with myself." Soon Dorothea discovered

> the pathetic stop, and I can't tell you how pathetic I was. I gave them floods of sentiment. I was wonderfully tender, and I could hear the most encouraging *ohs* and *ahs*. You know, the organ is a beautiful instrument; this one is astonishingly powerful, and it occurs to me that you must have been able to hear a few notes.[22]

Clement and Dorothea harmonized perfectly. Both conservatives, they agreed about politics, and their countries were allies. Dorothea's unique relationship with the imperial family did not escape Metternich. And an astute, well-placed contact in London could prove very useful. Dorothea, in turn, would operate her relationship with "the Coachman of Europe"* for her own political purposes.

"I have the misfortune of loving ambition, I love every feeling that pushes a man to go ahead," she confided to Clement.

"What a singular person you are, in all you say and thus in all you think," Metternich replied. Ambition worked so strongly in him, that he let Dorothea "share in my property."[23]

☙❧

Three days after the Nesselrodes' dinner a select group of diplomats, including Metternich and the Lievens, admired the scenic route leading from Aix-la-Chapelle to Europe's oldest and most famous thermal station. While the company relaxed after dinner in their private salon at Spa's leading hotel, Metternich amused them by reading aloud. Still, he managed to look at Countess Lieven "a lot, and we chatted pleasantly. You were tired from your long walk."[24] Next day Clement exerted his exceptional diplomatic skills to contrive that on the return journey he and Dorothea occupy a carriage alone.

On the following evening, October 28th, Prince Metternich formally called on

---

*So-called because Metternich drove the pan-European coalition of conservative countries.

Countess Lieven. "The hour I spent sitting at your feet, proved to me that the position was good. It seemed to me, on returning to my place, that I had known you for years." When he awoke on the 30th Clement felt cold and empty. In the interim Dorothea had come to his "lodging; you were in a fever—my love, you belonged to me!"[25]

"In a fever." Dorothea's fervent feeling, or her excuse to stay in her room until the coast cleared for her to slip away to Clement's bachelor* apartment, or both. He dared not hazard a clandestine visit. Disguise would be difficult and without it he risked instant recognition on the street, or worse, bumping into Dorothea's husband, even her sons. She, however, could easily envelop herself from head to foot in a dark cloak, and hide her face with a heavy veil. Anyone chancing to see an unknown female going into or emerging from Clement's rooms would only snicker.

> Good God! My love, I who know how to rejoice in so few things, do you understand what makes me feel true happiness, it is you, only you! My Clement, if you cease to love me, what will become of me? ... My dear friend, promise to love me as much as I love you; our lives are pledged in this promise.[26]

At last Dorothea Lieven had found a man she felt to be worthy of her, a man to whom she could give her whole heart, a man who would love her absolutely, a man who would fulfill her emotionally and intellectually as well as physically. Clement's instinctive understanding of her innermost thoughts gave Dorothea a special, a precious intimacy missing since her mother's death. His tender, aesthetic side fulfilled Dorothea's subconscious yearning for her father as much as Clement's powerful position appealed to her ambition. "My soul is so satisfied, so calm, how pleased I am about you and about myself.... I would not know how to imagine a life in which you were not the purpose."[27]

Clement had known many women; yet, he longed for one desirable more than simply as a woman and a socialite; he wanted a woman who would arouse his deepest feelings and engage his razor sharp and politically focused mind as well. His lengthy letters prove beyond any doubt that Dorothea did exactly that. "My happiness today is you. Your soul is full of common sense and your heart full of warmth." We "think alike, we have the same tastes, the same needs. You are as a woman, what I am as a man."[28]

Dorothea Lieven had found her soul mate.

She: "How amusing it is the way our ideas agree! You are so like me, you make me laugh; probably you think the same about me. We talk to each other about the same things; we think the same way about them; often I get your answer before I ask the question."[29]

He: "Why are your letters exactly like mine? Why do you write me almost the same words I have written you, and you have the air of knowing them whilst my letter is still in my room? Will such perfect identity of our beings be so complete that the same thought only finds the same expression in each of us, when a word, a single phrase will succeed in expressing what we feel?" Of all Clement had ever had of friendship, feeling, trust, even fellowship Dorothea best understood his mind. "I could write volumes, I could repeat to you a hundred times in one page that I love you."[30]

*Metternich traveled without his ailing wife.

Duty interrupted their idyll. Empress-mother Maria invited the Lievens to nearby Brussels, where she and Charlotte Lieven were visiting Maria's favorite daughter, the Grand Duchess Anna, and her husband the prince of Orange. So on November 4th Dorothea tore herself away from Aix-la-Chapelle. "It is impossible to see you go away without telling you what I feel," wrote Clement. "The story of *our* life is concentrated in so few moments. I have found you only to lose you! These few words contain the past, the present and perhaps the future. I have finished a period of my life in less than eight days."[31]

Tsar Alexander expected Count Lieven in Aix-la-Chapelle on the 12th. Under camouflage of a keen wish to again see her brother Constantine, Dorothea promised to do her utmost to accompany her husband.

On November 16th Clement thanked his countess

> a thousand times, for the wonderful day you let me spend yesterday. You gave alms to the poor; that is more than giving treasure to the rich. I saw you—I could tell you what I feel—I heard you tell me what I need so much—what I know and what I would like to learn every hour of my life! Am I so cold, my love? Am I the man you thought me before we knew each other?[32]

Daily, Dorothea rejoiced that "my life belongs to you, my good friend, my life, my heart all is yours, yours forever."[33] Daily, Clement loved her more. Never would "a man be *your lover* as I am." A rapport like theirs only existed once in life; they belonged together; she belonged to him. Clement would not give up Dorothea "for all the delight and fortune in the world. The only thing that exists for every man is happiness; my happiness is you."[34]

On November 18th Count Lieven accompanied the tsar on a visit his Württemberg relatives. Dorothea would await her husband at Brussels. Metternich wrote his wife that urgent state business summoned him to the Belgian capital. What, the astonished Austrian newspapers speculated, could possibly compel their chancellor to visit Brussels?

Dorothea and Clement stayed in the same hotel. Each signaled a free moment by sending the other an English newspaper. "The day you told me: *how well you know how to love*, I was the proudest man in the world,"[35] Clement exulted. At all costs Dorothea must "stay ill: that is to say the state of your health necessitates caution but does not deprive you of the ability to go out."[36]

Count Lieven arrived. Nonetheless, the lovers contrived to spend their fourth and final day together, if not alone. The duke of Wellington invited an extremely select party, including the Lievens and Metternich, on an outing to an undulating plain dotted with woods, fertile fields and fat, contented cattle. There Wellington guided his guests over what had, only three years before, been the bloody battlefield of Waterloo.

⁂☾⁃

"Love me, my good Clement, love me with all your heart: love me during the day, the night, always!!!"[37] Torn apart, and after such a short time, too, Dorothea and Clement consoled themselves with daily letters. That day Dorothea could only write at bedtime because her boys claimed her. She could not bear to send them away; nor could she end her day without a word to "my Clement." How sweet "to love you! So exquisite!"[38]

Clement wrote each evening after business ended. Neither choice nor pleasure drove him to write; need did, "and this need turns to happiness." Indeed, he sought "another word than 'write' when it comes to you. I speak to you, I chat with you, you are in front of me, above all, you are in me."[39] "You are my last thought when I go to sleep and my first when I awaken, you are that in all the moments when I am not forced to think of some duty." Even then, "your lover never forgets you."[40] He had dreamed of Dorothea all night. "I was next to you: you were kind, lovable, as you always are."[41]

Yet, despite the sheer delight of getting such ardent letters from the Continent's premier statesman, Dorothea felt uneasy. Clement's reputation could hardly be described as inspiring faith in his constancy. Princess Metternich took their children to Paris, whose climate proved healthier than Vienna for those suffering from a weak chest; Dorothea's Viennese friends wrote that Clement surrounded himself with beautiful, charming women.

Tormented, the countess confronted her lover. Metternich scoffed at the gossip; his demanding work, to say nothing of his love for her, absorbed Clement too deeply for female distraction. Then, his letters stopped.

Dorothea at once assumed that the wily chancellor had used this means to indicate that all had ended. "How can you give me nothing but the trouble of seeking to prove this is wrong?" Clement raged. "When I do not write, it is because I cannot, and I tell you so; the idea of making up stories about an act that can be explained quite naturally and with no trouble, is undignified for both of us."[42] Clement forbore to reproach Dorothea for having thought him capable of such trickery, because she had got satisfaction from unburdening herself. So by forgiving her for the entire theory, he proved his censure of it. And if she "had the ill luck in life to meet people capable of doing what you thought I had done, I pity you; but do not confuse me with them."[43]

Never would he admit it, but Clement's sharp words lodged in his conscience.

> I wrote you yesterday before I went to bed. As soon as I was asleep, I found myself with you, I do not know where, I spoke to you, and I saw that you asked a grand gentleman next to you who I was. Rather surprised I whispered in your ear: "How is it that you don't recognize me."

As the dream continued, Dorothea denied knowing Metternich, let alone having been at Aix-la-Chapelle and Spa. Frantically he asked Wellington what was the matter with her. The duke replied that a year ago Dorothea had married a "Mr. N" and with her marriage had forgotten everything. Surprise woke Metternich. "Then, I went back to sleep; I saw you again; there was no question of the former foolishness, but you were not yourself. You found fault with everything I could think of to say, and we ended with a real dispute about Rossini."[44] Still, Clement loved Dorothea as before. "How nice it would be," she would later write him, "to meet a man who did not mind saying: 'I was wrong!'"[45]

A friend arrived from Vienna. She threatened to tell Clement if Dorothea were to have any male distraction in London. They knew each other, Dorothea replied, and if Clement could not trust her, he would not love her. This feeling of "confidence that accompanies our love is such a joy. I know that I, better than you, have the right to boast of it, I have made great progress, and I had so far to come."[46]

Nonetheless, guilt tortured Dorothea immediately after Aix-la-Chapelle and Brussels. Unlike her previous affairs this liaison engaged her innermost emotions.

Dorothea's compelling love disturbed her loyalty, her deeply ingrained sense of duty, her allegiance to her husband and to the fabric of their marriage. Had Clement ever "been loved in your life, much loved by a heart to which yours cannot respond?"[47]

"You have been aware of a void inside yourself that you feel the need to fill; your husband is good, loyal, but he is not what a husband should be: the arbiter of his wife's destiny."[48] Hence, Dorothea would fail to find either in her home or in her husband what did not exist; indeed, she had barely emerged from childhood when she made a choice that, not unnaturally, turned out to be the wrong choice. Now, Clement declared, her senses needed

> to be seduced. They no longer get full pleasure; your senses are never offered what is put outside their sphere. The joys that only the senses feel, are like the effects of a chandelier. The rockets raise themselves, they throw off a day that must last forever; you think you are lifted up with them; all is beautiful and shining; even the environs borrow from their fires—and you find yourself again plunged into darkness. What makes *our life* is not transitory.[49]

Yes, he conceded, they were both wrong, both weak to look for and even more to submit to, happiness outside the home. So Dorothea must keep the domestic peace, must be "good, gentle, and delightful with" Lieven. Clement understood. He lacked Lieven's rights, "and he does not have those that belong to me. His line is other than mine: the two do not cross; why make him aware"[50] of it? Why, indeed? So Dorothea set aside her scruples, her guilt, her remorse, and gave in to her fervent feelings.

ഇറ

Towards the end of her life Dorothea Lieven devoted many months to meticulously arranging her voluminous papers. Among them her executors found some plain, paper-covered notebooks such as one can see in any stationery store. Into these she had copied sections of her letters to Clement, but omitted all evidence of intimacy. Dorothea burned the originals. Thanks, however, to the vigilance of the French secret police★ a few survived.

This one makes up for the many love letters Dorothea destroyed. If, she wrote a year after the Congress of Aix-la-Chapelle, "you had been here this summer, what beautiful and good opportunities to see each other at our leisure!" Business often called Lieven away. As often Dorothea lamented to herself, "If only he were here!!!" She visited Lord and Lady Jersey at their country estate. On retiring, she stood for some time on her balcony admiring a beautiful full moon. Dorothea heard steps in the next room. She did not know which guest was her neighbor but if Clement had come to the Jerseys it would have been him. Clement would have entered her balcony. They "would have whispered softly together; the image of what could have been persecuted me all night long, I closed the door to my balcony, I went to bed, I dreamed" a delightful dream. She saw her love.

> We spoke a great deal, and for fear we would be heard, you took me on your lap so you could speak to me more quietly; my dear Clement, I heard your heart beating, I felt it under my hand so strongly that I woke up, it was my own heart reacting to yours. Good God! My love, how it still beats at this moment.... Will my dream ever become reality?[51]

★ *Prince Metternich and Countess Lieven's clandestine correspondence (1818-1826) passed through Paris.*

7

Four Envelopes

Only a woman's heart knows real love. Her whole existence is love, what an inferior role in your career! My friend, you love me as much as a man can love. I thank you for that ... I thank God for having put these emotions in your heart; but I would not occupy any greater space were we together while as for me, I would forget the universe next to my Clement.[1]
—Dorothea Lieven

Hardly had Countess Lieven landed in England after her Continental idyll in autumn 1818 when a severe inflammation of the throat and lungs forced her to spend "a week almost beside my own coffin."[2] She blamed London's infamous fogs, fatigue from an endless whirl of social activities, and catching a chill on the choppy Channel crossing. The countess continued to feel unwell even after her illness subsided. She was pregnant.

Dorothea dreaded Metternich's reaction. He was not the father.

"My love, you have certainly profited by my lessons. I told you I wanted things to go smoothly within your home," Clement replied, his large sloped handwriting striding confidently across the pages. "I love you neither more nor less *single* or *double*. Pregnancies in marriage double the bonds but not the delights. Children bring happiness. My love, how can you think I would not want you to be happier? You want a girl." Tell "me you are happy with the idea of perhaps carrying one. The day she is born, tell me you are happy to have her. And I will be happy in your happiness."[3]

Dorothea convinced herself that she would fail to survive the birth of this child. And not without reason. In 1819 medical science, if science one could call it, was primitive. Even with the best of care women often died in childbirth; indeed, an identical fate recently had befallen Dorothea's friend the Princess Charlotte, heiress to Britain's throne.

On October 15, while her husband and sons were at the theater, Dorothea gave birth to a fourth boy.

Lieven at once wrote his mother as well as empress-mother Maria, who had said she wanted to be godmother to each of Dorothea's children. But the count left it up to Charlotte Lieven to arrange whether Maria would indeed extend her favor to this child. The old countess did ask; she even took it upon herself to request that the tsar be godfather. Both accepted. However, early in Dorothea's pregnancy the prince regent had, with total spontaneity, announced that he wished to be godfather. Dorothea could not, she explained to her elder brother, do otherwise than accept the regent's offer, so at the baptism he must hold the baby, who must be named George. But her mother-in-law blamed Dorothea's vanity for "this 'mishmash' inasmuch as it is impossible to have a second godfather when the Emperor has consented to act." If only the regent had forgotten! In the event, Russia deferred to Britain, but "either I was ill, or the Regent was away, and now that he is King there is at least three months' full mourning—during which there can be no question of baptism." So despite "this embarrassing wealth of godfathers, my poor child is not yet a Christian."[4]

Malicious tongues called little George Lieven "the child of the congress" in spite of his birth eleven months after Dorothea last saw Clement. And more. The king adored his namesake because he thought George resembled him. "Up to the present he says it as a joke; in a few days he will be saying it meaningfully; later he will let it be understood that he had good reasons for saying it; and, still later, he will persuade himself that he can really take credit—that is how his mind works." In fact, young George looked exactly like his grand-mother Countess Charlotte Lieven, "and there was never any likeness between her and his Britannic Majesty."[5]

"My little boy occupies me and amuses me very much," the doting Dorothea wrote her lover. "He has teeth and intelligence: that is a lot for six months."[6]

∞∞∞

Meanwhile, the months since Aix-la-Chapelle and Brussels drifted slowly by. And as much as their long daily letters allowed Dorothea and Clement to express their joy at the mysterious force that forged such a strong link between them, so, too, did this clandestine correspondence cause Dorothea constant concern.

> My husband dined out but will return, and I am not yet at the point where I can forget that. I do not like to boast of happiness, or give voice to my fears; but I cannot help being astonished that, for a year and a half, no accident has befallen our correspondence. Constrained as I am, surprises could occur any day.[7]

Especially as little secrecy surrounded the liaison. Sharp eyes had noticed the Austrian chancellor's attentions at Aix-la-Chapelle and Brussels. Dorothea had shared her happiness with her close friends; she showed some of Clement's letters to Harriet Granville, not to mention Emily Cowper, who delighted in amorous intrigues. The jungle telegraph did the rest. Clement even saw his picture coupled with Dorothea's in a small town stationer's shop window. It did not take long for Austrian ambassador Prince Esterhazy to confide to his subordinate Baron von Neumann[8]: "*I am sure now that she loves him, and that they are in a relationship.*"[9] Evidently most of London society knew; indeed, everyone seemed to know except Lieven.

Human beings are capable of all kinds of denial. He did know Dorothea and Metternich were friends, that they corresponded, for the lovers wrote an occasional "official" letter, which each could show to others. Yet, even if the jealous count suspected an affair between his wife and Metternich, he had no inkling about the depth of her love. Besides, Vienna lay far off, but Lieven could easily claim his conjugal rights.

"I lack the courage to argue, besides I detest arguing," and "if Aix and Brussels were worth the trouble of exposing myself London is not and I am resigned to that."[10] So Dorothea focused on creating harmony in her home, as much for her children as for herself. Still, the problems in her convenient marriage now combined with the need to mask her passion for Clement, causing yet another strain in Dorothea's relationship with her husband.

෮෮ඃ෬

"I am going to enter with you, my love, into a very *secret* and very *confidential*, brief development about the greatest interest in my life, that of having you here."[11] Soon after the lovers parted, Clement set schemes in motion to get Lieven transferred to Vienna. Now, the Austrian chancellor heard from an impeccable source "that Pozzo[12] is working covertly to get posted to Vienna. The Paris territory, which he has done so much to damage, seems untenable to him in the long term. *We would not receive him,* even if they wanted to send him, which I strongly doubt."[13] Clement had no need to specify what he wanted his lover to do.

Some time later Count Capo d'Istria, co-chief with Count Nesselrode of Russia's foreign service, visited London. Lieven told him that after seven years in England "he would accept another post with pleasure. Let us see what Capo will do with these projects," Dorothea reported to Clement, although she thought Nesselrode had more "influence on nominations for positions."[14]

Accordingly, after an appropriate interval Metternich wrote in confidence to his ambassador at St. Petersburg, fully intending that the Russians intercept his letter. They did. "Here is a letter for Nesselrode that I have designated *for him alone*. I have not written him for such a long time that I greatly fear he will think me changed towards him, so I am taking the opportunity" to speak with him a little. He may not balk at "showing you my letter. If he fails to do so of his own free will, do not ask. I praise him, I speak logically; I sputter a little, *very little*; I speak" of "Tatitscheff, whom I want to kill definitely for Vienna. A better choice" would be the worthy and loyal Lieven, who would agree with Austria's principles, "but they will not make it." They think "I *would deceive* Monsieur by means of Madame, and they are wrong!"

> I have no complaint against Golovkin, because boredom is not a cause of complaint in business. He truly understands nothing, neither what he hears nor what he writes, but that is all right, since you are at Petersburg. The fact is indisputable that there exists no more eminent nullity that his![15]

While this project hung in the balance Dorothea, not always knowing "how to tell you all I feel," or "how to speak to you of anything else,"[16] yearned for Clement. As she sat at her lace-covered dressing-table re-reading his latest letter, cut velvet curtains kept out the wicked winter wind, a cheery wood fire crackled in the hearth, and a pot of early pale pink hyacinths perfumed the room. Dorothea's personal maid interrupted to announce Baron von Neumann. He insisted on speaking with the countess at once. Neumann had come straight from foreign secretary Castlereagh who had given him a dispatch from the British ambassador at Vienna. It announced Metternich's imminent arrival in London. Dorothea began to tremble. "All the happiness, all the misery, worry that your stay would mean to me, appeared before my mind's eye." How "could your presence, the greatest of good things, give me anything else but vast joy? It is no less true that I tremble." To "see you again for so little time, to see you again to love you again; to rejoice and tremble every minute of the day—my Clement there is such a conflict of opposing feelings in my soul!" Dorothea struggled to reconcile her fears with her longings. "*Only be prudent* and all will go well," Neumann advised; but Dorothea would have liked to see prudence "recommended to a man who is going to be hanged and in truth the gallows and the steamboat that goes from Dover to Calais would be the same thing for me."[17]

Barely two days later: "Come, my Clement so that finally I can read in your eyes that you love me, and I can feel myself near to my friend. My God! There is so much happiness in this thought, that I am already getting a fever."[18]

When the hedgerows were hazy with new leaf and violets starred the banks Dorothea took her little George to a delightful spot. On one side of Primrose Hill

> you can see all of immense London, on the other Hampstead heath. I put my baby to sleep on the grass, and I sat down with my book. Foscolo's letters of Ortis, in Italian.* Do you know it? It is a sort of imitation of Werther,† but full of Italian grace and imagination. My good friend, a beautiful sun shone, I felt so contented in that lovely warm weather and most delightful greenery; that place had poetry, like my reading; then I was dragged into a totally anti-poetic event, pick-pockets were being chased right in front of where I sat. I had to leave my poor Ortis, in the middle of a really touching elegy. Will you come, one day, my friend, to Primrose Hill to defend me against pick-pockets?[19]

The delights of an English spring also inspired Austrian ambassador Esterhazy. He invited an elite party for an informal outing; they would wander, either on horseback or by carriage, in the blossom-laden countryside outside London, and stop at comfortable inns as their mood dictated. Two reasons motivated Dorothea's participation: she could scout out an assignation site; she would make this sort of excursion so fashionable that society would be eager "to go again when you come, *if you come!*"[20]

In the interim Sir Thomas Lawrence returned to London with his portraits of the century's famous men. Countess Lieven charmed the painter into promising to let her see his pictures immediately. "I will wear a large hat, I will wear a veil, no one will see my face, and I can cry, at my leisure. I say cry" because "I feel that is the sort of shock the sight of your features will give me. My God! All of you, all your expressiveness, and a painting!!!"[21] Instead, Dorothea wept with frustration. Etiquette precluded anyone from seeing Lawrence's portraits before they had been formally presented to the king.

Soon London simmered under a rare heat wave. Dorothea fled the sweltering city for the nearby village of Richmond, a "delicious spot! The loveliest in all this lovely England."[22] Here the Lievens, like other members of society, had their country residence. Stately old trees and graceful weeping willows lined the low-lying banks of the Thames as it meandered through the village. Herds of brown and white cattle grazed serenely in the flat, green meadows. Often, Dorothea stayed there alone with her children. Daybreak would see them all striding across the fields; then Dorothea worked in her room. After dinner, she took her boys to the banks of the

---

The very popular Last Letters of Jacopo Ortis by Italian poet Foscolo denounced Austria's ownership of Venetia. Refusing to swear allegiance to Austria, Foscolo lived in England.
†*Goethe's romantic hero in the* Sorrows of Young Werther.

Thames where often they hired a boat and were very gently rowed. That summer (1820) Richmond basked "peaceful, warm, everything is in flower, the air is fragrant. Why are you not here my Clement?"[23] Neumann could have brought him to a copse near the Lievens' house; with her husband in London Dorothea could easily have slipped out to meet her lover. But Clement stayed in Vienna.

∞∞

When lush red roses reached their full glory King George IV's relations with his wife riveted the attention of all England, and much of Europe besides.

Caroline, princess of Wales had, some years before, removed herself from London to her native Brunswick, where her spouse devoutly desired she stay. She disappointed him. High-spirited and sensuous, Caroline fully enjoyed flouncing her way around Europe, at the same time giving herself the satisfaction of outraging her husband. On his accession to the throne in spring 1820, however, the princess promptly returned to his realm to claim her queenly prerogatives. These King George resolved to deny her. He insisted on a divorce.

The Tory cabinet disagreed. Nonetheless, they were caught between the King's frenzied anger against his wife and the public's noisy disapproval of the divorce. Into this dilemma stepped His Majesty's Loyal Opposition; the Whigs maneuvered the divorce issue as a way to seize power. That prompted prime minister Lord Liverpool to introduce a bill depriving the queen of all her titles and rights, and dissolving her marriage with the king.

Meanwhile Dorothea Lieven might be parted from her Clement, but at least she could still beguile him. The lovers delighted in political plots and society gossip; as well, this royal scandal played directly to their shared sense of humor and cynical view of human nature. So Dorothea used the disgraceful spectacle of a society divorce, one involving reigning royalty no less, to entertain Clement. She did not divulge every salacious tidbit, but according to rumor Queen Caroline's handsome Italian lover was a woman, and at her trial before the House of Lords, the queen would prove it!

Countess Lieven got special permission to enter the august portals of the all-male House and, from the visitors' gallery, to watch the opening debate, "perhaps the most remarkable that has taken place for centuries—a Queen indicted by the highest tribunal of the Kingdom. As regards detail—a lawyer sprung from the lowest ranks of society, inveighing against the whole House; and that House, that Committee, those Ministers allowing themselves to be ridiculed by a little attorney."*[24]

The Lords recessed until August 17. Then,

> peers of the three realms have to be in Parliament at ten o'clock in the morning, under pain of imprisonment in the Tower, or of a fine of 500 guineas a day. Only septuagenarians are excused, and they will be the most punctual so as not to give away their age. What a trial we shall witness! Those grave spiritual lords, how will they take the pretty things they are going to hear?[25]

Countess Lieven would have been ecstatic had Parliament recessed for several months past August 17. Besides providing fodder for Clement's delectation, the royal divorce had serious implications. Conservative Russia and Austria wanted the conservative Tory government to stay in power. Once Parliament met, angry crowds

---

*Henry Peter Brougham, a Whig member of Parliament and noted barrister, represented the queen.

gathered in Parliament Square. The countess applauded foreign secretary Lord Castlereagh's admirable sang-froid in facing them down. "One ought always to show courage even if it is only through fright; it is the one infallible resource."[26]

Driving down elegant Bond Street at the fashionably crowded hour of two in the afternoon the countess met the queen sitting in a slow-moving state coach drawn by six horses, and with her usual escort—what Dorothea called an unruly throng but actually the common people whom the countess, nonetheless, considered decent. Although a veil completely covered Caroline's face the fastidious countess shuddered to see huge black eyebrows, as thick as two fingers together, and an exceedingly generous application of rouge and lipstick. The queen's escort stopped Countess Lieven's carriage; they ordered her servants to doff their hats, Dorothea to lower her window. But London was not St. Petersburg; Tsar Paul's police did not enforce these commands. Instead, shouting people encircled the carriage. Neither the countess nor her servants obeyed. And she inadvertently broke up the queen's escort, for half of them followed her to Lady Granville's door. They took honors in noise, but the haughty countess held honors in determination.

Political passion reached violent proportions. The Opposition expected revolution. Republicans promoted strident public demonstrations outside Parliament. One protest resulted in soldiers killing five men. Metternich would not learn about that from the newspapers. The ministerial press were not eager to brag about it, and the Republican papers did not want the episode to discourage people from going to the House.

Meanwhile, "the Italian witnesses are supplying not only the Press but even Society with all its jokes. Everyone is using the catchword 'Non mi ricordo.'"*[27]

Popular discontent plus party maneuvers seemed about to bring down the cabinet. Then, to Clement and Dorothea's unmitigated relief Parliament defeated the Divorce Bill.[28]

That same summer the Kingdom of Naples rose against its autocratic ruler. Concerned enough that the revolt might succeed, conservatives feared an even worse fate—its spread. Sitting next to Countess Lieven, the duke of Wellington seemed sunk in gentle slumber. "Devil take me, Prince Metternich must march," the great general suddenly exclaimed.

> He must advance all his troops against Naples. It will be five or six weeks before they are in a position to act. Meanwhile, he must warn his allies of what he is going to do. They will give their consent. He must crush this Italian revolution; but he must come out of it with clean hands.

Dorothea had not changed one syllable, she promised Clement. Wellington might "have neither the opportunity, nor the right, to convey his opinion to you,"[29] so he used Dorothea Lieven as an unofficial conduit.

Britain's foreign secretary did have the right to communicate directly with Metternich. Aloof and handsome with icy but polished manners, Robert Stewart, Viscount Castlereagh (later Lord Londonderry) could be charming with those he knew well. A fine diplomat, he and Metternich admired each other. They had cooperated at the Congress of Vienna; they agreed that legitimacy and the status quo guaranteed in the Concert of Europe could best keep peace on the contentious Continent.

---

*"*I do not remember.*"

Countess Lieven had immediately cultivated the powerful foreign secretary as part of her professional duty, but Castlereagh's strong, honorable character and sound common sense attracted her, too. In turn, Dorothea enchanted Castlereagh personally, and engaged him politically. A close friendship developed.

The Castlereaghs liked to entertain informally at their country house in the scenic Kent countryside, and often invited the Lievens. Passionately fond of music, Dorothea's host would sit next to her while she played the piano. The conservative foreign secretary even "insisted on waltzing with me—heavens, what hard work to keep the Minister in revolution!" While they were dancing, several couples went for a stroll in the beautifully landscaped gardens. "It was a dark night; the little paths were well screened with thick laurel bushes; and the great majority of the guests gave us the slip." Only "little girls, dancers of the caliber of my husband and the master of the house, a few old women"[30] and, Dorothea virtuously informed Clement, herself, remained in the ballroom.

Lady Castlereagh neither equaled her husband intellectually, nor especially interested herself in politics. Nonetheless, they were an extremely devoted couple.

The foreign secretary distrusted Austrian ambassador Esterhazy, who had cultivated a closeness to King George IV. Castlereagh preferred his not particularly able but at least trustworthy brother, the British ambassador at Vienna, as a conduit to Metternich. The latter, in turn, had as much if not more faith in Neumann, the ambassador's immediate subordinate, than in Esterhazy. As for Dorothea Lieven's part in the equation, Metternich judged her "very clear-headed in all matters of business."[31]

And Castlereagh trusted her. His colleagues would think it too official were he to write Metternich on this particular issue, but he could talk informally to a woman. Castlereagh "wants the point made clear to you," Dorothea impressed on Clement.

> I did not think it was right to offer to pass on the explanation to you; but as, after a long preamble, he spoke to me in great detail on the matter, I concluded that he wanted to kill two birds with one stone. Here is his speech: "We are in perfect agreement, Prince Metternich and I, on the fundamentals of every question; but, in the application of our views on the Eastern Question,[32] I find a shade of difference which makes me anxious to bring him round to my own point of view. He wants the rest of the affair entrusted to Commissioners."

Castlereagh thought the negotiations not far enough "'advanced to be entrusted to *unskilled* hands.'" Hence, the question must be handled by "'negotiators of the *greatest ability*. That is the idea I should like to be able to convey to him as strongly as possible, although I am not permitted to address myself directly to him on the subject.'"[33]

By now Dorothea Lieven knew that men in power valued her political acumen, not to mention her talent for expressing the meat of the matter in a few, well-chosen words.

Meanwhile, Europe's conservatives realized their worst fears. Revolution spread from Naples to Spain, Portugal, and Piedmont; Greece started its struggle for freedom from Ottoman rule. Always staunchly patriotic, Dorothea Lieven still had independent opinions. If, she wrote Clement, one examined the source of all the problems "convulsing the world, does one not come back to" Tsar Alexander? "Is it not his liberalism that has strengthened the democratic party in Europe?"[34]

Yes. At the end of 1820 Metternich rallied an all–European congress to resolve the danger of international revolution. He met the tsar informally, and alone. "We talk for hours together without ever disagreeing."[35] Metternich's arguments against revolution, let alone the folly of granting concessions lest they encourage more demands, fell on fertile soil. Dorothea's brother General Alexander Benckendorff had recently told his master about subversive liberal activities amongst certain secret societies in the officer corps. The tsar chose to ignore this disturbing news; and he refused to consider Benckendorff's proposal to create a special police force to monitor the disgruntled officers. Still, Benckendorff's information disquieted the tsar. And the nationalist leanings of his Polish subjects disillusioned him. Moreover, although the tsar approved of legitimate sovereigns granting constitutions (except in Russia), he did not go so far as to endorse their doing so under the duress of rebellion. This concatenation of circumstances played into Metternich's capable hands. At Troppau he convinced the tsar to renounce liberalism, and declare himself ready to follow Metternich. Tsar Alexander "and I understand one another thoroughly,"[36] Clement impressed on Dorothea.

Austria and Russia now agreed that the Powers must send armies to restore legitimate rulers. Castlereagh preferred non-intervention in the internal affairs of other states. So after Troppau, Britain and Russia began to diverge on an important question that, on the other hand, drew Austria and Russia closer.

Hence, for Dorothea Lieven, patriotism, ambition, and passion coalesced to open exciting new opportunities.

૪૦ભ૪

Of course she and Clement could scarcely risk sending their personally and politically sensitive secret correspondence by ordinary post, or even by the Austrian diplomatic pouch. So the master of machination devised a method. Dorothea sealed her letter in a plain, unaddressed envelope intended only for Clement, and gave it to Neumann at London's Austrian embassy. "I do not need to recommend the enclosure to your care, dear friend," Neumann wrote on the second envelope. His counterpart in Paris put this second envelope in a third addressed to Metternich's private secretary at Vienna; he placed the envelope in a fourth, unaddressed envelope, which he handed to Metternich. Clement used the system in reverse.

The lovers also used a cipher to disguise places, events, or people. Jokes, gossip and, mostly in Metternich's case, scornful comments about certain diplomats enlivened the serious political content of their correspondence. Then, too, each periodically penned an "official" letter, one Dorothea could show to her husband, and Metternich, to others.

This deeply rewarding clandestine correspondence gave Dorothea an outlet for her ardent emotions, and expanded her independence within her unsatisfying marriage. And exchanging daily letters with Europe's foremost statesman encouraged Dorothea's ambition, sharpened the flair for politics she had inherited from her mother, and enhanced her power. Secrecy confirmed personal as well as professional control.

She knew it. Dorothea Lieven dedicated time and energy to her letters. Metternich valued them for painting "a picture full of truth on events and on men."[37]

An expert questioner, an excellent listener, an exceptional observer, a woman of extraordinary intelligence, Dorothea Lieven's ability to enchant the hearts and engage the political thinking of decision-makers won their confidence. That earned her the right to take a legitimate part in the political dialogue.

8

Partners in Politics

How, *mon Prince*, did you come to think of using my letters in a report? I am overwhelmed by the honor you do them.... They must make an odd collection ... and the relationship between us is ... odd. As a result of seeing one another for a week, two years ago, here we are engaged in an intimate correspondence which ought to imply a whole lifetime of daily contacts. Some day ... people will wonder what we were about—whether it was love or politics.[1]

—Dorothea Lieven

When 1821 opened, almost three years had passed since Dorothea last saw her lover. Now, "I am going to run after you, I resign myself to this humiliation with all my heart."[2]

The Lievens agreed that their sons Alexander and Constantine should continue their education in Russia. Their father would escort them; he must also attend to personal business and renew his relations at court. Dorothea never even entertained the idea of exposing her sweet, gentle little George to such a strenuous journey, much less thought for one moment of leaving him in London. She would take George with her to the Continent where she intended to seek a cure for her rheumatism. Several friends planned to visit Rhineland spas, and Dorothea's younger brother Constantine served as Russian minister at nearby Stuttgart. "It would be easy for us to meet," Dorothea wrote Clement.[3] She needed to choose a spa in "the vicinity of some capital that has an Austrian mission, so I can stay in touch with you. I submit all this to your wish," but "I must see you."[4]

Metternich could not mount the steps of his traveling carriage "without some significance being attached to it, and it would not suit anyone if it was said that for him the Rhine had become a Capua!"[5]* pointed out Dorothea's close friend the duke of Wellington. She must be patient, he counseled, even prepared for a letdown. But Dorothea had faith in Clement finding "the right means to go somewhere, and me, I certainly will know how to get horses to take me there."[6]

ഇൗരു

* Hannibal of Carthage consistently defeated the Romans until he established his winter headquarters at Capua, in antiquity Italy's most luxurious city. When he left, defeats followed until Carthage lay in ruins and Hannibal lived in exile.

Bees were bumbling through heavily scented lilacs and lilies of the valley when Count Lieven escorted his wife and little son to Dover. Behind her stood the painful parting with her older boys. "You don't know what such a separation means to a mother—how all her thoughts are concentrated on it; how afraid she is of forgetting some piece of advice which might be useful," Dorothea wrote Clement. "Everything becomes important; and I felt that all my mind and all my time were not sufficient to think of everything and do everything."[7]

Dorothea had to face yet another farewell. "The force of habit is strong; and, now that I am deprived of his [Lieven's] presence and his protection, I forget that differences of character and disposition now and then cause me unpleasant moments. I wept bitterly when I left him; I am still in tears and feel quite lost."[8]

Indeed, traveling without her husband proved exhausting. "You have to think, you have to devote all your intelligence to arranging where to sleep and dine. What a method of broadening one's outlook!"[9]

Having paid a deadly dull duty visit to the Grand Duchess Anna and her husband, the prince of Orange, at Brussels, as well as calling on other members of the imperial family refreshing themselves at western watering places, Dorothea, hoping Clement could contrive to visit his nearby estate, settled at an exclusive Rhineland spa.

Schlangenbad lay in a verdant valley sheltered on the north by steep, densely wooded mountain slopes and bordered on the south by the busy Rhine river. Terraced vineyards, tiny winemaking villages that clung to the riverbanks, and huge hilltop castles surrounded the spa. Its baths enjoyed a superb reputation for easing rheumatism; called "the ladies' baths, they fortify the hands and whiten them, here is something that will do me good and give me pleasure,"[10] Dorothea wrote her husband.

"The baths and countryside are delicious, and in fine weather nothing is more magnificent, unfortunately good weather has been rare."[11] But little George Lieven always lifted his mother's spirits. He "is all my joy," she wrote.[12] And George's vocabulary waxed "so large that I do not have time to keep up with his language.... I find him a glowing presence."[13]

Nonetheless, duty continued to tie Clement to his desk. So after four weeks Dorothea deserted Schlangenbad for nearby Stuttgart, the city of her and her mother's exile thirty years before. General Constantine Benckendorff, Russia's minister to the Grand Duchy of Württemberg, eagerly anticipated his sister's visit. Not for one second would he entertain her idea of staying in a hotel, so Dorothea and her small son spent very pleasant days with the Benckendorffs. Constantine's little boy fell ill soon after his aunt and cousin left. Because, Dorothea reproved her brother, his children ate too many dishes. "Put them on a more simple diet; always *roast* meat, beef, lamb, or veal—but one kind only for dinner; with that potatoes" or "spinach, and then a tart or pudding; they will be perfectly satisfied with that if they are hungry." Too much rich food made the children eat more than they should. "Your children will have an entirely different appearance for neither has the proper complexion and all children's illnesses come from their stomachs."[14]

Tawny leaves were already floating down from the trees but Metternich still had not found the right means to meet his lover. So Countess Lieven's well-sprung carriage bore her north to Frankfurt to await her husband. "Rothschild[15] called at the crack of dawn today; all his house and correspondents put themselves out to help me. They are very like you in this regard,"[16] Dorothea flattered.

⁝

Meanwhile, Great Britain's King George IV descended on his realm of Hanover for his formal investiture as its ruler. Foreign secretary Lord Castlereagh of course accompanied his king. Metternich meant to use this occasion for one of those face-to-face meetings that served him so well. He and Castlereagh needed to discuss a thorny issue: the Eastern Question. In a bold bid for independence, the Greeks had taken up arms against their legitimate sovereign, the sultan of Turkey. Tsar Alexander wanted to help them militarily. Appalled at the prospect of Russia spreading her power in Eastern Europe, Austria and England had already painted a dread scenario for Alexander: if the Greeks succeeded, Russia's southern provinces would soon follow suit. So if Lieven joined Castlereagh and Metternich at Hanover, official representatives of the three powers could meet. That confluence of conditions brought Dorothea what she desperately wanted.

Calculating that Countess Lieven's presence would please King George, and put Metternich in a positive mood, Castlereagh sent an urgent invitation to Dorothea, sitting on pins and needles at Frankfurt. She set out immediately, arriving on October 20th (1821). Under pretext of conveying the Austrian emperor's official congratulations to King George, Metternich and an extremely distinguished entourage reached Hanover the same day.

The tsar's business delayed Lieven's arrival. So for eight precious days Dorothea and Clement made delicious love at night and wove diplomatic webs by day. Since the Hanoverians outdid themselves to entertain their king, whose extravagances exceeded theirs, the lovers met at many social functions, too.

Metternich now pulled the strings of Russian foreign policy, so he and Dorothea wanted Britain to hew to Austria and Russia's conservative line. King George held his cabinet in utter contempt; he blamed it for bungling his divorce and botching his wife's funeral. The king despised Castlereagh most of all, for fastidious Lady Castlereagh refused to recognize the King's buxom blonde mistress. So Clement and Dorothea got busy; they successfully contrived to reconcile the king with his conservative foreign secretary.

Count Lieven arrived on October 28th. The king immediately invited the Lievens, Metternich, and Castlereagh to a gargantuan repast that the extortionately paid French genius who ruled over the royal kitchens thought fit to set before his master. It began modestly enough with only two soups, immediately followed by turbot, lobsters, and trout. Fourteen entrées then made up the first course including loin of veal in a béchamel sauce, sweetbreads with stewed lettuce, and lamb cutlets reposing on a purée of French beans. The second course featured twenty-four dishes consisting of several varieties of roast fowl, six different joints of roast meat including hare and a hot haunch of venison, lobster salad, cherry tarts, and five other sweet dishes. During this dinner Lieven gratified his company with the news that Tsar Alexander had no plans to promote the Greek cause with guns.

Next day King George left Hanover with a small party including the Lievens. They and Metternich arrived in Frankfurt on November 5th. Five days later Metternich left for Vienna and the Lievens for London, but not before the lovers had laid their plans: to meet at the next all–European congress, scheduled to take place at Verona in September of the following year (1822).

Austria and Russia wanted King George to attend the Congress of Verona. He would fortify the conservative cause and, as a matter of course, bring his foreign secretary with him. Hence, were the king and Castlereagh again to visit Hanover, they could easily proceed to Verona. That would neatly circumvent parliamentary debate, even cabinet discussion, on their attendance.[17]

Dorothea Lieven understood English politics; Metternich excelled at intrigue. They concocted a plan. She would cajole the king into visiting Hanover again next summer.

With subtle flattery the countess catered to the king's pride, his love of pleasure, his immense vanity. She dwelt on the dangers of Jacobinism; she proved what a great moral effect the king of England's presence would have. Dorothea even dragged in her tsar; how he would cherish a chance to erase memories of his unfortunate state visit to London! Castlereagh liked the idea of his sovereign going to Hanover and from there to Verona. Concerned that the foreign secretary's keenness might cool, Dorothea urged Clement to make sure his ambassador kept Castlereagh and the king in favor of the journey.

Typically, Countess Lieven left nothing to chance. She and her husband were staying with King George at his "cottage" in Windsor forest. Shortly before Castlereagh came to discuss his plans with the king, Dorothea engaged George's mistress in private discussion. "Not an idea in her head; not a word to say for herself; nothing but a hand to accept pearls and diamonds with, and an enormous balcony to wear them on"[18]; still, the countess stood on excellent terms with Lady Conyngham. Impressing on her the great prestige her royal lover could gain among Continental statesmen were he to go to Germany next summer, Dorothea carefully sketched the need for Castlereagh to be at the congress, and the difficulty of getting him there without the king's presence at Hanover. Lady Conyngham swallowed everything.

On tenterhooks, the countess dined with Castlereagh that evening. Knowing how he liked to tease her, Dorothea waited patiently for the foreign secretary to divulge his news. "Tell him that I am hoping to see him soon," Castlereagh finally said. "I think of nothing," Dorothea exulted to her lover, "but our splendidly successful project."[19]

Alas, a prolonged and particularly painful attack of gout decided King George on summering in Scotland. Then Lady Conyngham and Whig leader Lord Grey met at a dinner. His party wanted Grey to get on friendly terms with the favorite so as to gain direct access to the king. Countess Lieven put a spoke in that wheel. Turning the full battery of her charm on Grey, she insisted that he sit next to her at dinner. By "the end of dessert, he was quite ready to believe I was encouraging him. When we went up to the drawing room, he came to sit by me again and did not leave." Suddenly, Lady Conyngham asked when Lord Londonderry* was going to the congress. Grey at once pricked up his ears: "'What? Londonderry? What Congress? Is there to be a Congress?' Lady Conyngham: 'but, of course.' *'If there is a Congress, there is mischief; send me to the Congress; I shall know what to do there.'* 'What would

---

* *Viscount Castlereagh had succeeded to his father's title, Marquis of Londonderry.*

you do?' 'Break it up immediately, and send the Holy Alliance to the devil.' Here's a nice mess," the countess lamented, "there will be questions in Parliament, and the last hope of seeing Londonderry go will disappear."[20]

Meanwhile, King George prepared to host an official dinner for visiting royalty. Not unnaturally he included the Londonderrys. George's mistress refused to attend if her arch-enemy, Lady Londonderry, did. If Lady Conyngham did not come, countered the king, he could not invite the visiting princess, which would be an insult. Lady Conyngham held firm. Her royal lover then conceived the brilliant idea of asking Countess Lieven to arbitrate. "Thank Heaven, a quarrel of two years' standing is ended, at any rate as far as appearances go," she regaled Metternich. "I can think of no more difficult job than getting round a woman's vanity, when one can appeal neither to her reason nor to her decent feelings."[21]

That a foreign ambassadress had secured his wife's invitation to a state dinner deeply humiliated Londonderry. He even confided to Dorothea that he might resign. Stupefied, she could only express her surprise that he would consider sacrificing to a women's quarrel his whole political existence, let alone the good he had done and might still do.

Dorothea and Londonderry now talked only "*tête-à-tête*; and then we never stop. I really believe he loves me with all his heart."[22] Clement must trust in the innocence of their friendship; she found Londonderry so entertaining because "you gave me a taste for his conversation."[23]

Meanwhile, the foreign secretary began to show irrational mistrust of those closest to him. Dorothea admitted to Metternich that her influence over the king might well disturb Londonderry, but he must realize that she had always used her power in his interest; he should thus forget her official position, and remember that Dorothea stood his friend.

Londonderry did. For a few weeks.

He then became abnormally sensitive about Lieven discussing business with Wellington, and fantasized that the Lievens might prefer him as foreign secretary—because the duke and Dorothea were close, and she was working to get him admitted to the king's favor. All this seemed credible, but lacked foundation. Dorothea could not fathom why Londonderry had become so suspicious. She thought she had an honest face; the foreign secretary must discern her true feeling of friendship for him.

In fact, Londonderry showed alarming signs of psychotic depression. He imagined himself the object of persecution—blackmail for the criminal offense of homosexuality—his violent temper outbursts terrified one and all. But he continued to gravitate to Dorothea's side in society and sought her out when she walked in Kensington Gardens. "His face lit up when he caught sight of me. I felt that he grew gentler with me, and he often told me so. Then he would allow himself to make the most intimate confidences. If I said a word to calm him about his ideas on his position— for it was always about his position that he spoke—he flew into a rage; and from that moment his tone would be bitter and ironical." Londonderry "became a kind of torment.... I felt attracted towards him; at the same time a certain terror overcome me whenever he grew angry"; but despite "that, I had a conviction that he felt real friendship towards me.[24]

To Dorothea Lieven's horror and distress, Londonderry committed suicide.

She lost a good friend, as well as a close connection to Britain's foreign secretary, "perhaps the only man in England who understood European politics, and whose principles as well as his inclinations urged him towards friendship with Austria" Dorothea commiserated with Clement. "Besides mourning Lord Londonderry as a friend, you have to mourn him as a Minister."[25]

Encouraged by his spouse, Lieven lost no time in approaching prime minister Lord Liverpool. "Londonderry is dead, but the reasons that required his attendance at Verona remain. Will someone be sent and who?" "I must first appoint a foreign secretary," Liverpool replied. "That decision is deferred until the King returns from Scotland."

"England surely would not want to show discourtesy towards Europe's sovereigns by keeping them waiting for an envoy," Dorothea prompted her husband. "Why not treat the choice of representative to Verona separately from that of foreign secretary?"

"I shall send Wellington to the Congress," confided the harried prime minister.

Dorothea liked the duke personally and thought him useful politically, but had little opinion of him as a diplomat, Metternich even less, but at least they could count on his conservatism. So Dorothea hastened to give Clement the good news via a note to her friend Emily Cowper's brother, posted at the Frankfurt embassy, asking him to let Metternich know at once. Emily liked to participate in Dorothea's intrigues and gladly enclosed the note in her own letter. Dorothea could not trust the news to Neumann at Austria's London embassy, since Liverpool had made Lieven promise to tell nobody in the British capital.

◈

Lord Londonderry's death created an immense chasm in the cabinet.

The talented, ambitious man destined to fill it represented all that Countess Lieven loathed. An upstart (his father had so far forgotten himself as to marry an actress), a liberal, a demagogue who meant to rely on popular support, George Canning even proposed to publish diplomatic correspondence!

The duke of Wellington, who relished titillating gossip with his like-minded friend Countess Lieven, regaled her about Canning. He had been with Caroline, princess of Wales "when, after the first year of their marriage, she received the famous letter from the Prince of Wales giving her freedom and taking back his." Caroline consulted Canning. He thought the letter gave her leave to do as she liked, "and they took advantage of it on the spot. I rather fancy," Dorothea added for Clement's delectation, "that might have happened even before the letter."[26] Regardless, Canning soon fell in love and married. The Cannings and Princess Caroline were friends; she stood godmother to their eldest son. So when, later, the king insisted on a divorce, Canning said he would resign his cabinet post rather than support any measure against Caroline. If Canning's earlier friendship with Princess Caroline had enraged her husband, this stance earned him the king's eternal enmity.

In addition, the Opposition hated Canning.

> The Ministers distrust him; those who want him do not like him. His personal following is a mere drop in the ocean; and, with that exception, there is not a soul in the United Kingdom who has the slightest respect for him. In spite of all these reasons for keeping him out, public opinion demands him.[27]

As much as Liverpool and Wellington mistrusted Canning's intellectual brilliance and feared his forceful personality, so, too, did they realize that the government's survival depended on Canning's ability and seniority, not to mention his dynamism and debating skill. Hence, the duke convinced the extremely reluctant king to appoint Canning.

Britain's new foreign secretary scorned congresses as much as he despised the Concert of Europe. Canning wanted the Congress of Verona to fail, and, to Countess Lieven and Metternich's dismay, his instructions to Wellington assured that it did.

ೞೞಛ

In autumn 1822 the diplomats deliberated for well over two months in the small, north Italian city standing on a fertile plain carpeted with orchards and vineyards, and watered by the burbling Adige river, which tumbles from the steep slopes and pink granite peaks of the nearby Dolomites. For centuries a prosperous trading center, Verona boasts ancient buildings, a well-preserved Roman amphitheater, and charming cobbled streets. As well, it is home to one of history's most famous romances. Verona's medieval town square features the balcony where Juliet (supposedly) welcomed Romeo.

Clement and his countess kept such constant company that her compatriots stigmatized Dorothea as "the Austrian." Russian ladies showed the proud countess "little respect, while speaking badly about her and keeping aloof," because of "the hatred they have sworn against Austrians, and suspicion of a liaison between the Countess and Metternich."[28]

Passionate love in romantic Verona profoundly satisfied Dorothea. Nevertheless, she could not under any circumstances tolerate calumny cast on her patriotism.

"The circle in which I live puts me in a position altogether comfortable to my curiosity and taste," Dorothea fired off to her brothers (Alexander with an important military command at St. Petersburg and Constantine, minister at Stuttgart). Foreign minister Count Nesselrode and Prince Metternich insisted on Countess Lieven opening her drawing-room each evening to give the diplomats an appropriate social venue; hence, she saw the most important and interesting people. Dorothea already knew "Metternich fairly well by meeting him on several occasions," she wrote with gross understatement,

> but here I have associated with him on the most friendly terms. The Duke of Wellington, too, who is the best and firmest of my English acquaintances, comes to see me constantly. These two stars, looked upon antithetically in the Emperor's antechamber, have completely deprived me of the society of my fellow-countrymen, so that at Verona I see all Europe except Russia.[29]

Yes, Nesselrode, and Russia's ambassadors to France and Austria did call daily, but other Russians perceived the countess as English because she had lived there for ten years, or Austrian because she saw Metternich so often. Tsar Alexander disapproved of this ill-will; indeed, there had been a totally futile attempt to make him share it. So the tsar continued to treat Countess Lieven with his usual kindness; "and I flatter myself that he quite understands me."[30]*

Countess Lieven's campaign won her a long, affectionate letter from empress-mother Maria; it included "a whole page of compliments and pretty speeches made

---

* *He might well. At Verona Tsar Alexander concentrated on his affair with the new Lord Londonderry's buxom wife.*

about me by the Emperor. I see from this that Verona, whatever you may have thought, was far from injuring me in his estimation,"[31] Dorothea crowed to Clement shortly after the congress.

Nonetheless, Verona proved that George Canning's rise meant a drop in Dorothea Lieven's power. This diminished her political value to Metternich.

Originally convened to tackle the tenacious Greek revolt, the Congress of Verona instead turned to a more pressing problem: Spain. Revolution still threatened its legitimist government. Neighboring France's reactionary regime declared itself ready to cross the Pyrenees with an army to restore Spain's legitimate king. And Tsar Alexander offered to deploy part of his enormous army in the peninsula. No-one relished the prospect of Russian soldiers marching across the Continent, or of Russian ships carrying them westward. If the Concert of Europe must intervene in Spain, the Powers preferred that France act on their behalf. Thus Austria, Prussia, and Russia united behind French intervention. In a move calculated to drive a wedge into the Concert of Europe, however, Canning instructed Wellington to insist frankly and forcefully that Great Britain would not interfere against revolutionary forces favoring constitutional government in Spain. Hence, Dorothea's closest English friend and political ally opposed her lover, her tsar, and her husband.

She had always questioned where her and Clement's love would lead. By now Dorothea realized that their chances of meeting were few and, even then, involved huge complications. Hence, their relationship as lovers had, at best, a dubious future. Admitting to this unpleasant truth caused Dorothea no little pain for she loved her soul-mate, craved his attentions. Still, there remained politics. So long as Metternich controlled Russian foreign policy, Dorothea's connection with him constituted a crucial asset, one she resolved to exploit in her drive to resuscitate "my diplomatic career."[32]

Countess Lieven's vehicle stood ready at hand.

9

The Cottage Coterie

I much prefer your letters to all the dispatches in the world.... You are among the small number of people who see things as they are, who seize the heart of everything.... You understand men so it is no surprise that you can do so much of their work.[1]

—Clement von Metternich

Countess Lieven returned from Verona at the end of 1822 to resume her place among the exclusive clique of diplomats who surrounded King George IV. The Cottage Coterie consisted of Russian ambassador Count Lieven, Austrian ambassador Prince Esterhazy and his first secretary Baron Neumann, Hanoverian minister Count Münster, sometimes the French ambassador, and Countess Lieven—the only woman.

The King often invited them to his "cottage" in ancient, scenic Windsor forest. Stuccoed and thatched in rustic style on the outside, exquisitely furnished at enormous cost on the inside, the Cottage provided the ultimate in comfort and elegance. Only the king's mistress Lady Conyngham, her complaisant husband, and a favored few including the Lievens stayed in the Cottage itself. They led a lazy, luxurious life. Rising at nine, Dorothea walked in the garden. After dressing she lunched with the king at eleven; they talked until one. She wrote letters for an hour, then joined the party for an outing in the forest, or on the lake. At four Dorothea dressed for dinner, in warm weather served in tents. Afterwards the piano; then écarté; bed at twelve. Conversation could occasionally be interesting, but considering Countess Lieven's rather caustic opinions of her host and his mistress, she usually found it "so stupid that one begins to doubt one's own intelligence."[2]

୫୦୯୫

After the debacle at the Congress of Verona the Cottage Coterie concentrated on keeping the king behind Austria and Russia's support of a French incursion into Spain to restore her legitimate ruler. That pitted the Coterie against foreign secretary George Canning, whose policy of non-intervention in Spain had provoked a split in the European alliance at Verona. France invaded Spain. To Tsar Alexander and Prince Metternich's fury, Canning forcefully and eloquently condemned French action in Parliament.

So starting in the spring of 1823, the Coterie focused its energies on a stratagem hatched in Metternich's fertile brain: "the plot to make Mr. Canning jump" (out of office). Dorothea Lieven fed the flames of reactionary King George's ire against his liberal-leaning foreign secretary, and invigorated the conservative duke of Wellington's doubt about Canning's policies.

In his cozy private parlor at the Cottage, King George and Countess Lieven sat comfortably engrossed in a long tête-à-tête. She flattered the vain British monarch into believing he had been missed at Verona; how he could benefit his realm by taking a hand in foreign policy because everyone distrusted Canning. She got the king to agree that Wellington's compliance with Canning's instructions to make clear that England refused to intervene against pro-constitutional groups in Spain, had been very disappointing.

Wellington often invited the Lievens to his country seat. The duke liked to take Dorothea on carriage drives through Stratfieldsaye's fine woods and superb park with its wild, white violets and beautiful vistas of the undulating Berkshire countryside. But since recurring and severe chest colds plagued Dorothea throughout that 1822–23 winter, it was in the duke's favorite room, his library, that she impressed on him how every Continental statesmen lacked confidence in Canning, how all his cabinet colleagues distrusted him, how all eyes—domestic and foreign—turned to Wellington as England's savior.

Dorothea got the duke to admit, she boasted to Metternich, that the results of his faithful execution of Canning's instructions at Verona turned out to be worse than at first appeared. Daily, England's separation from the Concert of Europe became more obvious—a misfortune for all but especially England. Indeed, Dorothea persisted, "For eight years, powers so dissimilar in their constitutions had been able to see eye to eye on all questions." Now, they must meet the spirit of revolution boldly. It affected all nations, although England less than others. Hence, Dorothea needled, "her lukewarmness at the moment."

"Do you take us for Jacobins?" Wellington exploded. "Damme I'll show you what I wrote about Spain; and you will see if M. de Metternich ever said anything stronger."[3] Next morning he showed Dorothea his letters. Although she transcribed them for Metternich from memory, Dorothea, in all justice, did urge Wellington to show the papers to Lieven and Esterhazy. The duke refused.

Metternich might suppose this conversation imposed "rather a strain on my virtue. You realize that a lesser woman would have been very happy" to have a monopoly of the duke's confidences.

> You can imagine, that, for a moment, I smiled to myself at the thought of being the direct channel of information interesting to my Court and to you. But, when I reflected what good it might do, I immediately sacrificed my vanity, and finally persuaded Wellington to show Esterhazy and my husband what he had read to me.[4]

Indeed, Dorothea succeeded in creating such contrition in the duke that he sought to make amends about Verona. And under her expert handling King George came to see Wellington as the only man he could trust. The cabinet paid little attention to foreign policy, but the ministers did have personal affection for the duke. So the countess felt confident that she and her Coterie cohorts might yet thwart Canning.

∞

"Always I have a temperature; my chest always troubles me; I am always in my dressing-gown. I read till my eyes are red."[5] It seemed to Dorothea that since her return from Verona she had hardly left her bedroom. During January's dark days a particularly virulent chest cold depressed Dorothea, for it forced her to decline a flattering invitation to the Cottage, thus keeping both Lievens from closer contact with the king.

And the constraints of ill health caused Dorothea constant worry about Lieven; whether he could keep proper track of all the new points that arose, whether he would mishandle the information she worked so hard to glean from her private sources: "at Court, the King and his mistress; in the cabinet, the Duke of Wellington; in the Opposition, Lord Grey; in the Canning party, Lady Granville."* Yes, managing the current annoyance between Canning and Russia needed "much skill on the part of all concerned to avoid rocks which beset the course of affairs."[6]

Another worry nagged Dorothea: her father. "I imagined myself with you and I doubt if I can long resist my wish to see you again and embrace you all." Such strong "emotion could well make me surmount the disgust I have for the journey,"[7] General Benckendorff wrote. "My first wishes are for you and yours."[8] Had his health allowed, the general would have sailed with a Russian fleet bound for France. "You can imagine my dear child," that "I would have been happy to again see my dear, my well-loved Dacha."[9]

"If only I could go to him! How much I think of it, how much I want it," Dorothea sighed. "My husband will not let me go until next year. He is afraid the journey would strain my health."[10] So Dorothea resolved that the following summer would see her in Riga.

Meanwhile, her father felt "very feeble." Still, "I am taking advantage dear and good Dacha to satisfy my dearest occupation, to write to you and say that my love for you is always the best living."[11] General Benckendorff never finished this letter. He died three days after suffering a severe stroke. During that time one of Dorothea's letters reached him and, Alexander comforted her, lightened their father's final hours. "I feel the need of writing to you often," she told Alexander, "and of drawing near to you as much as distance allows. It separates us one from another at a time when my heart and spirit are bowed down by sorrow. Your grief cannot be compared with mine, which will sadden all the future joys of my life."[12]

Of course it would. Because guilt aggravated Dorothea's grief. She had not visited, had not attended her father's deathbed; Dorothea felt she had failed him, had fallen short of her childhood attachment, of their special bond that had survived even into adulthood.

"For a week my heart and eyes have refused to write to you," Dorothea confided to her kindred spirit, her Clement.

> I have been overwhelmed by my loss. It took me by surprise, as if my father had not been old and infirm, and as if in the natural order of things he ought not to die before me. After twelve years separation, it has affected me more than if I had been always at his side. He always loved me more than his other children. He asked for me: he wanted to bless me again—it is irreparable, that is the real misery. This will be a grief to me for many a day. My dear old father![13]

---

*Lord Granville and George Canning had been close friends since their youth.

The shock of her father's death, her profound and penitent sorrow piling on top of frequent and feverish chest colds, not to mention the arduous political struggles of the Cottage Coterie, now coalesced. London's premier physician forbade the countess to risk spending the next winter in England. So the count informed foreign minister Nesselrode that he faced a long, sad separation from his wife. Lieven would stay in London while she journeyed south. If Dorothea recovered sufficiently in warm, sunny Italy the Lievens planned that she would "return to Russia at the start of next spring, where the presence of my sons necessitates the attendance of one or the other of us."[14]

"The presence of my sons." Nesselrode knew very well that their grandmother Countess Charlotte Lieven, let alone their uncle General Alexander Benckendorff, could assure the suitable progress of the Lieven boys' education. Hence, the Russian foreign minister would recognize his ambassador's implied message. The Lievens had something important to discuss, a matter so delicate that it must be broached in person; and Dorothea's return to St. Petersburg, ostensibly on account of her sons, would cause much less comment than if her husband went.

Italy, meanwhile, lay within Austria's sphere of influence, which would facilitate Metternich's presence. Lieven knew his wife stood on friendly terms with the Austrian chancellor, that they corresponded. Since the Lievens were hatching a dramatic shift in Russian policy, to sound out Metternich would be prudent. For that Dorothea had unique qualifications.

Besides, the loss of an important source of male comfort, her father, increased Dorothea's desire to see her soul-mate. On the other hand, she knew the change in Russian policy that she and her husband were pondering might mean a break with Metternich. Convinced of his own infallibility, the man who had told her he was "a man apart from most other men" would never tolerate any deviation from his policies. So seeing Clement meant as much to Dorothea politically as it did emotionally. He promised to meet her.

England's hedgerows were still green but trees already blazed in gold and flame when the countess set out for Italy. She had long outgrown her husband emotionally, let alone intellectually, but twenty-two years of wedlock, five children, the void left by her father's death, and loyalty to the fabric of her marriage gave Dorothea "a very heavy, very unhappy heart at leaving."[15]

Obstacles, expense, and often peril typified private travel abroad. On their return from Verona the Lievens had neared the English coast in pitch darkness. Heavy seas hindered the ship from docking. Dorothea decided on taking the small boat to reach shore. "There was no gangway, no rope ladder, nothing" to help get into it; "one had to wait for a wave to lift the cockle-shell high enough for one to throw oneself from the deck of the packet-boat into the arms of a waiting sailor. I managed very cleverly. When we got to shore, they had to run the boat aground"[16] and, as a result, winter's chilly waves drenched the hapless passengers from head to foot.

A lady of rank rarely traveled without male escort. Paul Lieven, Dorothea's eldest, accompanied her. The Lieven entourage also included George, as Dorothea would not for a moment think of parting from her precious little boy for the whole winter. She and her sons rode in the first carriage of their cavalcade. Upper servants—Dorothea's personal maid, Paul's valet, George's governess, and a courier to take care of travel arrangements—rode in the second. The third vehicle, piled high with luggage, conveyed more servants. Their duties included washing and ironing the bed linens without which no self-respecting traveler would dream of going abroad, for she could be sure of one thing: the inns provided damp, dirty sheets. When Dorothea's close friend the duke of Wellington went to Russia he took not only a bed, but also a mattress covered with heavy silk to prevent the ubiquitous bed-bugs from getting into it, and of a light color to facilitate detection of any adventurous vermin.

Hardly had Countess Lieven's comfortable traveling carriage drawn up in front of the finest hotel in Paris, her first stop, when Russian ambassador Count Pozzo di Borgo called. Consequently, twenty-four pages of Dorothea's unusually cramped handwriting summarized their conversation for Lieven; indeed, her daily letters to him bear strong witness to Dorothea's grasp of business, to say nothing of the diplomats' confidence in her.

Four-year-old George's droll speech and infectious excitement at crossing the Alps between France and Switzerland enlivened the long southeastward journey to Geneva. As they neared the city, Dorothea suffered a debilitating attack of food-poisoning. And Geneva turned out to be "the gloomiest place on earth, and certainly in the gloomiest weather I have ever seen." For two days the skies wept incessantly, with "such a fog that I have no idea whether there are a lake and mountains or not." In fact, "I am rather gloomy," Dorothea disclosed to Clement, for all "the wisdom in the world cannot control destiny. It does with us as it pleases; I wish it would be pleased to bring you to Italy while I am there."[17]

On the morning of her departure for Milan a glorious sun shone. It turned the lake, surrounded by a green and smiling countryside with beautiful autumnal trees and snow-capped mountains beyond, with Mont Blanc towering over the whole land-scape, into a lovely panorama. Still, Dorothea feared crossing the Simplon Pass, and with good reason. Snow in October is not unusual in the Alps, and a blinding flurry of large slippery flakes almost caused her carriage to over-turn as it negotiated the narrow, winding road that snaked up and over the pass.

"How beautiful, how beautiful!" Southern Switzerland's superb weather, its splendid mountains with their spectacular waterfalls, rich vineyards, and magnificent Lago Maggiore, its shore studded with well-kept villages and lovely gardens so elated the countess that she enjoyed several energetic walks along the lake.

೮〇೮

"Well, so I find you are not coming to Italy after all." Why then "did you ask me to come? Your letter was definite." And "I have left all my comforts, all the interests of my life, all my intellectual habits, for the sake of an alien sky which warms my body but leaves my mind utterly vacant." It "will turn to marble, like all those statues in the cathedral."[18]

Sunny Italy had one significant disadvantage. The repressive regimes ruling its several autonomous regions turned the country into a political backwater. Still, Dorothea Lieven had not the slightest intention of letting that affect her career. Clement must keep her "au courant" because she could correspond with her husband and Wellington only through the ordinary mail; if Clement failed her, the countess ran "the risk of relapsing into the conventional feminine role; and it seems to me that would be a pity."[19]

She visited La Scala—found the building magnificent, the opera disappointing—but without Metternich for motive spent little time in Milan before turning south. Florence bored Countess Lieven although she liked the opera, and the month of warm weather restored her health to such an extent that she could hardly believe her legs had ever hurt. Dorothea walked all over the quintessential Renaissance city, felt well, and looked so well that people laughed when she said that she had come to Italy for her health.

In December (1823) Dorothea reached Rome.

"We two should live happily in Rome. You are mad about it; I am quite ready to go mad; together, we should make a happy and harmonious household,"[20] Dorothea enticed Clement. She admired the aqueducts "as they stride away out of sight, nobly intersecting the Campagna"; the dome of St. Peter's brought her to tears; the Pantheon's interior, with its "light falling straight from the sky without any artificial interposition—the idea and the effect enrapture me."[21] And little George's reaction to Rome delighted his doting mother; he insisted that the evangelists supporting the Chair of St. Peter were Cossacks.

A strange silence emanated from Vienna.

"Where is your letter, what has become of it ? Haven't you written?" How "wicked you are, how hateful! I wish I could send my abuse as quickly as I say it. I am furious. To get no letters would be a calamity anywhere; but how much more of a calamity in Rome!"[22]

A sufficiently serious bout of pneumonia had stopped Clement's pen.

> Thank you for reassuring me about your health. Together with your health, resume your old habits. Write every day, and send me a letter every week. I beg you, moreover, to set me an example; for I should feel some diffidence about letting the whole of your diplomatic service into the secret that I show more eagerness than you do.[23]

Dorothea urged sun and fresh air, exercise, peace of mind, and distraction for Clement's recuperation; in other words—Rome. Leave Canning to his own devices, the countess impressed on the Coachman of Europe; Clement would never turn the foreign secretary into a minister after his own heart. Indeed, Britain's prosperity justified Canning. The "lower classes live in plenty. Trade flourishes. The nobility wallow in the lap of luxury." The "National Debt is being reduced; taxes are being abolished. Bread is cheap," Dorothea counseled. Even if Russia and Austria did frown on British foreign policy, "what does John Bull mind? He has his mug of beer. And what do the Ministers mind? They are at peace among themselves."[24]

"The journey to Milan is settled,"[25] Metternich wrote. He and his emperor would arrive there at the beginning of April. Dorothea delayed her return to London.

"We must achieve our goal fully; the hardest part has been overcome,"[26] Lieven wrote. "The hardest part." If Dorothea meant to approach Nesselrode with a bold new direction in Russian policy, she must first be strong enough to withstand the rigorous journey across Europe. With her return to London now postponed, Lieven wanted his wife go to Russia straight from Italy.

> It is impossible for me to treat George to Russia without exposing him to privation and fatigue, which will make me suffer more than anything that could affect me directly and basically, your mother doubtless would have pleasure in seeing him, but this small moment of satisfaction would be short and the *troubles* would be great and perhaps a distraction in my business.[27]

Note: business.

"The Italian journey is put off till the beginning of September. Important reasons have led to this decision. One of them is, that we now have such a good understanding with St. Petersburg that it would be awkward to increase our correspondence by going to a distance."[28] Clement could not, after all, meet Dorothea in Italy. And he had sent an explicit warning: Russian and Austrian cooperation against Canning had never been stronger.

Meanwhile, with his ailing wife still living in Paris and his lover residing in London, it could scarcely come as a surprise that the "Adonis of the Drawing-Room" showed interest in other women; indeed, Dorothea's Viennese correspondents reported that Clement had begun to show marked interest in one beautiful young lady. And he had not come to Italy. "You would not believe how beautiful Italy has made me. You are missing a great deal by not seeing me, and no doubt this is the Indian summer of my charm. Fogs and journeys will make me lose it all; and age will prevent a second miracle—what a pity!"[29]

Hurt, angry, disappointed but not altogether surprised, Dorothea steeled herself to separate passion from politics. She may have lost her lover, but Dorothea had not lost one shred of her ambition. The dwindling of her romance with Clement freed her of any constraint that emotion might put on her political plans. Meanwhile, the excitement of business awaited in London, and for that Metternich might yet prove extremely useful.

ဆာကဗ

Pink and purple peonies perfumed the ambient air when Dorothea disembarked at Dover. She found her ally, the conservative duke, depressed; her antagonist, the liberal Canning, at the summit of success. King George abused his foreign secretary but "might just as well have held his tongue for Madame de Lieven will have *rien de plus pressé*[30] than to make a good story of it to her Emperor and to Metternich" noted waspish Mrs. Arbuthnot. "As *folle de lui*[31] as ever," the countess, "having failed to find him in Italy, is off again to search for him."[32]

En route to Russia Dorothea planned to visit Metternich at his German estate. Johannisberg's castle towered over the Rhine, not far from Schlangenbad spa and the famous Lorelei rock, and commanded a magnificent view of the busy river and enchanting countryside. Business brought Clement to Johannisberg but only one item had significance, and it "wholly belonged to me!"[33] He and Dorothea differed over what they called "the hump": the Greeks' fight for freedom from Ottoman rule. Tsar Alexander found it a heaven sent opportunity, for if Russia aided her Greek co-religionists militarily, Russia would advance towards her historic goal: control of the Straits—the strategic waterways linking the Black Sea to the Mediterranean. Metternich feared that a Russo-Turkish war would threaten the multi-ethnic Austrian Empire by encouraging other nationalist movements in the Balkans, let alone extending Russian power in Eastern Europe at Austria's expense. Dorothea Lieven embraced the tsar's urge to weaken Turkey. "If I could speak to you for one hour," Metternich sighed, "how differently you would see things & how impossible it would be for you to see them otherwise!"[34]

Metternich might well have infinite confidence in his powers of persuasion at a face-to-face meeting, but this time he chose to ignore a telling factor, one Dorothea had already pointed out: Canning's strong position. Now the political sands were shifting, too. Whig leader Lord Grey called; Countess Lieven would be astonished at certain changes. Grey refused to say more. But the countess had a special talent for inspiring the confidence of prominent men; she charmed Grey into divulging that prime minister Lord Liverpool's health would require his retirement; Canning would succeed him; would get rid of colleagues who opposed him; the liberal Grey might join Canning as foreign secretary. Wellington had confirmed the probability of Liverpool's retirement; indeed, many Tories urged him to ready himself to be prime minister.

Instead of Dorothea's visit, Clement got her letter from Dover. She was pregnant. Although Dorothea suspected it before she left London, the doctors had no objection to her traveling. Nonetheless, the short journey from London to Dover forced Dorothea into bed. That made her trip to Russia seem absolutely absurd, even dangerous. So the Lievens decided to give up the idea—for the time being.

ଅଓଔ

Dorothea reasoned that Russia could benefit from Canning's strength. Yet, her tsar still stood shoulder-to-shoulder with Metternich in the conservative cause. So until she could discuss her idea first with Nesselrode, then with the tsar, practical politics demanded that the countess continue her partnership with Metternich. On balance, if her mission to Russia failed, alliance with him gave her a strong fallback position.

So Dorothea urged Clement to return to his good relations with Wellington. Still smarting from the coolness created at Verona, the duke found it difficult to discuss this subject with Dorothea but King George did not. In the snug intimacy of the Cottage, the king asked the countess to convince Wellington that he still had Metternich's confidence, and to convince the Austrian chancellor to hold out the olive branch. "You have no idea how capable he [the Duke] is in affairs and how right in principle; to what an extent he is our whole support; what services he does us ('us' means your Ambassador and mine)." Wellington "is the only check we have on Mr. Canning's follies. The latter hates; but he fears him."[35]

After roundly abusing Wellington's behavior at Verona, and virtuously blaming his attitude on a guilty conscience, Metternich condescended to write the duke and send him a gift—a case of Riesling wine from his Johannisberg estate. At the same time Dorothea should reassure the duke that Metternich liked him, spoke of him constantly, had forgotten Verona, and relied on him to save England and Europe from the bane of liberalism as he had saved them from the scourge of Napoleon.

Concomitantly, the countess disguised her hand with flirtation. If Clement paid attention to other women, she could return the compliment. The king, to his mistress's patently obvious annoyance, began to pay assiduous attention to plumply pregnant Dorothea. And when he arranged a hunting-party for the duke of York, that portly prince excused himself to take Dorothea for a drive. She laughed at the royal rivalry, but Lieven laughed louder. Staying at the Cottage during a sweltering September, several exalted personages went out on the lake in a small boat. Wedged between the bulky perspiring thighs of King George and his brother York, Dorothea told her husband in Russian that disgust and heat were making her ill. So Lieven insisted she sit beside him in the bow of the boat where, he diplomatically claimed, stronger breezes blew.

ଅଓଔ

Meanwhile, a huge scandal loomed. Canning discovered that Metternich had orchestrated "an intrigue with the Court here—of which Madame de Lieven was the organ—to change the politics of this government by changing *me*."[36]

Thanks to King George's blundering, Metternich's plot "to make Mr. Canning jump" had sprung to a premature conclusion. The king and Wellington had, via Austrian diplomats Esterhazy and Neumann, sent Metternich secret information or, as Canning put it, a letter with "some incredibly unadvised expressions."[37] And with the king's approval another cabinet minister asked Neumann that Metternich propose to provide the anti–Canningites with arms. Metternich did, but also instructed ambassador Esterhazy "to keep himself safe—to let Madame L. [Lieven] do all."[38]

Believing the plot doomed, Esterhazy leaked information. Canning found out.

In the interim, France, having restored Spain's Bourbon ruler, kept her troops at Madrid. If France gained influence over Spain it would, Canning resolved, be Spain without her wealthy South American colonies. He wanted to recognize their independence. The king, Wellington, Metternich, and the tsar opposed this move.

So Canning threatened to resign over the Spanish-American issue and to declare

> openly in the H. of C.*—taking care to keep safe my sources of intelligence—that I was driven from office by the Holy Alliance [Austria, Prussia, Russia]; and further, that the system ... [of] personal communications between the Sovereign and Foreign Ministers, was one under which no English Minister could do his duty. If, after such a denunciation and the debates which would have followed it, the L's and Est.† did not find London too hot for them, I know nothing of the present temper of the English nation.[39]

The king had no choice. Britain recognized Spain's former colonies as independent republics. And Countess Lieven diplomatically conceded that this move enhanced British prestige without doing any harm to the Continental powers.

She disliked Canning's liberalism, but that did not necessarily rule out Russia's making use of it. Still, an astute player does not discard an ace too early in the game. So Dorothea and Clement continued to correspond frequently; discuss politics fervently; gossip maliciously; and titillate with murmurings of love.

He: "Our liaison is a hundred times more true than those who only sustain themselves by such essentials as we lack!"[40]

"I write to you because I miss the joy of not writing to you. You have become a habit ... You are my second nature."[41]

She: "I brought the Ozarovskys here to show them" English country house life. "We are a large party"—"diplomats, Ministers, pretty women, jealous husbands, perfumed dandies, long dark corridors, chapels, towers, bats in the bed-curtains—everything you need for a romance, or, at any rate, for an affair. I am bored, because I am not having one."[42]

⋙⋘

Dorothea's sixth pregnancy raised her hope that this time (February 1825) she would give birth to a daughter. Her fifth son's arrival in the world caused his mother immense suffering; indeed, seventeen days after his delivery Dorothea's debility

---

*House of Commons.
†Lievens, Esterhazy.

proved so great that her doctors outlawed visitors. The Lievens named the boy Arthur, after his godfather the duke of Wellington.

Simultaneously, Clement arrived in Paris to attend his wife's deathbed. "There is nothing in the world I would not do for"[43] her. Since he considered wifehood a profession like any other, Clement, despite never having loved his wife, thought her "excellent, full of intelligence" and, he told Dorothea, uniting "all those qualities that make for inner" happiness. Now, "talking to the person who understands me" comforted the widower, and gave his soul-mate a value "no other person has acquired in my eyes."[44]

At this point Wellington confided a wonderful idea. Metternich should cross the Channel, land at Brighton where the duke and Dorothea would meet him, and from Brighton go straight to Windsor, thus avoiding Canning. Actually, long before Princess Metternich fell dangerously ill, her errant spouse had confided to Dorothea that, if the occasion suited, he might go to Paris and from there visit King George at either the Cottage or Brighton to put into play the face-to-face diplomacy which Metternich had polished to perfection. So Dorothea dropped a hint in the duke's ear. Now, she wrote Clement, Wellington's plan delighted him because it would please Metternich's friends and infuriate his enemy; indeed, the duke felt fully confident that Metternich would jump at it. But Dorothea advised Clement that she judged him too astute to jump at anything.

Dorothea played a devious game. Since her romance with Clement had now ended, she felt justified in giving full rein to the clarion call of ambition. So Dorothea continued to intrigue with Metternich against Canning; at the same time the Austrian chancellor told his ambassador to protect his own skin, and leave everything up to the countess. Concomitantly, she concocted a bold move to cooperate with Canning.

Dorothea had always been uncomfortable with Austrian domination of her country's foreign policy. "My love, you love me well, because you love Austria that you did not love," Clement wrote early in their relationship. "One of the delights of my life would be to see you loving Austria"[45] from conviction. Unhappily for him, that particular delight never materialized. Certainly the ambitious countess used Metternich's ascendancy over her tsar to advance her political purposes. Yet, like the humiliating Peace of Tilsit, Tsar Alexander's submission to Metternich chafed Dorothea Lieven's patriotic pride.

Even though parting from the delight of her life, her two adored little boys, proved to be a huge wrench, Dorothea left for Russia three months after baby Arthur's birth. She asked Metternich to recommend books to while away the tedium of her long overland journey. She would write him "from Frankfurt; I will write from Berlin; and then I shall desert you; for," Countess Dorothea Lieven challenged the Coachman of Europe, "I shall have other things to do."[46]

10

"The Living Dispatch"

It is a pity Countess Lieven wears skirts; she would have made an excellent diplomat.[1]

—Tsar Alexander I

Much water had flowed under London Bridge since Countess Dorothea Lieven last saw the cold Neva river. Yet, in 1825, vivid memories of the milieu she had rejected in her youth—the grinding round of glittering gaieties that constituted court life, the vicious intrigues, the compulsion for all courtiers to cede their self-respect and embody it in the Tsar of all the Russias—remained.

She reached her country's capital at the time of "white nights" (late June). The sun never fully leaves the sky, and shades of pink and mauve tinge the gray twilight of midnight's hours. St. Petersburg presented a challenge. Success would mean professional recognition, failure a huge setback, perhaps even relegating the countess to "the conventional female role."

Countess Lieven must captivate Tsar Alexander I, whose candid countenance and quick mind, her diary tells us, hid a considerable capacity for deceit. This Dorothea blamed on the sycophantic courtiers who surrounded him from birth. Alexander disliked and distrusted Europe's premier statesman, the man who described himself to Dorothea as "the mastiff among all my equals,"[2] but a common danger had united Metternich and the tsar. After Napoleon's defeat Alexander distanced himself from the Austrian chancellor. Resistance to revolutionary ideas drew them together again and, at the Congress of Troppau, the tsar pretended to forget his earlier distaste; Metternich's ingenuity did the rest. Alexander "passed suddenly from excess of Liberalism to an equally excessive Ultraism."[3]

In fact, Metternich "acquired an absolute empire over"[4] the tsar's mind. Then the Eastern Question erupted over the Greeks' ferocious fight for freedom from Ottoman rule. To Russia the Eastern Question had only one meaning: control of Turkey's capital, Constantinople, commanding two narrow waterways—the Bosphorus and Dardanelles—that connect the Black Sea to the Mediterranean. Unlimited

Opposite: **Alexander I. This notoriously suspicious tsar trusted Dorothea Lieven's political judgment. Artist: H. B. Monnier. Used by permission of the Slavic and Baltic Division, The New York Public Library, Astor, Lenox and Tilden Foundations.**

Пис: Монье, 1806   Peint par Monnier, 1806

Императоръ Александръ I   L'Empereur Alexandre I

access to the Mediterranean had been the major goal of Russian foreign policy for decades, a goal Alexander proved as ambitious to advance as his ancestors and, indeed, his successors.

Hence Russia supported independence for Greece as a way to weaken Turkey. Austria opposed. Metternich complacently considered the status quo, the 1815 Vienna Settlement he had crafted with Castlereagh and Talleyrand, and currently embodied in the Concert of Europe, as constituting the best assurance for peace. So Metternich sought to restrain Russia through procrastination over Greece.

Dorothea Lieven always felt uneasy about her country's consent to Austria's lead in foreign affairs; it offended her profound patriotic pride. To Dorothea's further dismay, Tsar Alexander entrusted to Metternich not only Russia's honor and interest in the Greek question, but also the "still more irritating question of our relations with Turkey."[5]

All "the Powers, more or less, seconded Austria in the aim of mystifying Russia; all had the same interest in preventing a rupture between that Power and the Porte."* Then George Canning, arguably England's greatest nineteenth century foreign secretary, "presented himself as the rival, and almost as the antagonist of Prince Metternich."[6]

Canning believed in national self-determination as the best way to preserve peace; hence, he favored independence for Greece. The British foreign secretary distrusted European entanglements, and hated Austria's reactionary policies. He chose to detach his country from the Concert of Europe. It "bridled England, and for that reason was repugnant to her insular pride."[7] Moreover, Metternich's failed plot to "make Mr. Canning jump" (out of office) caused Canning to consider the Austrian chancellor "the greatest rogue and liar on the Continent, perhaps in the civilized world."[8]

Countess Lieven grew to appreciate Canning as much for his brains, wit, and nimble diplomacy as for his political authority, which she now planned to turn to Russia's advantage. Dorothea admired the foreign secretary's adroit separation of Britain from the other Powers over French military action in Spain, and his skilful recognition of the Spanish American republics. She watched Canning's attempts, "sometimes by devious, and sometimes by direct methods," to draw Russia's attention to Austrian maneuvers to "bridle" Russia over Greece. But Tsar Alexander "saw only in these insinuations the aim of disuniting the two Imperial Courts."[9] He sacrificed the liberal Canning to the conservative Metternich.

Canning started to cultivate the countess on the eve of her departure; for if Russia insisted on fighting Turkey over Greece, Russia would want support. The tsar could hardly count on Austria, his rival in the Balkans, but Canning, seeking to widen the rift in the European alliance that his instructions to Wellington had successfully opened at Verona, saw cooperation with Russia over Greece as a chance to achieve exactly that.

"I am one of the small number of mobile diplomats known to history,"[10] Metternich smugly confided to Dorothea. His wife's terminal illness summoned him to Paris. There Metternich boasted about his influence over Tsar Alexander, of the

---

*The Ottoman government, known as "the Sublime Porte" because of its ornate ceremonial door. If the tsar marched on Constantinople, how, Dorothea Lieven asked, could they stop "him from throwing the Porte out of the window?" (British Library, Lieven Papers, Add. 47396, # 112–115, Oct. 4, 1823, D. Lieven to C. Lieven).

stratagems he used to make the tsar leave the Eastern Question entirely in his hands. Metternich's archenemy, Russian ambassador Count Pozzo di Borgo, carefully collected all these "*gasconnades* spread abroad without discernment and beyond measure,"[11] and gleefully sent them post-haste to St. Petersburg.

The diary that left posterity its most precise account of a tsar's assassination, that painted an unique picture of another tsar's disastrous state visit to London, accurately told the astounding story of its author's role in a diplomatic revolution.

⁞

Weeks of worry over her dear little George delayed Countess Lieven's departure. He suddenly fell seriously ill with "a high fever that, for eight days, did not leave him for one moment. This sickness is called infantine fever. It lasts more or less a long time, but one is never fully rid of it for one month."[12] Dorothea had a trundle bed set in her son's room. Day and night she soothed his hot little face and hands with a handkerchief soaked in lavender water, refreshed his thirst with lemonade and, spoonful by spoonful, coaxed him into drinking sustaining broth. Fatigue aggravated Dorothea's anguish, not to mention dread that baby Arthur might catch his brother's sickness; she became ill, too.

Only when the doctors declared George fully out of danger did his mother set out on her long north-eastward journey across the Continent. Jolting over bad roads for days on end, she passed the time in reading the books Metternich had recommended, and halted only once: at Stuttgart for a brief stay with her brother Constantine (Russian minister to the Grand Duchy of Württemberg) and his family.

"Has George recovered his strength? Is he is good spirits? For God's sake take care of this dear child. What is the maid doing and the rest of the household? I have no time to write to my *friends*. Make all the necessary excuses for me." Immediately on her arrival in St. Petersburg Dorothea begged her husband "not to let George go on a boat, he would again suffer his fever, or he could have an accident and I am afraid of everything more or less. What happiness to again see my dear little ones!"[13]

Her grown-up son, Paul, gratified Dorothea with a glowing report from his superiors at the foreign ministry. But what a disastrous idea to place Alexander and Constantine at Livonia's Dorpat University.[14] The boys' limited acquaintance with German made serious study impossible and now, their weak Russian hampered them at St. Petersburg's military college, explained Dorothea, as usual trying to soften her husband's severity towards his sons. Moreover, "poor Alexander is very ill. Everyone agrees he cannot stay in the army, his chest is abysmal." A "missed career and what to do? He has an excellent heart but little ability." A long "subject to discuss & it only causes me regrets."[15]

⁞

Meanwhile, the countess turned her attention to diplomacy. Success depended on a single factor: winning the confidence of that astute diplomat and supreme autocrat, Tsar Alexander. Dorothea's unique relationship with powerful empress-mother Maria, as well as her singular combination of talents, stood in her favor. The aura of divinity surrounding the tsar, not to mention the court's malicious machinations—not the least of them a carry-over from Verona: her compatriots' accusations about Dorothea's lack of patriotism—might daunt a lesser spirit.

I knew the invariable hostility of Prince Metternich to the Greek cause. I had more than once given him sincere warnings on the need ... [to end] the Eastern business in good faith, on the clear-sighted view of Russia in this business and on the danger of finally bringing the Emperor to recognize that he had been the dupe of difficulties improvised by Austria. My advice remained without result.[16]★

So the countess decided to tell the tsar "the truth, if he did me the honor to speak to me of his affairs."[17]

Countess Lieven set the scene with characteristic care. Before yielding to her foster-mother's urgent invitation to Pavlovsk, Empress Maria's enchanting summer palace outside the capital, Dorothea engaged her husband's chief, cautious foreign minister, Count Nesselrode, in a tête-à-tête. With delicate finesse Dorothea floated the idea of Anglo-Russian cooperation over Greece. Nesselrode liked it. He left Dorothea in "absolutely no doubt about his friendship for me and for you,"[18] she wrote Lieven. Indeed, during her brief stay in St. Petersburg Nesselrode twice visited the countess, and promised to come to Pavlovsk for further discussions.

The foreign minister saw Countess Lieven as a gift from the gods. He had a sound business relationship with his tsar, but Alexander had lately become interested in mysticism and holiness, so he "saw his ministers seldom; and only during work-time. His occupations in these days were pious readings."[19] Nor did master or minister make a habit of traveling abroad to meet their counterparts. Dorothea, on the other hand, had represented Russia in London for thirteen years. She had created an unique position for herself in England's politically permeated society; she had won the confidence of King George and his ministers. Then, too, she enjoyed a close friendship with Metternich. All that gave Dorothea's political judgment particular credibility; indeed, her letters to Nesselrode had already proved her diplomatic acumen at St. Petersburg. Countess Lieven had an intimate relationship with the powerful empress-mother. And her remarkable blend of abilities equipped Dorothea to navigate the unpredictable shoals of Alexander's mind. Last but by no means least, the countess could speak with the tsar in a manner his ministers could not. As a woman she could talk to Alexander informally. If she failed to convince him, Lieven and Nesselrode could safely dissociate themselves.

∞∞

Empress-mother Maria presided over the court at Pavlovsk. Designed to resemble a Roman country villa, the attractive summer palace sat in a beautifully landscaped park through which flowed a small river. Stately Finnish oaks shaded broad paths, German lime-trees bordered secluded walks, Dutch and English bulbs blossomed in manicured flower-beds. Not far away the tsar lived alone in Tsarskoe Selo's grand Catherine Palace, its baroque blue and white facade glittering with gold columns and pilasters. Mementos of his victories over Napoleon decorated the tsar's study, and a handsome malachite writing set reposed on his desk. Alexander received the countess with "the familiar good humor"[20] he had always shown her.

Still, Alexander's isolation in quasi-monastic solitude made him more suspicious than ever. The sight of even such a familiar face as Dorothea's seemed to embarrass him. She did "not know why, but this embarrassment gave me courage."[21]

★*Among Countess Lieven's unpublished papers are letters to Metternich (October to December, 1824) giving reasons for settling the Eastern Question to Russia's advantage.*

So during their tête-à-tête Dorothea applied the technique that, all her life, won her the trust of eminent men. "I answered his banal questions in such a way so as to interest him a little. By degrees he became more intimate." The tsar spoke only of business. Countess Lieven answered firmly, but with reserve, neither for nor against Canning, whom the tsar absolutely abhorred. "Put your foot down, Sire, and you will make the whole World tremble," coached the countess as Alexander commented on other countries' weaknesses. Dorothea encouraged the tsar to talk. He "spoke well, though without much distinction" and, despite his monasticism, "loved to be listened to."

"I left your sister a young woman; I have found her a stateswoman."[22]

Her tsar's gratifying recognition, graciously conveyed to Dorothea's elder brother, gave her confidence. Well aware of the pitfalls that pock-marked the court, the countess practiced extreme discretion and only mentioned business to Nesselrode. Indeed, her bold words to the tsar rather unnerved that cautious diplomat, but he recognized Dorothea's resolve, respected her reserve, and agreed with her views. So Nesselrode gave Dorothea some pointers on advancing what she described in her diary with gross understatement as "the vague idea which I had formed. It was reduced to this: to detach ourselves from Austria and re-approach England, for everything could be done by this double relation."[23]

ଽୠଓଷ

Alexander asked about Metternich's private opinions. Dorothea fed him enough to justify the annoyance he already felt towards the Austrian. And under her expert ministrations that annoyance grew, so much so that, in high anxiety, the Austrian ambassador hastened to Pavlovsk for a confidential consultation with the countess. "I send you herewith included a letter for Madame de Lieven," Metternich wrote his representative. "I beg you to give it to her *by your own hand into her hand*," for although the countess "thought very clearly in all matters of business," Metternich judged her "a little mistaken on Greece."[24]

If, Dorothea told the Austrian ambassador, Metternich "did not bestir himself to arrange our affairs with Turkey, conveniently, he could be sure that we would take up the matter ourselves."[25]

Meanwhile, Countess Lieven mended her fences. She impressed her patriotism on all and sundry, and the court rewarded her with flattering attention. "It was not worth the trouble to disparage me, since I was there only for a few weeks,"[26] Dorothea noted dryly.

Twice Tsar Alexander came to Pavlovsk to talk to the countess. They focused on foreign policy. He bombarded her with questions about Canning, which gave Dorothea dozens "of opportunities to put in allusions which all ended in advancing my theme."[27] It, the subtle countess noticed, began to turn into the tsar's theme.

Alexander faced a dilemma. Isolated from England as well as from his other allies on the Eastern Question, the tsar needed a partner. Could he make advances to England? The bitter rivalry between Canning and Metternich did give Alexander "a sort of guarantee, yet he did not wish to deliver anything to chance, and, compelled by the awkwardness of his position, he came to the strange decision to entrust to me the interest of a new political combination for Russia."[28]

ଽୠଓଷ

Dorothea had arranged to leave for London on August 31st at six in the morning. On the 30th she got a letter from Nesselrode. Tsar Alexander had given him a special commission; the foreign minister absolutely must see Countess Lieven "at the moment before you leave. Today is impossible at least unless you can see me after the Empress's soirée. Since I am sleeping here I could also see you tomorrow morning before your departure. Tell me which you prefer," but "tell no-one the reason for this visit."[29]

Agog with curiosity, Dorothea decided to delay her departure until ten the next morning; she would receive Nesselrode an hour before. Punctually at nine, the countess's footman threw open the elaborately carved mahogany double doors of the handsome apartment that, as the empress-mother's foster daughter, she occupied at Pavlovsk, and announced Count Nesselrode. As he and Dorothea seated themselves in chairs covered with figured, straw colored silk, conveniently placed on either side of the white marble fireplace, the foreign minister announced to the astounded countess "that he wished to have a conference with me in due form. He would speak as minister to minister." He "would give me word for word the dialogue he had had the evening before with" the tsar.

"Alexander. 'Madame de Lieven goes tomorrow: have you seen her much during her stay here?' 'Several times, Sire.' (There Count Nesselrode took precautions to conceal his frequent visits to me. The Emperor was very suspicious.)

"Alexander. 'If you have spoken with her you will have been satisfied. I have found her sensible on all questions. She judges fairly and without prejudices. An idea has come to me which I have been working out for some days. Could we not profit by her return to England to re-approach that Cabinet? She knows the influential persons in that country, she enjoys great consideration, she well knows the means to use her position to render the service I ask of her.'"[30]

Пис. Изабе, 1814 г. — Peint par Isabey, 1814

Графъ Карлъ Васильевичъ   Le Comte Charles Vassiliewitch
Нессельроде,   Nesselrode,
1780 — 1862   1780 — 1862

Count Charles Robert Nesselrode. Russian foreign minister, later chancellor. He relied on Dorothea Lieven's political acumen. Artist: L. G. E. Isabey. Used by permission of the Slavic and Baltic Division, The New York Public Library, Astor, Lenox and Tilden Foundations.

Russia's policy of restraint would soon rouse the Turks to action, Alexander continued. Nor could he stand on the side-lines for long. His people demanded war; so did his enormous army. The Powers had abandoned him;

every one of them had intrigued in Greece—except Russia. England should think of that. If she joined with Russia the two Powers could control matters, let alone settle the Eastern Question in the interests of Europe, and according to the laws of religion and humanity. That should be the basis of Nesselrode's instruction to Countess Lieven.

As a stateswoman she could understand that "we cannot make the least advances to England. That would not suit my dignity." But "we can make the Cabinet of England understand that, if it takes a step, it will not be repulsed, and that we shall always be ready to welcome its ideas."[31]

Finally, Tsar Alexander insisted that Nesselrode "take care to receive and to keep the secrecy of the interview you ask of her."[32]

Dorothea listened in amazement. "Here was the most cautious and discreet of Ministers compelled to entrust the most confidential, most intimate and most bold political projects to a woman."[33]

"How were we to begin," the countess asked, diplomatically cloaking her elation, "when we had shut our mouths to England?*

"A woman knows how to make people speak," Nesselrode replied. "And that is precisely why the Emperor considers you are a unique opportunity, and your presence here has been for him like a revelation. (Here was shown in its entirety the mystic faith of the Emperor),"[34] noted the countess wryly.

"The conversation between Count Nesselrode and me was gay and serious by turns, the conclusion was that I should obey and be very diligent." Dorothea moved gracefully across the room to seat herself at a small, round table intricately inlaid with rare woods. There she wrote out her instructions. Nesselrode read them: "That is the true wish of the Emperor, he is going to be attached to that idea, don't forget it for an instant!"[35]

A delicate issue then arose, one Dorothea must treat warily: respect for "the *paix de ménage*."[36] She and Nesselrode agreed to her telling Lieven everything, that he "take the question in hand, if I succeeded in putting it *au monde*."[37] The foreign minister would give Dorothea "a letter of credence to that effect"; otherwise, "all this would be incredible."[38]

So while Countess Lieven watched, Nesselrode wrote to her husband. "Believe all the bearer tells you." Ten minutes later the foreign minister escorted Dorothea to her carriage. "The Emperor had doubtless enjoined this piece of politeness, which agreed with his warning (to Nesselrode) only to see me at the moment of my departure."[39]

ಐಂಡ

Dorothea had no time to stop in Stuttgart now. She sped westward.

Not for one minute did the countess consider breaking her political tie to Metternich; if Canning rejected Russia's overture, Tsar Alexander might yet need Austrian friendship. The tsar "took me for a man; he treated me as one as regards confidence, and as a woman as regards attentions and consideration."[40] So Clement should trust Dorothea, should not insist on being right. Even were that the case, Metternich must not waste time in arguing; rather, he should concentrate on making peace with Alexander.

Furious at Canning, the tsar, several months before, forbade Lieven to mention Greece.

Dorothea Lieven had never met a man who could say "I was wrong." Metternich proved no exception; indeed, it would "have cost at least as much to his vanity as to his policy." So although Metternich disdained her arguments, Dorothea prudently persevered with "all the good faith I put into my political relationships with him."[41]

Concomitantly, the countess made sure that Nesselrode continued to distance himself from his friend and fellow conservative. She sent Nesselrode copies of Metternich's latest letters. In one he boasted that Nesselrode would fall to his knees in front of him, in thanks for all he did for Russia; in another Metternich cuttingly criticized St. Petersburg for dithering; and the third lauded to the heavens his own consistently wise policy. Such typically superb follow-through assured Nesselrode's support for the brilliant maneuver Dorothea had succeeded at planting in the tsar's mind.

She reached London in record time. Instantly summoning her copious charm and her diplomatic wiles, Dorothea faithfully, scrupulously, and without wounding her husband's delicate sensibilities gave him "the ideas you," she wrote Nesselrode, "developed for me in our last meeting." Lieven grasped Nesselrode's meaning perfectly, and would "wait for a judicious occasion."[42]

The count confirmed his wife's astounding story. She "put me in possession of the little letter you entrusted to her for me, and by which you authorize me to learn from her, by word of mouth, all the details of the last interview you had together."[43]

And Alexander wrote Nesselrode: "It is a pity Countess Lieven wears skirts; she would have made an excellent diplomat. Let us see where her negotiation will lead us."[44]

୫୦୧୫

Her westward dash made Dorothea ill. So her husband brought her to Brighton where Dorothea expected the bracing ocean breezes to speed her recovery. Nearby, Canning convalesced from a debilitating attack of gout. On October 25th Count and Countess Lieven paid him an unofficial visit.

From the moment he became foreign secretary, Canning had cultivated the countess; he meant to disrupt her partnership with Metternich. And despite Dorothea's discouragement, Canning persevered. That "made the work more easy when, in our turn, we had an interest in winning him over."[45]

With infinite subtlety, Dorothea now raised the question of Greece. As a woman she could do it informally. If Canning failed to react, Lieven could distance himself without jeopardizing his official position. The foreign secretary valued Greece's liberation less than the chance "to avail himself of this question as a lever to unite himself to us, and especially to keep us more certainly detached from Austria," Dorothea's diary declared. Indeed, Canning's "most powerful inward motive was the pleasure of circumventing Metternich."[46]

Her diary gave Lieven credit for cleverly leading Canning into the conversation he and Dorothea wanted. Then, breaking the nine months' silence over Greece, Lieven showed Canning papers that confirmed a deep divide between Russia and Austria. Moreover, he disclosed a secret document. It proved decisively that before the sultan of Turkey's Egyptian vassal Ibrahim Pasha had marched against the Greeks, the Porte had agreed to let Ibrahim keep whichever part of Greece he conquered; Ibrahim could also "ethnically cleanse" his new territory by deporting all its (Christian) Greek inhabitants to Egypt as slaves, and repopulating the area with (Muslim) Egyptians.[47]

Five days later the Lievens again visited Canning. Count Lieven revealed the astonishing initiative his wife had brought from Russia. Canning welcomed it. He immediately grasped that if Great Britain made advances to cooperate on Greece, Russia would encourage them, thereby breaking with Austria.

"I regard our affairs as going on well in this country," Lieven wrote Nesselrode on October 30th. "My conduct" will "prove that I have entered into the meaning of 'the living dispatch' you sent me."[48]

જીજી

In any crucial negotiation timing is vital; personality can make all the difference; and details are immensely important. Dorothea's dramatic idea that Russia take advantage of Canning's strength to cooperate with him over Greece was far too delicate to entrust to the diplomatic pouch. Success depended on personal diplomacy, diplomacy in the hands of a stateswoman, a woman with profound understanding of powerful men. And Tsar Alexander's astonishing decision was too significant, his overture too sensitive to trust to regular channels. A "living dispatch" guaranteed absolute reliability.

Hence Countess Lieven played the key role in a diplomatic revolution. It split the Holy Alliance, changed Anglo-Russian relations, facilitated Greek independence, and heralded the beginning of the end of the Ottoman Empire.

Dorothea Lieven had arrived at a watershed in her life. This remarkable episode meant that she at least equaled her husband in importance. The countess had won her place in the Great World.

11

"Realpolitik"

> Mde. de Lieven ... does not deny that her Court to Mr. Canning is for the purpose of attaining Political objects ... she avowed that upon principle she paid attention to those whose goodwill towards the Russian Government she thought important. She ... feels her preferences as well as others; but she does not think she is in a position in the country to indulge them to the exclusion of those who can be of use to the Russian Government.[1]
> —Duke of Wellington

The spectacular success of her mission to Russia catapulted Dorothea Lieven, at age forty, into a frenzy of political activity. It put her at the hub of an intricate and dramatic story: the birth of modern Greece.

Secret discussions between Count Lieven and Mr. Canning advanced the promising entente that "the living dispatch" initiated. Then in November 1825, Tsar Alexander I died suddenly. His death threw the delicate diplomatic balance into disorder.

Contrary to common expectation Dorothea Lieven's erstwhile lover, Grand Duke Constantine, did not succeed Alexander.[2] And an insurrection instantly welcomed their younger brother to the throne. Suppression of the Decembrist Revolt dominated the first months of his reign.

Tsar Nicholas I, Dorothea Lieven's new master, looked "the very ideal of a great monarch, of an autocrat over millions of the human race, full of a sense of his unique position, and in the habitual exercise of its immense and insuperable authority." His mien expressed a fearless and resolute will that might be fierce. His voice had "the intonation of a man accustomed to command, to see all other wills bend before his. It was impossible to look at that magnificent man without seeing and feeling that he was Russia."[3]

Interested only in the army and politics, considerably less charming and much more decisive than his eldest brother Alexander, "the Iron Tsar" had no use for any of the trappings of liberalism. On the contrary, he personified absolutism.

In an unusual move for a monarch, Nicholas fell deeply in love with his arranged bride, and she with him. Princess Louise of Prussia became the Empress Alexandra. At their court one spoke German rather than Russian, and Nicholas surrounded himself with men of German origin, particularly those he had known from his youth and felt he could trust, men like Dorothea's brother Alexander.

The new tsar admired Alexander Benckendorff's distinguished military record. A brave officer, and talented military administrator too, Dorothea's brother had risen to the rank of general. He had warned Tsar Alexander about secret societies plotting to act in favor of a constitution, and had advised that the tsar establish a special police force to monitor them. Tsar Alexander refused. Result: the Decembrist Revolt.

A typically loyal Baltic Baron, Benckendorff distinguished himself in crushing it. He then revived his idea of a special police force. Hence, in one of his first acts as tsar, Nicholas created Section III. It operated a vast and ubiquitous network of secret agents who pried into the actions, the speech, even the thoughts of every Russian. Benckendorff headed Section III from its birth until his death. He won widespread respect for his integrity, his decency, and his discretion in carrying out his often repugnant responsibilities.

"I heard with much interest and more pleasure of the new duties" that the tsar's "confidence imposed on you," applauded Alexander's proud sister. "Your position is a difficult one, but I can well understand that one gives one's self entirely to such a master—and when one's heart is in one's work difficulties disappear."[4] Benckendorff's position put him second in importance to the tsar, which enhanced his sister's influence at court.

So did Nicholas's tribute to his esteemed old governess, Charlotte Lieven. On the occasion of his coronation he created her a Princess and Highness. According to Russian custom, her descendants also took the title. One of Dorothea's London enemies considered "this promotion an insult to the British nation generally and to herself in particular."[5] But Princess Dorothea Lieven delighted in her elevated status, and felt especially proud that the tsar conferred "Highness" on no one else. At once, she ordered new stationery; it had a tasteful coronet engraved in the upper right hand corner, with "D.L." entwined beneath.

⅋Ↄᏻ

Martial young Nicholas meant to shake off Metternich's shackles over the Eastern Question, a move Princess Lieven had urged on his predecessor. Nicholas cared little for the Greeks, but their struggle for independence would provide an apt pretext for the war he fully intended to wage against Turkey.

Tsar Nicholas sought Britain's friendship, but to Princess Lieven's dismay an obstacle arose. "Turkish from head to foot,"[6] her close friend and political ally, the duke of Wellington, opposed George Canning with the king, in the Cabinet, and in Parliament.

Driven by ambition, Dorothea decided to advance the interests of the minister who favored Greek independence. Besides, she believed Wellington would recognize her resolve, indeed her professional responsibility, to promote Russia's goals.

No foreigner enjoyed King George IV's confidence as did the princess; no foreigner could "use more freely then I the diplomatic opportunities offered by these familiar relations with him." The king detested Canning, and Austrian ambassador Esterhazy, whom George liked, lost no occasion to put Canning in the king's bad graces. While Austria and Russia were close, Dorothea did not bother to hinder Esterhazy; on the contrary. Now, she subtly reminded the king of Canning's good points, and entertained him with examples of the foreign secretary's well-known wit. Consequently King George, for the first time, invited Canning to dine in the tasteful intimacy of his luxurious Cottage in Windsor forest. As always, the king gave one arm to his mistress Lady Conyngham and the other to his close friend Princess Lieven, seating them on either side of him. Then, before the rest of the party sat down, George broke precedent. In a loud voice he asked the princess to choose her neighbor on the other side. Dorothea promptly named Canning. Thus, after the ladies left the table, Canning found himself seated close to the king.

"Nothing escaped the King's very delicate tact." Canning "had very *gauche* manners and sinned against the etiquette of elegant society."[7] Interested in Canning's success so long as he acknowledged her assistance, Dorothea gave him snippets of advice, which the foreign secretary gratefully accepted. Princess Lieven preened herself on the results.

৪৩৫

Meanwhile, diplomatic protocol mandated that King George officially congratulate Tsar Nicholas on his coronation. Keen on catering to the Russians, Canning proposed sending Europe's hero to convey the king's good wishes. But Wellington had a serious ear infection. And at "the most severe time of year, they were going to make him cross all Europe, to find Polar ice at the end of his journey" merely to "address a compliment!"[8]

Canning really wanted Wellington to clinch the dramatic policy reversal that "the living dispatch" had opened: Britain and Russia would arrange independence for Greece without resorting to war. Canning meant to curb Russia through cooperation. And who could better dampen Tsar Nicholas's martial zeal than the victor of Waterloo? Or, as Dorothea put it: "side by side with the salaam the Duke is to make, he should come to an understanding on the question of Greece. He (Canning) will compromise him (the Duke) and mock him at the same time—a double pleasure."[9]

Wellington prided himself on knowing how to obey as well as command. "Loving activity and secrets, in the smallest as in the greatest things," promptly discarding "a principle for a fancy; a mixture of the great and the almost childish, of stiffness and feebleness; but, above all, recoiling before nothing, and not knowing what was impossible for him to do," the Duke, "without reflecting on his health or on policy,"[10] accepted the mission.

Lieven received the news "first with astonishment, and then, *literally*, with tears of pleasure, at having to announce to his Court such a proof of my resolution to carry into effect the system of renewed confidence which I opened to him in October."[11] Of course Canning could not tell his correspondent that "the living dispatch" had made possible his opening "the system of renewed confidence."

The Lievens and Canning spent January 31 to February 2 (1826) at Windsor with the king. Comfortably seated around a roaring fire as the steadily falling snow obscured vistas of the fine trees surrounding the Cottage, they crafted the finishing touches for Wellington's mission. The pro–Turkish duke should develop what had so far been Canning's secret discussions with the Lievens into an agreement on Greece. Britain would notify the Porte that if it made concessions over Greece, Russia would not wage war. If Turkey refused, the duke could tell Russia that Britain would stop, by force if necessary, the sultan's surrogate, Ibrahim Pasha, from effecting his egregious plan to "ethnically cleanse" any part of Greece.

In his luggage the duke carried three letters. With great tact they guided Dorothea's influential brother Alexander, her husband's chief, Count Nesselrode, and her still powerful foster-mother Empress Maria to appreciate Wellington's noble feelings (he applauded Nicholas's suppression of the liberal Decembrists) as much as his military fame. And Dorothea drilled the duke on the demands of court etiquette, not to mention her martial tsar's partiality for uniforms.

"Since my arrival here my time has passed entirely in ceremonies and receiving and paying" calls, Wellington wrote from the Russian court. "I change my Uniform several times" a day. "I have been most cordially received by the Emperor, his whole family, the Army &c., and am treated more as one of the family than as the Ambassador of a Foreign Power."[12]

Suddenly, the tsar summoned Prince Lieven to St. Petersburg. Speculation swirled.

"I cannot help thinking there is more in it than meets the eye," the princess tantalized Metternich; one did not summon a man from so far away without good cause. Dorothea had not the least idea whether Tsar Nicholas would keep her husband in London but she did know Lieven would "resist all proposals. He has not a spark of ambition in his make-up. He wishes to be of service"; but "in his own way; and that is possible only in his present post." For her part, Dorothea would be "very sorry if anything interfered with his career, as I could no longer accustom myself to any other."[13]

Tsar Nicholas wanted Lieven's help in the negotiations with Wellington. Buoyed by this proof of his new master's faith in him, the jealous prince felt justified in putting his increasingly prominent spouse in her place. Dorothea could keep the home fires burning, as a proper wife should, but when she insisted on a two-way information flow, Lieven sent only social vapidities. "You have never treated me so badly regarding letters as now," Dorothea reproached, and "you understand, meanwhile, that at present everything is grist."[14]

Still, Dorothea assured her punctilious husband that, despite his absence, she continued to observe official mourning for Tsar Alexander. "I have only done what is strictly necessary, only go to essential parties, only stay for quarter of an hour."[15] Very correctly dressed in black, she mingled with ministers and ambassadors at Lord Liverpool's formal dinner. The prime minister engaged Princess Lieven in a long discussion: Wellington and Nesselrode should agree quickly on Greece. "One must also strike *fairly*," Dorothea replied. Liverpool "returned to *quickly*." He spoke much of Tsar Nicholas, and the letter Wellington had brought him. "What comes from the heart carries a cachet in itself ... my letter must prove my personal attachment." The princess promised the prime minister that Nicholas knew it but, she prompted her husband, Liverpool "would attach more of a prize to know this from a higher authority than mine."[16] And Canning had visited, Dorothea wrote her spouse in invisible ink between the lines of a long paragraph about their little boys, purposely to express concern about disparities in Wellington's report of his first private meeting with the tsar. Canning got the impression that Nicholas had "not yet understood recent political events and that Nesselrode has not even advised him on how to establish optimal relations with the Duke."[17]

Meanwhile Lieven and Nesselrode presented the Greek question to Wellington in a new light. Far from patronizing rebellion in Greece, Russia wanted to control revolution and preserve stability. The conservative, pro–Turkish duke "entered under full sail into this order of ideas,"[18] Dorothea's diary tells us; indeed, she may well have been the muse who inspired them. "It is just as we foresaw and as we did so much we can be content,"[19] his wife congratulated Lieven.

ಌಗ

"The Duke is very pleased what do you say?" Canning asked the princess.

"I await to know what he is pleased about & want to know if you are."

"It seems as if I am obliged to be."[20]

The St. Petersburg Protocol (April 4, 1826) consolidated the bold stratagem Princess Lieven had initiated with Tsar Alexander. Before, Russia acted either alone, or with Austria and Prussia. Now, Russia would support British arbitration for an autonomous Greece nominally under Ottoman rule; if the Porte refused, the protocol agreed to "joint or separate" intervention.

Wellington had exceeded Canning's instructions. He committed his country to join Russia in what could easily turn out to be war, not to speak of having been hoodwinked into signing an agreement to detach Greece from the Ottoman Empire. If, Canning confided to the elated princess, the duke "had been more acute he would have played his cards better so as not to be the only one"[21] hoodwinked.

Driven, according to Dorothea, by his desire to outflank Metternich, Canning could certainly be satisfied at Austria's demotion to secondary status in the Eastern Question. And Metternich, infuriated at this diplomatic setback, sustained a painful personal bruise to his ego as well. His partner "in perfect rapport" of head and heart, "the being who belonged to" him, had disappointed.

Now the minister who, early in life at least, believed women had no place in politics, who disliked society, who never paid calls, visited Princess Lieven every Sunday. "When I have closed my door, he stays for at least one hour, he begins by speaking of current events, then we touch on other general questions," she teased Metternich. The previous day's tête-a-tête lasted "over two hours. I suspect he was making a kind of reconnaissance. He wanted to test my judgment and the capacity of my mind. He talked about everything, including you." If Canning hoped to find out anything, he departed empty-handed, but Dorothea took "a good look at him. He is quite as clever as they say. I fancy he is a man whom one might catch, but could never hold."[22]

Meanwhile Metternich, always wanting a woman in his life, paid noticeable attention to the very young lady who had taken his fancy two years before while Dorothea wintered without him in Rome. "So much for the constancy of men. Don't you think my reproaches are rather lukewarm?" Dorothea refused to wreak revenge. "So much for the folly of women." Yet, how strange for Clement to take notice "of a little girl! I should look funny, if I were to bother myself with a little boy!"[23]

Especially when she derived such immense satisfaction from the steady progress of what Dorothea saw as "*mon enfant*"—an independent Greece—let alone stoking the rampant speculation over her growing friendship with Canning. The tsar's representative and the foreign secretary found their minds well matched. "In the midst of company, his eyes meet mine. I know that look well," Dorothea taunted Clement, for they, too, had delighted in a shared sense of the ridiculous. "It means: 'Did you see the joke?' For he notices everything."[24]

Sentiment played no part in this sudden friendship. George Canning enjoyed the novel experience of conversing with an intellectual equal who, concomitantly, proved to be a charming woman. And Dorothea Lieven cultivated him because, as Wellington wrote in the introduction to this chapter, it served Russia's interest to do so.

ಬಂಧ

Before Russia and Britain could spring news of their protocol on the unsuspecting Continental chancelleries, England's cabinet must approve. Canning wanted to sound out the French government first. That did not suit the Russians; he should be in London when Lieven got back. "It is vital to the success of the business we negotiated together that they see and listen to each other," Nesselrode instructed Dorothea. "Your husband brings to that effort all the necessary skill." He "knows our most private thoughts."[25] Nesselrode had faith that Canning's proposed excursion to Paris would not take place. Nor did it.

"I find it difficult to explain to myself how with your sense of priorities & your knowledge of Henriette you can doubt the effect of your delay,"* Dorothea wrote Lieven. Their son George's puppy adored the master of the house; she had "no other idea in her head than your arrival, that is a rival in every way for me, I doubt that I think of you more than she does." Besides, Henriette's "patience is much less than mine & that is what you seem to forget." She "is so envious and susceptible!"[26]

While sitting at her inlaid cherry-wood writing table absorbed with letter composition, the princess got a surprise visit from the duke of Wellington. His distinctively large, spiky handwriting interrupted Dorothea's to recall to Lieven's "memory that we are *at a standstill* here until your arrival."[27] She continued:

> I throw myself at your knees to beg you to stay in Paris only for one day, take pity on me—I cannot go on, I do not know what to say, I anger you & do not comfort myself at all. I did not sleep for half an hour this night & there are still 12 nights & 12 days more because for the last time I want to believe you, you told me you would be here the 23. My husband, my good husband, you are my only joy on this earth, do not make me sad.[28]

Dorothea's sleepless night may have had more to do with little Arthur; he was teething. She brought him to town from Richmond to consult London's premier dentist. To Arthur's no less than to his anxious mother's relief, the dentist eased his discomfort.

Then a letter arrived from Vienna. Even after distance, time, and proximate attractions eroded passion, politics had bound Dorothea and Clement. Politics also drove them apart. Metternich's impending marriage now delivered the *coup de grâce*. This letter would be his last. "We should be hard put to it, you and I, to find in the whole world people of our own caliber," Dorothea replied. "Our hearts are well matched, our minds too; and our letters are very pleasant."[29]

ಬಂಧ

Soon afterwards prime minister Lord Liverpool suffered a serious stroke. Wellington and Canning vied to succeed him. King George would decide. Austrian ambassador Esterhazy exerted his influence in favor of the man who could be counted on to agree with Metternich's conservative policies. Princess Lieven promoted Canning's cause "with less reserve but also with more effect."[30]

---

*En route to London Lieven stopped at Berlin, Vienna, and Paris to explain the St. Petersburg Protocol to his colleagues.

That winter (1827) the Lievens fled London's writhing "pea soup" fogs for Brighton's salt-tanged breezes. Besides, the king and Canning were there, the latter recuperating from a debilitating illness. Daily, Dorothea took the convalescent for a drive along the ocean promenade. One morning Canning unburdened himself of a startling secret: he would resign if he did not become prime minister. One obstacle stood in his way. King George feared "the danger run by the Protestant Church if the Cabinet had an advocate of Catholic Emancipation as its Chief."[31] Canning had long favored Catholic Emancipation; he now disclosed that if the king appointed him prime minister, he would promise not to raise the issue. The foreign secretary followed this revelation with another: he would say nothing to the king. Dorothea Lieven "understood the meaning of his confidences."[32]

At this time the king's mistress, Lady Conyngham, concerned herself with religious issues although always, qualified Princess Lieven, "according to the proportion of her most limited mind." So the princess fed the favorite enough of Canning's confidences to serve her purpose. Concurrently, Dorothea used every suitable occasion to impress a salient fact on King George: Canning never mentioned the cabinet crisis, but the duke always did. "Naturally very proud, but a dissembler like all kings," George "listened to all this, felt it all, without letting it be seen, though I allowed myself to divine it."[33]

Weeks passed. On March 28th the king commanded Wellington and Canning to the Cottage. The Lievens were already there. King George did not appear in the dining-room to partake of the gargantuan breakfast set before his assembled guests. Instead, George conferred with the duke. At 2:30 the king and a smiling Wellington arrived at lunch; Canning looked drawn and upset.

After lunch the princess retired to her room to dress for an excursion through Windsor Forest's lovely unfolding greenery. The long coat of superfine merino wool, cinched at Dorothea's slender waist with a wide belt, trimmed down the front, along the bottom, and at the top of narrow slashed sleeves with a leaf motif, and her wide-brimmed hat decorated around the crown with stemmed flowers, shrieked of the latest Paris fashion. The party paired off in small, pony-drawn chaises. King George always went with Lady Conyngham. This time, "in his mood of finest malice," he turned to Princess Lieven and loudly said, "I am sure you and the Duke of Wellington would like to go out together." George knew Dorothea and the duke's friendship had deteriorated to the point where they had no desire to do so; the king then arranged the other pairs—omitting Canning. Dorothea thought he would explode. "At the moment of my keenest anxiety the King suddenly getting up, asked my husband to take Lady Conyngham, and himself squeezing Canning by the arm, said: "I want to talk with you, I shan't go out."[34]

Three hours later the company came back. Canning and the king were still closeted together. Now Wellington pulled a long face.

When Princess Lieven joined the other guests in the drawing-room, Canning pounced on her. "What do you know?" Astounded, she returned the question. Canning could not, he confided, understand what the king had in mind. Throughout that seemingly endless, elegantly-prepared dinner King George kept up a frustrating inscrutability. He took special pleasure in teasing the princess, who "willingly gave him this little satisfaction."[35]

After two more interminable weeks the king named the commoner prime minister.

ᏊᎧᏣᏃ

Canning named his and the Lievens' close friend, Lord Granville, foreign secretary.

Horrified, Harriet Granville called on Dorothea. With tears in her eyes, she begged her friend to use her influence to rescind Granville's appointment. Harriet eloquently argued her husband's superiority, as also his modesty. Indeed, she pleaded, he "was a marvel, but she much preferred that he should not be called upon to prove it!"[36]*

Dorothea obliged. But Britain still must have a foreign secretary. Prime minister and princess reviewed the possibilities. Suddenly Canning stopped and, with a laugh, asked Dorothea what she thought of Lord Dudley. Dorothea laughed louder.

> "Ah! if you nominate him I know someone who will be much enraged." Canning.
> "Who?" Princess. "Prince Metternich." Canning. "Are you sure of that?" Princess.
> "Perfectly sure. He cannot bear him. Don't you know, then, that they had *une querelle de salon*[37] at Vienna which makes them irreconcilable." Canning. "In that case I am decided. Lord Dudley is my man."[38]

ᏊᎧᏣᏃ

Meanwhile, the ferocity of the Greek fight for freedom demanded notice. Russia wanted to put teeth in the protocol. Wellington forcefully opposed. Canning meant to divert Russia from drawing Britain into its greater goal of weakening the Ottoman Empire. "Never at any moment" could the Lievens "flatter ourselves with having Canning sincerely and boldly with us."[39]

Indeed, only "with great difficulty, after a long time and by tricks and artifices"[40] did Dorothea and her husband get Canning to resume discussions on Greece. Consequently, Britain and Russia agreed to impress on the sultan that if he rejected negotiations with Greece, they would recognize its independence. This agreement and the St. Petersburg Protocol were then incorporated into the Treaty of London (July 6, 1827). Britain and Russia invited the other Powers to join them. France did. Austria and Prussia refused.

In August, Canning died. Lord Goderich succeeded him.

Russia's foreign minister could rely on the portraits Princess Lieven painted of the Goderich cabinet, she wrote her brother Alexander. They were a weak bunch, but at least the new ministers professed political principles dear to Russia, for they "have grown old in their distrust of Austria."[41]

Except one: the duke of Wellington. And he looked frostily on Princess Lieven. Wellington could not forgive her for having separated politics from personal friendship, for having preferred the minister friendly to the Greeks to the minister friendly to Russia's historic rivals, the Turks.

After six months in office the Goderich ministry died a natural death. King George named the duke prime minister. "With him the policy of Austria was enthroned anew."[42]

---

*As foreign secretary Lord Granville, a poor public speaker, would be required to defend government policy in Parliament.

12

Checkmate

> What a gloomy life I am leading! Is this really the way I ought to use my intelligence? I find that people stupider than I am have a hundred times more sense. Real intelligence consists in being happy, and I am not happy.[1]
> —Dorothea Lieven

The year 1828 opened inauspiciously for Princess Lieven. Her persistent pursuit of power and her promotion of the duke's rival had deeply offended Wellington. So his premiership promised to halt the upward trajectory of Princess Lieven's career. At the same time trauma tormented her domestic tranquility.

Dorothea's spectacular evolution from Lieven's discreet helpmate into a diplomat in her own right grated on all the tensions in their marriage. How galling for a proud woman, one with such exceptional aptitude, to be married to an inferior mate. How frustrating for an ambitious woman, one with professional aspirations, to be dependent on a lesser partner, for Dorothea practiced diplomacy behind the scenes.

Her enhanced professional status added to Lieven's earlier exasperation—over his wife's love affairs—and aggravated the inadequacy he already felt beside her superior talents. Besides, his wife's career challenged Lieven's conventional male superiority both within their marriage and vis-à-vis the world by which he set such store.

When rancorous shouting matches rocked the Russian embassy's private quarters, Dorothea fervently hoped her small sons were out of earshot. And as gray light from a glowering morning sky filtered through the chintz window curtains of Dorothea's small parlor, an emotionally-fraught quarrel brought both protagonists to their feet in tense confrontation across the polished mahogany table; then, Lieven slammed out of the room.

Why "these shocking relations that have been simmering between us for so long, that trouble our peace, that ruin our health? If we agreed on the true cause of our torments we might also find the means to stop them." But Lieven despaired of that. Dorothea's "deplorable disposition," her defiance, her incessant doubts about his diplomatic ability, her "irrational envy"[2] of his official position embittered their lives, exposed them to obnoxious scenes, and brought them the world's unwelcome attention.

> *Read this immediately, until you reach the end.* I did not lie when I said that I felt I was dying—you have nothing more pressing at this moment than to decide my fate—If you do not, deep down, feel any goodwill, or tenderness for me, decide on our

separation now. If you loved me it would cost you nothing to curb your temper; thus you cannot love me anymore, so it is useless for me to hope for one minute, for happiness. You were dedicated to mine—I only find love and devotion for you, in my soul. I promised them to you ... my heart and my pride are shocked at your harshness. I forgive you your lack of intuition—but I told you this morning that the effect of your insensitivity on me is the same—*mortal*. I think that for your own *well-being* it would be useful for us to separate. Consult yourself. The exercise need not be long. It turns on knowing if you love me enough to promise me sweetness, intimacy of heart, goodwill that makes a marriage happy, and that you could not, in justice, refuse; or if you do, of saying what follows. In that case we have seen one another for the last time.

Answer me for pity's sake for I feel that I am dying.[3]

Your answer makes me tremble, possibly it will kill me.... [For] you I have only love, do not

Arthur Wellesley, first duke of Wellington. He never forgave Princess Lieven for putting politics before personal friendship. Artist: Sir Thomas Lawrence. National Portrait Gallery, London.

hate me, do not make me suffer any more. God who knows my heart, knows it is ready to break. Let us come together again, my husband, and never quarrel. Let us make a vow and keep it. Only tell me you love me, I am full of tenderness for you.... If you have any religion, any pity, you will know how to apply this to your anger, and I beg you on my knees to forgive me. God knows what my fault has been; my only fault is to love too much.[4]

Desperate, Dorothea had no alternative; she must swallow her pride, again submit to her husband's jealous temper. Divorce, even formal separation, would mean the unthinkable—that Dorothea give up her children. It would cause a huge scandal, and to her, social status meant far too much ever to flout society's rules. Besides, as a practical matter, a single female bearing such a dreadful stigma could scarcely contemplate with composure a return to cold, strictly circumscribed St. Petersburg. Nor could she easily set up household as a single foreigner in London; the society she now so haughtily led would shun her, and she would have no status without her husband.

Dorothea Lieven had made a marriage of convenience. She sincerely believed she had kept to her part of the bargain: she had created a home, borne sons, conducted her affairs with discretion, and helped her husband's career. She honestly felt she had proved her love by doing her utmost to dispel Lieven's feelings of inadequacy by keeping as much as humanly possible in the background. She had no choice but to stay married. Without her husband Dorothea would have no career.

∞CI∞

While balancing on the tightrope of her marriage, Dorothea's former passion for Metternich crowded back into her life.

He had kept all Dorothea's letters neatly docketed in one specially designated drawer of his writing desk. Because Russia's relations with Austria had grown glacial, thanks to Metternich's fury over the Treaty of London which the Lievens had negotiated with Canning to confer independence on Greece, the princess feared that the wily Austrian chancellor would use her letters to discredit her.

If Lieven got wind of his wife's passion for Metternich, his current temper outbursts would be as nothing. And any hint of the personally compromising nature of those letters would destroy Dorothea's credibility at the Romanov court, especially with the powerful empress-mother, not to mention creating such a scandal in London that Lieven, who cared so much about what people said, could never live it down. And besides her cutting comments on King George's mistress, Lady Conyngham, the princess had often amused both herself and Metternich by poking fun at the king. Were her letters to fall into Austrian ambassador Esterhazy or secretary Neumann's hands, they would use them to kill Dorothea's influence over King George.

Frantic, Dorothea agonized over what to do. "Despite the coldness you have shown me recently, I still think of you as my friend," she wrote Wellington after another severe struggle with her pride. "If this title displeases you, I would have recourse to that of the most honest man I know. As such I invoke your help, the only that I can & that I would wish to use, in a matter I regard of the highest importance." This step "is completely necessary for me" and "it is *only* under your auspices that it can succeed."[5]

The princess had always treasured Wellington's friendship. His offense at her preference for Canning (the minister who favored Greece) over himself (the minister who favored Turkey) disappointed Dorothea, sure he would understand that professionalism had motivated her. Still, she firmly believed "you have kept for me the friendship which always honored me, & that I have not for a moment ceased to merit"; hence, "without scruple, without hesitation,"[6] Dorothea entrusted to the duke her letter to Metternich which requested that he return her letters in exchange for his.

Wellington should seal her letter in an envelope that he would personally address to Metternich.★ And "since there is everything to risk if my husband sees me receiving a letter from you that I will not let him see,"[7] Dorothea asked the duke to address his reply to her close friend and cohort in amorous intrigue, Emily, Lady Cowper.

Wellington answered at once. Dorothea, not he, had sacrificed their friendship— to her zealous exertions for Russia. Nonetheless, he would faithfully carry out her commission.

Grateful, relieved, Dorothea could still not swallow the duke's accusation about sacrifice; they must have a candid clarification. "I do not seek it because I feel myself guilty. I want it because my feelings towards you are today what they always were. If

---

★*Wellington enjoyed romantic intrigue, and knew about Dorothea's liaison with Metternich. Besides, the two conserative statesmen were as one in their resolve to maintain the integrity of the Ottoman Empire.*

the same motive inspires in you the same desire, you will let me know when we can speak to each other." A written arrangement would imply preceding correspondence so Dorothea asked the duke to call. If he did not find her at home, "your visit will be a legitimate excuse for me to write to you to ask you to fix a date."[8]

Misunderstandings arose.[9] So Dorothea prepared a draft for Emily to copy.

The princess, Emily wrote Wellington, lived in utter dread of finding herself in Metternich or Neumann's power but had complete faith in him, and felt rather miffed that he doubted it for one moment; indeed, "the greatest proof of confidence she can give, is the wish that all her letters should be in your possession." Thus, Dorothea proposed that Neumann bring her letters to Wellington's house. She would then take Metternich's letters there and when, in Wellington's presence, she had verified all the numbers on hers (if only one were missing, it could do her infinite harm), would give the duke all Metternich's letters, and take from the duke all hers. Dorothea felt "so very nervous upon the whole subject, & with so little opinion of the honor of either M. or N.* that it would be kind," cajoled good-natured Emily, "to get the letters as soon as possible into your hands to relieve her mind from the anxiety she suffers. N. can make no objection to this arrangement as M.'s letters would be in your power till she delivered her own."[10]

If, worldly-wise Emily concluded,

> there is any doubt of fair dealing on either side, the Man is bound in common courtesy to run the risk. Politically they may have an equal interest in the letters, but as a woman all the risk is on her side, because his reputation cannot suffer by any exposure, & to her it is everything.[11]

ഇൽ

Scarcely had Dorothea brushed through this battle when war broke out between Russia and Turkey. The Porte refused to grant Greece independence, so Tsar Nicholas all too willingly invoked the Treaty of London.† Princess Lieven rejoiced. Now her country would prove its worth.

But the duke seemed ready to break with Russia. And his cabinet colleagues, barely able to control their suspicion of Russian designs on Ottoman territory, "would give anything to get out of the Greek treaty, which they hate."[12] Nonetheless, Wellington blamed the Lievens' "misrepresentations of things here, and particularly respecting me," for the deterioration in Anglo-Russian relations. His ambassador must make clear to Tsar Nicholas that "we were not aware we had ever given cause of complaint"; must, moreover, not mention either the prince or princess, as "I can prove nothing."[13]

Besides their "misrepresentations," Wellington supposed the Lievens to be in the thick of every plot against his government, but refused to make a public complaint for "however strong the proofs, they cannot be produced in court."[14] A private complaint "would occasion more inconvenience than the Lievens can in a century," and a general complaint would be useless because if it caused Lieven's recall "we shall have to explain ourselves to society at least." The victor of Waterloo would "prefer to incur not only all the evil which Madame de Lieven can do me, but even all she would wish me, to having to explain my conduct upon any such subject."[15]

---

*Metternich, Neumann.
†The 1827 Treaty of London pledged Britain, Russia, and France to effect Greek independence, by force if necessary.

Regardless, the princess provided England's prime minister with plenty of provocation. "*Our* Minister,"[16] she boasted to her brother Alexander, was none other than Wellington's secretary at war.

Henry John Temple, Viscount Palmerston, had majestic height, a fine figure, and face to match. A year older than Dorothea, the charming bachelor rake had been one of the first to waltz with her at Almack's, and they were rumored to have enjoyed a brief fling during her early days in London. By now, however, "Lord Cupid" had settled into a more or less steady relationship with Dorothea's conveniently married intimate, Emily Cowper.

Serious financial problems plagued Palmerston. As unlucky at the gaming tables as in stock market speculation, he also faced charges of carelessness as a company director. Eventually, he extricated himself. How, surfaced much later when some members of Parliament charged Palmerston, then foreign secretary, with treason: working for Russia. Palmerston's accusers swore before a Parliamentary investigating committee that during his financial troubles he had been in Russia's pay; they deposed that Palmerston got money from Russia through an agent, Hart, who kept a gaming-house; that Princess Lieven had hired Hart to transfer funds to Palmerston by losing money to him at gambling; that Hart made two payments of £10,000 (some swore £15,000)[17] each. Then, when Palmerston became foreign secretary he appointed Hart as British consul in Leipzig and, Palmerston's accusers deposed, although Hart earned a disgraceful reputation Palmerston refused to dismiss him. The charge against Palmerston was never proved; nor was it ever disproved.

When Canning became prime minister Dorothea, deep in his confidence, suggested Palmerston for the new cabinet. Canning would have made him chancellor of the exchequer had his reputation not been "very much compromised by speculation on the Stock Exchange, of which fact," Dorothea's diary averred, "I was wholly ignorant."[18] Was she?

Canning kept Palmerston as secretary at war. He agreed with Canning over Greece, and "applied himself very keenly to questions of foreign policy"[19] for which, Dorothea noted, he showed great aptitude. Palmerston sought every occasion to interact with senior members of the diplomatic corps, whom he constantly met at the Lievens' house.

Then the Russo-Turkish war broke out. Most of Wellington's cabinet "loudly protested their partiality for Turkey. The Canningites were more Russian." They resigned. Now warming the Opposition bench in Parliament, Palmerston continued to support Russia's policy on the Eastern Question, and to speak as firmly as before in favor of Greek independence. "My husband and I did not fail to keep him to this line."[20]

The Lievens divulged private information. Palmerston used it to attack Tory policy in newspaper articles, and to hammer the government in Parliament.

And the princess gratified Palmerston's ambition to become a statesman by coaching him in diplomacy; she also drilled him to hate Metternich and beware Vienna. Pure politics drove the princess. Austria adamantly opposed Russia's aims on the Eastern Question.★

★Russia wanted to use Greek independence to weaken but not eliminate the Ottoman Empire, fearing that its collapse would unleash a greater danger: a Great Power struggle over the spoils. Metternich and Wellington wanted a srong Ottoman Empire to guard against Russian expansion. Hence, they encouraged the Porte to refuse Greece any iota of freedom.

ഇറ

Meanwhile, although the Duke of Wellington no longer called at the Russian embassy, his foreign secretary did.

George Hamilton Gordon, earl of Aberdeen, born in the same year as Dorothea Lieven had, at an early age, inherited vast acres spanning Scotland from the North Sea to the Atlantic. Dorothea met the reserved, cultured earl at her first ministerial dinner; he sat next to her at table. Their mutual wit, intellect, charm, and sense of humor made them get on well. During the Russo-Turkish war a select group, including Aberdeen and the Lievens, spent some summer days at Tunbridge Wells, an elegant spa lying in the wooded, gently rolling Kent countryside. Several impressive estates surrounded the spa. The Lievens drove out to see one. Aberdeen went along. But the owner had only "granted permission to see the place" to Russia, so "Lord Aberdeen had to resign himself for two whole hours to pass for a Russian subject. He played the part, however, with extreme good grace."[21]

Aberdeen would become one of Dorothea's firmest personal friends and political allies. Now, however, she despised him "as the most inept Minister of Foreign Affairs England has ever seen." Aberdeen earned this tribute because he served merely as Wellington's "passive instrument,"[22] functioning, at best, as "Chief Clerk in his office—but not more Minister of Foreign Affairs that I am,"[23] the princess told her influential brother Alexander for Nesselrode and the tsar's ears.

She also told "that dear simpleton of diplomacy," as Metternich called Aberdeen, and accused the English foreign secretary of following the Austrian chancellor's lead. Stung into a fury that burst through his usual cold reserve, and into a resolve that replaced his habitual diffidence, Aberdeen wished Dorothea's words could be heard in Parliament; there he would publicly declare them "altogether unfounded—that he was neither knave nor fool, and that one must be one or the other to have any regard for M. de Metternich. This," Dorothea concluded with becoming modesty, "is not bad for a beginning."[24]

ഇറ

Thanks to her delicate ministrations Metternich's once ardent admirer, King George, developed into "everything we could desire both for the Emperor and for Russia, and possibly he may show it all the more because his Ministers are so ill-disposed."[25] Dorothea knew that the constitution curbed the king's authority, but he still had a say in policy making, and could dismiss a minister. How regrettable, she needled, that Metternich led Britain's cabinet. "I give you my word that this shall not be,"[26] vowed the king.

The princess drew every arrow in her quiver. She pushed the reactionary duke of Cumberland, who had great influence over his brother King George, to promote the king's resistance to Wellington, "hoping in this way to turn the latter out."[27]

Cumberland conceived several schemes to unseat the duke and since he, his wife, and the princess were friends, many assumed she had a hand in each plot. Dorothea did charm Cumberland into confiding his plans. As well, she acted as an intermediary among the anti–Wellington factions for, Princess Lieven told her particular friend Lord Grey, "to *know* everything and to meddle in nothing are my chief duties."[28]

Posterity remembers Charles, Earl Grey for his passage of the great parliamentary reform bill but for much of the time Princess Lieven knew him, Grey led the

Whig Opposition to a succession of Tory governments. Cultivation of such a prominent public figure fell to Dorothea Lieven as a professional duty. It posed no hardship.

Charles Grey entered Parliament when Dorothea lay in her cradle, and instantly became prominent. Aloof yet charming, tall and dignified, with a long face, high forehead, firm, thin-lipped mouth, chiseled nose, and bushy eyebrows over large, piercing dark eyes, Grey personified patrician pride. A superb orator, he had "the most beautiful diction in the world, the noblest prose, the purest and most elegant style," the most dignified gestures; and Dorothea described Grey's voice as conveying "the resonance of bronze."[29]

Guarded and hesitant, Grey depended on others; often moody, sometimes insecure, he thrived on the stimulus of praise.

> My dear lord, your highest quality in my eyes has always been that you have the clearest, the most honest and the most open mind of any statesman I know, and at the same time the keenest foresight. Your greatest defect is that you do not allow yourself to be sufficiently guided by your own incontestable superiority of judgment.[30]

Dorothea Lieven achieved such influence over Grey that his Whig colleagues often viewed her askance.

Occasionally callous and egocentric in politics, Grey, nonetheless, had a profound sense of political integrity, let alone a stellar reputation for honor. And he held firm on core beliefs. So conversation between the liberal, staunchly British earl and the conservative, resolutely Russian princess could be counted on always to be lively. If Grey would promise to curb his imperious temper, not "talk louder than I do, we shall end by understanding one another," but, Dorothea warned, "if it is to be a strife of lung-power, I decline the contest."[31]

"Why is there this difference between us, when I believe our characters to be so well suited to one another in all other respects." Grey rued the years he had lost before finding "out how much I was formed to love and esteem you."[32]

A devoted parent of several sons and daughters, "Saint Flirt" had, before his marriage, fathered a daughter with the famous Georgiana, duchess of Devonshire; and he had several extra-marital liaisons. Sitting up in bed each morning the Whig earl would write to "my dearest Princess," then carefully perfume his letter with musk. Each afternoon he visited.

Dorothea basked in Grey's tenderness. She treasured a friendship that gave her the security to think aloud, a feeling usually "not to be looked for except between persons whose opinions agree on all points."[33]

Their love affair naturally added spice to their friendship, but their unique political association meant much more to them—and to us. After Grey's death his wife wanted to use his letters to the princess for a political memoir.

> It does not suit either me, or the memory of Lord Grey that today, when the deeds are recent, when the personalities that appear in our letters are still living, it does not suit, I say, either him, or me that it would be known to what point of intimacy and of confidence the leader of the opposition for ten years, the head of the government for four, found himself with a foreign ambassadress.[34]

This remarkable correspondence began during Dorothea's passion for Metternich, and waxed in intensity as her involvement with the Austrian chancellor waned.

Grey confided in Dorothea only on condition that no-one else saw his letters, and extracted her promise "that they *never* fall into other hands."[35]

When Parliament did not sit the earl retreated to his Northumberland estate. Howick stood in a wild, remote county of windy moors and vast woodlands on the Scottish border. There Grey relied on his friends for news, something the princess provided better than most. Close to the king, au courant through her husband, her social position, and her Europe-wide correspondence, Dorothea delighted in "conversing" freely with Grey about politics. Astute, pragmatic, accurate, she scrupulously separated speculation from fact.

To Dorothea's distress Grey, in a major speech, eloquently denounced Canning's policy of cooperation with Russia over Greece. He thought it might well make Greece dependent on Russia.

She esteemed him as a statesman, Dorothea flattered, but why must she endure the pain of finding Grey her "adversary on all the points that I have most at heart? And you are going even to attack the cause of these unhappy Greeks, for whom, in former times, you always" had "such sympathy!" only because "we wish to save them!"[36] So Dorothea would

> consider as personal anything you may say having a tendency to embarrass the fulfillment of the treaty [of London], which, in truth, I deem the sheet-anchor of Greek independence. You have there an avowal on my part, I will not say a menace— and I make it in all sincerity.

She could not conclude "with any words of friendship. This is a state of things that is very unnatural between us, and I request you not to let it last."[37]

"This, of course, precludes all discussion. I must submit to the penalty if I should be so unfortunate as to incur it; but in my turn I must add, not a threat, but the expression of a resolution equally sincere and equally firm," Grey instantly replied. "If our friendship is broken off on this ground, it never can be renewed.... I have written this with a degree of pain equal to what I experienced in reading your letter."[38]

After a prudent interval Dorothea placated; Russia would exert no more influence over a free Greece than any other Power, so why quarrel over the means. "I keep in mind what you" said and "am satisfied. Our wishes are identical—at least on this one subject."[39]

> It has happened to me, unfortunately, but too often in the course of a long life to differ from those whom I loved most in political opinions. But if unfortunate in this respect, I have been most fortunate in another, in having been able to maintain, in spite of these differences, the unbroken intercourse of private affection.[40]

Grey had taught his "dearest Princess" a valuable lesson.

Meanwhile, as Wellington's anger against the princess escalated, Grey worried that his friendship with Dorothea might be used to turn the king against her.⋆

> I have sometimes thought of this till I have almost convinced myself that I ought to relieve you from the *désagréments* to which you may be exposed. There is nothing so delightful to me as your correspondence; but great as is the pleasure, ... [and] great as the sacrifice of it would be, I am capable even of this, to avoid what might be attended with inconvenience to you.[41]

⋆*During the royal divorce proceedings Grey had exonerated Queen Caroline in Parliament. His speech commanded national admiration but earned Grey the king's undying enmity.*

"You understand me but little" if you think "me capable of accepting your offer," Dorothea at once answered. "Shall I give up the only true friend I possess and do so to please those who are certainly not my friends? Surely this would be baseness and folly combined."[42] All the duke's anger could not stop Dorothea from "continuing to regard you with affection, and even to write of it to you."[43]

"*Je suis tout à vous, de coeur et d'âme,*"[44] Grey replied.

The princess next put her shoulder to the uphill task of prying Grey out of his Northumberland fastness to attempt a defeat of the government. English politics "excite my curiosity and interest to the utmost, and it seems impossible that you should not sooner or later be called on to direct these," Dorothea flattered. "Take office, my dear lord: this is my great desire, and for England's sake." Her wish was disinterested, for Grey "would not then be to me what you are now; and I hardly know, on my side, whether I could be so frank" as now, for "we should both be official personages."[45]

> I think, of all pieces of foolishness, the greatest would be for England and Russia to find themselves at war. Too often, however, in this world small passions have brought about great evils, and in all Europe I do not see a single man at the head of affairs of a sufficiently commanding intellect, to bring fools to reason. I have said it once before, and I repeat it now: take office, my dear lord, ... [if] you wished it, you could become Premier.[46]

The distrust that Dorothea's logic inspired against Wellington's policy on the Eastern Question fortified Grey's own observations, and bred in him a growing belief that the government had blundered. So the duke thought to neutralize Grey by offering him a cabinet post. That offended the princess. She refused to listen to any "half measures for you. As I have already told you, the place you have to take is the first place."[47]

Lord Grey's caution prevailed over Princess Lieven's persistence. "I truly believe I would be better off to retire from my profession," Dorothea sighed to her intimate friend Emily Cowper. "It only exhausts me to no purpose."[48]

೩೦೦೮

To Princess Lieven's added distress, not to mention Europe's surprise, the war with Turkey began badly for Russia. So Tsar Nicholas and his closest confidant, Dorothea's elder brother Alexander, galloped to the front. Her younger brother, General Constantine Benckendorff, who, after the tragic death of his delicate young wife, had left diplomacy to re-join the army, commanded the Pravadi campaign. Because "my heart needs it," Constantine always "found a little minute to chat with" his "dear, dear Dorothea."[49] Then, the long weekly letters stopped. Dorothea blamed duty and the miserable mails, but a deadly fever epidemic had swept through the Russian army carrying Constantine with it.

"How little we know what we wish, or why we wish it—I, who was so eager for this war, had I but known what it would cost me!" Dorothea mourned. "The order of nature wills that we should lose our parents—but a brother, why need we be deprived of him so early?"[50] Constantine died in Alexander's arms, but her surviving brother had not the heart to tell Dorothea of their disaster; Nesselrode did.

"What do you expect me to think of your silence at such a time? From whom should I expect the sad but precious details, and some marks of affection, if not from you?" Four weeks before, immediately on getting "the sad, sad news," Dorothea had written. "My grief today is as keen as on the first day—it is more bitter perhaps, because of the total ignorance in which I have been left of the last moments of our dear incomparable Constantine."[51]

"Yes, dear Dascha, I will redouble, if possible, my amity and tenderness. I love you with all my soul," Alexander replied, in giving Dorothea the details she craved. He "would be so happy to see you again, embrace you, express all my attachment in living voice."[52]

While Dorothea grieved over the death of the sibling closest to her in interest and intellect, a courier brought more heartache. Empress-mother Maria had died. Like all her children, Maria's foster daughter loved and revered her. Dorothea lamented the loss of that maternal mantle of affection which her mother's best friend had spread over her.

The princess felt as if she were standing at the center of a black cloud. How, she asked Alexander, could a handful of mere Turks bring her magnificent tsar and his great army to a standstill, thereby shaking Europe's faith in Russian power. Indeed, Wellington's government had hardened its anti–Russian attitude; were it not for problems in Ireland, Dorothea thought the duke would have declared war on Russia the day he learnt that Tsar Nicholas had decided to blockade the Dardanelles. Unless their country won, and won quickly, Dorothea wrote her brother, "we must be on our guard at every moment against the vengeance which England will think only proper to take" on us because she believes "she has been duped in this business."[53]

No one knew better than Princess Lieven about England having been duped. Russia's diplomats hoodwinked Wellington into signing the St. Petersburg Protocol, which committed his country to "joint or separate" intervention should Turkey refuse to compromise over Greece. The Lievens then convinced Canning to fortify the protocol with the Treaty of London. Martial Tsar Nicholas meant all along to wage war against the Ottoman Empire; now he fought on behalf of the Treaty of London signatories!

That war orphaned Constantine Benckendorff's two children. The boy already lived with his uncle Alexander. But Alexander found himself in a quandary over his small niece; rather than exposing the delicate little girl to Russia's harsh winter, Constantine had left her in Stuttgart. Alexander now asked if Dorothea would take Marie until the spring.

A gusty wind spattered winter rain against the Russian embassy's window panes. In Dorothea's small private sitting-room cedar logs blazed cheerfully in the hearth, and warmth suffused her as she read her brother's letter. At last, at long last a daughter! A daughter who bore the same name as Dorothea's dead first-born, a daughter who looked like Dorothea, a daughter to whom she could pass on her knowledge, her wisdom; "my experience of life qualifies me for being a good guide to a young girl"[54]; a daughter with whom she could forge that special maternal bond, as her mother had, with her. "I am sure I can bring her up well, and I am still more sure I shall love her." With no "daughter of my own, all my care and love would be centered upon the dear child."[55] Dorothea wanted Marie for good.

Alexander all but agreed. Then, he began to waver. "I beseech you to decide to let me have that dear little Marie; it will be a new life for me and an interest and an occupation for every moment, which will be an advantage for her and a happiness for me."[56]

Why "do you refuse me, who have no daughter, a happiness which can only be profitable to the child?"[57] "You have offended me and wounded my feelings, my brother; the hurt you have done me will never be effaced. Never would our dear Constantine have been capable of treating me in such a way, but then he loved me."[58]

ഇ∙ഗ

During the 1828–29 winter lull in fighting Tsar Nicholas appointed a new commander-in-chief; so when melting mountain snows surged into swollen streams, Russia's army advanced rapidly through the Balkans. Stunned, Wellington and Aberdeen "would have resisted the march on Adrianople,[59] but Palmerston" and the Whigs, "intriguing with the Princess Lieven to turn the Duke out, succeeded in preventing any move in that direction."[60] Adrianople surrendered. The road to Constantinople lay open. Dreading Russian occupation of the Ottoman capital, the Powers persuaded the Porte to accept Russia's peace terms.

Meanwhile, the princess and Lord Aberdeen engaged in several satisfactory tête-à-têtes. After discussing the French ministry at some length she said: "In short, there is not a man of talent in the whole Government; they are all a pack of fools." Aberdeen answered: "Of which Government are you speaking—of ours, or of the French?" "There is no resisting a man who says such things,"[61] Dorothea noted.

She charmed the foreign secretary into confiding his private views which, the princess cynically observed to her brother, had doubtless been influenced by Russia's resounding military successes. Aberdeen's opinions might not be as generous towards Russia as she could wish, Dorothea conceded, but they did fully conform to Russian interests. True, Aberdeen did not direct British policy, "but as he has so few ideas of his own it is pretty clear that he never speaks but in accordance with the order of the day. This just now is wholly favorable to the Emperor's wishes." Benckendorff must, therefore, impress on Nesselrode that "he has within reach the principal *role*." What he wanted would be done. Dorothea did not express "exaggerated enthusiasm—I only say what is the precise truth."[62]

The Treaty of Adrianople (September 14, 1829) confirmed Russian supremacy in Eastern Europe. And to Dorothea's intense satisfaction, Russian arms convinced the Turks to accede to the Treaty of London. The Powers would settle details for an independent Greece at a conference to be held in the British capital.

ഇ∙ഗ

The end of Russia's war with Turkey concluded another war. Wellington's conservative government could, aside from Greece, be expected to satisfy Russia. So both the princess and the duke made advances, and a marked reconciliation took place. The prime minister resumed his regular visits to the Russian embassy for political discussions, often heated, with "this clever, intriguing, agreeable diplomatess."[63] Yet, their relationship never resumed its old intimacy. Wellington refused to separate personal friendship from politics; he never forgave Dorothea her ardent support of Canning, not to mention her energetic efforts against his government.

And the duke blamed Dorothea Lieven for the knotty diplomatic dilemma that dogged him. How to extricate Britain from the hated Treaty of London without being a joint guarantor, together with France and Russia, of Greek independence or, even worse, "leaving France and Russia joined in a common interest is more than I can tell. Mr. Canning and Madame de Lieven have much to answer for!"[64]

13

"I Was Very Strongly Involved ... in the Origin of Greece"

We have a King who just suits us because he does not suit the English Ministers. They will have the honor, but we shall get the profit. I hope that people at home will be satisfied with all ... we have done, and know ... we have toiled hard to obtain this result.[1]

—Dorothea Lieven

The climax of Dorothea Lieven's exhilarating role in the creation of Europe's newest nation-state opened at an English country house. Comfortable Claremont stood square and stately at the top of a slight incline. Green velvet lawns and lovely gardens surrounded the large white house, dappled deer grazed among groves of fine trees in the splendid park, and swans glided gracefully on a lake. Beyond, fertile fields and wooded hills stretched to the horizon. The Lievens were visiting Prince Leopold of Saxe-Coburg.

He and Dorothea had been friends since their youth when Leopold served as aide-de-camp to Tsar Alexander I; as well, she had been close to Leopold's wife, the Princess Charlotte, only child of King George IV. Charlotte's early death aborted a promising avenue of power for her ambitious husband. He, however, continued to live in England. When his mother-in-law Princess Caroline descended on London to claim her queenly rights, Leopold, not unnaturally, called on her. That incurred the eternal enmity of his father-in-law the king. George, moreover, deplored Leopold's liberal leanings.

The Russo-Turkish war had not yet broken out when, after a convivial dinner, Claremont's host engaged his old friend in an extensive discussion of the Eastern Question. Expressing an "ardor that contrasted vividly with his customary prudence," Leopold declared that Russia must "despise the bad temper of England, laugh at her threats, think of our own honor, not let our co-religionists die, and aid those poor Greeks at least by the indirect means of a war with the Porte."[2] This excessive eagerness piqued Dorothea's curiosity, so she charmed Leopold into confiding that he coveted the Greek crown.

As they carried their candles upstairs to their bedroom, Dorothea told her husband. He burst into derisive laughter, but Dorothea bet him that she would be proved right.

Tsar Nicholas's victorious armies neared Constantinople; the Wellington cabinet watched with scarcely veiled hostility. Fearing that Russian bayonets would dictate terms for Greece, Britain urged that an international conference settle details. The tsar's protégé, Count Capodistrias,[3] already in Athens leading the Greek government, wanted a hereditary constitutional monarchy; he asked that a king be chosen from the cadet branch of a reigning house. Greece's guarantors—Treaty of London signatories Britain, France, and Russia—agreed, provided this prince did not come from one of their royal families. So the laborious diplomatic process now taking place at the London conference on Greece "set every German ambition in movement."[4]★

Leopold's rocky relationship with his father-in-law King George, not to mention the King's jaundiced view of his son-in-law's liberalism, worked against him; nor, for that matter, did Leopold's liberal views exactly endear him to that pillar of conservatism, Tsar Nicholas. One woman, however, exerted remarkable influence over King George; at the same time Princess Lieven had unprecedented power, were she sufficiently convinced that Leopold's candidature could serve Russian interests, to propitiate the Romanov court.

ᘒᘔ

"In despair at heart" Princess Lieven's erstwhile lover, powerful Austrian chancellor Prince Metternich, always adamantly against an independent Greece, now, at least, wanted "to have his share of the cake," Dorothea's diary tells us. He inspired foreign secretary Lord Aberdeen to propose a German prince serving in Austria's military. France opposed. "One could not with decency recruit a King from"[5] Metternich's army. Russia supported France; so Aberdeen withdrew his nominee.

Soon everyone suggested other German princes, but no two diplomats agreed on any of them. Next, England proposed Prince Frederick of the Netherlands and, somewhat carelessly, Prince Leopold. The Romanov court liked Frederick, tied to it through marriage. Since his conversation with Dorothea Lieven at Claremont, however, Leopold had continued to confide his pro–Russian views to her. So she may very well have planted the seed of Leopold's suitability in Aberdeen's mind at one of their frequent and friendly private conversations.

France wanted a Catholic king to sit on the Greek throne, and refused England's suggestions. So Leopold crossed the Channel. At Paris he hired a secret agent to carry a letter to Capodistrias outlining his views on Greece, especially his personal offer to govern it. Capodistrias responded positively. Hence, Leopold appealed directly to the French king. He gave Leopold his support in return for Leopold's formal promise to "marry a Catholic princess and to bring up her children in that religion."[6] Officially, however, France supported Prince John of Saxony, England the Dutch prince Frederick. Deadlock.

Leopold's liberalism found little favor with England's conservative prime minister. Still, the duke of Wellington correctly thought his nomination could be presented to Parliament as "a success for the government, and of this the Duke had much need after our victories and our peace, towards which he had shown himself openly opposed and discontented,"[7] Dorothea's diary noted.

★*The ruling houses of Germany's many small states traditionally provided consorts for Europe's monarchs.*

Meanwhile, during the deadlock Princess Lieven had several tête-à-têtes with Lord Aberdeen. He came to realize that neither Prince John nor Prince Frederick could carry the vote of the Conference. So Aberdeen, Dorothea recorded with suitable modesty, "decided to end this comedy, and in agreement with the Duke of Wellington who wished absolutely to make a King," he "begged my husband to approach the French Government to get it to sacrifice its candidate on condition of England withdrawing hers," and "personally asked for the substitution of Prince Leopold. We were surprised and charmed at this overture."[8]

ಬಂಗ

At once "an episode occurred which is not worth telling" except to "put some historical persons on the stage."[9] Mecklenburg's grand duke and his brother Prince Charles (son-in-law to the king of Prussia) sent their brother-in-law the duke of Cumberland some startling news. The kings of both Prussia and France favored Prince Charles for Greece, but since neither king could intervene officially they consigned the matter to Cumberland. He told his brother the British king. Without the slightest inkling that the diplomats had agreed on Leopold, George commanded Aberdeen to push Prince Charles's candidacy.

The king's hedonism had by now caught up with him; George had grown so fat that he could no longer be hoisted onto his horse, let alone bear to have himself laced into his corsets. In poor health, averse to business, and displeased with his ministers to boot, the king saw them as seldom as possible; he preferred the company of intimates like Princess Lieven. George hated the Greek question; it suited him that his ministers said nothing about it. That suited Aberdeen, too. It especially suited Aberdeen to keep any whisper of Leopold's candidature from the king while he let it advance to the point where he could present his monarch with a *fait accompli*.

Cumberland told Lieven about the king's command. The ambassador and Aberdeen met several times, but to Lieven's surprise the foreign secretary made no mention of Prince Charles. "After a week my husband learnt that Lord Aberdeen had been to the King to complain of the obstinate resistance he had encountered from Prince Lieven."[10] Such adroit placement of blame for the certain failure of Prince Charles's candidacy at Lieven's doorstep stunned the ambassador, to say nothing of his spouse.

And as if that were not enough, Aberdeen capitalized on the king's anger at the ideas he, Aberdeen, "had just improvised and submitted" about Lieven, Dorothea's diary indignantly recorded. The foreign secretary informed his sovereign that for some time the Russian ambassador's "relations with and influence in England were such as to render him by no means agreeable to the Government." So Wellington and Aberdeen recommended a request for Lieven's recall. "In the keenness of his disappointment" about Prince Charles, the king "found nothing to say against this judgment."[11]

Tsar Nicholas did. With extreme tact, Count Nesselrode denied the British government's request.

Meanwhile, thanks to Dorothea's delicate handling King George developed a gratifying distrust of Aberdeen. Bolstered, therefore, by his wife's guarantee that he stood on safe ground, Lieven went on the warpath. "The choice of the Alliance was fixed," he told the king. Prince Leopold would reign in Greece. At first King George refused to believe Lieven; then he "affirmed with an oath that he would never permit it."[12]

The king summoned his foreign secretary. Well aware of Britain, France, and Russia's agreement that Greece's new ruler could not come from any of their royal families, the British monarch, who had always vigorously denied any relationship with his son-in-law now, with surprising energy bellowed: "If Leopold claims that he does not belong to the Royal Family, I affirm it."[13]

What a conundrum! The prince "derived all his importance from his position as" the king's son-in-law, "and boasted everywhere that he belonged to the Royal Family." Leopold now must prove the opposite. The king "had never wished to admit the relationship"; to stop Leopold from getting Greece, he now "claimed it with warmth."[14]

The lawyers upheld Leopold. How, the king then pressed Aberdeen, could his ministers be stupid enough to think well of such a clod? Because, answered the harried foreign secretary, Wellington wanted him. "Are you then Secretary of State of the Duke of Wellington and not of the King of England?" his Britannic Majesty roared. An apoplectic speech ensued. The king vowed never to let his ministers treat him with such lack of respect, never to agree to Leopold's nomination; if the duke found this a reason to resign, his sovereign cordially invited him to do so. Frightened out of his wits Leopold said he would renounce the Greek throne, "which had not yet been formally offered."[15]

At this time King George hated the duke and abused him to all and sundry because, after a long and intense tussle, the prime minister had won his sovereign's reluctant consent to enfranchise Catholics; all England knew how much that had outraged the king's strongly Protestant conscience. Subsequently, the king's "impotence had taken the form of indifference to all business."[16] That, however, did not prevent King George from frequently inviting his friend Princess Lieven to his cozy and luxurious Cottage in Windsor forest.

Wellington, meanwhile, stood so strong that he could afford to ignore the king's bad temper. The duke had a brief albeit frigid interview with King George, who "consented to *everything*" about Greece. The king even invited his ministers to a state dinner "to attest in the eyes of all the weakness of the King and the power of the subject."[17]

On January 30, 1830, the London Conference formally invited Prince Leopold to accept the Greek throne.

> Such is the simplicity of forms in England that the document emanating from the three first Cabinets in Europe, addressed on a solemn occasion to a sovereign elected to govern a New State, reached him the day after in the country by the coach, done up in a large brown paper with the small string which they use for parcels in England, and addressed to one of his *valets de chambre*. A pair of boots is sent with the same ceremony.[18]

Leopold wanted benefits for Greece. France and Russia agreed. But "he had to struggle *corps à corps*"[19] with England, showing "a judgment, an energy, and a cleverness of which none had ever suspected him."[20]

Crete, bitter battleground between Christians and Muslims, must be included in his new country, insisted Leopold. Determined to deny Greece every iota of territory, Wellington and Aberdeen demurred. Leopold asked Britain, France, and Russia at least to put the island's Greek population under their protection so as to end the war and massacre of Christians. "5,000 Turks would finish that," Aberdeen replied. "Indignant at this atrocious proposal, the Prince declared he would never consent to present himself to a new people under circumstances so horrible."[21] Long, tedious negotiations ensued. Leopold capitulated on the inclusion of Crete, but not on safeguards for its Greek population. He also insisted on financial aid, and the presence of a foreign force strong enough to protect the first actions of his government.

Britain balked. "What a set of people your Ministers are!" the princess, in peculiarly undiplomatic parlance, confided to her close friend, Opposition leader Lord Grey. "I must unburden my heart to someone, and you alone will not misunderstand me."[22] Leopold wanted to arrive in Greece bearing a boon that "his new subjects will recognize as due entirely to his personal efforts"; for "the very fact of his being the nominee of England will cause his sovereignty to be looked upon with suspicion, by a nation that has already had such good cause to reckon the present government of England as its enemy."[23]

Irritation between Prince Leopold and the Wellington government grew so great that the English diplomats refused to deal with him. Rumors flew thick and fast. While eating an excellent dinner at the Russian embassy, Lady Granville had "Greece on one side, so low and flat, so thin, that the log was a better King than that. Nobody knows what is to be, but he whispered it all in German to the Princess, who did not tell us anything."[24] At his wits' end, Aberdeen asked Lieven to take over the negotiations. And to Dorothea's gratification, on February 24 "the English Prince" put his formal acceptance of the Greek throne "into the hands of the Russian Ambassador."[25]

80С3

At this juncture the ailing English king as well as his heir, the duke of Clarence, fell gravely ill. A minority loomed in the person of a ten-year-old princess. Victoria's father, King George's brother the duke of Kent, had married Prince Leopold's sister. Kent's death left his only child heir to the throne after Clarence. With the life of both the king and Clarence in danger, Prince Leopold saw himself as regent for his young niece. And, Dorothea's diary noted, a close and well-connected friend of the prince's "cursed the day on which Leopold had engaged himself with Greece, since a more important part was reserved for him in England, and the moment was near. That made the Prince think."[26]

Meanwhile Greek prime minister Capodistrias, now seeing Leopold as a threat to his supremacy, started to impinge on the sovereign's power. As well, Capodistrias favored Leopold with several letters calculated to discourage his zest for the throne.

> My prince, a people heroic, great, generous but poor expects you: it must pay with its love for the sacrifices you are about to make for it. For they are great sacrifices. You are leaving your fine palaces for little thatched ones—your sumptuous repasts to eat black bread. It will be necessary to forget the pleasures of society, the comforts of your home.[27]

And when Leopold asked his banker to arrange to capitalize the sizeable revenue he enjoyed in England, Rothschild had to consult insurance companies. "They reckoned the Prince's life at seventeen years in England, but at seven in Greece, taking into account the climate and the dangers."[28]

So to Dorothea Lieven's dismay Prince Leopold officially and irrevocably renounced the Greek "throne, which he had coveted so much and accepted with such joy hardly three months before."[29]

This episode by no means indicated the end of Princess Lieven's efforts to elevate Prince Leopold onto a throne. In the meantime, the contentious question of borders for Greece stirred Dorothea to execute some nimble maneuvers.

Britain, France, and Russia had already agreed that Greece's northern frontier should extend from the west coast Gulf of Arta to the east coast Gulf of Volo (central Greece today). Now fearing that the country might fall under Russia's aegis, not to mention a strong wish to minimize the territorial loss that independent Greece would mean to the Ottoman Empire, the Wellington government reversed itself.

At the same time Whig Opposition leader Lord Grey, happily ensconced at his Northumberland estate, expected sooner or later to be called to office. Indeed, the political situation had become so fluid that pundits, including Dorothea Lieven, expected it to be sooner. Grey supported a free Greece, provided it did not fall under Russian domination.

Two days before Russia and Turkey signed the Treaty of Adrianople giving Greece the Arta-Volo boundary, Princess Lieven satisfied Lord Grey's condition. "Your Government now wishes to circumscribe the proposed Greek frontiers. We desire them to be those" the Powers originally agreed on. "Assuming that our victories have at last placed us in a position enabling us to carry out the wishes of the Allied Powers, I can hardly see why we should draw back." Wellington's wish that Greece now have less territory than his government had agreed to before had no basis in reason, equity, or political needs. Greece "is either to exist as a Power, or she is not to exist. If she is to be called into being, the country must be constituted in such a manner as to stand alone."[30]

"Nothing can be more futile than any haggling at this moment about the limits of Greece," Grey agreed. Hence, due to Dorothea's superb timing, Grey, on the day Russia and Turkey signed the Treaty of Adrianople guaranteeing Greek independence, plotted the Arta-Volo line on his map in the seclusion of his study at Howick. The "more extended frontier is certainly the right one. I am, therefore, decidedly for the boundary of Volo and Arta."[31]

Diplomatically curbing her glee Dorothea conceded that the frontier Grey indicated "might form a middle term," for England's about face on Arta-Volo had prompted Russia to counter with a demand that Greece be enlarged beyond it. But if the British ministers insisted on "their 'Morea'[32] they will get no business done at all, for Russia and France cannot agree to help you carry out such a piece of stupidity. *Your* frontier, however, shall not be forgotten.... I thank you for the suggestion."[33]

In the interim, a feverish chest cold assaulted the princess, so her husband removed her from foggy London to recover at Brighton. There, a bitter quarrel broke out—over "what people were saying": Dorothea inspired Lieven's most creative ideas at the conference. That exacerbated the prince's frustration at his wife's relationship with Grey. So Lieven betook himself to London in a huff.

Comfortably ensconced in a deep, cut-velvet-upholstered wingchair overlooking the sparkling indigo ocean, the princess opened her husband's letter. Instead of consoling her, it brought Dorothea to tears. "I repeat *in front of God* and I have too much religion to invoke him in vain, I know I am going crazy, in the name of God come, your presence perhaps will restore me." No one doubted Lieven's competence at the conference. "In the name of God do not say it any more" but "come my husband I beg of you, Wednesday will be *too late* ... come for the love of God, if God means anything to you—because I, I am nothing."[34]

No answer.

> I only ask you to let me know by your steward if I can expect you Tuesday or not—I think the latter more probable since the zeal and pleasure with which you left me proved only too well how you enjoy occasions for getting rid of me.
>
> Your children are well. As for my health, I hardly think it would interest you after what you said.[35]

The health of his "dearest Princess" did interest Grey. So did her letters. Princess Lieven put secret information in brackets because "{if I imagined any other than yourself *alone* read my letters, I should never dare write anything}."[36] The Arta-Volo boundary, which Dorothea consistently called "Lord Grey's frontier," so far represented "{only a project on our part}." Prince Lieven wanted "{nothing better than, by accepting this [Arta-Volo] as a mean term, to satisfy the susceptibilities of your Ministers; and, at the same time, I think it would}" benefit Greece. Yet, Lieven acted "{on his own responsibility, for it remains to be seen what the Emperor would say}."[37] If Tsar Nicholas agreed, Arta-Volo, by guaranteeing the Greeks' strength and freedom, would benefit all Europe. Hence "Grey's frontier" would "{play a great part, and that thus very peaceably}" at Howick he "{had the honor of laying down the boundaries of a new State}."[38]

Grey rather pettishly replied that Dorothea had no need of this super secrecy since he had already heard that Arta-Volo went by the name of "his" frontier. Still, Grey grumbled, he "certainly did not expect to be quoted."[39]

He had only himself to blame, Dorothea pointed out. He had written about "his idea" of the boundary to a friend, a British diplomat at Paris, who read Grey's letter to Russian ambassador Count Pozzo di Borgo.

"The epithet *Lord Grey's frontiers,* given to the new limits of Greece, was an expression agreed upon between Matuscewitz[40] and myself but in such strict confidence that in my husband's presence we had never even alluded to them under this name," Dorothea replied. "It would appear likely that between Matuscewitz and Pozzo" these "new limits also went by the name of *Lord Grey's frontiers,* and that Pozzo has proved less discreet than I have been."[41]

Regardless of who leaked the phrase "Lord Grey's frontiers," Dorothea Lieven's adroit diplomacy inspired the idea, gave it a name, and kept it in motion. And for a very good reason. If Grey came into power, as he most likely would, he could scarcely deny his own brainchild. And that is precisely what happened.

14

"*To Know* Everything and to Meddle in Nothing"

As there is no rule without its exception, I thought ... I was entitled to make one to the rule I have always observed of never meddling with the political matters of this capital. I assure you that I pass for being altogether ignorant of what is going on.[1]

—Dorothea Lieven

In 1830 Princess Lieven tore herself away from London, from her two small sons, and from political drama. As summer air breathed softly over England, King George's days dwindled; Lord Grey's day drew near. Concomitantly, Russia beckoned. Prince Lieven chafed to secure the lucrative estates he recently had inherited from his mother, but until the London Conference settled Greece, Dorothea kept his nose to the grindstone.

She, too, had come into a significant legacy, one that demanded attention. Tsar Nicholas showed that Dorothea's diligence on behalf of her country did not go unnoticed. At Princess Charlotte Lieven's death the tsar promoted Dorothea to her mother-in-law's prestigious position, one Dorothea's own mother had held: senior lady-in-waiting to the empress. Never, Princess Lieven told her brother with grateful tears, "has a like honor been received with greater emotion."[2]

Naturally Dorothea knew Nicholas and his wife Alexandra but not as tsar and tsaritsa. She must fortify her relations with them. The court favored its westernmost capital with its presence that summer, so the Lievens set out for Warsaw.

℘

Princess Lieven's energetic efforts against the duke of Wellington had not escaped her court's attention. So foreign minister Nesselrode instructed the princess to better her relations with the British government. And, of course, she must cultivate the new king. Lastly, Count Nesselrode and General Benckendorff candidly cautioned the princess against meddling in British politics.

Tsar Nicholas promoted Lieven interim foreign minister during Nesselrode's three month leave-of-absence, and honored Dorothea with an invitation to accompany the court to St. Petersburg. Her brother urged acceptance, but the princess itched to return to her children. Besides, King George's imminent death, the Wellington government's weakness, and rising public pressure for political reform made English politics far too fascinating to forgo for the vapid splendors of the Romanov court.

Flowers bloomed in colorful profusion under a pellucid sky when the Lievens, traveling in opposite directions, left Warsaw. Dorothea reached her first stop, Berlin, in "fifty-five hours—not very bad for a woman methinks."[3] News of King George's death awaited her.

Bowling along between Berlin and the British capital the princess suffered a common hazard of contemporary travel. Her carriage over-turned.

Suffering from such a severe back injury that she could barely walk, confined to the couch in her Richmond drawing-room, Dorothea, balancing her portable writing-table in her lap, kept up her Europe-wide correspondence. And received a steady stream of friends, diplomats, and politicians whose news enlivened her daily letters to Lieven.

Charles, second earl Grey. Great Britain's prime minister and his "dearest Princess" had a uniquely close personal and political relationship. Artist: Unknown (After Sir Thomas Lawrence.) National Portrait Gallery, London.

"You have no idea," tempted Lord Grey, "what a good nurse I am."[4] Her intimate friend urged Dorothea to recuperate in the bracing North Sea breezes of his beloved Howick. Instead the princess, like her mother, took her children with her to a seaside resort. Dorothea's doctor prescribed bathing in Brighton's sun-warmed salt-water, a well established remedy for easing muscle pain. Each morning Dorothea and her personal maid entered a bathing tent anchored on the beach. The maid helped her mistress undress and don long, baggy pantaloons and a woolen blouse, and confined her hair in a cap. When the fully clothed sufferer emerged, a brawny female attendant picked her up and carried her into the sea. Lightly holding Dorothea by only one or two fingers, she let the gently lapping waves take over. Several minutes later, grabbing Dorothea under the arms, the attendant bounced her up and down like a baby, and restored her to her maid.

The salutary effects of this treatment, not to mention King William IV[5] and his wife's marked kindness, decided the princess to extend her stay. Consequently, the king pontificated "in the most flattering way of the union of England and Russia, and of the impossibility of anything disturbing an understanding which both Powers had every interest to maintain. He fully recognizes the Emperor's merits and relies upon him absolutely."[6]

And since Dorothea Lieven recognized that only her husband had authority over her, she also told Alexander that Lieven would be pleased with the extremely satis-fying attentions that the king and queen showered on her. Indeed, Lieven would be gratified at his wife's relations with everyone.

That gratification would of course include his wife's excellent footing with the prime minister. Wellington went out of his way to visit Arthur (his godson) and George Lieven while their parents were at Warsaw. Dorothea's warm appreciation of the duke's kindness thawed their cold truce; a change, Dorothea told the envious Grey, due to Greece no longer coming between them. So Grey must not give this "*rap-prochement* an importance which it really has not. We see each other from time to time—that does not constitute intimacy."[7]

Indeed, Dorothea's imperious friend must be patient. Sea bathing did her back a world of good, but lately Dorothea had been absorbed in nursing her darling George, "so ill that I cannot move him from Brighton before to-morrow, and," she wrote Grey, impatiently awaiting her in the capital, "I am not sure of being able to take him all the way up to London without a rest."[8]

⅋⊙⅂

Meanwhile, momentous events caused every conservative heart to quake. Rev-olution broke out in France (July 1830) and roiled the Continent. In England long-festering discontent erupted. Laborers burned hayricks and smashed machinery to drive home their demands for higher wages; agitation for parliamentary reform swept the country. Riots broke out in London. Wellington ordered up troops. The "aris-tocracy rolls in wealth and luxury," Dorothea Lieven observed, but "the streets of London, the highways of the country, swarm with miserable creatures covered with rags, barefooted, having neither food nor shelter." That sight revolted the conserva-tive princess into an astonishing admission. "Were I one of these thousands of poor wretches I should be a democrat." Why "is it that no Government seems ever to have been able to find a remedy for this evil?"[9]

The Tory administration seemed solid, but political pundits agreed that the pres-ent turbulence called for reinforcement. Grey explained it so lucidly that Dorothea sent Alexander a translation: "perhaps the Emperor may deign to cast his eye over it."[10]

For months Princess Lieven had been pressing her hesitant friend to become prime minister, but now that revolution gripped the Continent she feared a Grey government might include liberals whose ideas the tsar would find hard to swallow. Still, Grey had both will and authority to rein in excessive liberalism. So Dorothea urged him to insist on the premiership while she pushed Palmerston to join the duke's cabinet. Although "somewhat difficult to manage,"[11] Dorothea told Alexander in what would turn out to be a huge understatement, Palmerston had favored Russia over Turkey on the Greek issue.

She stood completely "in the dark"[12] about whether Palmerston would enter Wellington's cabinet, Dorothea virtuously assured Alexander. Not quite true. Con-sidering, however, her brother and Nesselrode's warnings at Warsaw to confine her professional activities to more conventional ambassadorial duties than intriguing in cabinet making, one can scarcely blame Dorothea for keeping Alexander in the dark.

Under strictures of sworn secrecy the princess told Palmerston's lover, her inti-mate friend Emily, Countess Cowper, that the Tories were ready to conciliate; how far depended on the duke's political problems. He had "been debating *who* should undertake the negotiation, himself or Peel,[13] and has decided on himself." The princess preferred "the two P. P.* to listen to each other. If they agreed, all would go more than adequately."[14]

Before beginning her next paragraph Dorothea paused to sharpen her quill pen and dip it in the inkwell when a letter from Palmerston arrived. It left little hope that the negotiations would succeed. Palmerston could "count on my utmost and complete discretion just as I count on yours," the princess now addressed him directly. A cabinet member had confided to her that he considered "the matter well advanced. He holds tenaciously to success." Dorothea had delicately let fall her strong suspicion that Palmerston would want a senior cabinet post. The minister "observed that you do not constitute a party whose principles differ from those of the cabinet." Find, Dorothea pressed, "two or three Whigs and it will work! That would be a cabinet!" The minister agreed. "The Duke must go to the extreme of admitting that. And that extremity is possible."[15]

The princess begged Palmerston to burn her compromising letter immediately. He did not; nor, to her exasperation, did he join the Wellington cabinet.

Two weeks later the newly elected Parliament met. According to custom the king opened it with a speech expressing the government's views: he deplored revolution abroad and political unrest at home. A debate followed. Lord Grey spoke persuasively; parliamentary reform would save England from rebellion. What a detestable idea, Dorothea dissembled for her court's benefit; she would be sorry to see Grey prime minister. Still, in preparing her brother for the inevitable, she confidently assured Alexander that under Grey England would adhere to her treaties (the 1815 Vienna Settlement); they committed the Powers to maintain peace and to prevent, by force if necessary, France from aggrandizing her neighbors. The weak Wellington government would not.

A few days later King William IV asked Earl Grey to form a government.

৪৩০৫

Dorothea Lieven stood at the summit of power, a place no other female representative of a foreign government had achieved (or would achieve). And she had done it through her unique combination of talents. After so many years of operating behind the scenes the princess could preen herself. Instantly, she assumed the role of Egeria.

Alarmed at what a Whig administration might mean, the diplomatic corps lost no time in urging Princess Lieven to discourage Lord Grey from appointing a foreign secretary too steeped in liberalism. As for Lord Palmerston, the tables had turned. He immediately pressed the princess to induce Grey to give him the foreign office.

"I boldly promised to propose him to Lord Grey."[16]

When Grey paid his customary afternoon call, he found his Egeria sitting next to her drawing-room fireplace where a small wood fire burned. Seating himself on its other side, Grey said he had already decided. The princess felt "a little embarrassed because in reality Lord Lansdowne was a perfectly suitable choice, the most

---

*Peel (Sir Robert) and Palmerston.

moderate of all Whigs and the most in touch with foreign policy. However I did not fail to remark" that "the Cabinets of Europe were going to be very uneasy at" Whig rule, "and that as Lord Grey had every interest" in starting with "the goodwill of foreign Powers, I could assure him that nothing was more likely" to win "their confidence than to entrust foreign affairs to a man known" to have "moderate opinions, and not absolutely wearing the Whig livery."[17]

Lord Grey agreed. "But he asked me 'where can I find the man?'"[18]

"When I named Lord Palmerston" Lord Grey "recoiled."

The prime minister thought Palmerston "frivolous and pushing, and had taken no trouble to find out what solid qualities he could possess."[19] Although disposed to believe Dorothea's word that the foreign diplomats thought well of Palmerston, Grey questioned whether he quite deserved it. So prime minister and princess discussed the issue at length. They came to no conclusion.

"Palmerston awaited the *dénouement* with deep anxiety. He left me no peace. I was living at Richmond" but "came into town every day, and he galloped from one to the other of my residences. His obsession was keen, and my desire to serve him was also great."[20]

Meanwhile, Lansdowne declined the foreign office and proposed Palmerston.

On the morning of the day that the new ministry became official, Grey sat in his office writing out his list of cabinet members for the evening papers. A visitor interrupted, staying tête-à-tête with the prime minister for one and a half hours. At the end of that time Grey gave his sheet of paper to the person waiting in his ante-room on behalf of the press. One side listed Grey's initial cabinet; it did not include Palmerston. The other side listed Grey's final choice; next to foreign secretary, Grey had written Palmerston's name. There was no mistaking Grey's tall, elegant visitor.*

Lord Grey insisted that Dorothea promise to say nothing except to her brother, and then only in secret. So when the tsar's premier confidant saw his sister's full signature at the end of her letter, he must hold it against a flame to reveal the invisible ink. Grey "wished to give the Foreign Office to Lord Lansdowne. I suggested Palmerston, and Grey" agreed "in the hope that the choice would be agreeable to our Court. Have no fears," Dorothea righteously declared to her censorious brother, "not a soul here has the least idea of the influence by which this has been brought about."[21]

&⊃⊂3

The new French government sent a wily old hand to represent it in London. A living legend, short, slight, and limping, pale and extremely wrinkled with thickly powdered hair hanging straight to his shoulders, witty, charming Charles-Maurice de Périgord, Prince de Talleyrand, scion of one of France's noblest houses, arguably figured as the most brilliant diplomat of his day.

Having ably represented his country under the bewildering succession of governments that followed the 1789 revolution, Talleyrand eventually came to see Napoleon Bonaparte as detrimental to French interests, and helped bring about his downfall. Napoleon called his erstwhile foreign minister "de la merde dans un bas de soie."[22]

This story is based on an eye-witness account only divulged several years later. Mr. Scanlon, editor of the Courier, *waited in Grey's ante-room for the cabinet listing on behalf of all the evening papers. He received Grey's note with the two lists. He saw Princess Lieven go into and out of Grey's room.*

Disillusioned with the repressive regime of the restored Bourbons, the liberal-leaning Talleyrand withdrew into semi-retirement only to nurture, in 1830, the advent to the throne of Louis-Philippe, Duc d'Orléans, as constitutional king. Since Continental sovereigns failed to greet this new ruler, born of revolution, with any marked degree of enthusiasm, he and Talleyrand agreed that French foreign policy must focus on an alliance with the constitutional monarchy across the Channel. To win this difficult goal France needed an ambassador who combined ample political experience, utmost diplomatic skill, credible liberal opinions, and ingrained aristocratic manners. At age seventy-six Talleyrand undertook the task tailor-made for him.

Prince Talleyrand challenged Princess Lieven's influence over Lord Grey. Furthermore, Talleyrand's official hostess threatened the princess's social supremacy.

Semi-royal[23] and extremely wealthy in her own right, Dorothea, duchess of Dino, had married to oblige her family. At age fifteen she wed Talleyrand's nondescript nephew, heir to his vast fortune and future head of his powerful family but for all that, far beneath her in intellect and interests. Their union turned out to be miserable. Having presented her husband with two sons to carry on his distinguished name, the duchess followed her heart until such time as she proposed to divorce the lackluster duke and marry her lover. Dissuaded by intense family pressure, Dino then devoted herself to her uncle-by-marriage, forty years her senior. Rigidly respectable members of Europe's aristocracy preferred to persuade themselves that this "May-September" relationship was purely platonic, a somewhat surprising inference since Talleyrand's private life had for years fed society with salacious gossip. And Dino offended convention by exposing her marital problems—not only did she live apart from her dissolute spouse, but to protect her fortune, the duchess got a court-ordered financial separation.

The French embassy's new hostess proved a worthy foil for Princess Lieven's steel. In wit, intelligence, and conversation the two women were well matched, but Dino had the advantages of semi-royal status, youth, good looks (not pretty but often beautiful, her aquiline features, jet-black hair, large, luminous blue-gray eyes, and full, emphatic lips gave Dino an irresistibly seductive air), and Talleyrand's fame. On her side Dorothea Lieven had driving ambition, deep knowledge of English politics and society, a notable ability to enchant the minds and hearts of prominent men, and finer political acumen. When "age had tarnished the bloom of youth" she knew, Talleyrand wrote, "how to supply its place by great dignity, and exquisite manner, and a commanding air, which gave her a noble and somewhat haughty appearance, closely resembling the power she wields."[24]

Society anticipated some amusement in the rivalry between the Dorotheas. But they had too much in common not to respect each other; indeed, the two ladies became life-long friends. And, despite the differences dictated by their respective countries' foreign policy, so did the princess and Talleyrand.

ഇൗരു

France's July revolution sparked the adjacent Belgian provinces to revolt against their autocratic ruler, the king of the Netherlands. In Brussels street fighting erupted. France readied forces to support her neighbors. The Dutch king rallied his army and appealed to his allies. Prussia promised aid; Austria and Russia supported Prussia.

Seeking to conserve the status quo, to contain France no less than the pernicious influence of liberalism, Tsar Nicholas prepared to march across the Continent.

"For God's sake," Grey pressed, "urge against foreign interference" with "all your power; for if Prussia sends a single man across the frontier"[25] war would engulf Europe.

So Dorothea observed to her influential brother that although nations had learnt to use their might with growing confidence, governments had shown neither wisdom nor dynamism. Luckily, Russia had unique grounds for security: distance, relatively ignorant masses, ingrained religious devotion to the throne and, above all, an enlightened ruler who knew how to make himself both feared and loved. Still, "we belong to Europe and are bound by our treaties—shall we not thereby be dragged into the movement which is disturbing the world?" Should that happen, "will not the mere contact of our soldiers with the turbulent populations be a source of danger"?[26]

The Belgian revolt promised a protracted struggle with concomitant Great Power conflict. Since it came hard on the heels of a similar issue only recently resolved— Greece—the Powers agreed, in principle, to guarantee an independent, neutral Belgium. Their diplomats, again meeting in London, would settle knotty details.

Tsar Nicholas at once relieved Prince Lieven of his post as interim foreign minister. Back at his embassy the prince found his wife firmly ensconced as the prime minister's Egeria. And "everyone" seemed to be saying she was Russia's real ambassador. Lieven's barely subdued jealousy, let alone the frustration he felt over his inability to control his spouse, exploded. So ended Dorothea's three months' respite from the daily aggravations of her dysfunctional marriage.

Concomitantly, she grappled with a gnawing concern. Although Dorothea considered her soldier son Constantine the most promising of her three older boys, she worried about his difficulty in submitting to discipline. "Where is he? Who is his chief? Can you recommend him to the care of the latter?" Dorothea asked her brother.

> Can you get reports on his conduct—which, if good, may be passed on to my husband? Do keep an eye on him a little now and in the future. All this, dear Alexander, lies very close to a mother's heart. Write to me and tell me all you hear about my boy. My heart is very heavy on his account and I can only calm myself by the thought that you love me enough to make you take an interest in him.[27]

Throughout that worrisome winter (1830–1831) the princess continued to shuttle between her houses in quiet, rural Richmond and loud, lively London. "I am most anxious to hear that you have not suffered by coming here yesterday, or, what was much more dangerous, and an act of absolute insanity, by going out in an open carriage," Grey chided. "I have told you that you mismanage yourself dreadfully, though I never met with such proof of it before."[28]

"My malady is a violent cold, so bad that it has ended in blood-spitting, which somewhat alarms me."[29]

"I cannot believe you would go to Richmond in such weather, and shall, therefore, hope for an immediate answer that will relieve my anxiety. God bless you."[30]

☙ﭢ

The London conference agreed that Belgium should be a hereditary constitutional monarchy. Because rebellion in Poland had, unhappily for Tsar Nicholas although not for Europe, thwarted his plan to deploy his army to keep Belgium under Dutch domination, the "Iron Tsar" now wanted his brother-in-law Prince William of Orange, heir to the Dutch throne,[31] to become king of Europe's newest nation-state.

Dorothea Lieven's unpublished memoirs give a minutely written time-line of her initial activities on Prince William's behalf.

December 29, 1830: Dorothea discussed his candidacy with Palmerston. The foreign secretary wanted Prince Leopold of Coburg for Belgium. But Leopold had become less attractive to Russia than two years before when Dorothea helped him climb onto the Greek throne only to see him renounce it. Russia could keep a close eye on Greece, peopled with co-religionists and placed in eastern Europe. But far-off Belgium sat next to a danger spot: France. Besides Leopold's unsuitable liberal tendencies and, his engagement to a French princess did even less to recommend him to the tsar. Dorothea proved that only the prince of Orange "was practicable and profitable for the whole world."[32]

"My explication with Lord Grey January 1."[33]

January 2, 1831: Vandeweyer[34] told Palmerston that the Belgians would never accept Orange, and demanded Leopold within six days or—civil war. "*We* would never consent," Dorothea told Grey and Palmerston. "They explained that it would be done without us—I observed that they could do so but war would inevitably result."[35]

Consequently, Dorothea informed Nesselrode that Grey and Palmerston agreed to Orange—provided Austria and France did. Ably abetted by the duchess of Dino's dulcet charm, Talleyrand worked assiduously to unite Belgium to France; he wanted to put one of King Louis-Philippe's sons on the Belgian throne. But, the French ambassador informed his government, his industry foundered against constant obstacles: the most prominent—efforts on behalf of Orange "by Madame de Lieven, Lord Grey's particular friend."[36]

January 3rd: Talleyrand told Grey that France wanted to annex one of the Belgian provinces. On the 5th Vandeweyer said Belgium desired union with France, or at least to have a French prince to establish it tacitly. Grey said he wanted a prince who pleased everyone—or—war. Vandeweyer retorted that the mere mention of Orange's name would cause revolution in Belgium. His Egeria proved to Grey that Talleyrand and Vandeweyer were playing games with him. She advised Grey to be high-handed, even suggested "the language to use—my speech made an impression."[37]

January 6th: Grey summoned Talleyrand. If France entertained the slightest desire to conquer Belgium, France faced war with the Powers.

₧⁖

At this juncture Dorothea Lieven's diary told a surprising story. The princess of Orange, formerly Grand Duchess Anna, had known Dorothea since their youth. As an adolescent bride Dorothea had daily visited her mother-in-law's drawing-room and there met Charlotte Lieven's charges. Now Anna wrote in secret; not even Lieven must know. A Russian courier would deliver a portfolio containing all her assets[38] directly to Dorothea, so that if Prince William needed money, Dorothea could provide it. She "gave the portfolio sealed into the care of the Embassy, but kept the key."[39]

Immediately on arriving in London, Prince William of Orange called. Dorothea arranged that he and Grey meet at her house. They discussed several plans. One involved separating Holland and Belgium, giving the latter to William, and fomenting a movement in Brussels to proclaim him king. The prince agreed "to this conspiracy, but means were lacking. We [note the use of the first person plural] needed money, two or three important gentlemen" had "to be bought. Where could we find the money?"[40]

Lieven and Matuscewitz[41] thought Dorothea should dip into Grand Duchess Anna's ample portfolio, but she "refused to do anything unless the Prince asked me." Yet, Prince William remained unaware that Dorothea held his wife's wealth on his behalf. "We had to find some opportunity for letting him know."[42]

Dorothea's intimacy with the imperial family, to say nothing of her power to inspire confidences, soon yielded the desired result. William divulged his marital troubles, his bitter quarrels with Anna, his disgust at her envy, her tantrums. Anna had decent, even generous feelings, Dorothea averred as she showed William the portfolio and his wife's letter. Prince William began to cry. "Yes, that is Anna."

"Well, Monseigneur, you need money, ask it of me."

"On no account in the world. She means the money for my" needs. "I know well that Belgium is lost to my father, but is his son to take it from him? No! ... Anna would never pardon me."[43]

Dorothea duly informed the conference of William's scruples. Meanwhile, Belgium seemed about to offer itself to France. Horrified, "Lord Grey, Lord Palmerston, my husband, Matuscewitz all"[44] pressured the prince.

And the prime minister pressured Princess Lieven. Belgium's representatives had arrived to settle on a sovereign. Prince William "would be the best arrangement."[45] His party must at once prove its power. Otherwise, England could not continue to support a cause that would intensify discontent, and "excite the jealousy of France."[46]

"Artificial, rather weak and very ambitious," Orange "came to me to ask for 500,000 francs. I opened the portfolio in his presence and in that of other witnesses, and I told him I should inform the Princess of this payment."[47]

Prince William objected. If Anna knew, "all would be lost.... Her rigid probity would revolt, she would denounce the Brussels plot."

"Princess Lieven: 'But, Monseigneur, I cannot avoid giving her an account of what I have done with her money.'

"Orange: 'Wait, I beg you for the courier ... the matter will be settled at Brussels.' I consented to wait for the courier. The conspiracy failed."[48]

"I begged the Prince to allow me to write to his wife. He was afraid." A week later Dorothea received a haughty, angry letter from Anna. "Bills had been drawn upon her. She asked me for the account." Dorothea explained everything, returned the portfolio, and Orange "undertook to appease her. I do not know if he ever succeeded."[49]

After some weeks a courier came from Count Nesselrode. He brought startling news. The tsar "had just received an unintelligible letter from his sister, in which she denounced my husband" as "having stolen 500,000 francs from her."

"I begged my husband to leave the matter wholly to me." Dorothea sent Nesselrode the grand duchess's two letters. "I told him all that concerned me in this question, and I left it to the gentlemen in question to explain how the sum had been expended. I received a reply from Nesselrode with this sentence: 'I have shown your letter and the letters to him who has the right to see them. The only answer has been "my sister is mad."'"[50]

ജൗൽ

Many Belgians wanted the Duc de Nemours, a son of Louis Philippe, as their king. France agreed. Russia did not. "You will never permit it. Belgium under the Duc de Nemours is Belgium under France,"[51] Dorothea impressed on Grey. He must be firm, she coached her somewhat indecisive friend, or his reputation as prime minister of a great country would suffer. The French government would not dare accept the Nemours nomination if Grey made plain to Paris that England refused to recognize it. Grey did.

Fearing war if Louis-Philippe let his son accept the Belgian crown, Talleyrand advised his king to yield. Dorothea congratulated Grey on the happy result of his resolve; but he should not show "too much satisfaction for this would betray your secret." France would "discover *your* fear of going to war and this would give her an advantage over you."[52]

Talleyrand now promoted Louis-Philippe's nephew, the prince of Naples, for Belgium. Dorothea heard that Grey had agreed, but she refused to believe such folly. Russia would never consent; moreover, a stand-off meant the end of the Anglo-Russian alliance, "an alliance which forms the only sheet-anchor of Europe. And England alone the cause—and for what? Think what a fine business it would be for your adversaries."[53]

Two days later the princess learned that Britain's foreign office had nominated the Neapolitan prince—"the very height of absurdity—a Prince desired by no single Belgian, and whom France wishes to impose on Belgium and Europe." Was this the England that in 1815 had led the Powers in preventive actions against France? Would England now let France set up a "Neapolitan *lazzaroni*"[54] as king of a constitutional country? Dorothea's brains were "paralyzed in trying to understand your policy, if, indeed, it be possible that you should be contemplating any such arrangement."[55]

The following weekend Prince Leopold hosted a select party at Claremont, his comfortable country house. Among his guests were Princess Lieven and Lord Grey. Soon after, Britain again proposed Leopold for Belgium. This time Russia agreed. Grey and Palmerston liked Leopold for his liberal tendencies and friendship for the country he had long called home. They did not like his engagement to a French princess but that, and his liberalism, made Leopold palatable to Louis-Philippe and Talleyrand. Still deep in Leopold's confidence, Dorothea Lieven impressed on Nesselrode that Leopold had "correct" ideas. And she convinced Lieven and Matuscewitz that, with the prince of Orange out of the running, Leopold represented the most reasonable compromise.

"My husband wants me to recount to you," Dorothea wrote Nesselrode, "all that Prince Leopold came to tell me yesterday. Here is my very truthful recital.

"'Before leaving I wanted to prove to you again my respect for your Tsar and to tell you that whatever may be the needs of my position I shall'" always "'remember what I owe Russia, and the personal feelings that attach me to the Tsar.'"

Leopold knew, Dorothea replied, that Russia preferred a prince from the House of Orange, but as that proved "*impractical* certainly Your Royal Highness offered enough of a political and individual guarantee that the Tsar would appreciate."

Belgium's new king then averred that he hoped, bit by bit, to amend the country's "detestable constitution."[56]

The Russians insisted that the conference officially confirm Leopold. Impatient at these diplomatic niceties, Grey high-handedly decided, directly before a crucial parliamentary debate on Belgium, to recognize Leopold unilaterally. That would rupture the conference.

Sure of her facts, confident in her knowledge of men, Dorothea Lieven, immediately before the beginning of the debate, let Opposition leader the duke of Wellington surmise Russia's dissatisfaction with the prime minister's decision. "And on this inference he founded the appeal he made to Lord Grey in the House to go hand in hand with us, commending highly" the two Powers' cooperation thus far. Wellington's move infuriated Grey, but at the "Conference he gave way. It will not be broken up and we shall keep England within bounds. All this is so confidential," Dorothea cautioned her brother, "that I have not dared to speak of it to my husband. He is delighted with the result, but that is only because he is ignorant of the author."[57]

15

"I Only Display One Color ... I Am *Grey*"

So long as we live, there will never be a moment of peace in the world.
Hasten therefore to settle Belgium, Greece, and Poland.[1]
—Count Nesselrode to Princess Lieven

Dorothea Lieven distrusted democracy. Like most aristocrats she felt that "the mob" threatened political stability. The princess preferred monarchy. It safeguarded stability. Yet, Dorothea respected the power of political liberty. "In ten years all Europe will be constitutional," she had predicted to that pillar of Continental conservatism, Prince Metternich. "You will be the last to see it, but you will see it."[2]

The 1830 revolution brought France a constitutional monarchy. If, the princess wrote Grey, France refrained from the aggression with which it had favored Europe after 1789, no country had a right to interfere in France's internal affairs. Nonetheless, Dorothea feared "that revolutionary mania may extend yet further elsewhere."[3]

"I have never yet known a popular revolution that might not be ascribed to" government provocation, Grey replied. If governments were wise and moderate, they need not fear "revolutionary mania." Certainly France's example would encourage others. "But the security against this is not to be found in armies and Holy Alliances." (Austria, Russia, Prussia.) Instead of prompting governments "to measures for putting down public opinion by force, show them the necessity of setting to work to put their houses in order in time."[4]

Momentarily dropping her mantle of professional diplomat, Dorothea Lieven delivered herself of a surprising rejoinder. "There is not a word in your letter of which I do not approve, not a single opinion that I do not reciprocate."[5]

ಐಂಧ

Naked trees clattered in a chill north wind when Tsar Nicholas's Belgian policy drew the princess onto a delicate diplomatic tightrope. As 1831 waned the Great Power representatives sitting in conference concurred on a peace treaty ending hostilities between Holland and Belgium. But Tsar Nicholas's protégé the Dutch king, who had refused to recognize either Belgium's independence or Leopold as its sovereign, persuaded his brother-in-law the king of Prussia to delay ratification. The tsar, balked in his intent to aid Holland with arms, now decided on diplomacy. Nicholas followed Prussia's lead, because—rumor whispered—his "real" ambassador, Dorothea Lieven, opposed ratification.

"You have too much regard for me to do what would be so distressing to me personally," Lord Grey reproached the princess, "and too much care for the interests of your country to force this Government into a close connection with France," which would certainly result if "any of the four Powers withheld ratification."[6]

"You accuse me," riposted his Egeria,

> of encouraging the King of the Netherlands in his opposition, and I, therefore am the cause of the non-ratification the Treaty! Truly you invest me with an influence and an importance that is both curious and novel, such as would be capable, if exerted, of bringing about the disavowal of all that my husband has effected.[7]

When Grey told her such tattle, he surely forgot that Dorothea was Lieven's wife. Moreover, "why should the non-ratification of one of the four Powers throw you into the arms of France? Your inclination must indeed be great if so trifling an incident could entail so grave a decision." Did Grey "really think I can believe you when you thus threaten me? for this I should have to forget you were an Englishman, a clever man," and "a great statesman."[8]

Dorothea's signature combination of logic and flattery had its desired result. Nevertheless, Tsar Nicholas's policy troubled her.

Princess Lieven firmly believed that if autocratic Russia and constitutional Britain failed to stay on good terms, good-bye to the peace of Europe. Possibly the greatest diplomat of the day represented France in London. Ably abetted by the stellar social skills of his seductive niece-by-marriage the duchess of Dino, Prince Talleyrand would certainly use Russia's reluctance to ratify to advance his goal of an alliance with England, a move Tsar Nicholas would view with an extreme disfavor.

Princess Dorothea Lieven. In middle life. Artist: Gauci lithograph from a painting by Lucas. (c) Copyright the Trustees of the British Museum. Used by permission.

The princess shared the prime minister's frustration at the Dutch king's obstinacy; as well, she cherished Grey's friendship. Russia must ratify; yet, Dorothea must support her tsar's policy. She must also keep Russia and England in tandem; moreover, she must stop the country Nicholas hated as the hotbed of revolution, whose king he scorned as the son of revolution, from alliance with England.

So the tsar's "real" ambassador insisted that her powerful brother General Benckendorff, no less than foreign minister Nesselrode, must understand—must, moreover, make Tsar Nicholas understand—that England, having once recognized Leopold as king of Belgium could not, would not, dishonor herself by abandoning him. And Dorothea knew for sure that Wellington, leader of the Opposition Tories, agreed. Besides, did the tsar plan to "personally vindicate the pretensions of the King of the Netherlands? I don't believe it for a moment." Were Russia "to take up the personal interests of King William we shall lose England, who, unwilling to remain without allies, will throw herself into the arms of France, and Europe will be handed over to the united influence of these two Liberal Powers."[9]

Indeed, Prince Talleyrand's assiduous efforts to achieve a treaty with England had already alarmed London's diplomatic corps. And Russia's formal protest, Dorothea impressed on Nesselrode, made the British believe Russia took Talleyrand's proposal seriously. So although the princess thought it unlikely that foreign secretary Lord Palmerston would ally his country with France, she did not put it past him to let the idea float simply to arouse Russia's anxiety and, thus, propel her to ratify.

Not only that, the Tories attacked the government for failing to finish the Belgian issue. Angry, but anxious to avoid antagonizing Russia, Grey barely restrained himself from publicly blaming Russia's delay in ratifying. Still, Dorothea warned Nesselrode, the Tories would attack again. "Let them take care that they do not at last provoke me beyond my patience," Grey confided. "Ratify! ratify! ratify! there is no other conclusion."[10]

Seeking to settle the Belgian business, Britain and France, early in the new year (1832), ratified the treaty. Princess Lieven alerted Nesselrode that the ensuing parliamentary debate would focus on Russia's ratification. So Dorothea advised that if Tsar Nicholas's protégé the Dutch king had decided to reject the treaty, refuse to recognize Leopold, and wage war "at last a decisive statement should make this clear"; however, "peace is the first priority."[11]

∞∞∞

The princess and her two boys spent most of that winter at their country house; Lieven stayed in London to attend the conference. Richmond provided relief from London's swirling "pea-soupers," so bad for Dorothea's feverish chest colds; Richmond also served as a safety-valve for matrimonial stress.

"You were in town last Wednesday without taking any notice of me," Grey pouted. "This prevented my writing, not that I had anything to say, or any inducement to write, except the pleasure of communicating with you."[12]

"I came to town with Arthur, for the dentist, and for nothing else, and after changing horses returned here at once. I did not see a single soul."[13]

"Your note, which I received last night, did my heart good.... God bless you; love me a little, and believe me ever, dearest Princess, Yours most devotedly."[14]

"I truly appreciate what you say, and indeed deserve the affectionate regard you have for me."[15]

Meanwhile, Palmerston decided to vent his spleen at the Dutch king's stubborn refusal to recognize an independent and neutral Belgium, by replacing Britain's ambassador at the Hague with a lower level diplomat—a mere minister. Tsar Nicholas could hardly be expected to view this affront to his protégé with any pleasure.

This subject gave the Opposition a chance to challenge the prime minister in Parliament. Tory leaders Wellington and Aberdeen confided to the princess that they held "as I believe you do also," she prompted Grey, "that Holland is associated with a brilliant epoch in the history of England which it would be a shame for this country to forget."[16] Hence, Grey need only share his views with Palmerston for the foreign secretary to agree.

"Dearest," Dorothea also pressed her long-time intimate Emily Cowper, "you must save us in a question of personal diplomacy." Besides having giggled together over mutual indiscretions almost from the moment they became friends, the two women now shared a political interest through Emily's lover. Foreign secretary Palmerston based his objection to an ambassador at the Hague only on grounds of economy, Dorothea prompted. In the Dutch capital an ambassador with £5,000 a year would cut the most important figure next to the king. Palmerston wanted to appoint a minister with a salary of £3,600. Within Britain's budget of £140,000 to £150,000 Dorothea felt sure the foreign office could come up with the £1,400. "It would be a terrible shame to sacrifice a *principal* for such a small sum. I say principal, for since your revolution you have constantly kept an Ambassador at that Court." Lastly, Dorothea divulged Wellington and Aberdeen's plan of attack. (Grey's cabinet included not only Emily's lover, but also her brother.) Grey had given Dorothea the distinct impression that he stood somewhat in awe of Palmerston. "Be less craven than he is."[17] Regardless, Palmerston held firm.

⟡

When crocuses pushed their purple petals up through the thawing earth, Tsar Nicholas sent a special envoy to the Hague. General Alexis Orlov[18] must convince Holland's king to accept the decisions of the conference. If the king refused, Orlov had authority to declare: "Russia gives him no countenance, but recognizes as established facts both the independence and the neutrality of Belgium."[19] Gratified, Grey fervently hoped Orlov would carry out his commission firmly. He did—but failed to win over his quarry. So Orlov repaired to London to assure the conference of Russia's good faith.

Nonetheless, not until rhododendrons and azaleas blazed in full glory did Dorothea congratulate Nesselrode on Russia's ability now to keep friendship with England. Her country ratified what Dorothea, careful to avoid suspicion of having become "tainted" with liberalism, described to her chief as "this damned treaty, because damned it remains."[20]

Russia's ratification carried exclusions. Tsar Nicholas wanted the Powers to impose limits on Belgium's free navigation of the Scheldt river, an artery essential to Belgian commerce. So Britain decided to review its ratification. This new wrinkle stimulated the princess into some adroit maneuvers.

Welcome sunshine warmed the room where Dorothea, seated at her intricately inlaid cherry-wood writing table, dipped her pen into the standish and smoothed a sheet of crisp, cream-colored paper. She knew Orlov would call on Grey between one and two o'clock. She knew Grey would be at leisure from twelve to three. Why not call a cabinet meeting during that time, "and there take cognizance of the communications we have to make?" If Grey examined them in greater depth he would judge more favorably than heretofore. Everybody—Prussia, Austria, even France— wanted matters to be decided forthwith, and Orlov to bring the government's decision to Russia. "Again, all hold that our reservations *in no wise prevent* the exchange of the ratifications, and further, everybody" wanted this exchange to "take place immediately, for thereby the core of the matter would be irrevocably fixed."[21]

And if England did agree to re-ratify, Orlov, insisted the princess, must carry the news to Tsar Nicholas, "for his broad shoulders may carry a great deal more besides. He leaves tonight. I know M. de Talleyrand is extremely anxious that the affair should be settled,* and they will all petition you to summon a Council for to-day." Russia's reservations could be kept secret; "all that need be known would be the exchange of the ratifications, this giving an assurance" of "perfect agreement among the five Powers on a point of interest common to all, viz.: the peace and tranquility of Europe."[22]

"I shall be very glad to see Count Orlov at the hour you mention.... I am willing to consider everything in the best view that can be taken of it, and to remove, and not to increase, difficulties; but I am much and deeply grieved at the conduct of your Court. I agree with you in thinking it of great importance that Count Orlov" bring back the decision, but "am afraid this can hardly be, if he is to away to-night. Could he remain for a day or two. I would ask it as a personal favor if that would do any good."[23]

"I sent your note to Orlov, my dear lord, and he is quite ready" to "remain for a day or two longer; but the case presents a difficulty. The steamer for Hamburg sails to-night," the sole public means "of reaching Lübeck in time to catch the steamboat for St. Petersburg." Could the British government provide transport for the tsar's special envoy? "You have my thanks for the conciliatory disposition evinced by your letter." Orlov had "every confidence *in you*, and carries away a feeling of personal regard for you" that should content Grey, for "what he thinks they will also think in Russia."[24]

Before he called his cabinet meeting to order Grey asked the Admiralty for transport. Hardly had his meeting ended when Grey told Dorothea that he hoped Britain and Russia's ratifications could be exchanged at that evening's session of the conference. If so, Orlov might be able to leave at once. If not, he could take either the *Lightning* steamboat, or the *Comet*, which would be entirely at his orders; "it is not fitted up with accommodations for passengers, though it is an excellent vessel."[25] Orlov caught the commercial steamer.

Jubilant at her success Dorothea still made sure to follow up. Besides being glad to bear such good news, the tsar's special envoy bore an extremely pleasant memory of his stay in London, the princess praised Grey. Orlov especially appreciated how

---

Princess Lieven's friend the duchess of Dino served as Talleyrand's unofficial private secretary. Consequently, the princess boasted to Nesselrode that "France in London" had become a valuable source of information for Russia.

kindly his hosts, most notably Grey, had received him. Much gratified, the prime minister reiterated his desire to keep on good terms with Russia.

All this good fellowship notwithstanding, Tsar Nicholas insisted on the Scheldt exclusions to Russia's ratification. He counted on the vicissitudes of British politics to return the conservative duke of Wellington to power.

Even "if a Tory Administration should succeed, it would not last six months, and the government would fall," Grey thundered, "not into our hands, but into those of a party professing opinions far exceeding ours."[26] So the prime minister explicitly advised the princess to correct the impression held at St. Petersburg.

"It's a poor government, but God knows if others would make it better,"[27] Dorothea had already told her brother. The Whigs might blunder, but at least they wanted to be on good terms with Russia. So when Grey asked his confidante about the rumor that she had become a Tory, Dorothea replied that people would have to be "very clever ever to know whether I am Whig or Tory. I only display one color— that is, yours. I am *Grey*."[28]

80C3

Impatient to lay Belgium to rest as much for its own sake as to de-fang the Tories, Grey blamed Russia's insistence on its exclusions for prolonging the issue. Then, to further complicate matters, Prussia, which had always cast a jaundiced eye on the viability of a neutral Belgium, got jittery over Leopold's marriage to a French princess. So Prussia and Austria agreed to support Russia over the Scheldt exclusions. Exasperated, Grey told Dorothea her court must, in all honor, exert itself to resolve Belgium.

"You are wrong to blame *us*; we have done all we could." Russia had been consistent from the beginning. Only recently Grey wanted Belgium to give way; why not insist on it now? Talleyrand agreed, saying openly that since England and France had given Leopold his crown, they were entitled to expect some compliance. "Talleyrand is no Russian, and therefore his opinion need not be regarded with suspicion."[29]

Leopold had a right to insist on free navigation of the Scheldt, Grey persisted. So Dorothea blamed the chilly rain that soaked England that September for putting the prime minister in a bad mood.

"If you found traces of the bad weather in my letter, I must say your Highness in return does not appear to have written in a good humor,"[30] Grey retorted. To avoid more conflict he would refrain from answering his Egeria's forceful arguments.

"How much better it would be," she teased,

> if you were the Grand Turk! No more contradictions then. I should be afraid of the bowstring, and I should always agree with you. Admit that you are rather dogmatic in your opinions, and that the Whigs in general, with all their apparent Liberalism, have a great predisposition for turning autocrats.[31]

Grey should hurry back to London. "We will try and amuse each other, and laugh. It is part of one's business in this world, and laughing makes one keep one's health" as well. "My Highness salutes your Lordship" in "true and warmest friendship."[32]

80C3

As the princess and the prime minister sparred politically and flirted in friendship, the conference agreed to a modified treaty and settled Belgium's border. Belgium accepted both. Grudgingly acquiescing to the boundary, Holland rejected the treaty.

Palmerston and Talleyrand wanted the conference to force Dutch acceptance. Austria, Prussia, and Russia argued delay. England and France sent the Hague an ultimatum: withdraw all troops from Belgium by November 12 (1832), or else a British fleet would blockade the Dutch coast and a French army would drive the Dutch garrison from Antwerp, which Holland held in defiance of the conference.

"Why are you not at Stoke[33] while I am?" the princess pouted. During this, the season for country house visits, the press of business conveniently kept her suspicious spouse in London. Did Grey know what was happening to her? In fine weather she loved her "friends doubly, and I love you madly today."[34]

"I partake in all feelings with which fine weather inspires you. Here it has been delicious, and your letter arriving at a moment when I was enjoying it to the greatest degree, I responded to your concluding sentence with all my heart."[35]

From Stoke the princess went to Panshanger, the Cowpers' crenellated country residence; there she found the duchess of Dino, Prince Talleyrand, and Lord Palmerston. The man Dorothea had been instrumental in promoting to the foreign office despite his being "somewhat difficult to manage" had become distressingly suspicious of Russia. He belligerently blamed the tsar for Holland's resistance, and showed an undiplomatic tendency for hasty judgment. But despite Dorothea's best efforts Grey agreed with Palmerston. So on October 22 Britain and France signed a convention pledging to enforce their ultimatum to make Holland accept the decisions of the conference.

Three weeks later a French army crossed into Belgium, and a British fleet blockaded Holland. Grey prayed, he wrote the princess, that these actions would end soon, and in such a way as to continue the positive relations he consistently sought to cultivate between his country and Russia. Dorothea duly sent the prime minister's message to Nesselrode.

৩৩০৩

Prince Talleyrand sat alone in a corner of Panshanger's casual yet elegant drawing-room, "taking as usual his coffee at a little table," the princess regaled Nesselrode. She crossed the room to sit next to the French ambassador, "and here is our dialogue:

"I. 'Ah, well, Prince, amuse me! Tell me something!'

"P. T. 'This Belgium will never be a country.'" It is "'not a nation, two hundred protocols will never make a nation; It cannot hold together.'" It "'*will not last.*'

"I. 'But what comes afterwards?'

"P. T. 'Tell me yourself.'

"I. 'Oh, if you wish *my* opinion, Belgium will revert to Holland, or be partitioned.'

"P. T. 'Let's partition it; that will serve to pass the evening. Arrange that.'

"I. 'Nothing easier, we must satisfy everybody.'" There are "'some not concerned; neither Austria nor us.'

"P. T. 'There remains?'

"I. '*You*—a little; *Holland* much; *Prussia* probably, and then.'

Prince Charles-Maurice de Talleyrand Périg-ord. The greatest diplomat of his day. Princess Lieven's once adversary, always friend. Artist: William Henry Mote; Charles Knight; Auguste Gaspard. National Portrait Gallery, London.

"P. T. (*grasping his cane*). 'And then, who?'

"I. 'Oh, something to England. Antwerp for example!'

"P. T. (*strikes the floor with his cane, the table with his fist, so as to make the cup dance, and to attract the attention of the whole drawing-room*). 'Antwerp to England? Do you know what a revolting thing you say? What? England on the Continent? Madame, so long as there is a France, small as it is now, we will not, we cannot, have England on the Continent. You disgust me ... what you say is abominable.'

"I. 'Ah, well, my Prince, don't give her anything. It's all the same to me.'

"P. T. (*recovers himself a little*). 'Go on, go on, I see you are joking.'

"I. 'What! You realize that now!'

"P. T. 'But all the rest was so good. Well. I thank you for having come to chat with me. I did not know you were such a good sport; I see we can deal with you.'"[36]

Having artfully provoked this frank outburst, the princess concluded that the current goodwill between France and England could not last. Nor did it.

16

The Princess, the Prime Minister, and Poland

Mme. de Lieven of all women was the most feared, respected, sought after, and courted. Her political influence ... went side by side with an authority in society which no one dreamed of questioning.... Her house was the most select in London, and the one the *entrée* to which was the most valued.[1]

—The Duchess of Dino

The ... Polish envoy ... expressed surprise that this "old and ugly woman, with a red nose, should possess such influence and make everybody submit to her decrees." This is explained by her rare intellectual qualities, her dialectic skill, and her extraordinary pliancy in social intercourse ... she was not only an agreeable companion but a political force.[2]

—Prince Adam Czartoryski

Barely had the Belgian bid for independence begun when Poland blew up. Late in 1830 rebels attacked the Warsaw residence of their repressive king, Russia's Grand Duke Constantine, killing several of his officers. Citizens and soldiers joined the revolt. Constantine fled. Poland's interim government sought negotiations with Tsar Nicholas. He demanded instant and unconditional capitulation. The Poles refused. War.

Many in England, including the prime minister, sympathized with a nation fighting for freedom from foreign rule. Not Princess Lieven. Her tsar could never permit Polish independence; if one nation in Russia's vast, multi-ethnic empire broke free, others would follow. She convinced Grey that the tsar had no choice but to crush the revolt.

Indeed, despite the best efforts of Poland's primary support, Prince Talleyrand, the British government gave no thought to aiding the Poles. They had, after all, rebelled against Britain's ally, one she needed on a vital issue: creation of a stable, independent, and neutral Belgium across the narrow strip of water separating England from the Continent. So to Dorothea's satisfaction the Grey government, in public at least, supported Tsar Nicholas. What the Whigs thought and said in private, however, constituted quite another matter.

ॐ

145

By the way, my dear lord, take the trouble to get and read last evening's *Courier*,[3] and tell me candidly if you ever have seen anything more insulting and injurious than what is written here of a Sovereign and a Power in friendly alliance with England. The *Courier* frequently declares its statements to be *by authority;* now, it appears to me that the authority which sometimes inspires its articles might equally forbid [such items]. Pray think for one moment of the effect [these writings produce].[4]

Surely, Grey replied, Princess Lieven had lived long enough in England to realize that although angry at the article, he had "no power over that, or any other paper, in great circulation." Indeed, the popularity of Poland's cause gave the profit-driven newspapers a strong motive to support it. Nothing "could lead to more erroneous conclusions than a belief that any of these papers, on matters of general policy, speak the opinions of the Government."[5]

The princess also prodded the foreign secretary via his lover and her close friend Emily, Lady Cowper. Lord Palmerston thought the *Courier* article disgusting, he told Emily. Still, just because he could get the editor "to insert any article I wished today," Palmerston had "no means whatever of preventing him from inserting anything of quite a different kind tomorrow."[6] At least Dorothea derived satisfaction from sending Palmerston's letter to foreign minister Count Nesselrode.

ಬಿಂ

Meanwhile a severe cholera epidemic swept through Poland, taking Grand Duke Constantine, his Polish wife, and Russia's military commander with it. Hostilities ground to a halt. So the Polish government set its sights on London.

Not for a moment did Dorothea Lieven think England would help the Poles, for that would mean war with Russia. But the British government reception of Poland's delegation did disturb Dorothea. Would Grey and Palmerston want Russia's foreign minister to meet "an ambassador from O'Connell after he had led a rebellion in Ireland"? If Nesselrode "presumed to do such a thing the English Government would not fail to make loud remonstrances, and rightly so."[7]

At this point the Polish prime minister, courtly, white-haired Prince Adam Czartoryski,* legendary hero of Poland's independence, arrived to plead his country's cause. Educated in the liberal tradition of the Enlightenment, Prince Adam had, in his youth, visited London, where he made friends with several young Whigs including Charles Grey. The prime minister, who could be ruthless in politics, now told his old friend that although the British public sympathized with Poland, it had more interest in parliamentary reform and preservation of peace threatened by events closer to home: Belgium. Furthermore, Grey needed the tsar's cooperation on Belgium and, in general, desired good relations with Russia. Palmerston told Prince Adam that England stood by the Vienna Treaties, which did not guarantee a Polish constitution. To cap all, Princess Lieven reiterated throughout politically infused society that Tsar Nicholas would never let other Powers interfere in Poland, just as England would not allow foreign meddling in Ireland.

---

*Prince Adam bore the name of an honorable family famous in Polish history since the middle ages; he was probably an illegitimate son of Princess Isabel Czartoryski and the Russian Prince Nicholas Repnin. When Alexander became tsar, he made Czartoyskli foreign minister but, disappointed that the tsar's liberalism did not extend so far as to grant Poland independence, the prince left Russia's service—not, however, before he and Alexander's wife, the Empress Elizabeth, had become lovers; indeed, rumor accorded the Polish patriot paternity of Elizabeth's only child, a girl who died in infancy.

Furious nonetheless that Grey and Palmerston even received Czartoryski, which could be construed as semi-official recognition of Poland as independent, Nesselrode instructed Princess Lieven to make the English ministers negate what their actions might imply. "My heart tells me you will accomplish that."[8]

With deliberate intent Dorothea showed Grey a cold shoulder. He protested.

"It is quite true that my feelings to you yesterday were not what they have been for many past years," she conceded. "But you cannot be surprised, when I tell you that I heard of the exclamation with which you concluded the account you gave to a certain diplomatist" about Russia's military success at Warsaw: "'All is ended; and it is *most* unfortunate.' I no longer recognize the friend, still less do I recognize the statesman." For "the first time I feel a hesitation in writing to you; but when the heart is full one can find neither ideas nor words."[9]

Grey replied,

> *There is not one word of truth in the exclamation which is said to have escaped me.* I have never concealed from you, however, that I feel a good deal of compassion for these poor Poles. But it has never influenced the conduct which my public duty prescribed to me. I am not a little vexed at your so easily believing this absurd story, and at your being ready to withdraw the kindness which I had hoped did not depend altogether on our political agreement.[10]

Dorothea: "I should not have been so distressed," had "I cared less about you. Your note has obliterated all trace of the pain I had at heart. See, my dear lord, the extent of your power over me.... Your note made me feel happy again, and I thank you."[11]

The princess immediately sent this exchange to Nesselrode.

‰ℭℬ

When geraniums burst into bloom and a benign breeze stirred early roses, King William IV, clad in a rich scarlet velvet robe trimmed with ermine, a jeweled crown, and the broad sky blue ribbon of the Garter stretched across his ample person, would, according to custom, formally open Parliament with a speech outlining the government's views. While preparing the king's speech, Grey consulted his Egeria. One word caused her grave concern: the word "war." Grey wanted to use it in reference to Poland.

> It strikes me that this particular word, following upon "civil commotions"—the term employed to characterize the recent events in Italy—would imply that the Polish affair is of a different order to these. In point of fact the cases are identical. For it is an insurrection in Poland, just as it was an insurrection in Italy.

England had never used "war" when officially referring to Greece. "Strictly speaking, this word can only be applied to the acts of two belligerent Powers. The respective positions of Poland and Russia are quite different" because international treaties recognized the tsar as Poland's ruler; thus, "'war' is not applicable," noted the diplomat. And, the politician continued, "since it is most important that you should furnish no pretext of quibble to your enemies" who would jump on "war" to draw the government "into an embarrassing discussion, I judge it" in "your own interest even to avoid" using it. The word "'contest' or 'unfortunate events' might be substituted for the word 'war.' 'Contest' would embody the same idea, but would not give rise to the same inconvenient equivocation as 'war.'"[12]

No one could "appreciate more entirely than I do the delicacy and generosity of the confidence you have placed in me, and I look upon it as one of the many valued proofs of your friendly feeling towards us. Only grant me the word 'contest' in place of 'war,' and I shall be eternally grateful to you."[13] Grey did.

∞○∞

Russet leaves carpeted the ground when Warsaw fell to Russia's army (1831). And General Benckendorff had more good news. Having wholeheartedly entered into his sister's appeal to keep an eye on her wayward son Constantine, Benckendorff's protection "had not been without result. A thousand thanks for all you have done for my son." Dorothea counted on her brother "in the future as I have had good cause for counting upon you in the past."[14]

She had begged Benckendorff for a great favor: "to entreat Count Nesselrode to grant my son Alexander leave of absence for four months." A "worthy fellow, attentive to his duties and discreet," not "guilty of any extravagance beyond a visit to the Falls of Niagara and a trip to Africa," he had served "for five years without a break, with zeal and assiduity, the climate of Madrid at this season is most trying for the chest, and he is anxious to get away for a time."[15] Dorothea's second son spent part of his leave at London; then, at his mother's behest, Nesselrode posted Alexander to salubrious Naples.

Meanwhile, Russia's autocrat put Poland under martial law. Taking advantage of public outrage, Talleyrand, having failed to convince Britain to send troops to help the hapless Poles, now persuaded Palmerston to appeal jointly to the tsar for leniency.

"Why this uncalled for stupidity? Forgive the expression, but really there is no sense in it," Dorothea expostulated; Emily must make her lover see that the Anglo-French petition would "only create bad feeling, and it is a clumsy move."[16] England and France's gratuitous meddling served only to irritate "the iron Tsar," Dorothea impressed on Grey. The prime minister reacted, she reported to Nesselrode, with "a somewhat embarrassed air."[17]

Nothing daunted, Talleyrand then talked Palmerston into a joint request that the tsar grant Poland a constitution. Lieven formally communicated Nicholas's refusal to Grey. His reaction deeply distressed the prince, who at once unburdened himself to his wife.

With silk skirts hushing around her ankles, the princess swept into Grey's presence. "I began by reproaching him for sending my husband back to me in such a bad mood," she regaled Nesselrode. Grey protested that he had every right to express his opinion on a communication made to him. "This communication was completely confidential and correct," Dorothea countered, yet Grey had "neither appreciated nor recognized it." Russia had sent the same communication to France, he replied. Yes, the princess responded; her court had politely told France to mind your own business. To England, however, Russia had condescended to include "the confidence of our Cabinet's thoughts. You merit this distinction but it is also a great one." Hence, Lieven felt justifiably surprised at Grey having failed to give Russia's confidence its due. Obviously embarrassed, Grey, nonetheless, persisted that the Congress of Vienna signatories would want to see Poland given all Tsar Alexander had promised. Those promises ante-dated Poland's rebellion, Dorothea said; now only Tsar Nicholas had power to grant a constitution. He would give the Poles a new government; indeed, he would do more for them than they could dare dream of after such a revolt. "And I affirm to you that if today England declared war on him he would abide by his decision, be assured of that. Do you want to annoy the Tsar, to alienate him?"[18]

Voicing grave concern about the negative impression he had given Lieven—which Dorothea "did not omit to exaggerate" when "that served to play on" Grey's anxiety—the prime minister "hoped Lieven 'would not come to a hasty conclusion.' I replied that he knew his duty": "to report the truth to the Tsar." Having rescued her husband, Dorothea excused Grey. "We will see what he will do to repair his frivolities"[19]; she used that word because no other would suffice to describe a man who based politics on sentiment.

"Influenced by Madame de Lieven," the frustrated French ambassador noted, Lord Grey "sought for pretexts to avoid all intervention on the part of England."[20]

And Lieven received an intercepted dispatch that Czartoryski sent his London representative. It included: "'The influence that Princess Lieven exercises over Lord Grey is a disturbing circumstance for us. Can you not engage the Duchess of Dino to disabuse her of that position?' The Duchess of Dino tried mightily to please Lord Grey, who meanwhile did not prevent the conquest and submission of Poland,"[21] gloated the princess.

ɬɔƠ

Russia answered Prince Adam Czartoryski's star-crossed role in his country's fight for freedom by condemning him to death. Narrowly escaping the Russian net, Czartoryski wended his way westward with a false passport, and called on his old friend.

In great sympathy, Grey invited Prince Adam to dinner. "This feeling you ought not to object to, and I think you will not. It is impossible you should not have it yourself,"[22] the prime minister confided to his "dearest Princess" as 1832 opened.

"Your commiseration is most humane," she commended, but in welcoming Czartoryski to his home, Grey had "lost sight of this, namely, that a statesman is responsible to the public for his several acts; that it is neither sympathy nor affection that ought to dictate his line of conduct." With "every token of friendship and consideration which you would show to a foreigner of the highest distinction," England's prime minister received a "State criminal, convicted of high treason against his Sovereign—a sovereign who is the friend and ally of England." Indeed, after Lieven had struggled in tandem with England for a whole year to keep peace over Belgium, this rebel met with "a most flattering and encouraging reception from the head of the English Government!" Russia might well view that as an insult. "When Lord Grey is Premier of England, Lord Grey as a private person ceases to exist. Your actions now are those of England.... From my long and sincere friendship for you, you must also understand the disappointment and vexation I feel in reflecting that" the British government's "first hostile proceeding" against "my Court should have come from you—and that after our nineteen years' residence in your country. Indeed, you have deeply grieved me."[23]

Prince Lieven went further; he delivered a formal protest to Lord Palmerston.

"To anybody else my answer would have been short: that it neither became a foreign Minister to offer, nor me to receive, such a communication. But to *you* I cannot write in a harsh and peremptory tone," Grey replied. He reminded Dorothea that his government had been strictly neutral on Poland, had even urged France against sending troops. Hence, "I think I might have been exempted from such a representation as Prince Lieven has thought himself justified in making to another member of the Government, and not to me," on "a matter which would not have signified a rush, had he not by this proceeding raised it into importance."[24] The prime minister reminded the princess that he had met Czartoryski as a private person. "I am certainly aware of all the duties imposed on me as a Minister of the Crown,"[25] Grey huffed, but that did not mean they curtailed his personal contacts.

Despite his duty to keep relations between the two countries cordial, Lieven felt he must protest when the prime minister received a "state criminal." The ambassador had hoped a friendly explanation from Grey "might have placed him in a position to mitigate the painful impression this news must produce at the Russian Court."[26] Since Grey had left town, Lieven had no choice but to address the foreign secretary.

Yes, during Poland's rebellion Grey had done his "duty as a statesman and a man of honor scrupulously and with dignity," praised the princess. His certain knowledge of the tsar's appreciation, of Dorothea's sincere gratitude, made her vexation "the greater at seeing you depart from the judicious line of conduct you had hitherto adopted."[27]

An ambassador's duties did not include inquiring "into the dinner-parties of the Government to which he is accredited,"[28] Grey pettishly persisted. And an ambassador did not normally make a formal protest against the prime minister to another member of the government. Dorothea's recognition of his friendly conduct towards Russia and familiarity with his character should have protected him against a complaint like Lieven's.

Continuation of this quarrel could, the princess felt, easily destroy a precious friendship. The deed was done; she had made her point. After seven days of heated exchanges Dorothea thought the time had come time to move on. Not one of Grey's arguments—and there were many—convinced her; indeed, Dorothea felt "quite capable of refuting each and all of" them. But "I call to mind, and shall now turn to account, what my old governess told me when I quarreled with my brothers and sister: 'The least at fault ought to bring the quarrel to a close.'"[29]

⁖☍⁃

Meanwhile Tsar Nicholas's severity and, more to the point, the regrettable enthusiasm of his triumphant troops, provided grist for the mill of public opinion, which the sensation-hungry newspapers gleefully exploited. They treated their readers to graphic, if grossly exaggerated, accounts of Russian soldiers tearing screaming Polish children from their homes for "repatriation," to say nothing of the distraught mothers flinging themselves across the railway tracks in a vain attempt to stop the departing trains.

"Although I felt myself at boiling point,"[30] Dorothea Lieven forced herself to think logically. Opposition leader Wellington fully agreed with her about the ill-will of the Whig newspapers so Dorothea and Matuscewitz (still assisting Lieven at the conference on Belgium) drafted an article for the Tory press. Dorothea delivered it to the duke who, in turn, promised to give the paper to a reliable and capable henchman devoted to the Tory party. Unbeknownst to Wellington the princess, she assured her brother, had hatched this little plot with her husband's consent.

In the House of Commons a small but vocal group of pro–Polish radicals goaded the government incessantly over its Polish policy. In gruesome detail they described the horrors that thousands of Polish deportees suffered on their long march to Siberia. Denouncing the tsar as "Attila the Hun," and "scourge of God," they accused him of sending a hundred thousand children to live in Russia's interior, to forget their country, their language, and their families. Palmerston tried to defuse this torrid rhetoric, but had to avoid antagonizing members whose votes the government needed on other matters; so the foreign secretary merely expressed a wish for leniency. And when the Tories objected to government ministers allowing such language about a friendly foreign sovereign, Palmerston voiced deep regret but did not interrupt the speakers. Intensely disappointed, Dorothea Lieven expected at least staunch defense from her protégé.

ဆဝဌ

A year later (1833) the radicals moved to censure Russia's policy in Poland. Again they graphically described the tsar's "horrible cruelties." Since his grandmother Catherine the Great had participated in the partitions of Poland, the radicals heaped scorn on her as an "outrageous public prostitute" who had 5,000 lovers! And this time Palmerston went so far as to admit that the Russians had committed atrocities—albeit overstated.

Palmerston had indeed begun to prove himself "somewhat difficult to manage." Grey must not be allowed to echo his foreign secretary.

A dense fog blanketed London. Clutching lighted lanterns as they peered gingerly through the mid-morning murk, Princess Lieven's two liveried footmen carefully guided her smart town carriage to Number 10, Downing Street.

"*Lord Grey.* 'What would you have Lord Palmerston do? He has only this means to calm the clamor of the whole House.'

"*I.* 'After you yourselves aroused them by your protection of the rebels, your articles in the newspapers, your weakness and your ill-will that made you accept all the grossest lies.'

"*Lord Grey.* 'We certainly do not want to quarrel with you, but we have an opinion and we will not shirk from the occasion or the need to proclaim it.'

"*I.* 'No more than we, my lord, and we are going to prove it. But we did not start a controversy whose publicity could lead further than you wish.'

"*Lord Grey.* 'Why not give us the means to refute all accusations against you?'

"*I.* 'These means were given you some time ago, my lord. They remained barren. Lord Durham[31] brought'" from St. Petersburg "'"all that was needed to wipe out every one of those lies."'" Russia "'"thought a confidence given to a member of the English government would not be unprofitable for that government."'"

His Egeria's observation seemed somewhat to embarrass Grey. How, he countered, could Russia fail to answer the accounts of atrocities filling the newspapers?

I. "Because, my lord, we thought hardly anyone could believe that; and we busied ourselves little with it, blaming the Radicals—meanwhile in all good faith I must admit that I believe we should have replied to the lies with the truth. I am little inclined to enter into details of our administration in Poland but, for example, here is an explanation of one of the charges leveled against us. We want to abolish the Polish language now, here is the fact. The French language *in the schools* was meant. [What] business does the French language have in that Poland which belongs to Russia? We replaced French with Russian. Big sin."

"'Upon my word, you are right, but why did I not know that?'" Grey replied.

Again, my lord; I accompanied the Tsar on a visit to the Cadet College. There he called the Poles to him, these chosen children that the English claim the Tsar rejected, that he grilled and ate. And as if that were not enough, the English press portrayed them as orphans of loyal subjects; and again the boys, in reality loaded with the kindnesses, with the trust, with the best intentions of the Grand Duke Constantine were described as being forced, evening and morning to kiss his feet and to hold against their hearts the dagger which afterwards would kill them during the course of the war. The Tsar treated these children with greater goodness than all the others. For him they also had the same love; truly, I heard the Tsar ask them if they still spoke Polish and prompted them not to forget it. That my lord is what I saw, so when I heard these horrors repeated, and I saw how they were believed the blood boiled in my veins. Come and see my Tsar; so great, so humanitarian, so strong and you will understand how we must disdain everything that resembles a justification.

"Grey heard me with great interest, my ring of truth and my anger made a deep impression." He "repeated that we must explain our opinions better." The princess countered that he must help Russia, "and in so doing help himself, for mischief could result, surely national irritation" if "the scenes in Parliament recurred."

At that the prime minister reaffirmed his sincere concern to continue good relations with Russia. And the princess reiterated the tsar's wish to regain Russia's former intimacy with England. Yet, today the tsar accepted England's coolness, her suspicions, he accepted it all because he stood "strong enough and prepared enough to reply to everything; but certainly" neither he nor Russia could long sustain this kind of abuse.

Grey then gave Dorothea "a thousand professions of sincere friendship for us, for his desire for peace, finally," she ended her account to Nesselrode, "a child who perceives to have said and done foolishness, promised henceforward to be wise."[32]

⊗⃝⊗

Meanwhile Dorothea's friend Emily and her husband left London for the Riviera.

Princess: "Her departure is a real grief to me," and "I wish to goodness I could get someone who would undertake to love me during their absence, I would pay good wages."[33]

Prime minister: "I can well appreciate the loss you will sustain in Lady Cowper," and "I propose myself to supply the vacancy which this occasions. You say you will give good wages and I shall be very reasonable."[34]

Princess: Had Grey heard "the great news of all London—Lady Jersey running after Lord Palmerston?" He, "not a little touched by her enticing ways, paying her visits during his mornings, of two hours' duration, and then little dinners with her, and then going to the theater" together. "So much for the fidelity of men!"[35]

Prime minister: "Your account of Palmerston and Lady Jersey amused me" greatly. "May I not derive from it a hope that I, too, may again be taken into favor?"[36]

He was.

17

An Impossible Mission

"You have succeeded in inspiring confidence" with "prominent men" until
"now unknown in the annals of England."[1]
— Count Nesselrode to Princess Lieven

It seemed so simple. Hence, hardly had Lord Palmerston entered the hallowed
halls of the foreign office when he received a note from the princess. Tsar Nicholas
would be most pleased were the new Whig government to keep Britain's current
ambassador in St. Petersburg.

Dorothea had commended cosmopolitan Lord Heytesbury to her influential
brother Alexander. Independent-minded and candid, he would please the tsar, a particular benefit since Anglo-Russian relations were then strained over Greece. Heytesbury met Dorothea's expectation. Yet, she confided to the chief of Tsar Nicholas's
secret police, the London embassy had nary a hint about the nature of Heytesbury's
reports to his government. Russia, the princess prodded her brother, should take
advantage of Heytesbury's tendency toward carelessness. Soon, his "models of diplomacy, written with great intelligence and tact"[2] were edifying Nesselrode, the Lievens,
and Benckendorff.

Belgium and Poland, meanwhile, preoccupied the Powers. So Mehemet Ali, the
sultan of Turkey's ambitious Egyptian vassal, seized the moment. He demanded the
hereditary Pashalik of Damascus for his son Ibrahim. The Porte refused. Ibrahim
marched into Syria. His victory over the Turks threatened Constantinople. True to
tradition the Sultan appealed to the Powers. British and French attention still focused
on Belgium but the tsar had subdued Poland; he sent a fleet to the Bosphorus. Negotiations ensued. Nicholas withdrew his fleet but not before Russia and Turkey signed
the Treaty of Unkiar Skelessi (July 8, 1833). In effect it put Turkey under Russian
protection. And the provision that only Russian and Turkish warships could pass
through the Bosphorus and Dardanelles so incensed some English statesmen, most
notably Lord Palmerston and Sir Stratford Canning, that they developed an indeli-
ble suspicion of Russia.

Heytesbury, now ailing, asked to resign. The princess alerted Nesselrode that
Palmerston wanted to replace him with Stratford Canning. Protégé of his cousin
George Canning and an able diplomat, Stratford, having spent several years at Con-
stantinople, thought the Ottoman Empire must be preserved. He could therefore be

counted on to carry out Palmerston's policy of preventing any rise in Russian influence over the Porte. But Tsar Nicholas could scarcely be expected to greet the prospect of Stratford's appointment to his court with any marked degree of enthusiasm.

Indeed, Stratford's infamous and daily "ebullitions of temper and *touchiness*" made the tsar oppose his appointment, Britain's chargé d'affaires at the Russian capital wrote Palmerston. Nicholas would be put "under the disagreeable necessity of formally objecting to his nomination in case of its being pressed by your lordship."[3]

Shuddering at the mere mention of Stratford's name, Nesselrode relied on Dorothea Lieven to scotch his nomination. She showed Palmerston her chief's letter. Palmerston reacted positively. Dorothea congratulated herself.

୫୦୯୪

Meanwhile, tension over Russia's exclusions to ratification of the Belgian treaty, not to mention the Tsar's treatment of his rebellious Polish subjects, caused the Grey cabinet to send one of its members on a special mission to St. Petersburg.

Described by Princess Lieven as an "enraged Pole," Grey's son-in-law Lord Durham had, not once but three times, asked the cabinet to recognize Polish independence because that would please public opinion and the House of Commons. "Unhappily this is true up to a certain point,"[4] the scrupulous princess admitted to her court. She now advised Palmerston and Grey that sending Durham to St. Petersburg would pour salt on the wound opened by Stratford Canning's proposed appointment.

To no avail. Combining logic with charisma, therefore, Dorothea convinced Durham to oppose Stratford's appointment. Concomitantly, she told her court that Durham's mission offered a singular opportunity. If Nesselrode and Benckendorff, not to speak of the tsar, capitalized on Durham's proverbial vanity as well as Grey's preoccupation with his daughter Lady Durham, Russia could influence British policy. Alexander must show the Durhams every consideration. And if Nicholas gave Durham only half the attention Dorothea contrived for Count Orlov when he visited

Henry John Temple, third Viscount Palmerston. Great Britain's foreign secretary began his diplomatic career as Princess Lieven's protégé, but became her nemesis. Artist: George Richmond. Used by permission of The Faringdon Collection. Photograph: Photographic Survey, Courtauld Institute of Art.

London during the recent crisis over ratification of the Belgian treaty, Durham would be "ours, both by conviction and inclination."[5]

Consequently, the tsar's cordiality towards the Durhams gratified Grey and delighted Dorothea. Always assiduous in follow-up, she told Grey the Russians had him in mind when they paid flattering attention to his daughter and son-in-law. As well, Dorothea persisted, her compatriots admired Durham's political acumen and esteemed his frank and honest way of discussing business. Nesselrode, in particular, sang paeans to "the manner in which all the official business has been carried through."[6]

He might well. Taking their cue from the princess, Russia's diplomats completely converted the "enraged Pole." Nesselrode even advised Durham to share his new-found expertise with the Austrian and Prussian courts by visiting them on his way home. And to facilitate this journey Tsar Nicholas, a keen amateur sailor, conferred a singular favor on the Durhams—he offered them the use of his personal steam-yacht. Flattered, Durham asked Grey (rather than Palmerston as foreign office etiquette preferred) for permission. Thinking Durham might make a more malleable foreign secretary than the incumbent, Dorothea had been extolling him throughout London's politically permeated society. Now she told Grey and other influential Whigs how the government would benefit from Durham meeting German statesmen and hearing their opinions. Grey agreed.

Palmerston did not. He and Durham had never got along. Palmerston now saw Durham's enhanced credibility in foreign affairs, to say nothing of his pledge to Nesselrode to prevent Stratford Canning's appointment, as an implicit threat.

All this had much to do with the official announcement, a few weeks after Durham's return, that the new British ambassador to Russia would be Sir Stratford Canning.

⁖⁃⁃

Diplomatic etiquette dictated that before formally naming its ambassador, a government must consult the host cabinet. Britain's chargé d'affaires at St. Petersburg had warned Palmerston against nominating Stratford. Durham and both Lievens had told Palmerston the tsar would never accept him. Still the foreign secretary persisted.

"What a fragile memory" Palmerston had. He no longer remembered "promising me a year and a half ago, never to send us Stratford Canning,"[7] Dorothea wrote her chief.

Furthermore, Palmerston now explained to the princess that Russia was the only available ambassadorial post. If Stratford did not get it, the government would still have to pay his not insubstantial salary, which would cause awkward questions in Parliament. Besides, Stratford's seniority and ability, to say nothing of his conservative views, should please the tsar. Quite ready to concede the logic of Palmerston's argument, Dorothea, nevertheless, emphasized that Stratford's notoriously bad temper did not suit her court. So Palmerston must see how his insistence in sending a man "with whom we would have unpleasant dealings at the least showed us the intent to displease and thereby damage our relations. And that we definitely would refuse him; that it is really worth more not to expose himself to this extremity."[8]

> My dear Count [Nesselrode], you can boldly say no. Everyone finds Palmerston's behavior very uncivil and our right to refuse the man who displeases us absolutely

natural. I never thought he could push the matter to this extreme. That is why I considered it superfluous to speak to Lord Grey. Now I shall do it.[9]

To Dorothea's discomfiture, Grey, irked at the tsar over Belgium, agreed with Palmerston that England needed strong representation in Russia. Besides, he hardly wanted to hazard a breach with his foreign secretary over what was, basically, a minor matter.

It was very far from minor to Dorothea. If Britain had no ambassador at St. Petersburg, the tsar could never countenance keeping an ambassador in London. He must recall Prince Lieven. That would bring Dorothea's ten years of accomplishment, let alone her preceding years of preparation, crashing down in ruins.

She stood at the window of her chintz-curtained sitting-room in grim gray Panshanger, staring unseeingly at the leaden sky and frost-bitten lawns. The princess had already consulted her hostess and close friend Emily, Lady Cowper, about what to write to Emily's lover.

Dorothea wrote down, crossed out, and re-phrased the paragraphs of her letter to Palmerston. As much as her pride meant to her, Dorothea felt it would be a small sacrifice when her entire happiness hung in the balance. "A perhaps inevitable appointment for you, one you judge suitable for your master's service has found itself swept away by my Court's persistent refusal to see its relations with England delivered into the hands of one it considers capable of immediately jeopardizing them through factious irritability and mistrust.[10] I fully enter into" the quandary this "refusal causes you, and in this connection convey my sincere regret at the event which produced it. But allow me to believe" that "it does not deserve the more serious result merely because my Court has used the right your Cabinet and all others have to refuse an unwelcome ambassador. One judges an act on its intent but, my Court does not intend to disoblige the English government. Because of that, but of equal weight, as I am the first to admit, this will sweep along with it an abysmal burden for me, one that could and must lead to immense trouble. And that" is "where I come to the subject which propels me to address myself to your friendship with confidence.

"I frankly admit that all my dignity leaves me when I only think of the possibility of having to leave this country. Above all, this calamity could not come to me from those I have always thought my friends; I especially counted you among them. So I freely address myself to you as my friend. For me, leaving this England would be the cruelest fate. It would utterly upset my life, destroy all my pleasures. Spare me" such "adversity; let me owe you the continuation of a twenty-year happiness, and judge the faith I place in your friendship by the appeal I allow myself today. It would be mortifying if I erred in your feelings for me.

"Your honor and tact assure me of this letter's secrecy. You can truly understand that only one *single*, unique person can see it, the one who will convey it to you."[11]

Grey suggested a compromise. Appoint Stratford, now on a temporary mission at Madrid, although titled "His Britannic Majesty's Ambassador to the Tsar of all the Russias," permanent ambassador to Spain. Palmerston agreed. Stratford refused. Palmerston then proposed that if Russia received Stratford, he would promise very soon to replace him. Nesselrode hesitated. Count Orlov coveted the London embassy. He advised the tsar to hold firm.

On New Year's Eve (1832–3) Dorothea greeted Grey with good wishes for the coming year. She hoped to spend it in England. "The matter lies in your hands, and it seems to me that your friendship assures me it will turn out in accordance with my desires."[12]

> Let me return your good wishes for the New Year, and more especially that part of them which relates to your continuance here. Be assured that this wish is sincere, and from my heart. There is nothing I would not do, that honor and duty would allow me to do, to contribute to its fulfillment.

Nonetheless, the Russian court had put the British government in a situation "from which it does not depend upon us to extricate ourselves. Let me hope, therefore, that a pretension will not be insisted on," one "to which we cannot yield."[13]

Six months later the tsar summoned Princess Lieven. Urgent meetings with Grey and other prominent Whigs delayed her departure but did win "the most positive and satisfactory promises"[14] that Stratford would not go to Russia. Still, Palmerston held the trump card. He did not promise to appoint another ambassador. And if Britain had no ambassador in St. Petersburg, Tsar Nicholas must recall Prince Lieven.

Dorothea dreaded the hazards of a voyage across the stormy Baltic. So did Grey. He arranged that a British naval vessel carry his "dearest Princess" to Hamburg in comfort and safety. She arrived only "two days before the packet-boats were shipwrecked."[15]

The second segment of Dorothea's northward passage brought her directly to the tsar's favorite summer palace, built by his ancestor Peter the Great to rival Versailles. Proudly strutting the entire length of Peterhof's splendid white and gold Grand Palace, the wide stone balcony faces a fabulous vista of formal terraces, lovely gardens, and graceful fountains. The magnificent water jets of the Great Cascade splash sibilantly over several black and white checkered marble stages into a grand marble basin; halfway down are a double cascade and grotto flanked by more fountains, and gilded bronze statues. The water then flows smoothly through a channel set between manicured green lawns and a colonnade of small fountains, straight to the sparkling (when the summer sun shines) Gulf of Finland.

Nicholas sailed into the Gulf to meet Dorothea, and at once brought her to his wife's boudoir; indeed, the royal couple lavished kindness on the princess. Yet, the court's tedious round of military reviews, festivals, dinners, excursions, and balls, which forced Princess Lieven to dress four times daily, brought back with stunning effect the restricted life she had rejected in her youth.

At least Dorothea had her "good" son Alexander always at her side. And as senior lady-in-waiting to the tsaritsa despite her residence in London, the princess solidified her status at court by cultivating a closer relationship with that important lady. This, in turn, helped her combat Orlov and his "Russian" party at the foreign ministry. They distrusted, not entirely without reason, the princess's influence with the imperial family. Of course her success in preventing the permanent appointment of Orlov's friend Matuscewitz to the London embassy did little to endear her to Orlov; still, Dorothea succeeded in defusing his open derision of what he liked to call Lieven's ineptitude to such an extent that she advised her husband of the "very successful relationship"[16] she had established with Orlov.

And Nesselrode several times expressed full satisfaction with Lieven. Nicholas professed great pleasure with his ambassador's dispatches. The smooth relations Lieven had established with Grey's government gratified the tsar, who wished to stand well with England. He constantly spoke of Lieven "with the greatest goodness—everyone heaps me with friendship for you and of questions about you."[17]

All this flattering attention, which the tsar could trust Princess Lieven to propagate, intended to convey that if Palmerston persisted in forcing an unacceptable ambassador on the Romanov court, or did not appoint one at all, the Autocrat would deliver a crushing snub. He would deprive London of an eminently satisfactory ambassador.

ಌಕೞ

When the scent of sun-warmed flowers wafted through the ambient air Princess Lieven sailed southward. To her chagrin the prince failed to meet her at Dover, or to welcome her at either Richmond or London. And when he did find time to greet his spouse, Lieven's frustration with "what people were saying" about her political power in general, and diplomatic importance in particular, exploded in a cascade of bitter accusations.

"I am not the first woman in the world to involve herself in business," Dorothea wrote, to give tempers time to cool. "Every woman who has a little brains and skill does so, and husbands who recognize this benefit" profit, without feeling humiliated. Even so, when Lieven held his highest post, as Russia's foreign minister during Nesselrode's leave of absence, all Europe knew Dorothea to be far off in London. Besides, it would perhaps

> not be excessive to recall to your memory that the busiest periods of the Conference always took place when I was at Richmond, and what is more for the past four or five years, I have always spent six or eight months of the year totally removed from London. Was that how I carried out your business? Was that how I single-handedly gave you every small interesting idea. Did not I, on the contrary, with female curiosity seek to catch everything, good as well as bad, to the right and the left, news that even your stinginess agreed to be significant?[18]

What Prussian ambassador Bülow could sometimes not say to Lieven, he confided to Dorothea. Most recently he had spoken about Russia's ambassador at Paris,

> which I told you of four or five days ago and of which you strongly approved. Did this represent the sort of thing he could say to you? No. But according to my recollection these overtures had to reach you and attain their goal. This one example could apply to all the relations I have of this type and I ask you after that if Bülow could think you are effaced, and that it is I who carry out business?[19]

No. Bülow thought Dorothea a useful intermediary, so Lieven could only infer "that they are more afraid of you or" have more "respect for you than for me. Now, that is not humiliating."[20]

In all fairness to Lieven, Dorothea felt she must mention the Stratford Canning affair "for it is important to judge the merit of the question on its results." At Warsaw Dorothea asked Nesselrode,

> "What orders for London?" "Whatever happens in England, keep Heytesbury for us. That is my only commission." The ministry changed and I said to Grey: "I have only one thing to ask of you, leave Heytesbury at his post." "Speak to Palmerston." I spoke to Palmerston and he promised it.[21]

A few months later, as he and Dorothea watched the dancers twirling round the floor at a French embassy ball, Palmerston casually said:

> "Do you know that Heytesbury is asking to return?" "Oh! My God, whom are you giving us?" "Adair or Stratford Canning." Thereon, in writing to Nesselrode, I told him. A long letter replied, which you read at the time without comment, as well my encounter with Palmerston that I told you about, and the rest you know.[22]

Of course Nesselrode "could not have a single thought to reduce your importance in writing to me on a subject he considered completely mundane."[23]

Dorothea had shown her husband all Nesselrode's letters; she told him she would make use of the foreign minister's comments on Stratford Canning. "I showed them to John Russell [a prominent Whig], and told you of their positive effect on him. You did nothing but listen with interest." Then Dorothea showed Nesselrode's letters to Grey and told him the whole story.

> All this is simplicity itself and I would say of little importance. It has become an affair of state without being either Nesselrode's fault, or mine, or anyone's. It is Palmerston's stupidity, and certainly you have treated it as such in being totally indifferent. This truly cannot be your chief charge. Has it not happened twenty times in your life that you availed yourself of a woman as intermediary for much more important things that this and quite rightly too, so as not to make a big affair out of something that could more easily be done indirectly.[24]

As for her relations with Matuscewitz, Dorothea "need only cite a sentence from one of his last letters in which he asks me to thank you for the interesting ideas you sent him by your *private secretary*."[25]

Dorothea felt she had answered her husband's accusations with absolute truth; she would be ecstatic were her letter to help him face his position as well as hers. "Let me think you know enough to hold yourself in esteem and to appreciate your political position, the deference, the respect, the confidence your conduct of business has engendered in all who have dealt with you." Whatever Dorothea might do to displease her husband always gave her great pain, so now she sincerely affirmed her avoidance of

> all that could cause you the smallest and least discontent; but on your side, admit to yourself that the opinions you expressed this morning must be very far from others' thoughts; at the same time they must not stay for one moment more on your mind or trouble for an instant the peace and confidence of our relations.[26]

Although Dorothea continued steadfastly to aver that she had done nothing with which to reproach herself she did later, in her unpublished memoirs, acknowledge: "my husband never forgave me for the importance I had."[27]

80C3

Meanwhile, the princess preened herself on a development she had enthusiastically endorsed during her stay in Russia. The tsar and his Austrian counterpart, meeting at Münchengrätz, pledged to maintain the Ottoman Empire.[28] Palmerston, however, convinced himself that Münchengrätz signaled Russia and Austria's intent to partition Turkey's empire. That fueled his resolve to plant the staunchly pro–Turkish Stratford Canning in St. Petersburg.

Thus, when the British cabinet urged Palmerston to extend the olive branch and name another ambassador, the foreign secretary refused. He would rather resign.

No-one disputed England's right to nominate her ambassadors. No-one disputed the tsar's right of refusal. No-one could fathom Palmerston's flouting of fundamental diplomatic convention. No-one could comprehend his insistence on Stratford Canning's appointment in the teeth of the tsar's opposition.

Palmerston's lover blamed her friend. Dorothea's interference had provoked Palmerston to expostulate to Emily that "both *she* and her *Court* wanted to be taken down a peg."[29] But most harmful had been Dorothea going over Palmerston's head to appeal to Grey about Stratford Canning, to say nothing of challenging Palmerston on his "turf" by engaging Durham to "make a great clamor about it." Furious, the foreign secretary resolved to punish the powerful princess. She "had meddled more than she ought, and had made the matter personally embarrassing and disagreeable to him."[30] And if any truth existed in the Hart story—never proved yet never disproved—that some years before Palmerston had, when in financial straits, accepted a large sum of money from Russia through the princess, it is not difficult to see why the foreign secretary would be only too glad to see the last of her. "It has been proved to me," she confirmed in defeat, "that because of Lord Palmerston I had to leave, perhaps forever, that England which I loved so much."[31]

Cherry trees flowered in a profusion of pink when a Russian courier rode his weary horse into the forecourt of his country's London embassy. May 20, 1834, figured as one of the cruelest days in Dorothea Lieven's life. Her husband received the tsar's letter announcing his new assignment, the letter that made Lieven "lift his hands to heaven in joy, and mine, in grief."[32]

PART III

France, 1835–1857

18

"What a Country Is Mine"

My children and politics were the only subjects I cared for.[1]
—Dorothea Lieven

Tsar Nicholas honored Prince Lieven with the prestigious post of governor to the tsarevitch. As well as taking charge of the young man's household, Lieven would introduce him to the subtleties of diplomacy and European society. That might please the prince, but a return to the capital whose confines she had contrived to escape in her youth constituted calamity for the princess.

To live near her adored, esteemed tsar and tsaritsa, to bring up her two precious boys amidst her family, to live in her native land, "the object of my pride and of my love—for, dear Alexander, I love it well, and perhaps I have served it well also, in my long absence—at least I have striven to do so," would somewhat offset the loss of "a good climate, a wonderful social position, habits of luxury and comfort that I will never find anywhere else, and friends quite independent of politics."[2]

One doubt disturbed Dorothea's specious optimism: whether her life in Russia would be long-lasting. As she neared her fiftieth birthday menopause loomed, "the age in life at which our mother was taken from us—an age that needs care and precautions." Never in robust health, Dorothea must now, after twenty-two years, sustain St. Petersburg's noxious climate. Would the beginning of her life there also "be its end? I must put aside such thoughts, for I love life; but it comes back again and again and chills my heart."[3]

Something else chilled Dorothea Lieven's heart. Her ambition burned as brightly as ever, but she could scarcely expect St. Petersburg's intellectual strait-jacket, not to mention the monotonous court pantomime, to offer anything remotely approaching the political excitement of "this England, that I love so well."[4]

ಬಂದ

At the other end of Europe the tsar and his wife were "having a veritable celebration at seeing you, you and your husband soon arrive."[5] With sympathy and tact Empress Alexandra unfolded what lay in store.

Her senior lady-in-waiting must be sure bring some of those extremely comfortable English upholstered armchairs, which made such a welcome change from the

163

straight, wooden-backed Continental style. The furniture should be sturdy enough to withstand Russia's climate for, instead of living with the tsarevitch in one of his parents' palaces, the Lievens would have their own house where the princess could create a suitable social milieu for him. Alexandra too, hated Russia's long, frigid winter but bore it well, she concluded with a caveat: because her dear ones warmed her heart. "Promise me faithful conduct and you will find in me always the same."[6]

What blessed relief to be spared eternal court ritual! The princess started to plan. By creating such a refined and appealing drawing room that all, including the tsar and tsaritsa, would come to savor the pleasures of conversation, Dorothea aimed to restore the intellectual glory her country's capital had enjoyed under Catherine the Great. That, in turn, would attract foreigners by piquing their curiosity and giving it a worthy object. "All this fully occupies the Princess who has it in her to play this part well," her friend the duchess of Dino noted, "though it would be difficult anywhere, and doubly so in Russia, where thought is as much fettered as speech."[7]

Even so, Dorothea confidently expected the tsar's favor, Nesselrode's friendship, and her brother's position to lead to some political power and as much freedom, if freedom one could call it, as Russia allowed. But Dino foresaw a situation her friend refused to admit to herself: to "lose touch with the map of Europe," or "only be able to look at it through some very small spy-hole, which would certainly be for her a living death."[8]

಄ఞ

Roses replaced rhododendrons as the dreaded departure day crept closer, and her excited animation revealed Dorothea's growing anxiety. London hostesses outdid themselves in one good-bye gathering after another. The duchess of Sutherland organized a subscription among Dorothea's female friends for a farewell gift. After great agonizing, they decided on a gorgeous gold bracelet set with a single lustrous pearl, and inscribed with the two hundred participants' names. It "is in my eyes the greatest honor that has ever been paid me. How proud I am of it, and how happy, and yet how sad!"[9]

The most heart-rending farewell took place at the last moment. Barely able to control her sobs, the princess begged Lord Grey not to forget her, to promise to write often so she could continue to live a little in her beloved England. The prime minister tearfully reiterated "once more, and more than ever, the assurance of my unvarying and tender friendship. It seems as though I feel more for you now that ever I did; I cannot fully explain it." Grey begged his "dearest Princess" to "love me as I do you, sincerely and for ever."[10]

಄ఞ

Rough seas rendered the Lievens' weeklong crossing to Hamburg "execrable, everybody was ill, and I almost died of it." North from Hamburg a howling gale whipped the angry Baltic into huge waves that drove the Lievens' ship onto a rock near a desolate island. For ten long hours they hung between life and death. Fifteen-year-old George and his young brother Arthur thought it a splendid adventure, but their mother arrived in St. Petersburg "so weak that I cannot stand, with my back all broken, and not an idea left." Her bitterness grew daily. "Time brings healing to every grief, but what I have lost in this separation so wounds me that I hardly imagine I shall ever get the better of this sorrow."[11]

Too exhausted, too ill to pay her respects to the imperial couple, Dorothea rested in the capital while her husband hastened to court. When Nicholas and Alexandra received the princess in town, their warmth gave her hope. Nonetheless, "it remains to be seen how I shall get on in my dear native land. The climate, the manners, and the society," Dorothea confided dryly to Grey, "will all be somewhat of trials."[12]

So would her husband's position. No longer did Lieven have "such a great and honorable existence, with so much independence in life's everyday routine."[13] True, the prince could revel in his superior standing at court, could proudly display his diamond encrusted badge of office, his many impressive orders and medals glittering on the splendid, gold-braided dress uniform he wore to court functions. Yet, as a courtier, Prince Lieven existed only at the tsar's pleasure. That troubled the princess much more than the prince, for her status now fully depended on his. No personal dignity existed "near the Sun.★"[14]

Not even Nicholas and Alexandra's extremely flattering attention could compensate Dorothea for the drastic collapse of her power, for the cruel drop in her freedom.

ᔖᘓ

"No one cares for me here as you do—at any rate no one tells me they do—and I have now more need than ever of your friendship." Dorothea implored Grey to write "all the news you hear, and your opinions on it all," because "my heart is still in England."[15]

"How constantly I think of you, how much I regret you, and how strong and sincere is the attachment which I must always bear you," Grey replied. "God bless you."[16]

Her correspondence continued to give Dorothea some liberty, some crucial personal space in her dysfunctional marriage. Deprived of the life she loved, Dorothea now depended on her letters for support, for affection. "Of all the friends I have left in England, it is you who are the most constant in friendship," she told Grey.

Dorothea relied on him for political news especially as Emily Cowper's brother, Lord Melbourne, had become prime minister; her devoted swain, Lord Palmerston, still ruled the foreign office. "One must stand among the spectators to see the play fairly," declared the scrupulous princess; "the actors themselves cannot possibly judge of the effect."[17]

Her letters let her live, if only a little, in England. "Silence your scruples," she encouraged Emily, "by the thought that by the time your confidences reach me all the subjects at issue will be obsolete. Likewise, I would tell you all my secrets if I had any,"[18] for although St. Petersburg's luminaries flocked to Princess Lieven's drawing room, stimulating conversation lacked. She did meet some highly intelligent people—Prince Menschikoff, minister of marine; Ouvaroff, minister of public instruction; Prince Golitsin, friend and confidant of Tsars Alexander and Nicholas and her favorite, foreign minister Nesselrode. Four men and no women. What pitiful paucity after London!

And there were no friends. One does not easily, or quickly, forge new friendships at age fifty, and in the years when close personal ties are formed Dorothea

---

★Russians' name for their ruler.

Lieven lived far (in miles and mindset) from Russia. "People definitely must not forget me; above all they must not forget me abruptly; and among them all," Dorothea wrote Emily, "you must not subject me to oblivion. I would consider myself dead if you stopped writing." Emily's letter came next day; it proved that "you love me and think of me constantly."[19]

Her many friends sent their letters to London's Russian embassy. There Dorothea's eldest son, Paul, who could thank his mother's influence with Nesselrode for his position as attaché, made sure her mail reached her via the relative security of the diplomatic pouch. Russia's post office could be relied on only to arbitrarily open any letter. For this relentless vigilance his compatriots owed a debt of gratitude to General Count Alexander Benckendorff. His Third Section censored the written and spoken word. His spies were everywhere. Among the several well-dressed young men gracing social gatherings at least one, if not more, functioned as a police spy assigned to nose out any whiff of those pernicious Western ideas—like personal liberty—that Tsar Nicholas abhorred.

Court did not differ. And it consisted of one long exhaustion. Dinners with five or six people including the tsar occasionally broke Dorothea's daily tedium of formal dining alfresco in full evening dress at a long, elaborately set table with at least one hundred others. Games and dancing, then supper invariably followed. Each participant in this regal Romanov puppet show dressed according to rank. The tsaritsa's senior lady-in-waiting donned a narrow-waisted, scarlet velvet gown with long tapered sleeves and a train falling in soft graceful folds to her feet. Elaborately-wrought gold brocade embellished Dorothea's dress, cut modestly low over the breast, draped over the hips. But no matter how beautiful, her gown remained a uniform. Small wonder that the best dressed woman in London harbored bitter thoughts on her loss of freedom even in the choice of clothes.

Had she been twenty the princess might have amused herself at court soirées. Instead, "I turn my eyes to right and to left looking for succor but those who might aid me go and establish themselves at the whist-tables, where everybody has to play extremely well and stake extremely high."[20] The princess relished her rubber of whist, but absentmindedness occasionally made her revoke; so she refrained from playing. "Great entertainments afford but little pleasure or distraction; and as for friends, one does not find them in a Court,"[21] especially not at one so treacherous as Russia's.

⍟

While servants readied their house, the Lievens stayed at Tsarskoe Selo palace. Dorothea's drawing room windows overlooked well-kept gardens landscaped in the English style; they reminded her of Richmond, especially as she continued her English habit of taking her boys on early morning walks.

When the tsar was not in residence, Princess Lieven's social circle consisted only of the imperial children and their attendants. In the morning she visited the delightful little grand duchesses; at four she dined in her apartment, sometimes with guests; at eight she opened her drawing room to about a dozen people. The princess conversed, and made them converse. She liked to share her worldly wisdom with bright young people and, for the tsarevitch's sake, kept conversation light and amply sprinkled with amusing anecdotes. Somewhat to her surprise the shy but intelligent youth seemed to enjoy what most teen-agers might have thought rather dull.

At ten, servants laid an elaborate supper; at eleven the evening ended. Sabbath interrupted this dreary routine. Dorothea dined with the tsarevitch, and in the evening gave a dance for him. Yes, it reminded her of English country house living, but Dorothea missed all her good friends, to say nothing of England's gentle climate. This was a Russian October. Tsarskoe Selo's stately trees were still green, but snow already covered its manicured lawns as the princess uneasily contemplated the first winter in twenty-two years that she would have the misfortune to spend in Russia.

November saw the imperial couple back in their capital. And the Lievens moved into their exceedingly comfortable, modern house, one of the most handsome mansions to dignify the Quai Anglais, St. Petersburg's most fashionable street.

"At home" every evening, the highest ranking, most distinguished of the tsaritsa's ladies-in-waiting commanded what she considered suitable esteem. But although the fastidious princess saw plenty of people, she found no society.

Except the imperial couple. Nicholas did not normally favor notable, worldly women, but he enjoyed discussing European politics with Dorothea Lieven. Indeed, prominent Russians were no different from other men in finding her conversation fascinating. The princess talked about England's social condition, "the secret springs of individual Cabinets and their members, the course of negotiations." Only a rare diplomat "could vie with her in information, or in the masterly expositions."[22] Yet suspicious, provincial St. Petersburg society ultimately judged, not entirely wrongly, that Princess Lieven had lived too long abroad; her "liberal" views were not appreciated. In a country whose Autocrat controlled thought as well as action, Dorothea, used to English freedom, "neither found eager opponents nor satellites of her opinions." Highly ranked persons, who "ought to have been most intimate with her, remained estranged"; they failed to accord her the deference to which she had become accustomed. And Dorothea's politically-focused conversation fatigued "genuinely feminine natures."[23] The haughty princess, in turn, despised what she dubbed "the spider web" of St. Petersburg's gossip-riddled conversation.

ᏜᎾᎿᏕ

Unpopularity did not especially disturb Dorothea Lieven. Something else did. By mid–November two feet of snow stopped her daily walks with her young sons George and Arthur in the exclusive Summer Garden, a landscaped park in St. Petersburg's center where great trees and handsome marble statues lined graveled paths set among well-kept lawns. The ubiquitous snow and hazardous ice curtailed Dorothea's carriage drives. And cold froze the port, cutting Russia's sea passage to the West. That made her "realize what a very long way off I am from you," the princess wrote Grey, "and the knowledge of it goes to my heart."[24] Her husband's absence in Moscow with the tsarevitch made Dorothea feel lonely indeed, as the limiting life she had cast off in her youth relentlessly spread its dark cloud over her. Nothing in Russia could resign Dorothea to life under an autocrat who restricted politics and repressed opinion, to the narrow-mindedness and tedium of Russian society and, above all, to the severe check on her ambition.

By early December the bitter cold seemed to seep into Dorothea's very bones. Perplexed, her doctors pondered how to pull her through the winter. If only Grey could send "some of your soft English air when you send me your kind letters!"[25]

She only went out to wait on the empress. Princess Lieven's elegant town carriage, with the crest proudly emblazoned on its panels and thick fur rug covering the floor, now rested on sledge runners so that eight horses could convey her quickly and smoothly over the frozen, rutted snow to the nearby Winter Palace. In the small ante-chamber with its delicate, silk-paneled walls and French empire furnishings, the princess occupied herself until admitted to Alexandra's presence.

Soon, the relentless cold attacked Dorothea's lungs, reducing her to such a sorry state that her doctors insisted she travel south; they told the tsar that January might prove fatal if she stayed in St. Petersburg. Nicholas and Alexandra's concern, indeed that of the entire imperial family, deeply touched the poorly princess. "I was brought up by the Empress-mother and treated by her as her child. My relations with the whole Imperial family were thus very close."[26] Empress Maria had become a mother-substitute for grieving eleven-year-old Dorothea at her mother's death. Maria's sons and daughters now seemed to be the only real friends she had in her homeland; Dorothea loved them "as truly as though they were personages of a far less illustri-ous degree, and of my own kindred."[27] And, in a very real sense, they were.

Nicholas authorized Dorothea's immediate departure for a warm climate. Her husband and fifteen-year-old son George would escort her, but only as far as the frontier. Prince Lieven did not dream of leaving St. Petersburg for longer than he could possibly help. His situation suited him down to the ground. The prince had finally shed what for so long he felt to be the emasculating mantle of his wife's superiority. This consummate courtier had again earned a position at court on his own merits. So once outside Russia, Dorothea must seek southern sunshine on her own.

That daunting prospect prompted her to convince her doctors that she could "never bear up against the mental worries occasioned by being sent forth like an exile, alone, without husband or child, to run the gauntlet of bad inns on all the highroads of Europe." Diplomatic niceties forbad her return to England; Dorothea cared for no other country, nor did she have friends anywhere else. So she would "try and veg-etate here quietly in my rooms"[28] until March, then consult German physicians before continuing to Italy. Princess Lieven's doctors advised her to spend at least two suc-cessive winters outside Russia. She did not know where. Nor did Dorothea relish the gloomy thought of becoming a "vagabond, without my husband, without hearth and home, without George."[29]

⧉

Her husband had settled very happily into his old courtier habits, had resumed relations with several cronies among St. Petersburg's elite with whom he corresponded throughout his years in London; some of his siblings lived in the capital, too. So did Dorothea's sister. Kind-hearted, widowed Marie and Dorothea had grown apart, if, indeed, they had ever been close. Amply content to spend her life as a lady-in-wait-ing, Marie had no interest in politics, could not begin to comprehend what her sis-ter had lost in leaving England. So Dorothea would not be able to confide her misery to Marie or, for that matter, to censorious Alexander. The head of Tsar Nicholas's secret police could scarcely be expected to sympathize with his sister's aversion to life in Russia. And Lieven had, to his immense satisfaction, finally freed himself from the influence of powerful women. Having owed his early promotions to his strong-minded mother, having relied on his wife's superior talents during his twenty-five-year diplomatic career, the prince now stood on his own. Dorothea had been relegated to the role of a proper Russian wife, and St. Petersburg's strictures would make sure she stayed there. Her intellect and personality meant little; Dorothea's status utterly depended on her husband.

Lieven loved his new position, not to speak of his life at court; he delighted in all the elaborate Christmas and New Year festivities. Dorothea gave an English dinner party at Christmas. Emily must tell Lady Holland that her Christmas pudding "played its part to perfection: it blazed brilliantly ... thank her a thousand times and give her all my love. I keep her little gift always on my table with my other English keepsakes."[30]

Two weeks later Dorothea's door opened only to the imperial family. Otherwise,

> twice a day I hazard a walk around my rooms. The rest of the time I am confined to a corner, & there they keep me in an artificial atmosphere which is supposed to resemble the English climate, ... [using] buckets of hot water, constantly refilled, and placed on each side of me. That is how they hope to maintain me until spring.[31]

Everyone around her enjoyed life. Only Dorothea lay "sick, lonely, sad, abandoned even by those who should be taking some care of me."[32] Indeed, her arid life seemed to cast all the evils of Dorothea's dysfunctional marriage into stark relief.

Did Grey know the greatest source of his friend's pleasure? Putting in order "all my voluminous correspondences with my friends; and among them all" Grey's letters came first. Dorothea delighted in re-reading "and arranging them. You have made me very rich, my dear lord. Your letters are the history of times we have lived through." Since "I must live in future on my souvenirs, you can judge how much value I set on all this."[33]

Without mental activity, for her eyes now failed Dorothea at night and darkness fell at three in the afternoon, forbidden to go out, she had plenty of time to reflect on the statesmen she had known, the events she had experienced—a tsar's assassination, another's ill-starred visit to London, her role in the birth of modern Greece. So as snowflakes whispered against her windows, the princess started to write her memoirs.

Still feeling and looking miserable in February, Princess Lieven pulled herself together and, for the tsarevitch's sake, began to receive people as well as to give parties two or three times a week. Empress Alexandra insisted on reviewing the invitation lists for, she told the proud princess whose exclusive house had been the envy of every London hostess, she must know with whom her son would socialize.

Alexandra and her husband created a sensation when they came to Princess Lieven's parties unannounced. And the imperial presence turned out to be extremely "opportune for the foreign diplomats, who are hardly ever admitted to Court and the grand soirées, but whom I invite to my house." With the recent brouhaha over Russian "atrocities" in Poland at the forefront of her mind, Dorothea delighted in strangers seeing "at first hand what is very good for them to know"[34]: that Nicholas and his family were exceedingly distinguished.

Her distinguished guests notwithstanding, it was English politics that pierced the gloom of Princess Lieven's bleak existence. She still considered Emily incapable of making an impartial statement, and her Tory correspondents were too sanguine, so Dorothea slaked her thirst with foreign newspapers and Grey's letters. He had left office soon after circumstances cut short Dorothea's career, and now the Whig elder statesman complained that Palmerston ignored him. Scarcely surprised, the princess, sure Palmerston had driven her and her husband away, rued her failure to open Grey's eyes. Had he only listened to her, "it would all have been so different. But let us leave the past—we cannot bring it back."[35]

Nevertheless, as she sat alone in the long, dark days of St. Petersburg's endless winter, Dorothea could not help but reminisce. Did Emily remember that "the most piquant parties took place before the opening of Parliament"? How fascinating to observe everyone treading so warily. "The scene is vivid in my mind's eye this year."[36]

Lord Melbourne's Whig ministry fell; the duke of Wellington became prime minister until the general election. Sir Robert Peel, Tory leader in the House of Commons, sent the princess a copy of his speech to his constituents. It outlined the new Conservatism. Peel accepted recent electoral reform, but insisted on attention to present institutions so that recognized rights would be kept, proven abuses corrected, and rightful complaints rectified. Dorothea Lieven judged the "Tamworth Manifesto" extremely well done.

She suffered for days on end as the dismal winter dragged on, the skies always shadowed, always gray, her surroundings a wilderness of snow and ice. Her husband gave not the slightest thought to sacrificing his way of life to suit his wife. Then March blew in.

☙◊❧

Before Dorothea could gather herself together for travel George, the apple of her eye, born and brought up in England, used to the care of London's finest physicians, stranger to St. Petersburg's noxious climate, caught scarlet fever. Quarantine now enveloped the elegant house on the Quai Anglais.

From a low chair at his bedside Dorothea kept vigil over her darling day and night. She bathed his burning body, changed his sweat-soaked sheets, plumped up his rumpled pillows, coaxed sustaining broth or soothing barley water down his red, swollen throat, did her utmost to ease his frightening delirium.

George died.

Can any sorrow "ever be greater? My poor little son George! They want me now to leave Petersburg at once and I only hope I may have the strength to get off. Today I can do nothing but cry. My son will always know where I am so send your letters to his care. And pray do not cease writing," for "now more than ever do I need your friendship."[37]

"How can I write, or what can I say to you? Yet write I must, to relieve myself by the expression of the feelings which your dreadful affliction has occasioned." At this terrible time Grey would not mention "any other subject, nor can I expect you to write more than a line, if even that is not too painful to you, to give me some account of your health, for which I feel, impaired as it already was, an increasing anxiety."[38]

Already bitter at losing the life she loved, Dorothea viewed the death of her adored George as a blow almost too severe to bear. Or so it seemed.

In the depths of grief, grief only a mother can fathom, Dorothea, at her doctors' insistence, agreed to leave for a warmer climate one week after George's funeral. "On the very day before I was to set out, my Arthur, my poor Arthur suddenly falls ill, and in twenty-four hours he, too, was at death's door. Only think how I was placed! Do you not marvel that I did not either die or go mad?"[39]

Dorothea battled with death over her youngest child's fragile, fever-racked body for fourteen days and nights.

> During the last fortnight the danger has been at its height, and even now I am not without grave anxiety. He is still in bed, and this is the eighteenth day of the fever. I have never left his room; I have done nothing but watch him and nurse him, and I am writing you this from his bedside. It is a wonder to me that he is still alive, and that I, too, am not dead of fatigue."[40]

Grey's letters momentarily twinkled through her misery, diverted her mind. "England interests me now as ever and in spite of all that I have gone through,"[41] Dorothea acknowledged gratefully.

"To say how constantly and how anxiously I have thought of you, how sincerely and how deeply I have sympathized in all your distresses, is quite impossible."[42] Grey had buried more than one child. He now invited Arthur and his exhausted mother to convalesce in the bracing ocean breezes of Howick, his extremely comfortable Northumberland mansion standing in pretty grounds amidst rolling green moorlands only a mile from the North Sea. Famous for its hospitality, Howick would allow Dorothea the comfort of friends, the advantages of superior medical advice, and a healthy climate.

Arthur recovered quickly. His mother kept him amused with games and puzzles; she read aloud from his favorite books. When the doctors let Arthur sit up out of bed for an hour each day, Dorothea felt able to turn over her night vigil to a competent nurse. Then, Arthur suffered a sudden relapse. His mother held him over a basin as he vomited incessantly. St. Petersburg's best physicians tried everything. "Arthur told me he was dying; poor angel! He felt the hand of death upon him; and I have had to survive him."[43]

∞∞∞

Barely nine months before, Dorothea Lieven had landed in Russia with her career in shreds. Now also frail in body and stricken in spirit she set forth on her sad journey south. "I have lost everything," she mourned to Metternich, whose ready sympathy for his former soul-mate had jolted him into shattering his nine-year silence. "There are few people capable of understanding all that the heart can contain of anguish. You are perhaps one of them, and who speaks to me like them." Metternich, too, had buried children. Yet, as a man, he had his profession to give him

> some consolation—there is none for me. My life is destroyed. Finished. A desperate instinct drives me away from horrible surroundings. Here I am thrown into Europe, without plan, without purpose. I do not know where I am going. I am looking for friends—and when I meet them, I find that it is no great matter!
>
> I want nothing more than to die, to keep my dignity until then, and to be reunited with the angels I have lost.[44]

19

The Path to Paris

Even at this present moment I hardly believe it can be true—Never to see my children more; all the joy, all the occupation of my daily life gone, and nothing left for my heart to love![1]

—Dorothea Lieven

Early on a crisp, 1835 April morning, the Lievens' crested traveling carriage stood in the frozen slush outside their somber house on the Quai Anglais. Barely a few days before, the princess had buried her youngest child. Prince Lieven wrenched himself away from his court duties for only as long as it would take to escort his stricken spouse over several hundred miles of Russia's badly rutted roads to the Prussian frontier. There, after thirty-five years of marriage, six children, a shared profession, let alone their recent tragedy, Lieven "snatched away" his protection, leaving Dorothea to face "an indefinite separation and a vague future that is very difficult very difficult."[2]

From their day of parting the prince pressed his grieving wife to return to "our *dear homeland*."[3] "I try to obey you, to calm myself," she insisted, but "that is not happening," that "is not going to happen at all, that will never happen my disaster is too great."[4]

৪৩৫৪

Dorothea Lieven now reaped the benefit of past kindness. In her early days at London she had befriended the newly married duchess of Cumberland, whom society snubbed for having been divorced. Eventually, the duchess returned to the dear familiarity of her native Germany. She now sent her luxuriously appointed carriage to meet Dorothea at the border and convey her westward across Prussia to Berlin.

There her friend welcomed Dorothea into the spacious apartment she had prepared in her son Prince Frederick of Prussia's mansion, and made sure Dorothea had every attention. Still, the sorrowing princess felt "it would be so easy" to die. "I do not know why death does not come and take me."[5] "Why am I not yet lying beside my two angels? They are at rest, I suffer."[6]

Suffering "all the anguish that the human heart can bear," Dorothea began "the most distressing of letters. Dear, kind friend," she asked Emily, "can you believe I am still alive after my brutal disasters? You who know me—picture me on this earth without George, without Arthur. With nothing to interest me—separated from my husband," far from "my friends, without solace, without intellectual resources," confronting alone the frightening prospect of an unclear future. "To see my children die! To hear dear Arthur tell me, 'I am dying.' No, it is too horrible."[7]

Surrounded by kind people but not her intimates, the fastidious princess so sought diversion that she received everyone. But despite distractions, Dorothea constantly thought "*they* must be coming home from their walk," a "small detail of the routine of *their* life occurs to my mind, and then, all of a sudden, it all flashes back, and I seem to see two graves, that rise up in my sight and stand before me, and my heart is as though turned to stone."[8] Dorothea implored her devoted Grey to write often, to tell her "everything. I feel the only chance of keeping my mind from brooding is in turning my thought to affairs in England. My only consolation is in your friendship."[9]

Her distress over her firstborn, her little Marie's death, had been too deep to articulate, and although Dorothea soon bore sturdy sons, she never got over her daughter's death. Nor, despite her anguished outpourings, did Dorothea ever fully recover from the deaths of her two youngest boys. "I can neither write, nor say all that this day makes me feel, after eleven years, it is just as sharp, sharper perhaps than in the moment itself."[10]

George and Arthur had been part of her core being. "To lose *both* my children, children whom I passionately adored, as perhaps few other mothers have ever adored their children. And still to live on when they are both dead, dead—under my very eyes."[11] Sons Dorothea still had, "but my children are all dead and gone."[12]

Guilt, irrational but nonetheless real, aggravated her anguish. Dorothea's youngest did not die on some far-off battlefield. They were in their mother's care, dependent on her, their protection her most basic duty. Born in England, named after their godfathers King George IV and the duke of Wellington, George and Arthur were bound up in Dorothea's precious memories of her life's happiest moments. Had she but succeeded over that impossible Stratford Canning affair the Lievens would still be in England, her boys not exposed to St. Petersburg's unhealthy climate, and to strange, let alone inferior physicians. "There are some names I cannot pronounce, not even write,"—her mother, her daughter, her young sons—"trifling memories, but so harrowing! I lock up all of that," Dorothea later confessed. "I am afraid of myself, of the sound of my voice. That is how I am" and "how I shall always stay."[13]

In her greatest need Dorothea craved her friends, especially men she judged her equals, men like Grey who could provide an anchor. "So that the mind is worth something I need neither amusement nor solitude. I need the mind of others for me to have my own. I do not understand *myself* opposite my thoughts. It is as if I were nothing at all."[14]

Groping to restore some stability, order to her life, Dorothea sought among her friends for one whose tragedies matched hers. "You and *you alone* came into my mind."[15]

Princess Lieven had always liked Lord Aberdeen. Despite her disgust at his anti–Russian attitude over Greece, they agreed politically. And she knew he could again become foreign secretary. So while the Tory earl tended his Scottish acres, the princess had offered to send him London news, for the world "always goes on regardless of whose hands hold the reins of government."[16] Aberdeen liked Dorothea. Her offer flattered him. He accepted. By the time Princess Lieven left England they were firm friends.

"How I would please you, my lord, because today I understand you." Aberdeen had buried two wives and four daughters. "But you are a man, you have the duties of your profession; I, I have nothing but my weakness and my tears. If only God would take pity on me, and call me to Him." Tell "me, teach me, how to bear my unhappiness. Resignation has not yet entered into my heart." She begged Aberdeen not to forget her. "My heart needs friendship, my mind is still susceptible to distraction. Your politics interest me."[17]

Even in life's greatest calamities some semblance of inner peace comes from

> the sincere commiseration of those whom we esteem; and as you have taught me to think that I deserve some portion of your friendship, I entreat you to believe that there is no person who more deeply sympathizes with you, or who more sincerely prays for the success of all those means which are in any degree calculated to alleviate your suffering. Having said this, I feel that I can add nothing more to any good purpose; and I will therefore turn to other subjects, which, under ordinary circumstances, might excite your interest.[18]

Aberdeen knew the princess would forgive his not renewing the sad subject that preoccupied her, sure she understood that his apparent cruelty meant kindness. Deeply grateful "for what you said to me and for what you did not say," Dorothea found Aberdeen's silence more agreeable "than all the words of the earth's happy ones."[19]

೫ОСൠ

Mired in misery, aching with rheumatism, too distraught to decide her next move, Princess Lieven languished in Berlin for a month. "I feel most anxious that you should adopt some plan which may afford some diversion to your thoughts, and procure you the comfort of your real friends," Grey worried. "Where is this to be found but in England, which is your second country?"[20] He urged her return. So did her bosom friend Emily. "I yearn to go there with all my heart," but "sorrow tires people & and they would cool towards me—then I would really have lost *everything*. I shall come when I am more at peace, when people can still love me for myself, for my company, and not out of compassion."[21]

Princess Lieven had kept her pride. By mid–May she resolved to try the healing waters of Europe's premier spa. Her friend the duchess of Dino promised to come to Baden-Baden; the Nesselrodes would be there too.

In the consoling company of her eldest son, Paul, on special leave from the London embassy, the princess headed southwest via Wittenberg, Frankfurt, and the picturesque old university town of Heidelberg. "Everything is beautiful and cozy and comfortable, it is a good thing to travel in a lovely civilized country like this."[22] Medieval towns with cobbled streets and half-timbered houses, strongly reminiscent of illustrations from *Grimm's Fairy Tales*, dotted the densely wooded hills and verdant valleys of Germany's famous Black Forest, whose thick growth of pine trees appeared pitch black after dark. Dorothea thought this part of her mother's native land "the loveliest country in the world, where the air is of the purest and most healthgiving description."[23]

Her magnificent route would, Dorothea wrote her husband, have given him great pleasure. "For me it is gloom rather than delight." With infinite sadness she reflected that "I have *no-one* with whom I can share diversion."[24] Lieven, at least, had his profession to distract him. Tsar Nicholas had again appointed the prince interim foreign minister for the three months Count Nesselrode needed to recover his health at Baden-Baden.

Famous for its curative waters since Roman times, Baden-Baden now figured as one of the aristocracy's favorite summer haunts. It offered Dorothea several cures for easing her rheumatism. As well she could socialize while sipping restorative albeit foul-tasting water at the pump room, and stroll in the park promenade among handsome trees, exotic shrubs, brilliantly hued roses, rhododendrons, and azaleas on the banks of the Oosbach river that rustled through town. The surrounding hills offered countless outings to dramatic waterfalls, sparkling mountain lakes, and prosperous villages nestling amid row upon tidy row of grape vines. Concerts and theatres tempted, too.

Dorothea sought a different diversion. Disappointed at Baden's dearth of politically minded visitors, she resorted to her correspondence. "Everyone here," Dorothea wrote Emily, sister of the prime minister and long-time lover of the foreign secretary, "wants William Russell to be assigned to Berlin. He is known and liked there."[25] Then the duchess of Dino arrived. As one in their hatred of Palmerston, the princess and Talleyrand's confidante loved to discuss politics. And Dino, too, had suffered the death of a child; she acted as Dorothea's "sick nurse, my distraction, finally everything."[26]

Princess Lieven's past glory and present tragedy attracted Baden's high society; yet, "she finds nothing but a cruel void in the distraction she demands of everyone," the duchess of Dino noted. Her friend had "lost her way and wanders at large. She is not resigned, and finds no pleasure in her regrets." Baden's healing waters and beautiful scenery gave the grieving princess no joy.

> She lives in the street, in public places, talks inconsequentially, and never listens, laughs, cries and acts at a venture, asks questions without interest in the answers. This misery is the worse, as four months of sorrow have not taught her patience. She is already astonished that her regrets have lasted so long; but, as she will not submit herself to trouble, it will not wear itself out; she prolongs it by struggling against it. In the combat sorrow triumphs and the victim cries out, but the sound is discordant and awakes no sympathetic echo in the hearts of others. I have seen people, one after another, cease to pity her and care for her: she saw it too and was humiliated. She seemed grateful to me for continuing to be kind.[27]

Such jagged pain, not to mention Dorothea's irrational guilt over her boys' deaths, signaled danger—of depression. And her frail health, now bearing the added burden of menopause with its disturbing physical changes and perplexing emotional fragility, exacerbated Dorothea's mental condition.

Everything upset her. The princess missed her son Paul terribly when his leave ended, especially as his brother Alexander, whose indifferent health had prompted Dorothea to get him a diplomatic posting at warm sunny Naples, could not immediately replace Paul at her side. And as if her youngest surviving son had not given Dorothea heartache throughout his life, he picked the present to deal her another blow. She had always thought Constantine the most capable of her three older boys, but this scion of diligent Baltic Barons proved disappointingly lazy and disobedient. Dorothea hailed his entry into a strict St. Petersburg boarding school with considerable relief; and General Alexander Benckendorff's readiness to deal sternly with his way-ward nephew reassured her, for Dorothea felt that Constantine needed strict super-vision. At the same time she begged her brother to write about the slightest improvement; for Dorothea wanted to give Constantine's stern father positive proof that some good did exist in this son.

All that discipline had little salutary effect on Constantine Lieven. He now got himself into serious trouble, not for the first time, over gambling and women. Lieven, however, this time refused to rescue him, and Constantine had to resign his com-mission in the army. How could Constantine so far forget himself when his father held such a high position at court? scolded the irate prince, always concerned with what people would say. And had Constantine thought of the additional grief he caused his poor mother?

Not long afterwards the princess suffered "such a strong hemorrhage that for some hours my heart beat in vain."[28] This first of several severe hemorrhages served as a frightening reminder of her mother's last illness. Dorothea's daily letters to Lieven, crammed with political news calculated to be of use to the interim foreign minister, news gleaned at Baden and through her correspondence with leading lights in every European capital, stopped. Confined to bed, weak and ill, Dorothea, nonethe-less, came to a decision. Her only salvation, the one way to drown her grief, lay in mental diversion.

Lieven had promised his wife an ample allowance. She could travel where she pleased. "If I am mistaken about England, it will be time to go mad. I would like to spend the autumn and beginning of winter," the country-house season, in England, the princess wrote Lady Cowper. To avoid harrowing memories of London, Dorothea planned to go north to Grey's hospitable Howick; from there she would accept Aberdeen's invitation to Scotland. Later Dorothea would turn south, but could not face Richmond or Panshanger, the Cowpers' country seat where they and the Lievens—with all their children—had spent so many happy days. While her cruel, poignant grief persisted, Dorothea felt an urgent need for distraction. "But I dare ask, what about my poor victims who would have to put up with the sight of my sad-ness. Can I impose such pain on them? & so my courage for England leaves me."[29] Nevertheless, Dorothea asked Emily to arrange country house visits that assured her a warm welcome and compatible company.

To her utter astonishment Emily's July 21st reply* elaborated on "what she deems good reasons for preventing my coming to England!" Dorothea indignantly wrote Grey.

> And she cites, as the most cogent of these, Lord Palmerston. By this I am to under-stand that it is made a condition of my coming, that I should show all manner of ado-ration for him, seeing that *his high position* would render my stay in England very unpleasant in case I refused to treat him as a friend. Truly love must be very blind to urge anyone to such indelicacy of conduct as this.[30]

Dorothea could not bring herself to answer Emily. Meanwhile, the latter wrote again. "Your son [Paul] and I had a long talk about your future." We "agreed that only two places come into question for you—Naples for your health, or else Paris." Naples would be a new venue; "it is so bright and beautiful and so fascinating."[31]

*This letter is lost.

Emily neglected to mention that the capital of southern Italy's Kingdom of the Two Sicilies could scarcely qualify as one of Europe's more lively centers of political activity. If Dorothea had disparaged Rome as a political backwater when she wintered there ten years ago, she would be highly unlikely to rate Naples any better.

In Paris, Emily continued with sound common sense, "you would have many friends and certainly, more distraction and society, a choice that would suit you better and besides, a constant stream of acquaintances and friends from every country" of Europe. In Dorothea's position, Emily would choose Paris. "You need to live in the middle of nonstop news and political activity—and in Paris there are more travelers than anywhere else—and more country house owners. I think your memories of England are too fresh—and that would tear at your heart. It is much better to keep England for the future, until time has calmed the bitterness of your"[32] sorrow.

Dorothea's long silence worried her friend. "Can it be possible that my advice to postpone your visit here has offended you? Can you doubt that my first desire would be to beg you to come at once," Emily wrote.

> I feared for your sake the ... [memories that] would beset you everywhere here, especially where your fondness and intimacies were engaged. Is it possible that you have closed your eyes to what cannot fail to distress you. And that after an absence of less than a year! ... Nothing will make me believe this to be the cause of your silence. You could not be so unjust towards me—you could not so misjudge my friendship and attachment![33]

Had she answered Emily's July 21st letter immediately, "I would have lamented it later," Dorothea replied. "Today I am more at peace—I can" suppress "the memory of what wounded me then." She loved Emily and needed her love. Emily must continue to send news but never again mention the July 21st letter. "I have lost too much, do not deprive me of my faith in your friendship."[34]

"I am very troubled by your silence," Emily wrote in the meantime. "You told me that disaster had made you nervous and distraught, but I never thought it could put you at the point of so misreading my friendship for you, and my loyalty." Since Dorothea had begged Emily for advice, "could I do otherwise than give you my candid counsel, and is it not very unfair" of you "to resent me for doing that? I could easily be wrong; it may be that you would feel happier here now than anywhere else, and everyone is the best judge of their own business. If you really think this then in God's name come. You know I will do anything in the world for you.... I am in despair to think I should have hurt you, and you must blame it on gaucherie but not on bad intent."[35]

"Do not accuse me of injustice, I never deserved such a reproach from you,"[36] Dorothea replied. "Your advice to stay away lest England evoke feelings of sadness" did not upset me. "Your letter treating this subject as a personal matter, did. You must allow me to deny that Lord P[almerston] is entitled to influence my position in England, and also permit me to speak frankly, so that everything is clear between us; & let me also reiterate my fervent prayer that this subject be closed between us."[37]

ಬೃೋಡ

Despondent and debilitated, Dorothea had been dictating her letters to a secretary. After admonishing Lieven for the distress his eight day silence inflicted on her

frail health, she now scrawled some lines whose excessive size, to say nothing of illeg-
ibility, bore mute witness to her sorry state.

> I have put myself into the hands of the Princess of Orange's doctor. [He had saved
> the life of Tsar Nicholas's brother-in-law, the Prince of Orange.] He is an extremely
> intelligent and able man and seems to understand my mental condition, which is
> killing me. I have not yet come to any definite decision, but his opinion is absolutely
> against Italy; so France and England remain.[38]

Dorothea enclosed the doctor's diagnosis. She asked Lieven to show it to her
influential brother.

With scarcely veiled sarcasm Lieven complimented Dorothea on her choice of
a doctor perceptive enough to diagnose that her state of mind caused her physical
infirmity. While expressing distress at his wife's condition, the prince wrote coldly
that she had only herself to blame. She had congenial company, she had her loving
son Alexander, what more could she want? Dorothea must get a grip on herself.

Meanwhile, among her many callers the princess had been pleasantly surprised
to meet a cousin on her mother's side, a widowed Mme. de Mentzingen, née Schilling,
very noble, very poor, with numerous children including delightful daughters. Always
drawn to promising young people, Dorothea invited one "to keep me company *chez
moi* during my stay at Baden. She is lovely and good. Like those splendid beauties
who make such a superb impression in London and are unknown at home. She is
eighteen years old."[39]

Her "niece" Marie de Mentzingen pleased the princess to such an extent that
she invited the girl to be her companion. So gentle, so solicitous of her "aunt," "so
perfectly naïve and innocent, so modest and so pretty. It is truly uplifting both morally
and physically."[40] Marie in some way filled the place, not only by virtue of her name,
of Dorothea's dead daughter and of her late brother Constantine's little Marie, the
daughter who might have been.

☞☜

Rain dripped dejectedly into puddles. Dorothea's cure ended. Duty recalled
Alexander Lieven to Naples. Acquaintances were going. Prince Lieven and General
Count Benckendorff insisted that the time had come for Dorothea to return to Russia. Her brother advised Tsarskoe Selo, so lovely in autumn. "You forget," Dorothea
replied, that "long before my misery it was decided that I must remove myself from
the Russian climate for a year and a half. You surely do not think my health fares
better today than then."[41]

Indeed, Dorothea felt her tragedy entitled her to seek solace where she chose;
so her brother, who enjoyed all life's blessings, must "enter into the heart of an
unhappy woman, and no one is more so than I am. I had everything; I have nothing
left."[42]

Memories were too fresh, too painful to return to England. The princess simply could not reconcile her former political power with her present lot; and her mourning, not to mention her health, precluded any prominent role in society.

There remained Paris. Princess Lieven's doctors liked its mild climate. She anticipated its lively politics. And Dorothea had good friends in Paris—Prince Talleyrand,
recently retired from the London embassy, and his niece the duchess of Dino;

Austrian ambassador Count Apponyi and his wife whom she knew from Rome; Russian ambassador Count Pahlen, a Baltic Baron and family friend; and last but not least British ambassador Lord Granville. "I wanted to tell you how happy Ly. Granville was at the thought of your coming here" and "for her sake how much I wish it may be the case," Harriet's brother encouraged. "It is so seldom that she sees a friend here." And "you will be near us with the power of seeing as many or as few as you like."[43]

At age fifty Dorothea Lieven found new and notable courage. "I favor frailty over forcefulness in a woman. It is more feminine."[44] Nonetheless, under her "feminine" frailty there breathed a forceful will to live what was left of her life on terms of her own choosing. Dorothea's return to Russia had brought home with all too painful clarity that if she wanted a career, she must achieve it on her own. Lieven might be happy in his new position, but it no longer afforded his spouse any chance to satisfy her ambition. All she had left in Russia were two pathetically small graves and an empty marriage.

Seeking solace for her soul, distraction for her mind, and ease for her "poor body," Princess Lieven set out for Paris.

20

The Struggle to Stay in Paris

Though I was a stranger in Paris, my true compatriots were the members of the diplomatic corps there, as they had been in every other capital. A sort of freemasonry united past and present diplomats. They had seen, or heard, much of one another; they are a kind of race apart, formed out of all nations.[1]

—Dorothea Lieven

My husband's company does not suit my mind, or perhaps my heart, but he is someone who loves me, to whom I belong, who is concerned about me. It is intimacy, habit, private life, all that is essential, so sweet for a woman![2]

—Dorothea Lieven

When, in 1835, brisk autumn air burnished leaves into bronze, Princess Lieven arrived at Paris. Ancient capital of a rich, powerful nation that for centuries dominated Europe, home to Europe's great intellectual movement, the Enlightenment, Paris also meant revolution. The 1789 cataclysm shaped the course of history, the 1830 upheaval landed Louis-Philippe on the throne as constitutional monarch. The first ten years of his reign saw fifteen ministries succeed one another. Such volatility gave the ambitious princess ample scope to operate.

Parisian society differed strikingly from what she had spurned in St. Petersburg and loved in London. Tightly interwoven, English politics and society were still controlled by an ingrained, wealthy, landed aristocracy that the Revolution destroyed in France. In its place arose an aristocracy of merit—of brains like the historian François Guizot, of money like the Rothschilds, of ability like Adolphe Thiers, and the fittest noble survivors of the Terror like the Duc de Broglie.

This energetic new aristocracy needed a meeting-place. Parisian salons had strong roots entrenched in the grand tradition of the Enlightenment when they were centers of culture and politics, when the ability to converse meant everything. Great ladies not only led fashion, they led conversation; no man could rise to repute without the setting of a salon, and women ruled them all. That gifted, aristocratic young priest Talleyrand first attracted attention in the pre–Revolutionary salons; that bright young bourgeois Guizot first drew notice in the Restoration salons. They conversed brilliantly. So did Dorothea Lieven.

ഇൻൽ

She accepted Prince Talleyrand and the duchess of Dino's invitation to break her journey from Baden-Baden to Paris at Valençay, Talleyrand's royally magnificent estate. That brought the wrath of Russia's Autocrat crashing down on the unsuspecting princess's head. How could she have failed to realize, Nesselrode admonished at Nicholas's explicit command, that the tsar had always seen Talleyrand as Russia's enemy.

Nicholas hated France, hotbed of revolution. He scorned its "usurper" king. And if Princess Lieven's visit to Valençay were not bad enough, her preference for Paris over St. Petersburg proved even more painful for the tsar to swallow.

Dorothea had told her brother of her intent to come to Paris, had given her reasons. He approved. Besides, "I do not in truth know what harm I could do in going to Valençay. Our relations with M. de Talleyrand were close in London because you and he were official persons," a flabbergasted Dorothea wrote Lieven. "Today he no

Nicholas I. The "Iron Tsar" denounced Dorothea Lieven as the only person who ever dared to defy him. Artist: Unknown. Used by permission of the Slavic and Baltic Division, The New York Public Library, Astor, Lenox and Tilden Foundations.

longer is and as for me I am nothing; to me he is a valued acquaintance, and at age 50, I think to be able to choose my connections in society. I made that one under your auspices. You never forbade me" Valençay. "I need not account for my actions except to you. I tell you all" my plans. "I remember only my deep eternal grief; and the respect, the love, the obedience I vow to you until the last day of my life."[3]

Having treated Prince Lieven, in public, to "an indirect tirade about the ladies who settle in Paris, so much so that I could hardly keep standing," the Autocrat, in private, expressed great satisfaction at Lieven's relations with his son; next, Nicholas tackled "the dangerous subject" in "the most friendly language but did not hide his distress." Explaining his wife's motives, Lieven emphasized that she certainly had not chosen Paris "with the idea of acting against his wish"; if it "stayed firm you would submit." Nicholas "agreed to your remaining for the winter." A few days later the tsar, tsarevitch, and Lieven dined alone. In "a delightful and good mood, and I dare think as friendly towards me as I could wish," Nicholas spoke "of you, however only for news. Then he asked about each of my sons."[4] Lieven underlined what Dorothea knew all too well: the tsar's favor meant everything.

ഇൻൽ

Princess Lieven settled into a spacious furnished apartment in the elegant "la Terrasse" building on the rue de Rivoli, at the center of fashionable Paris. Each morning a ravishing view of the Tuileries Garden greeted Dorothea and, she beguiled her husband, so did the lovely, still warm, October sun that daily flooded her rooms. Sitting up in bed facing the balconied window, Dorothea filled her morning with reading her mail and the newspapers, including English journals with which Emily Cowper kept her comfortably supplied. So many letters came that although the princess wrote quickly, her replies seemed to her always to be late. Still, she would welcome more letters; they occupied her mind.

A lively exchange, with Lords Aberdeen and Grey among others, crisscrossed the Channel. Political punditry edified Alexander Benckendorff. Politics, social tidbits, and her activities crowded the long daily letter to Lieven. His wife showed the world a cheerful face but on what would have been her adored George's sixteenth birthday Dorothea doubted if she could ever "support all the emotions this day reawakens in me."[5]

At 2 P.M. she received visitors. Afterwards Dorothea went for a walk, usually along one of the well-kept paths in the Bois de Boulogne. Her willowy figure clad only in black to mark eternal mourning for George and Arthur, Dorothea wore a chic, wasp-waisted walking dress with tapered bodice, sloping shoulders, puffed sleeves, and full swishing skirts. An astrakhan-lined cape kept her warm; a lozenge shaped bonnet, decorated with black ostrich feathers, framed her face in a flattering oval. Sometimes old Talleyrand went along. He sat in his carriage and the princess walked while they laughed and chatted. At other times desperate, her heart bursting with memories, Dorothea walked despite "torrents of rain; I like to brave all that. My health lets me, and my mind is better so."[6] Lieven must forgive her for burdening him with such suffocating misery, but she could confide in no one else.

Except God.

> Yesterday I spent about three hours at Church. I received communion with more than 300 people, almost all of them [poor]. I returned with my heart more satisfied than after any other communion—my niece [Marie de Mentzingen] accompanied me with religious piety.... I spent a sad night, the last of my angel Arthur. In a few hours it will be a year to the day since he ceased to live. Oh! my good husband, how the memory of each minute is pressed into my memory. What frightful moments![7]

৪৩৫৪

Dorothea never ceased to support her sons. Extremely able and making great strides, Paul, posted at the London embassy thanks to his mother, now counted on his father's position and "the feeling your experience must give you of what could be done for a man's career at a propitious time."[8] Tell Paul, Lieven testily replied, to be patient.

Lacking diplomatic skill but not intelligence, Alexander, epitome of character and decency, profited daily from practical experience at Naples, where Nesselrode had assigned him after Dorothea asked that her weak-chested son be posted to a mild climate.

Lieven now asked his wife to tell their sons that he wanted to give them a large estate. "Both begged me to dissuade you" in "general terms without explaining their motives which I must examine and interpret. I understand the difficulty of managing this property from a distance, and I grasp perfectly" how Paul's career and Alexander's health made regular visits to Russia impossible. Lieven often had problems with peasants. "What will it be for your sons? Then there are worries about bad crops. Finally a thousand things that render revenue precarious. Your sons beg you via my voice to renounce this project. As you have created it" to "increase their income, complete the idea" by giving each a larger allowance. "Make them happy and independent, since it depends on you that will be your solace, for they are the sole interest left to us."[9]

Their mother's potent mixture of reason, cajolery, and prodding produced a larger income for Paul and Alexander within the year.

Constantine had already been forced to resign his commission in the army due to trouble over gambling and women. Still, those around her wayward third son, Dorothea averred with maternal faith, considered him basically good and honest. Lieven wanted Constantine to manage his two new estates if the young man "gained the experience to be in charge without prejudicing our common interest."[10]

Suddenly, Constantine removed himself, his servants, and his belongings from his father's acres telling no one, least of all his long-suffering parent, his destination. Eventually he surfaced in a small town where Lieven sent him the interior ministry's "summons from the court of justice—no reply." Then, "soldiers' widows, generals' menservants, inn-keepers—all his creditors"[11] appealed to the prince for repayment.

Without so much as consulting his wife, Lieven resorted to a well-worn way out of family woes. He had Constantine banished to America.

⁎

Princess Lieven "knew all the secret annals of diplomacy; she could tell anecdotes ... with pungent ease." No one could better "paint a character or unravel an intrigue."[12] That master of diplomacy and conversation, Prince Talleyrand, graced Dorothea's drawing-room every evening. Prime minister Duc de Broglie and his wife paid her flattering attention. The most prominent public men—Thiers, Berryer, and Guizot came. Dorothea especially liked upright Count Molé. But she curtailed her growing circle because although her allowance assured a life of ease, it could not cover large scale socializing; nor did Dorothea have the strength. Hardly had she greeted some distinguished guests one evening when, suddenly, her "words and breath failed" and within "a quarter of an hour I was so ill, that I thought I would die. I truly frightened everyone."[13]

"The pleasantest women in Paris"[14] visited Princess Lieven. Daily, she saw the duchess of Dino and Countess Apponyi, the Austrian ambassador's wife—Dorothea appreciated her kindness, acumen, and tact which a crushing politeness hid from most people; and Lady Harriet Granville, wife of the British ambassador. Only the English, Dorothea confided to Grey, resumed friendships exactly where they left off. Absorbed in conversation or sharing sociable silence, Harriet and Dorothea walked in the Bois, or sat in some secluded spot on the banks of the Seine to admire the scenery. Harriet judged her old friend "really more liked than I think it is easy for a foreign woman to be."[15]

Frail health and mourning forced the princess to decline several flattering invitations to dine with the royal family until Louis-Philippe bade her to a very small dinner. His and the queen's attentions were too many to describe to Lieven. Neither fervent nor tactlessly lively, the clever, conservative king showed great knowledge of men, and listened patiently. "On all these points," Dorothea disclosed to Grey, "he is not at all French."[16]

She began to enjoy small dinners (six people at most), always in political circles. Talleyrand and Dino invited her on the duchess's saint's day, the Roman Catholic feast of St. Dorothy; much to Princess Lieven's surprise, both Dorotheas got gifts. Dinners at Talleyrand's mansion were always delightful. A noted gourmet, he employed the finest chef in Paris. And he invited the political powers, so conversation sparkled.

Of course Marie de Mentzingen's social life occupied her aunt.* Younger visitors to Dorothea's salon at once gravitated towards the beautiful Marie, and when the butler brought in the tea tray, she pleased their elders by pouring "tea like a Goddess."[17] Lady Granville presented Marie at court. The visiting duchess of Sutherland, she who had organized that handsome farewell gift of a gold bracelet from Dorothea's London friends, chaperoned Marie to a magnificent ball given by the Rothschilds.

☙◊ଓ

Princess Lieven had been living in Paris for only a few months when a disagreement between Thiers and de Broglie shook the ministry. Deep in the king's confidence, Talleyrand promoted Thiers for prime minister and the princess sang his praises in her salon, not to mention giving him excellent press in her Europe-wide correspondence only because, Dorothea told her friends, she wanted to keep her political skills from rusting.

Perhaps. From the day she arrived in Paris, the princess reminded her husband of their last conversation, of his promise: when his term as the tsarevitch's governor ended, he would return to the foreign ministry, a "useful way to spend your life in pleasure & comfort, & in the interest of your health and mine. A noble existence, a home, those are my only" wishes. "I am sick of life, I will always be, but at least it should be a little eased."[18]

Leaving Russia, replied the prince, would involve major monetary concessions. So he must wait at least until autumn, when management of his estates would be ordered.

Delighted that her husband still meant to join her, Dorothea pressed him to do so now, this winter (1835–36), for his health, his wish to see her—in Italy, Nice, wherever the sun shed warmth. In soliciting the tsar's permission Lieven could even "allow a glimpse of the chance to bring me back with you, if that chance could serve your purpose."[19]

Thiers's premiership gave Dorothea her opening. Two years before, Talleyrand had negotiated an alliance with foreign secretary Palmerston, a development Tsar Nicholas viewed with extreme disfavor. Talleyrand now wanted to move France closer to Russia.

Within three days of ambassador Granville's receipt of Palmerston's order to express to King Louis-Philippe Britain's concern that the Thiers ministry meant an

---

*Princess Lieven exerted herself to help the whole de Mentzingen family. She got Lieven to sponsor Marie's three young brothers; he placed two in Russia's prestigious naval academy and the older in a prominent regiment. As well, Dorothea coaxed her husband to give the boys an allowance.

end to the alliance, Dorothea whetted her husband's appetite with a verbatim account of the meeting.

She then summarized Talleyrand's confidence: it would be easy for the new French government to "give a different turn to European affairs. Thiers's positive bias could give us great advantage if seized now. He is good for us now, & bad, decidedly bad, for England."[20]

French policy could be changed with resolve and some—not much—skill, qualities Russian ambassador Count Pahlen lacked. Moreover, he constantly told Dorothea how he hated diplomacy, would be happy to quit. Meanwhile Thiers "could become Russia's friend, but we must want it, & not treat him rudely & disdainfully."[21]

"Never will I greet that cad,"[22] Pahlen told the princess. Rather than demolishing her ambassador Dorothea applied diplomacy. "Finally since yesterday they are in business, we shall see if Pahlen can bring some good manners to it. He has difficulty digesting small stature, bad fashion" and a hoarse voice. Once he knew Thiers better, Dorothea felt sure Pahlen would "get fully used"[23] to him. Indeed, so used to Thiers did Pahlen become that he led the pro–Thiers faction among Paris diplomats.

"Pahlen is perfect for me, & I can say I am perfect for him, & I think he feels it. That is tacitly admitted." Dorothea purposely refrained from asking questions, "& everyone comes to tell me everything, for some have had the experience that they profit from it."[24]

Thus did the princess prove to her spouse that his country needed him in Paris. Dorothea liked her new life. Yet, she missed a man's support and protection. She had a husband. Dorothea had invested thirty-five years, let alone great mental, physical, and emotional energy in her marriage. She wanted Lieven with her. He fit into her life; indeed, the eminently presentable, distinguished, aloof diplomat and courtier would be an asset.

Lieven's laconic reply merely expressed grave reservations about his wife getting too mixed up in politics, thus reminding Dorothea that even at age fifty she must submit to his moral authority, to his "superior male wisdom." Indeed, Lieven rejoiced at no longer having to labor in his wife's shadow. And Nicholas's keen interest in the Lievens as "not only individuals belonging to his Court, but as people admitted to his closest circle"[25] so gratified the prince that he did not seek the tsar's permission to travel, or to return to the foreign ministry. Rather, Lieven impressed on his wife that such favored mortals as they, must adapt their attitude and actions to the exalted position their master had seen fit to confer on them.

&ОСЗ

The Autocrat approved of Princess Lieven's decision leave Paris for the salubrious effects of summertime in Baden-Baden. En route she again visited Valençay. Set in splendid surroundings with miles of lovely shaded paths through its forests, an avenue of magnificent chestnut trees led to Talleyrand's moated Renaissance chateau. Inside, formal grandeur ruled, but the duchess of Dino arranged for every conceivable comfort. A steady stream of traveling musicians and acting troupes entertained and, although frail, Talleyrand still loved society and politics. Since Dorothea knew every diplomatic luminary of the past twenty years, she and her host conversed endlessly about past and present. As for the future, Dorothea told Lieven that misery made her feel the same age as the octogenarian prince.

She left Valençay in floods of tears. "How can I live after so much misery. I endure such terrible times, times when I only think of dying." If Lieven failed to lighten her life by coming to meet her in the autumn, Dorothea would "seek a Lutheran convent, some place of refuge to finish my days. I shall not be a charge on you or on anyone. To live abandoned, separated from my husband, from my sons, running from town to town, from country to country is so degrading."[26]

Despite the soothing baths, the daily doses of therapeutic water, walks in the lovely countryside or on the manicured paths that meandered among the colorful flowers and exotic shrubs of Baden's river promenade, Dorothea's health deteriorated. "My face frightens me. I arrived so white and with a little weight, in my fashion. Now I am thin, yellow, red a miserable complexion." Rheumatism crippled her arms. And day and night Dorothea "perspired out poison."[27]

After two months of perplexing silence Lieven favored his wife with a letter whose frost matched its brevity. "Since that cold" letter "I am again without news!" How could Lieven find "the courage to leave me for 4 weeks without a word." Dorothea had lost her "children, will I also lose my husband? My husband, pity me. Come to meet your poor wife. Can Court life satisfy your soul, your dignity as a man? Ask yourself these questions, if ever you have time to reflect. You will be very much" changed "if you can answer yes."[28]

Neither his position nor his intentions, began Lieven's eagerly awaited letter, had altered since "you left me." (Note: "you left me," not "we parted.")

However, at the time when (the following April, 1837) he expected his estates to assure a steady income,* Prince Lieven must escort the tsarevitch on an extended tour of his patrimony. If the prince resigned then, he could never "justify such an act in the eyes of the world; but above all in the eyes of our two eldest sons. They would lose a useful helper, and such an improper step could even result in angry ideas."[29]† What appalling ingratitude towards the tsar, worse towards the tsarevitch. At the end of that young man's foreign tour in the following year, however, his governor's duty would almost be done.

In the meantime,

> I leave you full freedom to choose your place of residence, except the prohibited place. You are too sensible, I am sure, to expose yourself lightly to the most dire results of such scorn for [the Tsar's wishes]. Not only would your existence at Paris prove an acute blow; but you would basically compromise your future.[30]
>
> Your rank, your relations with the Imperial family, your husband's position, and factors too superfluous to specify, differentiate you from other Russian ladies traveling abroad. Your presence in a great capital attracts the attention of the curious public, gives birth to a thousand false ideas that nourish the newspapers, and the spiteful.[31]‡

---

*Lieven regularly sent money to his London bankers, Harman & Co.; at the end of 1836 he had about $2,500,000 in London.

†A Russian noble's property always stood at risk of confiscation due to the Autocrat's arbitrary removal of favor—what Lieven euphemistically called "angry ideas."

‡The free French press had welcomed the princess to Paris by describing her as Russia's real ambassador at London; as Metternich's mistress and unofficial ambassador for Austria; the prince regent's mistress, he had even fathered one of her sons! She had been a close (the papers insinuated varying degrees of intimacy, often with less than Gallic gallantry) friend of Aberdeen, Canning, Castlereagh, Grey, and Wellington; she had contrived to put Leopold of Coburg on the Belgian throne.

St. Petersburg had criticized some of Dorothea's remarks—probably exaggerated—but "your words are repeated while no one remembers the gossip of others."[32]

> It is no doubt extremely annoying that the problematic place is precisely the one you prefer! [But] is it in a noisy capital, in the society of strangers that one finds consolation, real comfort for deep sadness? You found distraction in fleetingly forgetting your sorrow; but not lasting peace.[33]

Having "weighed everything only in your interest, I am *convinced* that your best course is immediate return to Russia. My two winters here make me confident that with great care you could stand the cold. These six months of snow are worse in thought than in fact." [34]

"If I were you, I would not hesitate for an instant." Again, Lieven did not want "to impose any constraint, not even to thwart your decisions, with one exception—an exception dictated by urgent duty. I rely as much on your mind as on your heart, and I am at peace."[35]

১৩৬৩

Two more years of doubt about her future horrified Dorothea no less than her husband's callous advice to return to Russia. How could he have forgotten his last word "in the carriage on our sad journey, you were determined then to keep it. You understood the impossibility of my ever thinking to return there alive." Lieven had wanted to decrease his duties to the tsarevitch at the end of a year, "even to use my absence as the natural pretext for a leave you could interpret into an indefinite absence."[36] No one knew better than Dorothea what training and habit meant, that in sacrificing his health and liberty Lieven wanted to preserve his fortune and assure his sons' future. He had agreed about "the frivolity of Petersburg life, the total absence of rational ideas, this spending of all strength without one useful goal,"[37] where self-respect existed only "as much as the Sun and favor allow." Who knew "better than you what is due to oneself!" How often Dorothea thought of her husband's happiness in England, of his important and praiseworthy life. It could never compare to the present. "Because whatever honorific title you bear it is only that."[38]

To calm herself, the princess drove through lovely summer foliage to her favorite spot in the Black Forest. As she contemplated crystal clear water cascading through towering rocks high on a stunning, densely wooded mountainside, Dorothea mentally composed a crucial letter.

She put its delivery into the powerful hands of her brother, together with her doctor's affidavit: only the mild Parisian climate could assuage Princess Lieven's suffering. Lieven got copies of both documents. So did the tsaritsa.

"Sire, I would no longer seek to beg Y.I.M.* to remember my miseries did I not find myself in need of imploring you for an act of humanity."

Her doctor's opinion, supported by all who saw her pitiful condition, mandated Dorothea's initial decision to go to Paris. Cholera had closed Italy; it still did. England, as Nicholas could well comprehend, stood beyond the pale. Everyone agreed on "a mild climate and mental distraction, my habit for 25 years, as the best & only possible relief for my poor body & bruised spirit." Paris

---

Your Imperial Majesty.

succeeded beyond my hopes. It soothed the irritation of my nerves, & gradually made my every ill disappear. I found all the mental resources that made up the habit of my life. More than one very old friend, comfort, their interest; a constant society that continued the memories of my former life, finally, in the only solace to which my mind responded, my health visibly recovered, my poor heart found a little distraction from my misery. [Had she] thought my stay in this city could displease Y.I.M. it would be the only motive that could make me leave a place where I felt such marked relief.[39]

After eight days in Baden all Dorothea's former symptoms returned in so aggravated a fashion that "today the doctor refused to visit me if I prolonged my stay in Germany, and insisted on my return to Paris as the last hope."

I stay abroad for my health. Y.I.M. knows what I have gone through. He knows I saw my life of 22 years broken off. He knows that hardly had I returned to Russia when the result of our climate showed itself in the most brutal fashion. He knows how I lost everything at once, my two dear children, who made all the joy, all the interest, all the occupation of my life! I tore myself from places that could offer me only the most horrible memories. In one cruel moment I was separated from my husband, he who wished to soften the misery of my poor life with his care. He sacrifices to you Sire, what his religion & his heart impose on him. I am alone in the world.[40]

"Sire, my life is henceforth awful. If my duty is to live it, let me ease it by the means experience has shown me. My stay in Paris is not a question of choice, but of dire need; seen from this aspect Y.I.M. will not refuse to sanction it.

"You allow me to believe, Sire, that my useless existence still means something in the eyes of the sovereign, the man who has honored me with his goodness, with his confidence, I say with his friendship."[41]

Meanwhile, Lieven's failure to acknowledge his wife's medical testimonial strained all bounds. Surely he did not think Dorothea capable of lying about her health, of inducing a doctor to give a false certificate.

I felt relatively well in Paris, menstruated regularly. As soon as I arrived at Baden everything stopped, my nerves resumed their distress my nights were awful, I swear I had not one *without insomnia,* suffering. Rheumatism first on the chest, then the back and now for almost 6 weeks [both arms]. "I cannot put a shawl on my shoulders by myself and need constant help to make the least motion.[42]

The doctor forbade Naples, Germany, and especially Russia. He urged Dorothea's immediate return to Paris. "I would be really sad if *my husband* did not believe me!"[43]

Weeks went by. No word from the imperial lips; no word from Lieven. Dorothea's miseries multiplied. Baden turned horribly humid and cold. She returned to Paris.

৪৩৫৪

Stark naked trees swayed in the Tuileries Garden outside Princess Lieven's window. Scarcely had she seated herself in a favorite winged armchair covered in green damask, when Count Pahlen arrived. That morning a courier had galloped into the cobbled courtyard of Russia's embassy. His bag included a letter from General Count Benckendorff to his sister; it contained the Autocrat's reply. Alexander's insistence on entrusting so sacred a communication only to a Russian courier had retarded Dorothea's receipt of her tsar's precious words. She favored her husband with an annotated copy.

Alexander: The tsar read Dorothea's letter "with the interest he continues to show for all that concerns a member of the family" his mother held in such affection.

Dorothea: "Besides this sacred memory, I would have thought I had personally earned the right to a little of the Tsar's interest and goodness; I think it even more because he often & amply showed it to me. My brother takes care to prove me wrong."

Alexander: "You were in Paris before your request to go there could have arrived here; so you do not seek permission." Dorothea should have waited "for it, before again starting on" a journey "that the first time displeased the Tsar."

Dorothea: Her letter explained her doctor's order for a quick return to Paris. "Thus I solicited the Tsar's *sanction*, which I could not doubt from the minute he realized the state of my health & all my reasons. I could not wait for his *permission*." Like the present letter, it would have been delayed for weeks, exposing "me to an interim stay in some small German town, and travel in the worst season of the year."

Alexander: The tsar recommended Vienna. It offered "the same distractions you seek at Paris," since diplomats were "just as numerous there as at the French capital."

Dorothea: "If the Tsar had deigned to read the doctor's opinion, he would have seen that he forbad me the German climate and Vienna in winter is one of the worst places. Also, I know no one there but Prince Metternich, one does not go to look for new friends at age 52! One of the reasons I prefer Paris is its proximity to England which means I live in the middle of my most well-liked acquaintances. My letter expressed that very well."[44]

Alexander: "Anyway H. M. [His Majesty] forbids you nothing, and gives you liberty to do as you like regretting only that your habits and tastes estrange you from your country, your husband, & all those who have proved their interest and friendship!!"[45]

Dorothea: "The Tsar cannot have forgotten that even before my disasters, my health estranged me from my country. And he knows that today it prolongs my absence."[46]

Alexander: "Such an elevated and loving heart as yours should have found more genuine comfort under the aegis of your household gods, had you offered them a hundredth of the sacrifices and care you have lavished in pleasing far from their foyers."

Dorothea: "What are the sacrifices & cares I have lavished in pleasing far from my foyers?" Deeply hurt, she thought her brother's words proved "I have fully failed to reconcile myself to his goodwill. So it seems my faculties of pleasing were hardly enough for that terrain, for certainly my goodwill was there, and I thought to have given proof of it."[47]

"H. M. forbids you nothing, and gives you liberty to do as you like." To Dorothea's acute distress, the tsar failed to "temper his severity by one word of interest or kindness."[48]

೫၆ನ

The princess endured desperate days, days when she cried frenetically over her sorry plight, about the profusion of past joy; "the images are so frightful, they tear my soul apart, & I return to them constantly. I ask God in his grace to help me."[49] She suffered lonely days. She bore days of debilitating illness. Yet, Paris began to feel like home.

By the time its distinctive year-end glow swathed the city, and the steel-toned Seine matched the massive cauliflower clouds drifting above, Princess Lieven, "in great beauty and high spirits,"[50] presided over an exclusive salon. Those she saw socially every day—the Granvilles, Apponyis, Pahlen, Talleyrand, Dino—senior diplomats, English visitors, and prominent politicians formed its nucleus. "Some of the most violent antagonists have occasionally joined in amicable and curious discussion."[51] To have "Berryer and Molé *tête à trois*,[52] looking daggers at each other" would have killed the English ambassadress, but the princess knew "what's what and gets out of every difficulty."[53]

She operated like "a planet that has satellites, for it is her profession to be a planet, but making no move to attract them" wrote a Paris newspaper. With "the calm of power, the security of an acquired right, the patience of a desire that feels its power" the princess knew "how to wait because she has foresight. In her no turmoil, nothing that feeds intrigue, nothing like political pomposity."

She spoke "not to impose her opinion," but "to give you the chance to express yours." Her society represented the politics of a "lofty civilization, politics elegant, simple, cool, the talk of a salon" where "all ideas are represented equally, where old systems are still respected, where the first news is already known."

The princess had "chosen the only political role that suits her style; she does not act; she inspires those who would act; she does not make politics, she allows politics to go through her," and "in her salon, *she reigns but does not govern*."[54]

⁖⁗

Meanwhile a severe cold, rheumatism, and boils had been plaguing the prince for months. Still, he would escort the tsarevitch from Siberia to the Black Sea to inspect his patrimony, returning to the capital in November. Lieven then intended to meet his wife.

Instead, the tsarevitch set out on his grueling journey without his governor. Illness confined Lieven to his rooms. In May, north winds blew a colossal accumulation of ice onto the Neva, and blocked the canal beneath the beleaguered prince's windows. "The temperature and air match this moving glacier."[55] On the other side of Europe bright sunshine and gently blowing breezes bore the fragrance of horse chestnuts and azaleas into Dorothea's room as she sat up in bed with her window to the balcony open.

And despite eternal grief, she felt strong enough to cross the Channel to "that beautiful land, those laughing landscapes, everything I adored when I had my angels, what to do without them!"[56] The Sutherlands promised to arrange everything. Dorothea's friends rejoiced. She would be in London by July 1st; after two weeks Princess Lieven would head north to Howick and Scotland, then three months of country house visits.

Benckendorff saw nothing wrong in his sister's plan; nor did Lieven. Yet, "I have perhaps been wrong in not frankly admitting all I had to suffer for your" two stays in Paris. Lieven implored his wife not "to expose yourself, nor deliver me to the most dire results of a similar decision. Do not think I exaggerate, or write under some" influence. "Do not put yourself under any illusion," but "reflect on it calmly and seriously, I beg of you again."[57]

This thunderbolt broke Dorothea's fragile tranquility, her hands and knees shook.

"I am not strong; I think to be if my life runs gently, but not when my mind is agitated." The "mind of a reasonable being, and mine looks for logic and reason in everything, comes to a full stop in front of such baffling" persecution. "'Forget me and let me live in peace.' Good God my friend, this is not addressed to you; I need not say it to you. The only appeal I dare address to you is this: Do not forget how much you once felt alarmed."[58]

᠔᠓

Dorothea Lieven's bid for freedom exposed the taut fragility of her marriage. Always frustrated at his inability to control his intellectually superior spouse, Lieven now asserted his authority by refusing to admit her need to live in Paris. Dorothea had for years dammed her frustration at being dependent on an intellectually inferior mate; she submitted. Her tragedy, she now felt, entitled her to seek comfort where she could. This standoff eroded whatever remained of the intimacy, the emotional and mental bonds vital to a healthy evolution of the Lievens' marriage. Meanwhile, a new and not altogether unexpected element entered into the delicately calibrated equilibrium of their union.

21

"You Are Not Alone"

> Before embarking yesterday, I fell to my knees. I prayed to God. I had so
> often asked Him to let me die! Yesterday I begged Him to let me live, so
> that I may keep the heart I have found.[1]
>
> —Dorothea Lieven

The most promising man in public life naturally gravitated to Princess Lieven's
salon, and they met socially as well. Piercingly fine, large eyes dominated his sharp,
clever face with its full lips, Roman nose, and decided chin; he held his head and
shoulders high, to compensate for a lack of inches. At age fifty, twice-widowed
François Guizot stood on the brink of a brilliant career.

Born into a Protestant bourgeois family, Guizot lost his father to the guillotine
during the Revolution; his mother fled to Geneva with her children. François returned
to his native land to study law. The politically ambitious young man frequented the
Paris salons where his outstanding conversation drew notice. But Guizot's pen earned
him the modern history chair at the Sorbonne.

His faith in constitutional monarchy made Guizot's lectures the center of political opposition to the reactionary Restoration regime. King Louis-Philippe appointed
him minister of education.

"Yesterday I attended the finest possible spectacle; the debate between revolutionary democratic and conservative principles," Dorothea wrote her husband. Guizot
"had the best triumph imaginable. Never have I heard conservatism addressed with
such conviction" and "eloquence. He electrified the Chamber. One cannot conceive
of a more lively display, nor a more flattering moment for a man."[2] Guizot's impressive mind and principled political beliefs engaged the exacting princess; his proud,
upright character attracted her. And although he chose to show the world a stern,
aloof demeanor, a smile, albeit slight and rarely seen, revealed a sense of humor that
appealed to Dorothea's lively disposition.

Not until she had been living in Paris for well over a year did Dorothea Lieven
and François Guizot become more than mere acquaintances. Early in 1837 Guizot's
visits to Dorothea's salon stopped when his eldest son succumbed to a serious illness.

"Among all the expressions of sympathy you have received in the midst of such
great adversity excuse me for the vanity of thinking my compassion would mean

something to you? I have bought dearly the right to enter more than anyone else into your grief," the Princess commiserated. "I looked for villains when heaven so cruelly struck me. If your heart is searching in its turn, think of me who is one hundred times more unhappy than you, unhappy at the end of two years as I was on the first day and to whom God in the meantime has sent the strength to support his terrible decrees."[3]

Guizot's reply greatly moved Dorothea. Engraved in her thoughts, its words "do me good. There is indeed someone who understands my sorrow."[4] At this time of terrible anniversaries—the deaths of her boys—Dorothea sought both sympathy and distraction. "I dread and desire to see you. Tell me the day and hour you can come; I shall be sure to be at home, and alone." Their sadness seemed to form a bond between them. "Teach me to find strength in my heart. What charity that would be!"[5]

Guizot had not given her "time, or else I did not know how to take it," to say how his visit touched her. "I prize your company more than any" other. "You are a man, you are strong. Me I am weak, very weak. Excuse me for daring thus to talk to you about myself; but it seems to me that I inspire a little interest in you, come and show it to me more often."[6] He did.

Gravure de François Guizot par Louis Calamatta d'après le portrait de Paul Delaroche

Collection Particulière. Photo de François Louchet

François Guizot. Historian and statesman. Dorothea Lieven's third and last great love. Artist: Louis Calamatta. Private Collection.

On June 15th the former premier hosted an extremely select dinner party. Torchères illuminated the corners of his dining-room; its great crystal chandelier blazed. Clusters of candles shed warm light on white damask, shining silver, and fine porcelain; liveried footmen in white curled wigs offered tempting dishes. Dorothea and Guizot were seated next to each other. The lively princess seemed preoccupied, sadness lurked in her expressive dark eyes; indeed, her troubled mien deeply moved her neighbor. And no wonder. About to leave for London, she had just received Lieven's edict against returning to Paris for the third time. Dorothea and Guizot's conversation at that fateful dinner drew them much closer.

He: "We hardly knew each other," had only "caught a glimpse of each other." All "we did not know, all we did not say to each other, it seemed to us we already knew, we had said it to each other a thousand times."[7]

She: "You are not alone." Those words "sum up the rest of my life and were it to end today I bless you for granting me the sweetness of hearing them, because I believe you, I need to believe you."[8]

Nine days later a mutual acquaintance invited some friends to Châtenay, her country estate. Guizot and the princess walked on graveled paths meandering among flowerbeds whose brightly colored blossoms scented the soft summer air, strolled around manicured lawns and through shady groves, and sat together on a stone bench under the spreading limbs of a sturdy old tree.

"You of such a grand nature, such an elevated, agreeable mind, such an alive heart, such a passionate and gentle character! You came to where I am, in mourning, desolate," searching "in your pain for a little comfort, in your boredom for a little distraction," a "superior being forever sad, alone. And one day, you let me see, told me I would comfort you, I would raise you again, you would love me, you do love me, and we would once more find, you and I, I and you, the intimacy, the happiness that surpasses, that dominates everything on earth."[9]

As a full moon sailed regally across the sapphire sky, Princess Lieven's carriage conveyed them back to Paris. She and Guizot pledged "eternal union."

೫୦ଓଃ

Princess Lieven left for London on a golden July morning. En route to the coast she devoured some letters Guizot had sent: his correspondence with his wives. Dorothea looked for history, what she had been doing on that particular day; she looked for romance; it affected her deeply. Indeed, Dorothea felt a full range of emotions. "They were not always sweet. Oh! My God, how few brains I have besides those minds. I am rather embarrassed. Then I tell myself other things count, and I am reassured."[10]

While awaiting a favorable tide Dorothea opened a letter from Lieven which had been lining her pocket since Paris. "I feel myself very sad today, I have never felt so sad,"[11] her husband had written on June 15th, the day full of meaning for Dorothea and François. Lieven's words threw his wife's emotions into terrible turmoil. She already had powerful motives for returning to Paris before June 15th added another. Yet, duty demanded that Dorothea submit to her husband.

I am impatient to place the sea between myself and France. I hope to recover a little peace in England. I have great need of it. I seem to have a fever. Oh! ... [how] I want to speak to you, to listen to you! You would return order to my mind. It has such ideas! So much sadness, so much joy, so much doubt about my future! It is in chaos, my heart cannot cope. It is so full, so full.[12]

Splendid weather and calm seas favored the princess. Walking on deck she watched "that white line which my eye saw almost up to the moment of entering Dover." When "they told me we were arriving, I turned to the other side and my eyes filled with tears. This island where I felt happy for so long, such a clear, gentle, serene happiness." Britain's border officials welcomed Princess Lieven. After dining at Dover she stopped merely to change horses; the coaching-inns greeted her with fruit and flowers. "Only verse lacked," but "John Bull would not do that!"[13]

All Dorothea's Whig friends had gathered for a grand welcome dinner at London's answer to Versailles, but Big Ben had already chimed eleven times before her mud-spattered carriage drew up in front of the duke of Sutherland's regal residence. So only the duke and duchess, and Paul Lieven were on hand. Completely bowled over by the emotion of the moment Dorothea entered Stafford House. Stepping through the classical hall with its marbled walls and Corinthian columns, she ascended the magnificent rectangular staircase, and "embraced the Duke, thinking to embrace my son, my limbs did not support me. The fatigue, the beating of my heart on entering London, everything that fills my heart, all of it stunned me."[14] Another time, admonished Guizot, "do not take anybody for your son."[15]

After a good laugh, a good chat, and some supper the Sutherlands escorted Dorothea to her apartment—drawing-room, bedroom, and dressing room. When Paul at last left his mother, her chaotic heart allowed her little sleep. Next morning Dorothea barely wrote François about her journey, because she dared not succumb "to the sweetness of describing my emotions. It would carry me away, bewilder me, I would not know where to stop; I would say too little, I would say too much."[16]

഼ഓ

The Whig Sutherlands hosted a splendid Tory dinner in Princess Lieven's honor. She and the duke of Wellington plunged into an orgy of reminiscences on a subject dear to them both: the court of King George IV. Lord Aberdeen glued himself to her side. Dorothea told him she had opened Milton (because Guizot had quoted him) and recited the lines to Aberdeen. They "put him in absolute rapture. I did not think of him while saying them, doubtless he did not think of me while hearing them.

"God is thy law—thou mine."

Aberdeen found this more beautiful:

"He for God only, she for God in him."[17]

Dorothea liked the second idea of this verse, but was less happy with the first—the woman would have nothing while giving up everything. Did Guizot agree? Yes.

Soon, her churning emotions and menopausal condition chafed each other into illness. After another serious hemorrhage Dorothea declined several grand dinners. They were too tiring; one rarely sat down to eat before nine o'clock. She had attended such a dinner one month to the day after June 15th. "It was warm, I asked to have the window open. A beautiful moon, very round, very clear, caused me abominable distractions." Please, the princess implored Guizot, "excuse me the moon."[18]

She now received only a few close friends. Lord Grey called daily. Lord Aberdeen and the princess had always liked each other; no more than that, she assured Guizot. She could talk to Aberdeen as she could to him, although it needed greater effort, because Aberdeen hated speaking of his calamities. He had been

> very happy in his life, happy as you were. He lost everything: two wives, four children, each at the age of sixteen. He is a walking tragedy. My trials have enlarged the taste he always had in my company, for the unhappy find each other.... [This] preface is to reach what you have guessed. I recognize in Lord Aberdeen the same symptoms that, during the last few months, I have been surprised to find in myself.[19]

Aberdeen now knew that Dorothea did not stand "alone in the world, that a noble heart has accepted the mission of consoling mine." He received this confidence like "a typical Englishman; a few trivial words, a very strong handshake as usual, and he left me."[20]

Next day Aberdeen requested a few minutes in private, asked to speak in English rather than French, to assure that he make himself clearly understood. Afraid

Dorothea had mistaken his silence, he wanted her to know of his strong affection, his deep feeling for her; nobody could comprehend and partake in her trials as he could. Happy to think her sorrows soothed, he begged Dorothea not to forget him. His traveling carriage stood at the door; before he left for his Scottish acres Aberdeen had one request: "to kiss my hand for the first time in his life." He took Dorothea's hand, kept it for a moment and left. What "singular providence made the 15th of June and decided the fate of my life."[21]

The princess supposed Aberdeen would be foreign secretary if the Tories returned to power. She knew he and Guizot would get along. Both basically serious, both having suffered the death of dear ones, both believing in constitutional monarchy based on conservative principles like limited suffrage, each man stood firmly in favor of upholding the highest standards in public life.

So far Guizot's political focus had been purely domestic. His relationship with Dorothea Lieven would now inevitably pique his interest in foreign policy, a development the princess fostered for her own sake as well as for that of her ambitious lover; he would never become a statesman without foreign affairs experience. So Dorothea "introduced" Aberdeen and Guizot by sending Aberdeen extracts from Guizot's letters. Were Aberdeen ever again to hold office, he wrote Dorothea, he would like to work with Guizot, "a man who would inspire confidence, and whom I could truly respect."[22]

৪০৫৪

Meanwhile, horrible doubt. "What have I done with my reason, with my dignity, with the little intelligence I thought I had? Everything seems to have left me at once. I completely gave in to a few moments of happiness, it was too much, too sudden; it must have turned my head." Dorothea had fled from François "thinking to recover a little calm, to get used to my joy, and, indeed, I saw in your letters what to do in the face of my harrowing memories, and to support a parting that cost me more than I showed. All this proved true for eight days, eight days only, but your letters were there. I have had no" more. "Are you suffering" too? "Why have you not found a way to end these tortures we endure? I say *we*; am I wrong?"[23]

Their daily letters took advantage of the "four envelopes" method Dorothea had learned from Metternich and, thanks to Harriet Granville, crossed the Channel in the relative security of England's diplomatic pouch. But the French post had been slow to carry Dorothea's letters from Paris to Guizot's country residence.* Assuming that the attentions of her English friends, especially Aberdeen, had weakened Dorothea's interest in him, François stopped writing. When his lover's letters did finally reach him he "reread twenty times those words full of imagination, for you so sad, for me so tender." Begging her to forgive his egotistical joy, François fervently thanked Dorothea for having relieved him about Aberdeen. Even before her departure that name caused him the most concern. Dorothea simply could not conceive of her attraction for a sad and serious man. "In your look, your tone, in those conversations where your lofty intelligence, so simple, so free, your soul so proudly moved, so sensitive to great things, so uncaring of small ones, full of so much sympathy and so much disdain, blaze with such dignity and abandon!"[24]

Guizot always spent summer and autumn with his family (his three young children and indomitable if cantankerous mother, who ran his household) at his country house, Val-Richer, in Calvados.

As she sat tête-à-tête with Wellington the princess suddenly felt a small piece of paper slipped between her hands. Her attention vanished, if not her tact; the duke stayed for another hour. At last, at last she could "read, I kissed. I still suffocate, with joy and complete pleasure." Overcome with jubilation, "I die of anger or I die of joy. I am a very frail creature. Why so much soul, so much passion in such a feeble body"? Dorothea "reread a thousand times these so sweet and piercing words. You asked me to forgive the worry you caused me? Oh! You can truly see that these torments are worth happiness to me! I love my torments, I love my joys, because all of them come from you."[25]

℮Ↄ

There remained Prince Lieven. In a letter his colleague Count Orlov (on a special mission to England) hand-delivered, the prince told his wife that instead of joining the tsarevitch on his six month tour throughout the length and breadth of Russia, Lieven's various ailments had brought him to ask Orlov to petition Tsar Nicholas on his behalf for sick leave. So by the time Dorothea read his letter, Lieven would be making his way to Marienbad, the Bohemian spa famous for relieving kidney disorders. Then the prince would go to nearby Ischl to see if salt baths could cure the boils that had been bothering him for months. In late September he would be free to meet his wife, but probably not in France. The prince would proceed to Italy to choose winter quarters for his charge and himself. Dorothea knew Rome. She detested Naples. "You do not generally like journeys, perhaps today you will prove to me otherwise, prove also all I hold most dear simply for myself."[26]

"What a different welcome I would have given this letter two months ago!" Why, "at the start of my new life does M. de Lieven, who must naturally return to Siberia, at the end of the earth, draw closer," why does "his desire to see me grow stronger now than during our two years of separation!" Although her thoughts made Dorothea sad, even contrite, she felt no need to elaborate on the subject because François understood her perfectly. "Another life has begun for me, a life that does not erase my sorrows, but makes me forget, makes me no longer understand that old life."[27]

Her husband and brother had hardly proved themselves sympathetic to Dorothea's need to live in Paris. Orlov had brains and stood close to the tsar; besides, he enjoyed as much so-called freedom as Russia allowed. So Dorothea invited him to stately Stafford House. As warm sun streamed in at her parlor windows, the butler poured wine from a cut-glass decanter and handed freshly-baked biscuits. Then, when he had discreetly shut the door behind him, Princess Lieven got down to business. Her frail health absolutely prevented her from going on any long journey to meet Lieven; even the short one to London had made her ill. Orlov knew exactly what she meant. Never had the princess "left a negotiation as well satisfied as I was with that one."[28] They agreed that she would listen to Orlov, not her husband. "That is novel but that is how it is." She would at once "return to the place that pleases me."[29]

Dorothea Lieven had traversed a long and bumpy road since wrestling, during her early passion for Metternich, with disloyalty to her husband. She must now arrange to meet him. Orlov chose Dieppe, the fashionable Normandy seaside resort. Since Lieven had asked Orlov to petition the tsar to grant him leave, Dorothea felt sure, she impressed on her spouse, that he would agree to Dieppe. Orlov had seen her state of health, how she had lost weight and deteriorated since coming to London. Orlov knew the life she led in Paris; indeed, he could not "conceive of any other for me even though my separation from you must continue because he finds me absolutely authorized according to the terms"[30] of the tsar's words cited verbatim in Alexander Benckendorff's letter. Since ill health forced Dorothea to cancel her country house visits and return to France immediately, they should meet there. Dieppe or Le Havre would fit into Lieven's itinerary. His wife awaited his "orders. North or South of Paris? and when?"[31]

Orlov interrupted. He came to say goodbye. Dorothea declared herself, as well she might, "very pleased with him." Then, putting Lieven plainly on notice: "We are close as well, and closer than ever so I embraced him a little."[32]

⁎⁎⁎

Some three weeks after she landed in England, Princess Lieven's son Paul and her friend Lady Cowper escorted her to Dover. Dorothea had always appreciated the practicality permeating Emily's charm and social sophistication. As the ladies sat in a private parlor sipping coffee while they awaited embarkation, Emily earnestly advised her friend to give up Guizot so as to avoid aggravating any further Lieven's fury at her return to Paris.

An extremely choppy Channel followed by another severe hemorrhage kept Dorothea at Boulogne for five days. She agonized over what kind of welcome to give Lieven. For two and a half years she had shown "the most tender wish to be reunited with him," had most sincerely begged him to come. Those "are the thoughts that kill me!"[33]

In Paris the princess resumed her agreeable routine—with a difference. "My strength is returning. The pleasure I find in this is to be able to tell you so. Last evening was cool; I like that better than heat." On returning from her walk, Dorothea "sat down at the piano; I found much Rossini in my head; I think this would suit you."[34]

Dorothea Lieven had fallen in love for the third and last time. Paris now meant a profoundly fulfilling blend of politics and passion: independent power through her salon, personal happiness with François Guizot. His and Dorothea Lieven's "eternal union" would not be unique *in* Paris, but it would be unique *to* Paris.

She had found a man who matched her intellectually, and who satisfied her craving for intimate, tender, quasi-maternal love. Now as never before, she needed a man who would nurture, guide, and support her through thick and thin.

She: "You were wrong to tell me to stay as I am—instead, encourage me to become more moderate, more patient, to deliver myself less to fleeting impulse, to play more peacefully with the happiness Heaven has sent me, to resign myself to inevitable irritations. I reason with myself admirably, I think myself certain of my action, and five minutes later, I shipwreck myself. Help me, guide me."[35]

He: "You are tired, very tired. Lean on me. I too, I am often tired, more often than I say; and I need to lean on you, need at least to be sure I can if fatigue weighs too heavily on me. Yes, I need you."[36]

To feel needed. Dorothea Lieven's sons led independent lives. Her young children were dead. Her husband's pleasure in his position at court proved his ability to get along admirably without her. Dorothea's union with François gave her a gratifying outlet for her maternal instincts and, above all, made her feel that she mattered.

> I see not only what is there, but everything going on with you when you write, if your hand is shaking, if your heart is beating, if your aspect is troubled or calm, your mood lively or sad. And without thinking about it I reply less to what you say than to what I see in your writing, in your words.... [When] we returned from Châtenay, I was near you, I was speaking to you, you were speaking to me. I did not look at the sky, the moon, the valley. I did not ask them to complete my happiness. It was complete, immense.[37]

Dorothea Lieven had chosen well. François Guizot understood her better than any previous beloved. "I defy you to invent in your mind, to find in your woman's heart, something I do not understand."[38] Passion enveloped their relationship, politics informed it. Nevertheless, this dutiful daughter of loyal Baltic Barons broke with tradition. She did not submit to her husband. The princess returned to Paris for the third time.

22

"Make Her Obey"

You, the simple sight of you brightens my whole being, your least word charms me, and the memory of your words, only the memory plunges me into ecstasy, you cannot sate me; it is not in your power to quench me, to fill my soul. All of you ravishes it.... I aspire with endless passion to this profuse joy that comes from you, that each time it comes, promises me more than it has yet given and inspires yet more unsatisfied desires.[1]

—François Guizot

Good God, what a letter! I have reread it, I will reread it every day until the end of my life; yes, every day. It occupies a place nothing has yet occupied. It will always be there, near me, on me, on this heart, to which it reveals the joys of paradise.[2]

—Dorothea Lieven

Princess Lieven's recovery, in late summer 1837, from her London journey soon sustained a jolt. The prince faced his wife's defiance with a fiat: leave Paris forthwith. It made her "physically ill because all upset is risky for me now. It made me morally ill which is even worse, for I found my husband" basically "ready to sacrifice his wife to the Court's pleasure. That is not the elevated ethical character I knew in happier times."[3]

As an adolescent bride during the harrowing weeks leading up to Tsar Paul's assassination, Dorothea had watched while Lieven "willingly" extended his convalescence to escape unwelcome duties. Pleading ill health, she now refused to leave Paris and sent her husband a new medical testimonial.[4] Princess Lieven's Paris physician prescribed complete mental and physical rest; he specifically forbad travel.

The princess felt perfectly justified. She had always done her matrimonial duty. Lieven must do his: provide support and comfort. And although Dorothea had begun her bold bid to live her life as she chose before ever François Guizot entered it, his presence strengthened her resolve to stay in Paris.

Sitting in her green armchair at the window of her parlor overlooking the Tuileries Garden, the princess pored over the poignant words Guizot penned so precisely on large leaves of cream-colored letter paper. She dreaded lest her dejection over the stand-off with Lieven try her lover's patience. That showed a miserable pattern, François replied, "of seeing love hesitate, recoil, hide or flee in front of duress, fury, a serious obstacle, great ennui, political interest." His and Dorothea's love "truly meant *for better or for worse*."[5]

To Dorothea's delight, Guizot briefly deserted his country residence. "Do you know how Calvin's austere disciple wants to advance himself? Do you know what the great orator did during his few days in Paris?" asked *Le Temps* on September 18th. "He was in love" with "a very seductive person, very clever, influential, and very well known, a lady of rank, a princess," a real "power in diplomacy." Despite "the beloved one's charms, which would explain the Puritan doctrinaire's fondness as fully inspired by her eyes, I regret to destroy perhaps an illusion, his love is like a political ploy. Yet, despite all he seems to be enjoying his role of *cicisbeo* to his chancellery goddess. She had a little illness." He "spent all his days seated at the bedside of the beautiful convalescent." This "ardor has changed all the lover's foreign policy views."[6]

Princess Lieven dreaded the repercussions, as well she might. Tsar Nicholas would be furious that Guizot's rivals entangled her in their schemes. In Russia she stood as "the first lady because of my rank, because of my position at the Palace, and even more" because she belonged to the imperial family. Hence the tsar's wrath "at seeing this country of revolution *honored* by my presence." François must not dare to laugh, as Dorothea had "a great desire to do, it is in deadly earnest."[7]

It was. The article confirmed rumors that had reached Prince Lieven, and stirred his ready jealousy into a frenzy. His wife's liaison with a Frenchman, a mere bourgeois at that, prominent in a polity the tsar spurned, a legislature the tsar loathed, punctured the prince's pride where it mattered most: his position at court. Lieven tore up Dorothea's medical testimonial unread, flew into a rage at the mere mention of her presence in Paris. He damned the idea of meeting at Dieppe, refused to set foot in France. The prince urged Dorothea to consider her duties as a wife and mother, to reflect that her defiance would jeopardize her precious social status, her future. "Let me know at once if you intend" to "meet me or not." Lieven would be held "answerable for the decisions I must make as a result." Were Dorothea to delay, "I must make a decision, no matter how distasteful."[8]

> I was fourteen when I married him, he is twelve years older than me, he quite naturally became my master because I was little more than a child. I very soon sensed the advantage I have over him; but that first impression stayed, and I tremble, yes, I tremble when I receive these letters.[9]

"If you decline my invitation, I will find myself forced, in duty, to deny you all financial support," Lieven threatened on October 1. "If I have no reply within three weeks, I shall be obliged to act as if that is your refusal."[10]

Two weeks later François returned from the country. What blissful relief to discuss her dilemma with him. Dorothea decided to ask two powerful men—chancellor Count Nesselrode, always her friend, and Count Orlov, her recent ally—to intercede.

If in eight days, the princess wrote Orlov, she had not left Paris to meet her husband, he would cut her off without a penny.

> That is the extreme to which he has taken his pledge to the Tsar to force me to leave France at any price, for his letters leave me in no doubt that he must account to the Tsar for decisions he makes about me. My letters and the doctors' opinions have reached him; clearly he wants me to leave, dead or alive.[11]

Lieven "must have construed the Tsar's vague word as absolute." In a brief error of judgment his strong sense of duty made him try to coerce "my submission in an exceedingly clumsy way very unseemly to me, very unseemly to the Tsar." No,

Nicholas could not have "sunk so far as to command my husband to such conduct towards his wife." The tsar "would not be the cause of discord in a household united for thirty-seven years."[12]

"My words are disbelieved; the doctor's testimonial insufficient"; thus, "today I claim my right" to ask "a capable expert here to assure himself of the accuracy of my assertions."

> If it is sworn that I am not in a state to leave, I ask the Tsar's protection; I ask him to make my husband understand his mistake in thinking to please the Tsar by casting his wife into the dilemma of risking her life by leaving, or enduring misery by staying. In any case, I accept this as a last resort.*

"The world cannot understand such an inexplicable act. As for me, I am not an obscure person. I live under the eyes of my friends, and you know that I have them. They seek reasons at the highest level for the persecution they see overwhelming me."[13]†

Dorothea underlined the power of public opinion to her brother. He had, moreover, always been exactly what she expressed in that "crushing moment when I got into the carriage to follow the coffin of one of my children, and to precede the other.... You have been for me a father, a brother, a husband. You always will be, won't you?"[14] She recalled when their minds moved in tandem, when Alexander vowed: "'if ever your husband threatens you, refer him to me; I am there to protect you.' The moment has come! protect me!"[15] But Alexander absolutely failed to comprehend, indeed took personally, his sister's rejection of Russia. And she "should not be surprised if after so many years of superiority over him, your husband revenges himself."[16]

> If it is true that I am superior to my husband, can I help it? For many years I have used this superiority in his service. It has been exceptionally advantageous for him, and now that it no longer helps him he has decided to punish me.... I have nothing with which to reproach myself vis-à-vis my husband.[17]

Helping her husband in his career had, after all, been part of her wifely duty, a duty she had done well. Yes, she had had lovers, but she played by the rules; always discreet, she had respected the sanctity of the family, had borne Lieven sons to carry on his name. Now, his turn had come. How could her husband, the man of honor, the gentleman, the father of her children write her such letters. "I examined your position, mine; my reason rejected it; my heart instantly denied believing you capable of the other brutality you threaten."[18] Dorothea could not judge what went on between Lieven and his master since the prince told her nothing; had the threat of Siberia, or property confiscation forced Lieven to such conduct? Regardless, Dorothea would stay in Paris for she felt too infirm to leave. The tragic loss of her children, her frail health entitled her to find comfort where she could. Lieven must support her decision, must allow her the means to afford her customary lifestyle as his wife. "I never thought that after 37 years of union you could put your wife in need, & I blame the Tsar for your threat."[19]

---

*Although not untypical, Dorothea's tact, let alone her logic, must have owed something to fear that the tsar would confiscate her considerable (close to $1,000,000) assets in Russia.
†This veiled threat would resonate. Sophisticated Europeans still thought Russians little better than barbarians who assassinated their tsars, committed unspeakable brutalities in battle and, generally, could barely comport themselves in civilized society.

ഇഗ

Late one evening, as autumn rain fell with bleak resolve, the princess's butler announced Prince Lieven. Dorothea's heart dropped. Her son Alexander entered. Having met his father at Baden-Baden, he brought Lieven's final word. "It is up to you!" thundered the prince. "Paris reduces me to using this language! So remove yourself from there."[20]

How awful for Alexander to be "caught between father and mother in such a thorny situation,"[21] to have to report Tsar Nicholas's words. "'Your wife hurts my honor and my dignity, she alone ever dared defy my authority. Make her obey, if you fail, I myself will reduce her to dust.'"[22]

Prince Lieven greeted 1838 by ordering his banker to stop all payments.

Princess Lieven's independent means* allowed her to hold out. And her letter to Orlov, not to mention her warning to Benckendorff about public opinion, bore fruit. Tsar Nicholas left Dorothea's Russian assets alone.

After a three month hiatus Prince Lieven, wintering with the tsarevitch at Naples, again took up his pen. Agreeing with his wife's words: "'Let us no longer speak about this black cloud hovering between us; let us no longer speak of the past,'" the prince admitted his keen interest in her health, to say nothing of his fault in ignoring it, but warned against "getting used to the idea that one can only live healthily in Paris. That is the illness I gravely doubt."[23] Dorothea should seriously consider spending her winters in warm, sunny Naples. There the Lievens could combine Italian luxury and English comfort in a custom built house. Duty and desire would, naturally, draw the prince to St. Petersburg in summer; Dorothea could accompany him or visit spas, even England.

"What on earth would you find to do in Italy?" cried a habitué of Princess Lieven's salon. "You could ask no one to give you news except the Apollo Belvedere, and if he refused you would say, 'Wretch, away with you!' This sally made everyone laugh including"[24] the princess.

Nonetheless, she wandered in a wilderness of worry over her future. "I feel like crying twenty times" a day. "Where shall I find courage?"[25] Lieven's "neglect, his weakness, the Tsar's cruelty, all this throws terror into my soul, despair."[26] Dorothea asked her husband to reflect "on intimacy, on tenderness up to the day you took your order from the Tsar and let a higher wish interfere in our relations!" Lieven had, in his own hand, written Alexander Benckendorff that he had no objection to Dorothea living in Paris. "Only in submission to the Tsar's order did you start to take a course towards me that I will not let myself describe because my wording in truth could only hurt you." Dorothea begged her husband to end their stand-off: "tell me where I am or where we are."[27] Silence.

ഇഗ

Meanwhile, she thought it high time to move out of her furnished apartment, to create her own home. Guizot's man of business found three possible houses each with a pretty garden, in a fashionable section of the Left Bank.

The area may have been suitable as far as aristocratic neighbors went, but the

---

*Besides her Russian assets the Princess had almost $500,000 in England.

princess had no intention of removing herself from the center of politics. "At times my thoughts seek you with infinitely more affection than other times," she wrote Guizot. "Yesterday you occupied me more than usual. You were not there for me to tell you. I had no pen or paper to write you. My vivid impressions were lost for you. We must be together, always together, then nothing would be lost. I had a lovely time on a charming walk yesterday, but alone, all alone, that is so sad! In the wood I admired unrivaled spider webs. What wonderful work. But the spider is also alone in the midst of this superb web"; he "likes to be alone. I do not."[28] Life in a house and garden with François would please Dorothea, but not alone.

At the same time "M. de Talleyrand is failing visibly; he feels it too, and it makes him very melancholy," Dorothea wrote her faithful old friend Lord Grey. "I go and see him almost every day, for it keeps him amused."[29] After Talleyrand's death his heirs sold his splendid mansion located at the heart of Paris, a mere step from the major embassies and seat of government, to James Rothschild, founder of the French branch of Europe's famous banking family.* When Dorothea heard that Rothschild planned to convert 2, rue St. Florentin, into the most popular form of dwelling in Paris, she began negotiations for a long-term lease on prime space—the corner mezzanine apartment.

Princess Lieven's visitors entered a handsomely proportioned hall topped with a painted dome. Wide marble steps bounded by a black and gold banister led to the mezzanine floor. Splendid marble statues graced the stairwell, the whole hall strongly reminiscent of St. Petersburg's palaces. But then the Hôtel Talleyrand typified the eighteenth century architecture that Peter the Great chose for his capital.

A dignified butler greeted the princess's guests in a generous foyer; he bowed them into either her private parlor with its delicately painted wall panels, or the grand drawing-room with its big corner sofa facing the window, and cozy clusters of couches, chairs, and occasional tables where, each evening, Dorothea held her salon. This spacious, square corner room, like all others in the apartment, had intricately inlaid parquet floors, gilded ceiling moldings, a handsome marble fireplace, and a mirror stretching from mantelpiece to ceiling and spanning the width of the fireplace. Shimmering chandeliers and wall sconces lit the rooms all of whose large windows overlooked the Tuileries Garden and the Place de la Concorde. Princess Lieven's bedroom (formerly Talleyrand's library), dressing-room, and guest room occupied the other corner of her apartment. In between stood the dining-room and small parlor. A corridor separated these rooms from the servants' quarters and kitchen.

❧

With the arrival of warm weather Princess Lieven's intimates, including Guizot, forsook Paris for the country. Her medical testimonial forbad travel. For the first time in her life Dorothea felt utterly alone. Even after she and Lieven parted at the Prussian border, he had been a presence, albeit in the background. Her husband's silence now made Dorothea feel truly abandoned.

Yes, both she and François were "sad, very sad. But I much more than you. You have children to bring up, you have your country, you have public duties, a great career in front of you." He should think of all she had lost.

After World War Two, the Rothschilds sold the Hôtel Talleyrand to the United States. It now houses the American embassy.

When I am next to you I am less gloomy, sometimes even forget my miseries. But when I am face-to-face with myself, alone! Oh! How terrible. I feel it all the more because I see no end to this awful [situation].... My heart is so full of love, of gratitude but again, I have lost too much, too much, and where I should expect support and solace only ice and severity confront me.[30]

Dorothea's desolation deepened as her state of limbo dragged on. At night everything seemed so much worse. After the oppressive heat broke, Dorothea took long walks in the leafy shade of her favorite Bois de Boulogne, hoping vigorous exercise would induce sleep. It did not. She started to menstruate heavily. Everything tired the poorly princess. Then the question of money raised its ugly head. True, Dorothea had private means, but how long could she, must she hold out. "And the dreadful, ever-present idea of economies naturally makes me tremble. Is it possible?"[31]

Desperate, Dorothea begged François for advice. The more he thought about it, the more he believed she should meet Lieven at Baden. Dorothea had "done all that could be done from afar and by writing." Evidently she would "not resolve this bad situation except by seeing and speaking yourself." So Dorothea must steel herself "to go on the attack."[32]

You send me to Baden very lightly. You forget everything. You even forget I cannot budge; that officially at least that is established.... [All] the past will be like a comedy if I make this journey. You forget that once out of France I could not return. You know that perfectly, you have told me so a hundred times. And you send me to Baden!

You are bored with me, want to get rid of me. I am not all that I seemed to you at first.... [At] the bottom of my heart is sadness, eternal sadness, sadness that had been covered with wonder, the joy of having found you. Time will naturally erase the first of these feelings. The second lasts, but more calmly, because it is more permanent. There is indeed in my heart sadness and you. That is the truth.

The fact is moreover that I have burdened you a little, that for you as for me, you would be very easy were I relieved of my present woes, that you advise Baden as a possible means ... [if it fails,] you need no longer listen to my complaints, put up with my faults.

And note well, I do not reproach you, I find you are right, a little right.... I love you more than I say. I excuse you, you, from the bottom of my heart. I remember with tender gratitude your constant kindness, I humbly recognize and regret my vivacity, my whims. I imagine that sometimes I bore you, but I cannot imagine your ceasing to love me.

My heart is very attached to you, my mind is very submissive to your mind, if I lose you, I have nothing left.... You give me the only joy I can have here below, the perfect intimacy of thoughts, of the heart, you want to subject me to losing them?[33]

"Since June 15, my mind and heart have not left you for one minute," answered François after he allowed a good night's sleep to temper the fury of his first reaction.

You entered, and entered with infinite charm, into the utmost recesses of my soul. You gratified ... [me] in all I have in me that is most private, most demanding, most insatiable, ... [and that] I revealed to you. And you exposed it all to your emotions, to your perception, to your words, in seeing you reborn and reviving, and unfolding, in front of my love, your beautiful nature rejuvenated, I flattered myself that I restored you, and I in turn received from you, not only joy, but a great rapture capable of satisfying two wounded souls for life.[34]

Having lived with dry and fickle hearts Dorothea doubted true affection. François showed her the trust inherent in her nature, made her find in him "what you had not found anywhere but in yourself."[35]

If these words failed to soothe a troubled soul, the next satisfied a longing as old as Dorothea's engagement when, at age fourteen, she promised to submit to Lieven.

> What are you saying [,that] your mind is very submissive to my mind? Is it your submission I want? I scorn submission, I scorn every trait, every act of inferiority. I am only happy in equality. I want an equal nature as well as an equal affection. I want to live at the same level and in full liberty with the one I love. I want to feel at the same time her independence and her union with me, her dignity and her abandon.[36]

೮೦೦೪

In the cruel, cold light of a cloudy October morning the princess sat comfortably in bed; as usual, her personal maid brought a tray laden with breakfast and the early mail. Dorothea sifted through her letters. She snatched an envelope she had addressed to her son Constantine. It returned from America with the word "dead" scrawled across. Heartbroken at Constantine's banishment two years before, distraught over the cause for Lieven's draconian act (Constantine's compulsive drinking and gambling), Dorothea felt that despite his sins, Constantine remained her child. So she had continued to correspond with him. Constantine had died in June;[37] by July the news reached Lieven. He did not tell his wife.

"To think of poor, poor Constantine, so ill-used, so deserted during his life, and disowned by his father after his death,"[38] Dorothea mourned to her devoted Grey. "Overwhelmed by news of a fresh sorrow," the grieving mother did not even know where and how this son had died. Lieven "left *me* in total ignorance"; apparently he wanted "me to learn it in the brutal manner I have just done! He thought neither of his wife nor of his"[39] children. "What a sorry spectacle for my sons, and how they will feel it!"[40]

All summer long the prince had enjoyed Continental society. No one "ever noticed in his demeanor or dress the slightest mark of mourning. And then to *me*, the boy's mother, he does not write, because I am out of favor at Court." Russia "is indeed a horrible country when a man must thus abdicate all natural sentiments, and shrink in fulfilling the most common and sacred duties of life,"[41] the proud patriot confided to Grey in the midst of her profound maternal sorrow.

Princess Lieven's Parisian friends, particularly Lady Granville, proved fantastic, Dorothea wrote Emily. Intimately acquainted with her friend's private concerns, Harriet realized that this latest hardship provided a chance to help. She felt

> that a man incapable of any normal feeling, of any reverence for God, must still value the respect of his fellow-men. She has thus written to ask those of my friends who are in Italy & who are going to spend the winter with my husband, to show in their behavior their opinion of him and me, and by overwhelming him with proof of their interest in me, proof of my grief, to force him so to speak to show some interest in me, and make him understand that decency at least mandates a change in his manner towards me.[42]

Emily jumped at the chance to join in her friend's defense, but Dorothea wanted to wait until Lieven answered a missive of similar ilk that the duchess of Dino had dispatched. Among other items it informed Lieven that his wife knew about Constantine.

"What people were saying" had the desired effect. However, far from showing grief, Lieven's crude letter invited his sorrowing spouse to rejoice with him in a happy release!

Some weeks later Dorothea received a letter from her son Alexander, who had joined his father and the tsarevitch at Rome. Lieven had "definitely decided to come to Paris as soon as possible after the Tsarevitch's European tour, and to spend the winter there." This gave Dorothea "the first contented moment in many years, and above all in the past year and a half! These eighteen months have been very sad, very painful in every possible way! But finally I can forget the pain. I want to forget it all, and deliver myself to the prospect of happiness at having you near me." In the meantime "I urge you to write."[43]

"We are about to arrive at the age when one thinks of the last act of the Drama," Lieven wrote, but did not send his letter.* "The gift of insight that you have in a high degree releases me from a long and hurtful explanation which probably would neither interest nor satisfy you." When they met, husband and wife must ignore external influences and resolve the question: "Is it together? Is it apart that we go through this last act?"[44]

Although many husbands turned a blind eye to their wives' liaisons, Dorothea could scarcely expect the jealous prince to develop into a complaisant husband at this stage; nor, given his master's prejudice, would he be likely to settle in Paris. She, on the other hand, would not give up her home, her political power, or her "eternal union" with Guizot. So Dorothea doubtless counted on Lieven's loyalty to the fabric of their marriage, his dread of scandal, and her powers of persuasion to cajole him into maintaining the façade of their union while they spent much of the year apart.

On January 16, 1839, the princess received another letter from Alexander. His father had fallen ill.[45] Dorothea instantly expressed her concern and reiterated her desire for a reunion. She promised to write regularly—Alexander had mentioned his father's pleasure in her letters. And Dorothea thanked her husband for reinstating her allowance. Meanwhile, Prince Christopher Lieven died suddenly on the 10th.

୫୬୯୦

"She feels it—naturally deeply—just as you knew her to be, and much more than those who do not see her in these moments, when all is laid open, would ever believe her" capable of, Harriet Granville wrote her brother. "Tenderness for whatever called for it in the past, forgetfulness of every cloud, on her knees with torrents of tears, hoping" she had "not often given pain, failed in kindness."[46] To protect her friend from prying eyes, Harriet carried Dorothea off to the British embassy where a calm courtyard isolated the honey-colored house from city noise.

"My insides are being torn out of me," Dorothea wrote her compassionate friend Aberdeen. "I have known the most bitter sufferings of life." The deaths of her boys were still "the most vivid, the most harrowing, the most frightful memory, just as on the first day!" This new blow made Dorothea "cry with less bitterness, but I cry sincerely. We traveled through life together, I did not know it except with him—married at fourteen years, thirty-eight years of union. The joys, the pains of life, we shared everything."[47]

Lieven kept the letter among his private papers; Dorothea received it after his death.

In spring her two surviving sons set off for Russia to settle their father's estate. The tsar received Paul and Alexander as members of his own family, but not once did the Autocrat mention Dorothea. "It is as though I were dead. So much for my expectations!"[48] she confided to Grey. There would be no pension for Prince Lieven's widow.

Moreover, the prince left no will. He had, on the other hand, told Dorothea and their sons that he meant to leave her the money he had in England.* English law made the widow sole heir if no will existed. But it turned out that capital belonging to a deceased Russian came under Russian law; all heirs inherited. Dorothea regretted this, "less for the affluence it would have given me than for a reason to hold on to some of my illusions!"[49]

Lieven had failed to provide for his wife. Rich, no longer young, exposed over a long period to the hazards of travel, the punctilious prince, moreover, hardly had robust health. He knew Russian law would make outright disinheritance difficult; and such a dire step would create a huge scandal. As well, Lieven realized that influence, rather than legal precedent, ruled Russia's judicial system. His wife did not enjoy court favor; his sons did. Thus, intestacy. It curtailed his widow's inheritance without incurring dishonor, not to speak of society's censure. Jealousy had added fuel to the fury of that revenge which her husband exacted for Dorothea's years of "superiority" over him.

Worst of all, Lieven's intestacy pitted the princess against her sons. The eldest asked his mother for her power of attorney; she hated the idea of treating directly with her children about money, so Dorothea gave the power of attorney to her brother. "Paul worked himself into such irritation, that he left without saying goodbye, and declared to me via his brother that I would never see him again."[50] Not only that, Paul's subsequent behavior caused his mother great heartache. He may have sided with his father in his parents' final stand-off, but his mother's unstinting devotion to Paul had never wavered.

Frightful insecurity about her finances, the horrifying thought of humiliation, of discomfort at perhaps having to change her lifestyle as she faced old age, plagued the princess. She decided to sell her diamonds. Lady Cowper promised to

> do my utmost to sell them as favorably as possible, and it will be a happiness for me to give you such proof of my friendship and to feel that I have a chance to be of use to you. I shall confer with the three people whom you name—I will ascertain their ceiling; and then see if I can place at least some of the diamonds with certain people who may be prepared to pay more.[51]

Meanwhile, Dorothea suffered hideous insomnia; corpses haunted her dreams; elevated pulse and excessive fatigue puzzled her doctors and plunged the princess into despair.

ঙরজ

"There is yet peace, even for her, if she will but tread in its path,"[52] Harriet Granville soothed. So since Lieven's death freed his widow to travel, when balmy breezes bore the scent of honeysuckle the beleaguered princess sought relief at Baden-Baden. Her doctor recommended a serene life—not simple when Paul stopped payment of his father's allowance, to say nothing of out-flanking his uncle Benckendorff

*About $3,500,000.

by having some of Lieven's estates under-valued, some of his holdings left out of the overall appraisal, and halting shipment of his mother's household effects. The prescription of a daily glass of sweet ass milk rich in vitamins and minerals proved somewhat easier to swallow.

Princess Lieven rose at six. She watched a gorgeous blue sky emerge from the deep dark green of the Black Forest's tall fir trees while she drank her pleasant, tepid ass milk delivered fresh from the farm. Then she walked for an hour, and rested. Half past seven found Dorothea taking a warm curative bath; afterwards came breakfast, letter-writing, dressing, and another walk. She ate luncheon, read one of the several books François had selected from his extensive library, went for a drive in her open carriage, sometimes with the duchess of Dino or Countess Nesselrode. (Dorothea pursued a delicate matter with Marya Nesselrode, one close to a mother's heart: promotion of Paul's promising diplomatic career—and that despite his despicable behavior over Lieven's estate.) Later the princess rested in a lawn chair amidst the refreshing greenery of her hotel garden. She ate dinner, her main meal, at four. At five the post brought letters and newspapers; they occupied her for an hour. After another long carriage ride, Dorothea sat in the garden's warm, fragrant dusk until her nine o'clock bedtime.

This regime resulted in more relaxing nights, but during the day loneliness swamped the princess. She thought to reach some peace when she took her favorite walk—at an old castle set among gigantic rocks and superb trees high on a splendid mountain, but even that excursion into the pine-scented woods failed to soothe.

July thunderstorms, pouring rain plopping endlessly into puddles, and unseasonal cold caused Princess Lieven's doctor to cancel all baths. She could not budge outdoors. By early August financial worries had fretted Dorothea's nerves to flinders. Sleepless at night, exhausted during the day, she fell ill. How Dorothea missed François, his encompassing love, his soothing presence, his sensible advice, his ability to chase away her gloom. Sick and miserable, the princess left Baden.

ॐ

By the time traumatic 1839 shuddered to a close, Princess Lieven's finances were settled in "neither a very bad nor very good"[53] way, she confided to Lady Granville. A stipend the princess's sons paid in return for her ceding all claim to those sections of Lieven's properties which she had inherited, revenue from her share of Lieven's English capital, and her own money made up Dorothea's relatively modest annual income of sixty thousand francs.*

It sufficed. The princess held her salon, known as "the listening post of Europe," in her elegant, comfortable home at 2, rue St. Florentin. "There is not one ray of sunshine that does not reach it, not one breeze that does not blow, not one bird that does not sing for you."[54] Guizot's private secretary reviewed her lease, his financial advisor made sure the upholsterer gave a fair price. The duchess of Dino counseled on furnishing familiar rooms. Princess Lieven bought a piano, new carpets, scoured the antique shops for furniture with the able assistance of Lady Granville, and asked her sister Marie to send one hundred of her books from St. Petersburg by the first available transport. A companion and servants assured every comfort; Dorothea kept

---

*Paul and Alexander Lieven each inherited three times as much as their mother.

her own carriage and horses; had a box at the opera; dressed in the latest mode. She visited London and patronized fashionable resorts; during the warm months she rented a house outside Paris.

Above all, Princess Lieven prevailed over "the misfortunes and injustices" she had suffered, to resolve the central conflict in her life. By winning her long, grueling struggle for independence, Dorothea achieved a deeply satisfying blend of passion and politics.

23

"A Perfect Union"

My heart is such a confusion of politics and love that it is quite laughable.[1]
—Dorothea Lieven

On a superb summer Sunday in 1840 two middle-aged lovers sat side-by-side on straight-backed rosewood chairs upholstered with ivory brocade, under the lavishly ornamented and gilded coffered ceiling of a small room in one of London's grand private mansions. A gentle breeze blew in at the windows whose corded crimson velvet curtains shaded the bright sunshine. "I do not know how to speak of the subject on which I am so talkative," the princess wrote Guizot a few days before, "because this subject has become so immense, so intimate; it has taken such a character of sanctity and of passion that it cannot enter into letters."[2] With simple, symbolic ceremony they gravely read together from the Bible; they pledged to each other everything they had, for eternity; they exchanged rings. Without any witness, without official sanction of either church or state, Dorothea Lieven and François Guizot entered into "a union in front of heaven."[3]

Never had he given her

> a bad moment; all you say to me is so good, so loving, so tender. I want to be worthy of it, I am worthy, because my heart is so grateful, so full of love.... I never want to leave you.... I think of you incessantly, more than ever—you who are no illusion, you who are my whole truth, truth that I cherish, that I will cherish all my life—Tell me you love me, say it to me often.[4]

He did.

❧☙

A crisis over the Eastern Question landed them in London. Egyptian Pasha Mehemet Ali decided to emulate the Greeks, to liberate Egypt as well as Syria from Ottoman rule. The Porte refused. Mehemet marched against his suzerain, the sultan. France backed the successful pasha so as to solidify her grip on neighboring North African colonies, notably Algeria. Russia jumped at the chance to encroach on the Ottoman Empire through a promise of protection under the Treaty of Unkiar Skelessi (1833). Alarmed at the prospect of Turkey under Russian aegis and North Africa under French, British foreign secretary Lord Palmerston invited the Powers to reassess the Eastern Question at a conference; their ambassadors would represent them. France judged its ambassador unequal to the task. So when 1840 opened, the French government replaced him.

Despite his focus on domestic politics, François Guizot always liked to listen to his princess "chat about my old trade of diplomacy and about England, a country"[5] he greatly admired. Concomitantly, the diplomats disliked constantly meeting a staunch adversary of the government in Princess Lieven's salon; yet, they did like to come. She must choose. Loath to give up either the diplomats or Guizot, Dorothea invited him to visit when the diplomats did not. He agreed; but vowed to arrange that "'the Ambassadors will be only too glad to meet me in your salon.' A year later he obtained the Embassy to London, and six months after the portfolio of Foreign Affairs. He has often since" said "that this change of vocation in public affairs had no other origin than this."[6]

⁂ℂℂ

Guizot knew next to nothing of diplomacy, and of England only through academics. To discern "each nuance of the customs, the people, to appreciate every meaning of the results of what seems at the first blink of the eye to be of little import you must live in England for a long time."[7] Princess Lieven had one month to impart the vast expertise she had amassed during her twenty-two-year career in London.

As she and Guizot sat on either side of the cheerfully crackling fire in her silk-paneled small parlor, Dorothea conveyed an incredible amount—England's unique blend of politics and society, diplomatic niceties like "the implication of the least words, the smallest steps in the most important business."[8] François insisted that his Egeria constantly reiterate her advice, so a steady stream flowed from her daily letters. "You live in a glass house"[9]; the infinitely subtle, observant, and curious English saw everything while at the same time giving the impression that they noticed nothing.

Thanks to his princess's preparations the new French ambassador made a stunning debut in the crème de la crème of society. Yet, Dorothea's elite social circle had undergone one significant change. Her close friend Emily had been widowed. After a decent interval Emily let her long-time lover's persistent wooing, not to mention her emotions, overcome her family's opposition and rigid Victorian scruples on the eternality of widowhood. "Tell Lord Palmerston I look back to the good time of our closeness with sincerity and joy. I want his friendship again, I readily promise him mine,"[10] Dorothea, turning necessity into virtue, wrote Emily on her marriage. Now Lady Palmerston wrote that her husband liked Guizot, thought they could do business together.

Some careless words then wafted across the Channel. "You must not admire the unfamiliar too much," and "above all, above all, you must not say so," scolded the princess. "Be very sparing of definite opinions regardless"[11] of the subject. Adolescent Dorothea had first taught herself discretion at Tsar Paul's treacherous court, later by observing the diplomats at Berlin; indeed, she had learned the importance of listening and observing at her mother's knee. "Watch the others a little," Dorothea now advised her lover. Diplomacy is "a profession like any other, and one only learns by doing."[12]

How, then, to guarantee the success of Guizot's first official dinner? Besides asking British ambassador Granville to bless her seating plan, Dorothea advised a trial dinner. The embassy kitchen could rehearse its talents on the diplomatic corps—one did not serve them everything of prime quality. À propos food, François must "not to eat so much. Your after-dinner sleep is due to that. It is insufferable. I shall be even more angry if you gain weight than you are if I get thinner. I find it dreadful for a man to have an embonpoint."[13]

His vigilant Egeria vetoed accepting minor invitations. "You see the results, no pleasure, no use, tiring you and robbing me of the time you promised to write volumes! I am still waiting for the volumes! No doubt you are busy, very busy, but you knew you would be when you made those promises."[14] Nor must Guizot be bothered with hostesses who had been giving boring parties for the last half century. "There are forty old ladies like that; you are not accredited to them."[15] Even worse, Guizot had graced the house of a man he met in Paris whose wife, unbeknownst to the ambassador, embodied "all that is lascivious in London." Prince Lieven "would rather have gone swimming in the Thames than dine with those people, and he had at least as much of a name for sobriety as you."[16] If Guizot accepted every dinner invitation, rebuked Dorothea, those in high society would hardly deem it an honor for him to dine with them. As for reciprocating, Dorothea defied François to compose a suitable dinner that included the lascivious lady. No self-respecting woman would come; nor would many men.

How could her star pupil shame the exacting princess with such a gaffe. Piqued in her professional pride, Dorothea drummed into Guizot that his position demanded more prudence. An ambassador must hold himself high, could not visit people of no social standing unless they were famous. Love, for truth no less than for François, drove her strong language. "Do you believe I love you? Oh! My God!"[17]

Princess Lieven's counsel turned Guizot into his country's ambassador, rather than merely its envoy. "If I am prudent I owe it to you."[18]

଼ଡ଼ଓଷ

She had already "introduced" Guizot to her Tory friend Lord Aberdeen by sending him Guizot's articles, and passing on Aberdeen's positive reactions. Dorothea now wrote Aberdeen that Guizot wanted to meet him. So the typically diffident earl "made a greater exertion to make his acquaintance than is usual with me, and I have been well repaid."[19] The two men spoke "almost with trust," with "trust but no confidences, isn't that so?" Guizot wrote his Egeria. "You are right. It is a profession one must learn."[20]

The ice proved harder to crack with another of Dorothea's old friends. Guizot's grave but brilliant mind would please Lord Grey, she introduced, but the Whig elder statesman wanted to judge for himself. So the princess advised Guizot that the Greys "would be most amenable to an advance, & you do not lower yourself by making an advance to a woman."[21] Guizot thus told Grey he greatly desired the honor of meeting Lady Grey. Gratified, Grey said she would be "at home" the next evening; if Guizot cared to call, Grey himself would make the introduction. After that the two men got on famously.

Despite his Egeria's warning that Palmerston could easily cause problems, Guizot's first private meeting with the foreign secretary satisfied him. How he wanted to discuss it with Dorothea, "first for my pleasure, but also for my profit. You cannot know how much confidence I have in your judgment. It was huge when I left Paris. It has grown since I am in London."[22] Guizot gave no details, for despite his and Dorothea's corresponding via the "four envelopes" method, if only one letter fell into the wrong hands, the worst sort of public scandal would ensue. This reticence "most certainly displeases me as much as you," for "your opinions, your opinions every minute on the least details, you always at my side, that is a delightful illumination."[23]

ʚ◦ɞ

A miasma now menaced Dorothea. Unlike his elder brother Paul, her son Alexander had kept up relations with his mother. Now on holiday in England, Alexander had an accident. It threatened his life. Dreading that God would claim yet another child, Dorothea begged Guizot to speak with Alexander's doctor. He did not; nor did he visit Alexander. Dorothea reproached. François explained. His valet checked with Alexander's valet twice daily; overt inquiries would result in the inevitable gossip which, Guizot knew, would disturb Dorothea much more that himself.

Guizot then sent good news, but two friends wrote that Alexander's doctor still judged him in mortal danger. Frantic, Dorothea scolded François for failing to give her all the facts. She then apologized for this "perhaps" unjust accusation; nonetheless, Dorothea refused to admit that her judgment had been hasty and deserved censure. Yes, François acknowledged, he should have asked Alexander's doctor for daily bulletins; still, his lover's scolding punished him too cruelly.

Would François retaliate, would he take offense at her sudden spurt of envy on reading a newspaper account of the beautiful young ladies who had graced the Queen's ball? Did Guizot speak only with Grey and Wellington during the six hours he stayed at Buckingham Palace? Her lover had insisted Dorothea tell him everything in her heart.

> Perhaps you make me repent my frankness. Do you know what I think? One must speak with this severity when one is nearby; nearby, because one can so quickly delete, explain. Oh! Nearby, I know very well you would not be offended! You would be the opposite! You would see there is depth, warmth, behind my words. I have a lot more to say.[24]

Dorothea must, François replied, ask Emily about his ennui at Buckingham Palace. "Thank you for being bored at the ball where I thought you were amusing yourself; I am ready to beat myself for thinking it, and even more for writing you about it."[25] His Dorothea knew very well that François rejected her picking a quarrel about balls and young women and, to prove his point, the busy French ambassador quoted from a favorite poet: "'Since the Lord gave me the desire of my heart in my dearest Mary, the rest of the sex are no more to me than the tulips in the garden.' If that does not please you, I will never speak to you of tulips I find beautiful."[26] "What a letter! How I love you, how I bless you. Speak to me of tulips as much as you wish." Pleasure suffocated Dorothea, and "what pleasure! My heart is jumping with joy. Oh! How young my heart is!"[27]

ʚ◦ɞ

On the diplomatic front England and France were far apart. Prime minister Thiers supported Mehemet Ali's claim to an autonomous Egypt and Syria. Palmerston upheld the Sultan's refusal. Seeking to isolate France, Russia decided to let the Treaty of Unkiar Skelessi lapse and work with the other Powers to protect the Ottoman Empire against Mehemet. Hence, Russian ambassador to London Baron von Brunnow, abetted by his Austrian and Prussian colleagues, set out to convince Palmerston to sign a Four Powers agreement without France. Guizot repeatedly told Thiers that unless France compromised the Powers would act without her, but the prime minister refused.

Meanwhile, Princess Lieven got ready to visit London, which she had promised her friends to do well before Guizot's appointment. But in the current diplomatic climate Princess Lieven's out-of-favor status at the Romanov court reacted strongly on the sycophantic Russian ambassador; moreover, Brunnow feared his compatriot's legendary abilities. Thoroughly alarmed, he shared his trepidation with Lady Palmerston, and cautioned the foreign secretary's wife to keep Princess Lieven at a distance.

So Emily advised her friend that since Guizot's colleagues at the French embassy envied her influence and the diplomatic corps dreaded her descent on London—indeed, stood ready to interpret negatively her every innocent move—Dorothea, to avoid provoking these factions, should postpone her visit until after Parliament had risen and society left London.

Guizot thought the idea ludicrous. So did Dorothea. Her independence let her ignore the whims of fools—like Brunnow. She had no intention of meddling in politics. Since Dorothea was coming to see her friends, she wanted be in London when they were. And she meant to complete the sale of her diamonds, a transaction Emily had initiated at Dorothea's behest the previous year, shortly after Lieven's death. "I do not generally mention this detail, but my finances are not so flourishing that I can afford to forget it."[28]

"I would be *personally* very angry if, for reasons of prudence or any other, you would find it wise to change what I have wanted for so long,"[29] Emily conceded. Dorothea took this to mean officialdom preferred delay or cancellation, but Emily would turn a blind eye.

Her friends welcomed the princess with great affection, so Brunnow had to beat a hasty, if temporary, retreat from society, which approved of Dorothea's manner towards Guizot as "very good and friendly without being particular."[30] The diplomatic corps quickly shed its alarm, but Brunnow warned Palmerston. "Beware Mme. de Lieven, Mad. de Lieven is not a Russian. Mad. de Lieven is an emissary of France; the least word said to her will find its way to the French Embassy."[31] Yet Emily Palmerston heard from Paris that there they reviled her friend for being completely Russian. "Does not this cross fire give one the measure and value of these absurd reports and of all those who make them?"[32]

Lady Palmerston knew for sure that the princess kept out of politics, but Russian foreign minister Nesselrode asked his wife to keep her eyes and ears open. Certainly, Marya Nesselrode reported, Brunnow had been absurdly panic-stricken about Princess Lieven's arrival. Suspicions were rife and easily exaggerated, but absolutely no proof existed about "the monstrous behavior of which the Princess is accused."[33]

⊗⊘⊗

Prime minister Thiers stood firm. Hence, Palmerston took advantage of Russia's cooperation. Britain joined Russia, Austria, and Prussia in the Treaty of London

(July 15, 1840). It imposed a compromise on both combatants and guaranteed future Great Power protection to the Ottoman empire.

France's humiliating exclusion from the Concert of Europe caused a conflagration. Thiers ruptured his country's entente with England. The ministerial press beat the drums of war; the radical press threatened violence. Strikes and riots broke out. By now back in the French capital, Guizot's "most faithful mirror, the most unclouded possible,"[34] she whose letters, since the day he left for London, let him live a little in Paris, reported that the diplomats predicted revolution, followed by the war Dorothea dreaded. It would threaten European stability, not to mention her residence in Paris as a Russian subject.

So the princess pushed her powerful English friends to promote peace. At the same time Guizot's allies urged him to lead the anti-war deputies in the Chamber. The country stood against war; King Louis-Philippe feared it would complicate the domestic situation and endanger his throne. "I fully approve of your decision to stay a stranger to all intrigue, and your absence will be the strongest possible proof of it. But I cannot conceive that you will not be here for the discussion" of the king's address, Dorothea advised. "I speak in the interest of your political position."[35]

Uneasy about internal instability, Guizot requested permission to participate in the opening debate (October 28). In the interim the king, seeking to avoid war and curb the incendiary effect of rampant chauvinism, dismissed his bellicose prime minister.

Guizot's moment had come. More of an intellectual than a politician, dedicated to clear, simple ideas based on his passion for right and truth, Guizot epitomized the policy of the *juste milieu*—the golden mean between anarchy (democracy) and privilege. "I have reread many times the longest of your letters," wrote his Egeria. "It is from a very honest man, but with a poor head for politics. Really, to fragment the parties even more at a time when their multiplicity makes the situation dangerous and government impossible, is not common sense. It is homeopathy."[36]

Dorothea expected François immediately upon arrival,

> but here is what I wish to settle into the bargain, that you will not see anyone before you have seen me; even if only for 10 minutes. This is not for the pleasure of seeing you one minute earlier, it is more serious. I do not want you to take a side, or only let it be suspected, before I talk with you.[37]

François should leave his carriage in a side street and hire a hackney to come to 2, rue St. Florentin; he must risk nothing that could cause scandal.

Guizot's private secretary met him at Calais. Since no one could possibly intercept the letter he carried, Dorothea yielded to the unbridled delight of using the familiar style:* "My well-beloved, I would like to send you some words of love that are as vivid and tender as I feel. I am happy, I am full of anguish, the anguish of pleasure. I am waiting for you," worried. "Excitement is said to be growing in the streets, that there will be some agitation tomorrow." How "vile to be trembling at such a happy moment!

"My love, you will come to me at once. At least if you arrive *after* ten o'clock in the morning or *before* ten thirty at night, you must come to me right away. I must

---

Due to the constant danger of letters going astray, the princess and Guizot used the formal vous. *This rare letter uses the intimate* tu.

speak to you before you see anyone" else. "Your place at table will be set; do not let me dine alone. My dear well-beloved, how happy we are going to be! How I love you, how I love you! What a poor affair these words are! How I will say them to you! Come, my dearly-beloved. I do not know how to talk to you about anything at this moment; I do not wish to stop this intimate style." Goodbye "my well-beloved, the most loved of mortals."[38]

Guizot arrived on October 26. He accepted the foreign affairs portfolio with conditions: his political allies would sit in the cabinet; he would lead the government in the Chamber of Deputies; he would be de facto prime minister.

ଔଡଔ

Soon after, Dorothea Lieven and Marya Nesselrode went for a drive in the Bois de Boulogne. Was it true, Marya asked, that Dorothea would soon marry Guizot? The princess burst out laughing. "Oh! My dear," she said, "can you see me announced as Madame Guizot?"

"I have heard some people" say "we were married in secret." After Dorothea's death Guizot begged his friend Aberdeen to deny this rumor "absolutely. Nothing secret suited us, neither the one nor the other. Moreover, I never married anybody without giving her my name which she took as hers. We each had our reasons."[39]

If she gave up "Princess Lieven," Dorothea would deny her Russianness—her heritage, her patriotism, her position in European society, and her unique intimacy with the imperial family which, despite her out-of-favor status at court, still stood, still meant much to her. As "Madame Guizot" she would be French, her life subsumed into her husband's, her salon his, her position, her power, dependent on his. Marriage would end her independence.

And if the princess committed the cardinal sin of marrying a bourgeois Frenchman, the tsar might well confiscate her Russian assets. In any case, Guizot's chronically slender income could scarcely support Dorothea in her accustomed style.

Besides, he had a family. Guizot's mother had been an integral part of his household during her son's marriages, and neither of his wives got along with her. The cantankerous old lady now ran Guizot's household and brought up his children. She received Princess Lieven most graciously but diplomatic relations never blossomed into friendship. "You are, you, in my home for my mother above all, an object of immense envy."[40]

So this middle-aged couple lived apart but were always together. They saw each other two, three times daily. Otherwise, letters flowed frequently. And on Sunday, August 30, 1840, they committed to each other in a private ceremony. "Yesterday I went to the Italian opera: *Lucia di Lammermoor*. In the first act a ravishing duo," a "love scene; they exchanged rings that they placed on their fingers; a union before heaven; such a likeness that it affected me all evening long."[41]

So different from the convenient marriage Dorothea contracted at age fourteen, this union raised no reservations, although it did cause emotional turmoil. And this time her partner gave Dorothea the nurturing love she craved and, indeed, craved to return.

He: "Do not have confused emotions. Everything is yours. Everything is mine; everything we can give each other. Never has a gift been more complete. I too, had confused feelings. Now, I no longer have them; I will never again have them."[42]

She: "Sunday it will be four weeks since the 30 ... I repeat the *30* with so much passion."[43]

> Sunday is a beautiful day, a holy day. I love it. Nothing refreshes the soul like placing oneself in harmony under the eye, the hand, the shelter of God. That is security; that is eternity for affection and joy. You have a pious heart. I was enchanted on the day I discovered [it].... My heart is so full of you, so full for you![44]

"Dearest well-beloved, tomorrow, tomorrow." Tomorrow "eight weeks have gone by since we so solemnly gave the one to the other, for this life, for eternity!"[45]

He: "Nothing is so delightful as this complete, continuous, minute communication of all one thinks, feels, knows, learns; this total abolition of all solitude, of all reticence, of all silence, of all constraint; the perfect truth, the perfect freedom, the perfect union!"[46]

24

The Entente Cordiale

> If you were a man, you would be called to the highest destiny. With your
> head and your heart, one could do anything.[1]
> —Prince Metternich to Princess Lieven

The foreign minister Dorothea Lieven had such a strong hand in shaping had
been in office barely a year when Britain's Whig government fell (1841). Scarcely had
the new Tory foreign secretary settled into office when he sent his first confidential
communication to his French counterpart. Would Princess Lieven convey Lord
Aberdeen's great pleasure at working with Monsieur Guizot?

Based on a friendship the princess had initiated and fostered, the entente cordiale between England and France now flourished through a crucial personal link.
Dorothea Lieven's new role also fit her "Russian interest; for surely whatever may
be our antipathies or our preferences, we want and need peace like all the world."
The recent ado over French exclusion from the Treaty of London proved that for
peace "to exist London and Paris must get on well together."[2]

⁎)(℣

Meanwhile, the Princess rented a country house near Paris for the warm months.
Standing on a shady height, Beauséjour's spacious villas, each set in a generous garden, faced a large and handsomely landscaped park, reminding Dorothea of Richmond in layout, peace, and location. She could dine at Beauséjour, then open her
salon if enough people were in town to make it worthwhile.

Would Guizot tell her butler to prepare a "fire in my drawing-room and the
room where I dress myself?" That "proves I am cold."[3]

"There will be a fire in the two rooms." The "windows are open for a shadow
of sun.... Come, come, we will talk and I shall make you warm again."[4]

Guizot went to Beauséjour every evening after the Chamber adjourned, returning to Paris next morning. "We are so *eingelebt*,[5] (do you know what this word
means?), that we need not ask anything of each other; we anticipate each other."[6]
They walked together in the park, dined and, deep in conversation, walked again;
Beauséjour meant "chez nous."[7,8]

They had plenty to discuss. Guizot must do something, the princess insisted,
about the right of search (a nation's ability to stop another's merchant vessels at sea

219

George Hamilton Gordon, fourth earl of Aberdeen. British foreign secretary, later prime minister. Princess Lieven's close friend and political ally. Artist: John Partridge. National Portrait Gallery, London.

to look for, and set free, African slaves). While still foreign secretary, Palmerston had convinced the Powers to agree to a treaty replacing the old, limited (on the number of each nation's ships seeking slaves) right of search, with unlimited right. When the Whig government began to wobble, Palmerston asked Guizot to sign the treaty while he still held office. But Guizot, already smarting from one of Palmerston's needlessly abrasive dispatches, had just sustained another gratuitous affront. In a major address to his constituents at Tiverton, Palmerston contrasted what he chose to call British benevolence in Asia with French cruelty in Algeria.

So "Lord Guizot" brusquely refused Palmerston's request. Thereupon Britain's senior diplomat, Henry Bulwer, betook himself to Beauséjour. He confided his extreme reluctance to forward Guizot's gruff reply—with good reason, Dorothea wrote François. She suggested that, instead, Bulwer send Guizot's tactful note to himself. In taking Palmerston's "demarche for what it is, a real apology for his misdeeds, you can show yourself satisfied, and at the last minute make a graceful" gesture. "You must admit that I am a good person; here I am almost his advocate!"[9]

Guizot stubbornly delayed signature until Aberdeen took office.

The new treaty's lack of numeric limits heightened French suspicions that it served solely as an excuse for England to consolidate her naval supremacy. And, in feeding these fears, Guizot's strident opposition failed to contradict the entirely erroneous belief that the right of search belonged exclusively to England. Hence, the Chamber crushed a motion to ratify the right of search treaty.

This meant merely a temporary setback, Princess Lieven placated her old friend the brilliant Whig barrister, Lord Brougham. He had led the successful parliamentary fight to abolish slavery throughout the British empire, and now lent his powerful voice to end the trade. Guizot must first dissipate the implacable resentment raised by the recent Treaty of London, and the rancor stimulated by Palmerston's gratuitously tactless words at Tiverton.

Dorothea chose stronger language to convey the same message to Aberdeen, adding that the antagonistic newspaper articles Palmerston inspired, perhaps even penned, against King Louis-Philippe fueled the fire. So Aberdeen and prime minister Sir Robert Peel gratified Guizot by announcing French non-ratification to Parliament in what the princess praised as totally appropriate terms. And Brougham's equally impressive speech, expressing "such flattering feelings for the nation, so pacific, so sincere, so eloquent,"[10] delighted the French foreign minister. For this benefit he owed his indefatigable Egeria no small thanks.

∞∞

Meanwhile, a storm gathered gale force around a lush tropical island. France placed a protectorate over Tahiti, where George Pritchard, an English Protestant missionary, had gained great influence over the government. Although Aberdeen recognized French hegemony on the island, and Guizot promised equal treatment for Protestant and Catholic missionaries, Pritchard incited the Tahitians against the French administration. So the French incarcerated him. Locked in a wooden blockhouse, confined to a tiny, filthy room under three inches of mud, furnished with only a mattress, Pritchard spent sixteen hours without ventilation, sanitation, food, water, or his family's knowledge.

What Dorothea Lieven denounced as "the disgrace of Tahiti"[11] generated jingoistic fury on both sides of the Channel.

While Tahiti seethed and the right of search simmered, Queen Victoria paid a state visit to King Louis-Philippe at his summer palace, the Château d'Eu, the first time in centuries that a British monarch had set foot in France. Guizot agreed with his Egeria that every last detail must be meticulously planned. Then why, she scolded, snatch a few days in the country with his family? "Forgive me for returning to this subject. But truly I want to *impress on your mind* how vital it is for you. I realize all your joys at Val-Richer, and am trying harder not to be envious," but his mother, seeing his workload, "will let you go for she knows politics is her real rival."[12]

Guizot returned to Paris. A stream of advice then flowed to him at Eu. Do "not appear irritated, but a little aloof," so Aberdeen "knows you want your due." That "can only have a positive effect on such an upright and proud spirit as his."[13] "I hope you are on a close and secure footing and he takes away the idea that he can always count on your word."[14] "Remember that the English Ministers' positive language in Parliament truly contributed to calm French foolishness."[15]

Meanwhile Austria and Prussia's ambassadors dined with the princess at Beauséjour. Would the queen, they mused, honor Louis-Philippe with Great Britain's highest award, the Order of the Garter? That would certainly be a slap in the face to their courts. "Make sure the King is given the Garter," coached Guizot's Egeria. "Begin by giving Prince Albert (Victoria's husband) the Cordon Rouge. Promise me that you will not forget."[16]

What a positive impact the immense honor of Victoria's visit had made in France, the princess followed up with Aberdeen; and Guizot's excellent memory of his meetings with the foreign secretary had given him such great confidence. Aberdeen must feel the same for "these impressions between two men like you, are always reciprocal."[17]

They were. Yet, a minor matter like Tahiti had waxed major because it affected all France's most delicate national sensitivities, Dorothea explained to her English friends. Guizot must vie with violent press reaction, the Opposition's drumbeat that the entente cordiale merely meant giving in to England, and popular clamor for war.

ം∞ങ

Trouble also menaced in the Mediterranean: in the east over Dorothea Lieven's "enfant." The Greeks, rebelling against King Otto's repressive rule, demanded a constitution. Britain and France agreed that Otto must grant one. Aberdeen asked the princess to convey his accord with any French proposal; Guizot requested, through Dorothea, that Aberdeen line up Russia and Austria.

By now, however, the princess exercised independent influence in Russia. Although she had officially resigned her diplomatic duties vis-à-vis the Russian foreign office,[18] patriotism and ambition impelled Dorothea to mend fences with the Iron Tsar. She had renewed her correspondence with her highly-placed brother. Alexander acknowledged his sister's "interesting letters and thank you for them exceedingly."[19]

Then Russian ambassador Brunnow's totally baseless accusation, that Princess Lieven used her stay in London to spy for France, reached the Romanov court. She had only herself to blame, Alexander admonished, because she made no secret of her liaison with Guizot.* And why not, riposted Dorothea, they were both independent.

Still, that had nothing to do with her outrage at seeing the tsar's envoy denounce her to the British government as a traitor; at seeing this slander spread to other cabinets; at seeing the trust of her closest friends shaken. "The Tsar does not believe it; the Tsar would never believe it; for the Tsar knows me," Dorothea told Emily Palmerston; and Alexander should have echoed it, instead of siding with Brunnow. Nicholas did better. "The Tsar knows I am a loyal subject; and when others doubted it," he sent a "goodwill memory."†

> Tell the Tsar that pertinence doubles great favors. My heart thanks him for the favor, my mind for the timing. But if my heart is satisfied, my honor is not.... [To doubt] I am the Tsar's devoted subject is to dishonor me; to say it is to dishonor me; and the Tsaritsa's lady-of-honor cannot stay under such a slur.

Dorothea demanded a retraction. "I need it or something to confirm to others that I have never merited such odious suspicions." She asked Alexander "to place this letter under the Tsar's eyes."[20]

---

* General Count Alexander Benckendorff was a good one to talk. He had several notorious extra-marital affairs, and died in the arms of a mistress.
†Via Alexander's wife. Their daughter Annette married an Austrian diplomat posted at Paris, so Countess Benckendorff often visited.

Soon Princess Lieven's scrawl again dashed over large sheets of paper as she drafted and re-drafted her letters to Alexander. Resumption of intimate correspondence between sister and brother proved Dorothea's vindication.

And, she told Emily Palmerston, Russia's autocrat allowed his favored aide-de-camp Constantine Benckendorff, son of Dorothea's closest sibling who had succumbed so tragically during the Russo-Turkish war, to spend a few months with her. "You cannot conceive what a delightful young man he is, & so kind to me, so caring, so warmhearted."[21] Destined for diplomacy, Constantine became a worthy substitute for Dorothea's son of the same name who died in America, far from the mother whose faith in his basic decency never wavered. Always drawn to promising young people, Dorothea grew very attached to her nephew.

"My profession demands precise knowledge gained by attentive observing and listening."[22] Greece pre-occupied the princess. "Perhaps the memory of its origin, in which I was very strongly involved adds interest." Guizot's government had advised King Otto to grant a constitution "while making maximum effort to have *the most monarchical possible*. France will help him."[23] Aberdeen agreed. Tsar Nicholas's dislike of revolutions and constitutions, concluded Dorothea, gave London and Paris valid reason to doubt Russia's good intentions.* The Powers agreed to cooperate.

In the western Mediterranean, Morocco menaced. France began to colonize neighboring Algeria; Algerian rebels found material help in Morocco. Guizot publicly pledged that if war broke out France would not keep any Moroccan territory; still, Aberdeen feared that jingoists in the Chamber might override Guizot's promise. A French fleet bombarded Tangier and occupied an important commercial center. British anger, already at fever pitch over the right of search and "disgrace of Tahiti," escalated.

Dorothea's intimate knowledge of English politics lent particular credibility to her clarification of Britain's position for Guizot's trusted friends. They helped her to induce some flexibility in the stubborn foreign minister.

8003

In the middle of these excitements Princess Lieven abandoned Beauséjour's beautiful blue delphiniums for the attractions of the Black Forest. She went to meet her brother. Alexander had a fatal and inoperable growth, but medical opinion judged him in no imminent danger.

Barely had Dorothea arrived at Baden-Baden when "a ghost, a skeleton, something that makes you recoil in horror"[24] entered her suite; brother and sister embraced in heartbreaking silence. Next day Alexander felt too weak to leave his rooms, "not a window open, an air of sadness even in the furniture." His "daughters around him not knowing what to say."† Dorothea "enlivened him a little, but it greatly tired him. It is a sorry sight. I have never seen its like, and must pull myself together" so as not to "dwindle as well."[25]

Dorothea derived some comfort from the universal respect shown to Alexander

---

*The king and Guizot's political allies at first feared that his and Dorothea's "strange relationship, so unwisely entered, sustained" would result in political problems, but soon saw that their fears were unfounded; even Guizot's enemies confessed that they no longer believed the princess "betrayed Guizot, neither to Tsar Nicholas nor to any cabinet" (Rémusat, Mémoires, vol. iv, pp. 41–43).
†Alexander's wife stayed away because he had traveled to Germany with his mistress who, in the presence of her lover's daughters and sister, decorously withdrew to a neighboring spa.

despite his "barbarous title"[26] as head of the tsar's secret police. And Baden's enchant-ing beauty, which surpassed "everything you can imagine in loveliness and laugh-ter,"[27] brought her a little solace too, especially when her caring nephew Constantine took Dorothea on her favorite carriage drives. Still, she felt utterly helpless to ease her brother's terrible agony and, even worse, useless, for his three daughters nursed him. "I want to distract his mind, I try all kinds of conversation,"[28] but not even mem-ories of their youth animated Alexander.

"I miss you everywhere, at each hour, in the middle of the sweetest family life as in the solitude of my office," Guizot wrote. "I said it to you in our first moments; I reiterate it to you in our last; that intimacy is for me above all else."[29]

"Yes, I love you so much, *at least* as much as you love me," Dorothea replied. "And I miss you *even more* than you miss me. That is quite clear, that is quite understood, for you have so much—and I, I have nothing, nothing but you! You *alone* in the world."[30]

Some weeks later Dorothea received "the world's most touching letter"[31] from Constantine. "I was and am truly sad about my brother's death. He is the last of my family, I am the only one left. This thought" is "a great sadness."[*][32]

In deep mourning, the princess closed her salon. Next day she "walked in the Bois de Boulogne for an hour. I needed air," Dorothea told Guizot. "My morning was massacred. Everyone came, and I had so much to write to Russia."[33] Daily after dinner (usually eaten in the late afternoon) and through the evening, Dorothea com-forted her niece Annette, Alexander's married daughter.

∂◑ℭ෴

Concomitantly, Guizot suffered an acute attack of kidney stones, causing his princess such anxiety that she fretted herself into illness. So when the still weak for-eign minister accompanied his king on a state visit to Windsor Castle, Dorothea daily reminded him to keep his diet, purge himself with lemonade, and wear his warm coat against treacherous autumn chills. And she begged Aberdeen to spare Guizot "fatigues and late nights at Court. Give him in return as much as you can of your conversation and continue your friendship for him"; that "will do him good."[34]

His debilitating illness robbed Guizot of his appetite for business, so his Egeria bent her diplomatic skills, not to mention her knowledge of English politics, to the task of preventing Tahiti, Morocco, or the right of search from disrupting the entente. Thus when Guizot and Aberdeen shared a couch beside the blazing fire in a small room at Windsor for private conversation, the French foreign minister introduced new ideas on the issue that "continued to excite evil heads and even good ones."[35] Soon after, England and France reached agreement[†] on the right of search.

What, the princess prompted, if in parting Guizot said to Aberdeen:

*Princess Lieven's sister Marie Schevitsch, lady-in-waiting at court and widow of a general, had died suddenly three years before. Dorothea told Harriet Granville that Marie had been "an excellent woman, a thousand times better than I can write," always good and kind to Dorothea. Much distressed at her death, Dorothea took com-fort in Alexander's words: "what remains of her is acclaimed with regret and tears. They surround her as if she still lives. Rich and poor fill her room, old and young are on their knees and kiss her hands. Poor Marie, she gave all, also all the blessings" (The National Archives of the UK: Public Record Office (PRO) 30/29 Leveson-Gower Papers; Subseries within PRO 30/29 Countess Granville, correspondence from Princess Lieven, 195, Dec. 13, 1841, Lieven to Granville).

†A new convention abolished the incendiary unlimited right of search. Instead, an English and a French squadron, each stationed on the west African coast and acting jointly, backed by treaties with local chiefs to let the sailors land, stopped the egregious trade.

"We know each other well, we have tested each other, our political conduct is the same; as long as we are ministers, we shall practice peace, good entente. The day a real difficulty arises and we really fear diplomacy will not resolve it, let us promise, before the last extremity, to meet."

Since neither country wanted war, each would know that the two men would exhaust all avenues to save them from it. "'In any case, we will have done our duty.'"[36]

"Your final speech to Lord Aberdeen is excellent, and I shall follow it."[37]

80CB

France and Morocco made peace on terms that satisfied England, but Tahiti festered. "It is all very well for you to talk about right, it is no less true that the episode was terribly cruel, and the English minister forced to ask you for splendid reparation. But what is stopping you from giving it?" rebuked Guizot's Egeria. If one had "done this to an important Frenchman, and you must admit Pritchard had importance, on that island, think of the outcry here." For "a nation as civilized as yours, these atrocious acts are shameful."[38]

Aberdeen could not, the princess pressed, let such an absurd cause as Tahiti destroy the entente. Guizot had bravely gone to the limit on reparations for Pritchard, "but the limit is drawn; he will retreat if England demands more than his conscience tells him is just."[39]

England and France agreed on the indemnity, and France officially apologized.

Gossip still married Dorothea and Guizot secretly, but Marya Nesselrode swore only that he was "much more devoted to her and more tender than ever. Despite his press of business he often goes to see" her, "listens to her, follows her advice, and is as obedient as a schoolboy. She rejoices at his progress in world affairs and plumes herself about it."[40]

80CB

"They say this summer was not lovely. I found it delightful," Guizot told his princess. At Beauséjour every evening, returning to the foreign ministry next morning, "we have never lived so close to one another. In one month, we shall do so again."[41] Dorothea's eyes—the lids, not her vision—were causing trouble so when buttercups burnished the meadows, she crossed the Channel for medical treatment.

Abnormally large lettering lamented Dorothea's despair at her slow improvement. "You lack the strength relative to the height, the vibrancy of your soul; you are like those beautiful poplars so tall so thin, that the least wind sways and bends. You bend as much under the small burdens as under the big ones." That sometimes taxed Guizot, but "knowing you as I do, loving you as I do, it is up to me to help you carry"[42] every load. Dorothea must draw on his greater strength. And must remember: "you have in yourself, at the base of your soul, much sense and valor, which you found in the worst extremity."[43]

Her eyes improved. And the London season, the society of her exalted circle, put the princess in her "element and I never enjoyed myself so much."[44]

Her eldest son was one reason. The combined cajolery of Dorothea's friend Emily Palmerston and Alexander Lieven, who had not estranged himself from his mother, acted on Paul's conscience. He lived in London and, on the last day of her previous

visit, called on his mother for the first time since their clash over Lieven's will. She
had not reproached Paul, had made neither him nor herself unhappy. Dorothea acted
on her own advice—to treat her son "as men in general must be treated; expect little, and ask less."[45]

ஐஒ

"God bless you, dearest. May he bless you as I love you!" Guizot greeted on
New Year's Day, 1846. "I am coming to tell you myself. At 11 o'clock. How are you
this morning? I hope your cold will soon disappear. It is mild, but you should stay
indoors."[46]

"You do not know how touched, moved, I am, how I love you even more,"
Dorothea wrote on the March anniversary of her boys' deaths. "This year, the days
of the week coincide with the dates.... How poignant and tender your words are."[47]

Some months later the Tory government began to totter. Disgusted at Palmerston's cavalier treatment of France over the 1840 Treaty of London, let alone his constant barrage in the press and Parliament against what he dubbed Aberdeen's policy
of concession to that country, some prominent Whigs refused to join a government
in which Palmerston held the foreign office. So to prove his goodwill towards France,
Palmerston and his lady graced Paris with a visit.

Irises and wisteria bloomed in the Tuileries Garden outside Princess Lieven's
windows when an extremely select group of guests assembled under the elegant crystal chandelier, its cut-glass ornaments sparkling with rainbows, for a formal dinner
"served in the Russian style and very good,"[48] with which the princess honored Lord
and Lady Palmerston. And true to the prudent diplomacy Dorothea had taught herself, she convinced an exceptionally wary Guizot to make sure his reluctant king
received the Englishman.

Soon Palmerston confirmed Dorothea Lieven's worst fears. He returned to the
foreign office.

Guizot had gone to his country residence, there to mastermind a crucial election. The princess conferred with Britain's senior diplomat in the leafy shade of
Beauséjour's linden trees. Who should marry Spain's sixteen-year-old Queen Isabella
and her younger sister the Infanta Louisa? Control of the Spanish throne meant control of the country and a major presence in the Mediterranean. Continuing centuries
of Anglo-French conflict over Spain, King Louis-Philippe wanted his son, the duc
de Montpensier, to marry one of the sisters; England preferred Queen Victoria's
cousin, Prince Leopold of Coburg.

"I have a thousand things to tell you," Guizot wrote his princess before meeting Aberdeen during Queen Victoria's visit to the Château d'Eu, "your advice to take,
for I need your advice. There is no way to write all that."[49] So he and Dorothea discussed the Spanish Marriages when she induced him to return to Paris from the
country to prepare for Eu. There Aberdeen and Guizot reached a satisfactory
arrangement.[50]

Then Palmerston returned to the foreign office. At once he sent official instructions to his minister at Madrid. These instructions, for the first time, formally recognized Coburg as a candidate for the queen's hand. Thereby Palmerston broke the
Eu agreement.

"It is now about not quarreling with England over this, but also not to have a beaten air about it. That is the question, a difficult one,"[51] cautioned Guizot's Egeria.

In the interim, he won his election. "How that would seem cold and dry and empty were I to think of it alone, were I to work on it alone!" Guizot exulted. There "is no life so full, no great affairs, that can suffice alone, without affection. I love you, you love me; you are with me in all; and all pleases me with you."[52]

Unbeknownst to the euphoric French foreign minister, Palmerston meanwhile officially and unofficially urged his minister at Madrid to push Coburg for one of the royal sisters, and to prevent Montpensier from marrying either. Concomitantly deep skepticism—born of bitter experience—about Palmerston's intention to keep the entente caused a confident Guizot to convince King Louis-Philippe that Palmerston's instructions meant that the King's Eu promise no longer held; France must press for a Spanish prince to marry the queen and Montpensier, the infanta.

They did. A storm of fury, carefully stoked by Palmerston, erupted in England. It ended the entente cordiale. And his cavalier conduct over the Spanish Marriages perpetuated Princess Lieven's anger at the man she blamed for her husband's recall and, consequently, her ensuing tragedies.

∞∞

In Dorothea Lieven's day personal relations meant much more in diplomacy than they do now although national interest, as always, determined foreign policy. As the crucial personal link in the entente cordiale, Dorothea prodded each country towards understanding the other on potentially divisive issues. And her correspondence with Aberdeen provided a reliable channel of private communication between the two governments.

The Spanish Marriages proved that such an entente could not survive Palmerston's breezy, abrasive modus operandi.

Despite Guizot's elation over what he considered his great diplomatic coup, the marriages failed to stem his growing unpopularity. France thirsted for military glory; Guizot gave his country peace, prosperity, stability, and parliamentary government. Eventually a string of bad harvests upset domestic affluence. Food supplies decreased, prices increased. A financial crisis followed, then depression. Unemployment rose. Discontent spread. Agitation for universal (male) suffrage turned serious. Strictly principled in politics, Guizot had never courted popularity; moreover, he relied on the dictates of his intellect rather than political expediency. A staunch liberal, he firmly believed that the French constitution must rest on a restricted franchise. Guizot cracked down on public protests.

On February 20, 1848, the mayor of Paris and the police chief circulated among the luminaries in Princess Lieven's salon. She asked about the unsettled situation. "Come here, Monsieur," the princess called to Guizot, sitting on a sofa at the other end of the room deep in conversation with the British ambassador. "Listen to what these gentlemen say."

"Is it for this that you interrupted my conversation?" Guizot commented. "These "gentlemen should calm themselves; then they and you can sleep peacefully."[53]

Parisians raised barricades in the streets. Troops fired. They killed several citizens. Guizot resigned. King Louis-Philippe abdicated. Revolution again roiled France.

25

"You ... Are a Model of Order"

> She had become a celebrity ... The greatest air, the grandest manners ... a true Princess but with simple and natural dignity; nothing of awkwardness, of artifice, or of the theatrical; always dressed in the best taste and always in accordance with her age.[1]
> —Princess Lieven's friend Lady Holland

The 1848 revolution shattered Dorothea Lieven's well-ordered life.

Fighting raged all over Paris. Tricolor flags flew. "*Liberté, Egalité, Fraternité*" festooned every surface. Day and night the princess heard massive crowds of marchers; they clamored for war against Russia; they sang the *Marseillaise*; they chanted "*vive la république*," "*à bas le roi*," and "*à bas Guizot*."[2]

Throughout Princess Lieven's neighborhood furious mobs felled trees, ripped up paving stones, tore out pipes, smashed fountains, wrecked delivery wagons, overturned buses, and broke off iron fences from the fronts of noble houses to build barricades. Hordes of people pillaged the butchers, bakers, and wine merchants. Well armed citizens patrolled the streets; horrified, Dorothea heard how they stopped a man who ventured out in his carriage, forced him to descend, and hacked his vehicle to pieces to pile onto the barricades.

The boulevards around 2, rue st. Florentin, ran with blood. Princess Lieven could have watched the fusillade on the Place de la Concorde from her windows, had she dared to stand in so exposed a position. To leave Paris meant risking damaged railroad tracks, burned bridges, and the ubiquitous patrols of armed citizens. Vivid memories of 1789 shuddered through every aristocratic mind.

"I beg you not to go to the" Chamber. "You are in no condition to speak, you will only worsen it by going out. I already feel great remorse in letting you come to see me."[3] Dorothea trembled for Guizot's health and safety, not to mention her own. Everyone knew about "Guizot's Russian Princess."

"I entreat you, my dear Baron," she scrawled in pencil to her friend Meyendorff, Russian minister at Berlin, "to get a reference for me to no matter which authority at Cologne in case I need to resort to going there.... I feel myself so abandoned!"[4]

"You have no need for any reference at Cologne I know people there—& I will not abandon you."[5]

As a dull winter drizzle dripped from gloomy skies, Dorothea, afraid to stay in her apartment any longer, took out her jewels and gold and sewed them into the panels of her wide, horsehair petticoat. Enveloped in her maid's thick cloak and heavy veil, she then made her way on foot to the house of friends.

"I do not yet clearly see what can be done for you, for me, for my children," wrote Guizot from his hiding place. "When will I see you and how? ... I need to know what you think, what you can contrive, if you can contrive. Me, I think of nothing else. I was wrong, I believe about everything, everything."

"P. S. I re-open this" letter. "Your note really earned all my friendship. God knows if it is still good for" anything. "You have done well."[6]

Thanks to Dorothea, her love escaped from France disguised as valet to a German diplomat. Once assured of Guizot's safety, Dorothea returned to her apartment to pack.

"Dearest well-beloved. What a situation! How my heart is broken. Yours is strong. Guard your health, guard yourself—let us pray to God. Let us hope.

"I leave tomorrow, I think, for I must be sure about the status of the railway. I go with an unknown, sure husband.

"I am writing to you from *chez moi*, do you understand what I felt in returning to this room, oh my God, my God!

"Adieu, adieu, dearest of happiness, you know how I love you! Will we see one another? Think of that moment ... You do not know all the friends you have, and how your name in honored. I also, have found truly caring friends.... God bless you dearest."[7]

The princess traversed Paris to the Left Bank home of her trusted friends Austrian ambassador Count Apponyi and his countess. From there another intimate escorted her to the house of an English artist. With the help of some excellent make-up and a voluminous if not exactly fashionable cloak and large poke bonnet, Dorothea disguised herself as his wife. To her dismay they had to travel to the coast by a modern method she had so far managed to avoid—the railway. Then they crossed the choppy, gray-green Channel to safety.

৪৩েৎ

A refugee at age sixty-three, when a woman wants a settled life, Princess Lieven spent her mostly miserable eighteen month exile in England. Its humidity aggravated her rheumatism; inch-high writing laboring across green stationery* bore mute witness to recurring eye trouble. Pride held the princess to her customary lifestyle but expensive England's luxurious hotels, let alone payment of rent on her Paris apartment so as not to lose it, severely strained Dorothea's purse. And she missed Guizot terribly. Living modestly in a London suburb curtailed frequent visits to his princess, comfortably ensconced in fashionable Piccadilly's premier hotel. Short of money, he tutored his children to save it, began to write a history of England to earn it. That left even less time for Dorothea.

Yet, like an old war horse who rears its head and paws the ground at the trumpets' charge to battle, Princess Lieven responded to the clarion call of politics. The chaos of revolution, her harrowing flight, the pressures of exile were as nothing next to Dorothea Lieven's self-respect.

---

* *The princess used green paper to alleviate eye strain.*

She opened her salon in her hotel suite. Aberdeen and Guizot came daily. Prime minister John Russell and foreign secretary Palmerston visited regularly; so did Russian ambassador Brunnow now that the tsar had ceased to look askance at the princess. Indeed, London's political elite flocked to what Paris prized as the "observatory of Europe"[8] to exchange the latest news about stirring events sweeping the Continent.

Soon after Princess Lieven reached England, revolution struck Vienna. Its citizens forced a constitution on their unwilling emperor; Czech, Hungarian, Italian, and Rumanian nationalists declared their independence. For thirty years Austria's chancellor and Europe's premier statesman, the man whom Dorothea Lieven told, "you will be the last to see a constitution, but you will see one," the man she said would never admit to having been wrong, fell from power. Prince Metternich and his family fled to London.

> I expect from you, my Prince, not only your card, but the sign of a more friendly souvenir. You did not come again. I inquired. I was told your health prevents you from going out.... [Would] you like me to visit you? I would be truly pleased to see you again but I must know if this pleasure is shared.[9]

It was. So a dignified old lady called on the Metternichs. Stately and imposing, wearing an enormous hat and carrying a huge fan, dressed entirely in black but, nonetheless, the epitome of elegance, Princess Lieven "looked as if she had stepped out of some ancestral portrait," recalled Metternich's young grand-daughter. The princess hardly deigned "to glance at us poor earthworms."[10]

Barely had the princess and Metternich exchanged greetings when the Continent's epic struggle between conservatism and liberalism absorbed the erstwhile lovers. Their conversation resumed its old intensity, at least as regards politics, as if there had been no twenty-two-year break. When not together, they kept their footmen busy with delivering notes. Not even her eye trouble or the rheumatism that too often confined her to bed could stop Princess Lieven's pen when the excitement of politics beckoned.

By the time roses displayed their full glory, London's fumes chased the princess to Richmond. For three weeks she relished the company of her attentive son Alexander. Afterwards, Dorothea found the stormy skies and chilly rain of a typical English summer exactly suited to her black mood, which her unsettled situation, let alone the prospect of spending the winter in England, did little to improve.

"Do you recognize this date?" Dorothea asked Guizot. Why were they always separated on their anniversary, August 30th? "At last you are coming the day after tomorrow, & that makes me forgive" everything. "I shall meet you myself at Putney bridge, Saturday. It will be an outing. I shall be there at 4.30. You know I am punctual."[11]

"What a shame not to have been together yesterday the 30th! In England! We shall talk everything over on Saturday."[12]

⊰⊱

Princess Lieven heaved a huge sigh of relief when resurgent conservatism restored the Hapsburg Empire at the end of 1848. And she swelled with patriotic pride when a Russian army helped Austria crush Hungary's stubborn revolt. Its leaders (four of them Poles and, thus, Russian subjects) fled south through the Balkans to Constantinople. Exercising his treaty rights, the tsar demanded their extradition—or—war. Palmerston advised the sultan to refuse; if Russia attacked, Britain would fight.

Many conservatives, including Opposition leader Aberdeen, counted on the princess to convince prime minister Lord John Russell to curb Palmerston. Lord John often drove out to Richmond for the pleasure of discussing politics with his old friend the princess. "What stayed with me in my conversations is that Lord John does not reject criticisms of Lord Palmerston, that he voluntarily admits your praises,"[13] she wrote Aberdeen. And when Russell's wife, enthusiastic supporter of the Hungarian rebels, joined him, as she often did, the princess paid flattering attention to Lady John, who had immense influence over her uxorious spouse. Hence, Lord John promised the princess that the foreign office would send a conciliatory dispatch to St. Petersburg, and one to Constantinople expressing only limited British support.

֍

Meanwhile, universal male suffrage elected Prince Louis Napoleon Bonaparte[14] president of the French republic. This reassured Princess Lieven. Louis Napoleon might not be blessed with a surfeit of talent, but his despotic tendencies boded well for stability; France would surely become an empire. Indeed, Louis Napoleon restored enough order for Guizot to return to France, although not yet enough for his princess; anyway, cholera raged in Paris. "The only sure thing is separation, and for quite enough time," she lamented. "How can you expect me not to cry?"[15]

"This is our anniversary. Why are we not spending the day together? When shall we see each other again? Cholera at London. Cholera at Paris, at Boulogne, all over." Whether or not to return to Paris caused the princess sleepless nights. "It seems one can get used to anything, but I do not want to plunge into a cholera climate."[16] Besides, in balmy August 1849, Dorothea, staying at the Star and Garter hotel on breezy Richmond Hill, delighted in lively company—the Metternichs, the Palmerstons—"I also see a lot of John Russell. All the rest of the foreign colony daily, from top to bottom."[17]

Except one. Dorothea sorely missed François. Her eyes precluded writing at length, but she did write daily. When a thunderstorm soaked him François had only himself to blame, Dorothea scolded; he should have known to take an umbrella.

Meanwhile, a pressing problem claimed her attention. The princess arranged her hair in fashionably long ringlets framing her face, and a chignon of false hair. The latest creations came from Paris. "I have just received the impatiently awaited parcel but alas, you did not see it was blond hair, it is brown, dark brown that I want," Dorothea wrote her friend Lady Holland.* She returned the useless wig, begging her friend for the patience to send another. "I do not know what to do if I do not have my hair."[18]

֍

"I am counting on Madame de Lieven to put me back somewhat into the mainstream of world events,"[19] wrote one former French ambassador to another. So when

---

Lady Holland owned an apartment in Paris; her husband, son of the Hollands who held court at Holland House in Princess Lieven's London heyday, had retired from the diplomatic service.

glossy brown chestnuts tumbled from the trees Princess Lieven's servants got busy. They polished the crystal chandeliers until they sparkled and the grand mirrors that graced every fireplace until they gleamed, they whisked the dust sheets off the furniture, and they summoned the piano tuner to the corner mezzanine apartment at 2, rue St. Florentin.

Rough seas rendered Dorothea Lieven's last Channel crossing a misery. After several days rest at Boulogne, the princess, buffeted by strong emotion at coming "home," physically beaten and mentally battered by exile, not to mention a four month parting from Guizot, gratefully inhaled her first breath of soft Paris air.

Three days later her habitués again rested their gloved hands on the black and gold wrought-iron banister rail as they mounted the wide marble staircase leading to "the observatory of Europe." And Princess Lieven, wearing "a toque of black velvet with white feathers, which is the last word of fashion,"[20] went everywhere in society to attract all shades of opinion to her salon.

"Your enemies say you would never dare to visit my salon," the princess challenged a government minister, one of Louis Napoleon's earliest and most loyal supporters. Although itching to prove his opponents wrong, Persigny replied: "I hate those who wish the government ill, and rarely visit salons." But, noted an Austrian diplomat,

> I who know the maneuvers of Madame de Lieven, the indefatigable, the insinuating, the tenacious, the intriguer, the impossible to discourage, to rebut, ... I know he will end by giving in to her advances; she puts men under a duty to yield to her or pass for being badly brought up, rude, having no savoir-faire, lacking in what is due to an old lady, a great lady to whom all the ministers, all the most distinguished men, even all the Sovereigns give homage. You do not want to be in her bad books, and you go there.[21]

Her salon stood as Dorothea Lieven's sole source of power now that Guizot, who always scorned the greed and turmoil of politics, had happily resumed his intellectual activities. It "is really interesting, and completely special,"[22] enthused Russia's Empress Alexandra soon after the princess re-invigorated their correspondence by offering her tsaritsa regular political news. Alexandra came to count on the "so fascinating, so unique, so diverse content of these always so eagerly awaited green pages."[23] Indeed, Dorothea's weekly letters gave Alexandra

> *delightful* moments, because they *enchant* for *that certain something*, which only you have. To say a lot in a few words is already a great talent but to say it well and with such acumen is an even greater quality. No one else but you [has that], my dear and *faithful correspondent*."[24]
>
> The Tsar and I eagerly await your ideas and amusing anecdotes.[25]

Her salon empowered Princess Lieven to play an exciting part in politics. Don Pacifico★ and other British subjects had monetary claims against the Greek government, so Palmerston ordered a squadron to Athens, and told his minister to use it to extract the money from Greece. Declaring a blockade of the Greek coast, Wyse demanded full reparation for Don Pacifico et al. This "gunboat diplomacy" outraged

---

★*A Portuguese Jew born at Gibraltar, Don Pacifico held a British passport. He lived in Athens; when an anti–Semitic mob destroyed his house, the Greek police did nothing. Don Pacifico asked the British minister to support his claim for damages against the Greek government.*

many in England, not to mention France and Russia, Britain's co-guarantors of Greek independence.

The Tories had been denouncing Palmerston's high-handed conduct of their country's foreign policy for months. Aberdeen, in particular, considered courtesy and resolve not incompatible in foreign policy. Dorothea Lieven agreed. Palmerston's breezy brand of diplomacy offended her profound sense of professional decorum, and his speeches, although not necessarily his actions, showed a disquieting tendency to encourage democracy. She had long ago learned to separate personal feelings from politics, but deep down Dorothea hated Palmerston for contriving her husband's recall and thus indirectly causing her resultant tragedies. So despite recent intimate dinners with the Palmerstons at Richmond's Star and Garter hotel, Dorothea leapt at the chance to damage the foreign secretary.

Aberdeen could not ascertain any details of Wyse's demands, but had faith in Dorothea. He asked her for an accurate account "on *Monday morning.*"[26]

"I guarantee *perfect accuracy....* My London correspondent,* whom you know, assures me that the whole cabinet sanctioned and ordered" the ultimatum. "I will write you again tomorrow. I have asked for the accounts you want."[27]

"We are waiting for Greek news. Without some fresh incident, I do not see how we can follow up on our attack.... I rather believe that some communication took place between the Greek government and Mr. Wyse."[28] Aberdeen asked for it. Dorothea obliged.

Meanwhile Greece appealed to France. France agreed to mediate. Britain accepted. Aberdeen wanted to know what the French government really saw as the mediator's mission. Baron Gros's "instructions (known for a certainty) told him Greece very probably was right on all points, and he must not keep quiet if he finds this to be so, but" must persuade Greece to cede "on one or two points to open a door of retreat to England,"[29] promptly answered the princess, citing an impeccable source.

On March 26 Gros presented his proposals. Greece accepted. On April 8 Wyse made more demands. On April 27 Greece gave in to them. Meanwhile, on April 19 London and Paris had agreed to Gros's March 26 proposals.

Naturally preferring Greece's April 27 submission, Palmerston repudiated his April 19 agreement with France. On May 15 France recalled her ambassador in protest. On the 16th Palmerston denied the recall in Parliament. That day the French foreign minister read aloud, in the Chamber, the letter of recall formally presented to Palmerston on the 15th. Admirably armed by Princess Lieven, Aberdeen convinced the House of Lords to censure the government's policy on Greece.

Jubilation made Dorothea "ill. Three mustard plasters in the night, and my doctor all night in front of my bed, not a moment of sleep. To die of joy, very good. But to be ill from joy" is "neither said nor done!"[30]

Queen Victoria and many prominent public men besides, pressed prime minister Lord John Russell to remove Palmerston. Fearing that his government would fall, Lord John, instead, denounced in the House of Commons "a foreign cabal at work,

---

*An old and fast friend of Princess Lieven's, and a regular correspondent, the witty, aristocratic, politically astute Charles Greville, familiar through his official position as clerk of the Privy Council with all the workings of government.

which has endeavored to impose upon the public of England false statements, which for the sake of its own ends has raised unfounded suspicions with respect to the foreign policy of England, and which endeavors to overturn that foreign policy."[31] Russell's blatant jingoism had its desired effect.

In blaming the princess for "this storm got up in Paris,"[32] Palmerston paid a lopsided compliment to the power of the woman he hated, the woman he termed "the Tambour-Major of Paris." Yes, the princess wanted Palmerston's fall—out of personal revenge and political conviction. But the Opposition stirred up the "storm," as proved by a small sampling of Aberdeen's demands for information. Dorothea Lieven gladly armed the Tories, but Palmerston's "gunboat diplomacy" forced the battle.

It had unforeseen results. Dorothea asked her friend Emily Palmerston to sponsor a musician whom the princess favored.

> You ask me to oblige you, as if that were a feeling which could still remain to me, after all I have *heard* & all that I *know*. I am much more disposed to send you some evil, which you try incessantly to do us. My God! Is it possible to behave so! After a friendship of 38 years, and all the proofs of devotion & friendship I have always given you.
>
> What pains me most is that I can no longer remember the past without finding you in the middle of all my memories. I would like to forget you.[33]

"Must I reply or keep quiet?" Dorothea asked Guizot. "Regardless, I shall laugh."[34] Such long-standing friendship demanded a serious reply, he advised.

> "I always thought one could separate friendship from politics. I have done so with you ever since the time long ago when I totally disapproved of Lord Palmerston's policy; I never hid it from you. But for all that is personal to you, even for what is personal to your husband, politics apart, I always stayed your old and true friend, and I did not omit, I think, any occasion to prove it. Now you seem to think I cannot be so and that political differences must prevent friendship. I regret it; I shall not change my mind. I want you to return to my way of thinking. That is all I can do today."
> That is better than laughing. One must not laugh in the face of an old friend, ridiculously but seriously angry.[35]

Dorothea agreed.

⊗⊗⊗

Excitement over Don Pacifico piling on top of the pressures of exile took a predictable toll. Inch-high handwriting now toiled over Dorothea's green stationery. And chest pains plagued the princess. Her doctors advised spas.

"What a story my journey is & what a start at Ems!"[36] Famous as a medicinal spa for upper respiratory ailments, Bad Ems, with its many hot springs, lies in western Germany's lovely Lahntal, near Koblenz. Untamed nature overlooked the Lahn river flowing between steeply wooded banks sprinkled with ancient castles, and charming old villages that snuggle into the surrounding greenery. The princess traveled via Brussels and Cologne, then sailed along the scenic Rhine, "the University of Bonn with me ... singing atrocious songs."[37]

Arriving exhausted, she spent

> two hours going from door to door asking for lodging not one—nowhere *one* room. Finally in a tobacconist shop beside the engraver one room two beds my lady's maid

and me. Not one servant in that house. My son [Paul], my doctor, my three maids each one scattered in some barns I know not where.[38]

Four maids! Over her long, lace-trimmed pantalettes their mistress wore a rigid wool and horsehair underskirt several yards in circumference then, a second petticoat padded from the knees down and boned above. A white petticoat with several starched flounces came next and finally, a muslin underskirt over which the modish princess wore her full-skirted gown. To maintain the walking, driving, morning, afternoon, and evening dresses, not to mention under and outer wear, and the bed linen that the fastidious princess deemed essential, busied many hands.

Her personal physician, ably abetted by Ems resident expertise, prescribed drinking the waters, bathing in the curative springs, keeping a diet, and walking. Dorothea delighted in the superb countryside although not necessarily the spa's huge crowds. Guizot came, and so did her nephew Constantine Benckendorff, now a diplomat deep in the tsar's confidence. Alexander Lieven visited, too. Like his mother a keen observer and shrewd judge of character who knew everything and everyone, his presence gave her particular pleasure.

Superb weather greeted the princess at Schlangenbad, the delightful small spa near Frankfurt that she first enjoyed so many years ago, when she went to the Continent to meet Metternich. On her way back from Schlangenbad, he welcomed Dorothea at his castle on the Rhine—twenty-seven years after pregnancy aborted what should have been her first visit. The princess enjoyed herself so much that she promised to return soon.

ಬಂದಿ

Princess Lieven did patronize Schlangenbad again but in 1852 had neither the time to visit Prince Metternich and his plump, good-natured wife on her way there, nor the energy on her way back. The princess went to Schlangenbad to meet the Empress Alexandra.

Her brother's death had dealt a blow to Dorothea Lieven's influence at court, which she instantly took steps to rectify. Russia's minister at Berlin, Baron Peter von Meyendorff, born at Riga eleven years after Dorothea, stood on excellent terms with both the tsaritsa and his fellow Baltic Baron, chancellor Nesselrode. Meyendorff and the princess had corresponded sporadically before Alexander Benckendorff's death. Afterwards, "I heartily accept the exchange you propose," Meyendorff answered to Dorothea's suggestion that they put pen to paper regularly, "I shall write at length about my information."[39] As well, Dorothea sent her letters to the tsaritsa via Russia's diplomatic pouch bound for Berlin, recommending that Meyendorff read them before forwarding to St. Petersburg. There Alexandra shared Dorothea's letters with her husband.

At Schlangenbad the tsaritsa's court fawned all over Princess Lieven. She spent every morning with Alexandra in what the tsaritsa described as "pleasant, so *comfortable* society"; sometimes Dorothea read aloud from the note-books containing her memoirs, or the two ladies indulged in "good conversations, devoted and true friendship that the heart feels."[40] Hence Dorothea, distressed that her son Paul lacked a profession (he had resigned from the foreign service), tactfully dropped a hint to Alexandra—with positive results.

During another long tête-à-tête the tsaritsa showed her senior lady-in-waiting so much friendship, such great interest, that Dorothea "touched on the possible guarantees."★[41] Alexandra promised to do her utmost. "She told me that, and I believe"[42] her. And despite Guizot's misgivings, his princess turned out to be right.

Her eighteen month exile in England had severely strained Dorothea's purse, so a pension from the Russian treasury would be particularly welcome. And tangible recognition of lifelong service gratified Princess Lieven's pride, to say nothing of setting the seal on the return to her birthright: full court favor.

Even at Schlangenbad court custom demanded that the tsaritsa's highest-ranking lady-in-waiting attend grand soirées. And instead of obeying her doctor's order to rest between her mornings with Alexandra and her evenings with the court, Dorothea received a steady stream of exalted visitors, among them three "princesses whose names I am still trying to find out. I must stop that or I will be dead."[43] So she dined "chez moi tête-à-tête with Meyendorff." Recently promoted ambassador to Vienna, the man Dorothea Lieven deemed Russia's most able diplomat "adores me, & I adore him also; we are going to spend our time together. What things we already have to tell each other. I showed him your letter for," Dorothea flattered François, "he is very enthusiastic about you."[44]

Despite the exhaustion of court life, "I am very content that I have come. A precious memory & security for the future."[45] Indeed, Alexandra welcomed Dorothea's "green letters" even more "than before, for we understand and like each other better. This *reunion* re-warmed our hearts for" one another. "I know that under the *political* Princess Lieven there is *another* who belongs to me and to God."[46]

Schlangenbad also confirmed "a higher goodwill for me."[47] Dorothea Lieven had regained Tsar Nicholas's trust. Her self-respect and resolve had carried the princess through the upheaval of revolution and into a reordering of her life.

★ *A life pension for the princess as Alexandra's senior lady-in-waiting, possibly also as Prince Lieven's widow.*

26

The Last Act of the Drama

She is a stateswoman and a great lady in all the vicissitudes of life.[1]
—Count Joseph Hübner, Austrian ambassador to France

In 1853 a physically frail but mentally vigorous old lady plied her power quite alone. Her husband had died; her lovers had left diplomacy. No man stood at Dorothea Lieven's side when the Eastern Question again erupted. It provided a poignant setting for the ultimate drama in Princess Lieven's extraordinary career.

National priorities caused the Crimean War. For decades Britain had opposed Russia's relentless drive through the Ottoman Balkans towards control of Constantinople and the Straits. The new French government sought status. True to tradition, the Turks took advantage of their rivalries.

Personalities played no small part. As the princess predicted when he got himself elected president of the republic, France's Louis Napoleon metamorphosed into Emperor Napoleon III. He wanted to ground his dynasty in glory.

"An incomprehensible Trinity"[2] (Dorothea Lieven's description) governed Great Britain. Whig Lords John Russell and Palmerston, former prime minister and foreign secretary respectively, held senior positions* in a coalition cabinet led by Princess Lieven's old and close friend Tory Lord Aberdeen. Palmerston wanted to curb Russian power in the eastern Mediterranean; as home secretary he promoted a Russophobia impossible had he headed the foreign office. Aberdeen, too, sought to restrain Russia but disagreed with Palmerston's gratuitous belligerence. Confident the princess would convey his message to her court, the prime minister promised to spare no effort "to preserve peace, if it be possible."[3]

Tsar Nicholas seemed set on humbling Turkey—either with arms or diplomacy. Chancellor Nesselrode, Russian ambassador to Vienna Meyendorff, and Princess Lieven advised against war. She warned her friend and Count Nesselrode's confidant, Baron Meyendorff, that England and France would fight Russia in the Black Sea to block the spread of Russian influence in the Mediterranean. And the princess sent Meyendorff a letter written to her "almost under Lord Clarendon's dictation."[4]† It

---

Palmerston had to be given a cabinet post but the queen and Aberdeen, among others, refused to have him at the foreign office.
†*Princess Lieven meant a letter from her old friend and constant correspondent Charles Greville, clerk of the Privy Council, and a close friend of foreign secretary Clarendon.*

237

urged exploration of every diplomatic avenue before deciding on war. Dorothea underlined the British message: an impeccable and highly-placed source assured her of the French emperor's pacific intentions.

Louis Napoleon and Charles Auguste, Comte de Morny, had the same mother. Twenty-five years Princess Lieven's junior, Morny resulted from a clandestine love affair between her old friend Talleyrand's illegitimate son, and the Emperor Napoleon's step-daughter, married to Louis Bonaparte, once king of Holland. Brought up in the cream of society, the intelligent, ambitious Morny's ineffable charm, excellent conversation, and exquisite manners pleased the fastidious princess. And he enjoyed the company of women. One of Morny's many mistresses, the Belgian ambassador's wife, helped him amass a fortune when he returned to Paris after a distinguished military career and got himself elected to the Chamber of Deputies. A habitué of Princess Lieven's salon, Morny consistently advocated a return to the empire; he now stood second in importance to his half-brother.

Princess Dorothea Lieven. In old age. Artist: Delessert. Private Collection.

Their country, unlike England with its powerful war party led by the implacable and popular Palmerston, had no war party; and French public opinion opposed war with Russia. Realizing the difficulty, if not impossibility, of Russia prevailing against both France (with, arguably, the Continent's strongest army) and Britain (possessor of the world's premier navy), the princess encouraged her court to reach accommodation with France by reporting every well-substantiated indication of Napoleon's pacific tendencies and French anti-war feeling.

The Crimean War (1854–1856) devastated Dorothea. She had always dreaded war as a danger to stability. Now her adopted country and her beloved England were allied against her homeland. Fully independent, yet close to the imperial family, Princess

Lieven felt that duty demanded her departure from Paris. "Vagabond, at my age!"[5] (sixty-eight).

∞

"What anguish to have to leave you, to have to leave everything!"[6] the princess mourned for the first and last time, on the dank and bitter day of her arrival in Belgium's small, provincial capital; she and Guizot had agreed not to increase their mutual misery at having to part by writing about it. "The weather is frigid and everything has such an unhappy air!"[7] Brussels's damp climate and Dorothea's draughty hotel suite aggravated her ailments, especially the weak chest that had plagued her throughout life. How she missed her home, her friends, the stimulation of a vibrant cosmopolitan capital "so beautiful, so charming, so green, so nourishing, the air so gentle, and the conversation! And *you* twice a day, what paradise!"[8] François and Dorothea's love, their intimacy of heart and mind, had grown deeper, stronger, "from day to day more true! For time is needed to fully establish truth, even in the most intimate friendship."[9]

Despite her miseries, and they were many, this ailing yet resolute old lady lost no time in turning her depressing exile to splendid advantage. Many travelers passed through neutral Belgium's capital. Russia's Paris and London embassies had moved there, too. And diplomats, especially the British and French, could visit Princess Lieven's salon without constraint. So Dorothea's daily "green letters" to Empress Alexandra conveyed vital information, as they had for Nesselrode and Benckendorff during her London heyday—with one basic difference: Russia had no diplomatic relations with France or Britain.

"I have the honor to send Your Imperial Majesty a copy of a letter I received this morning from Morny," the most influential man in France next to his half-brother the emperor. "We stay in correspondence, it is a crucial and direct thread, and in the Emperor Napoleon's entourage or more his close circle, he is the only one on whom I fully rely."[10]

Naturally, neutral governments offered an indirect link between belligerents, but her court could depend on Princess Lieven as both direct and timely. So her "green letters" gave Dorothea's last years pleasure and interest; they "doubled this tender respectful affection I have for Your Imperial Majesty they sometimes give my Tsar pleasure: I love my letters."[11]

The princess realized their importance. She kept copies.

∞

Fragrant horse chestnut blooms had faded by the time poorly Princess Lieven escaped humid Brussels to recruit her strength at Bad Ems. But a nasty cold rain settled in, with the sky "no more *black* than the bottom of my heart."[12] The princess yearned for Paris, but peace seemed far out of reach.*

Two months later England and France agreed to peace negotiations based on Four Points. Concomitantly, the princess proposed a congress. "If talking leads to something, good. If it fails, you resume fighting. Meanwhile there is always a chance of accord if you are face to face. Why not advise your master to initiate this idea?"[13]

---

*By now the British had blockaded Russia's Baltic and Black Sea ports, and British and French forces had invaded the Crimea with the aim of taking Russia's premier Black Sea naval base, Sevastopol.

Count Morny liked the concept of a congress, but it could not come from France. Princess Lieven should suggest the notion to her court when winter weather halted fighting.

Meanwhile she followed her cure, took the baths, walked weather permitting, dined at three, went for a long carriage drive; received at eight but conversation proved lackluster; retired at ten. Then Count Morny arrived. Consequently, Ems improved, so much so that Dorothea put off her departure. Although weak from a serious illness, the urbane, witty count could still converse with consummate charm. "He spends his days with me, and our exchanges always give me something to put on paper."[14] In the evenings "we make music. He sings exquisitely."[15]

Feeling a little better, the princess proceeded to Schlangenbad. Hardly had she descended from her carriage when Prussia's crown prince called. (Neutral Prussia led the effort to persuade Russia to accept the Four Points.) Extremely close to his sister the tsaritsa, he urged Dorothea to impress on her the benefits of peace. "Oh my God I am preaching it in a desert for such a long time,"[16] Dorothea lamented to Guizot.

Tsar Nicholas rejected the Four Points.

Because of wording. "As a result we believe you do not seriously want peace." England must "use much gentler language. You say we are too sensitive, but the strong have become the weak. If one wants to soften, come to a resolution one will know how to manage it; the French language," Dorothea flattered Morny, "lends itself so well to that."[17]

"The strong have become the weak." The princess had striven against war. Always patriotic but never blindly, she now strove for peace. Dorothea Lieven knew Russia had little chance to prevail against both Britain and France.*

✠

"*Never* have I been so discouraged and sad."[18] In September the vastly outnumbered Russians, fighting bravely at the river Alma, inflicted heavy losses on the victors. Concomitantly, unseasonal cold drove Dorothea from Schlangenbad. Brussels hotels offered not one free room, Princess Lieven's lodging resembled a tomb, and houses rented only by the year—a dismal prospect. The frail princess had trouble sleeping, walking; she lost weight, and her wracking cough worsened. Without "rest, comfort, material pleasure, my friends, my routine, my mental resources, my doctors," her home, the Parisian climate, "I weep, I weep, and I perish."[19]

Wretched, old, feeble she might be, but that did not stop the princess from conferring at length with Lord Lansdowne, one of Aberdeen's coalition cabinet and fully conversant with his country's foreign policy. They focused on peace, Dorothea impressed on the tsaritsa. And Guizot's logic intensified Lansdowne's "natural penchant for peace," Dorothea told Meyendorff, now a member of the tsar's crown council.[20] Guizot gave Lansdowne ideas (first discussed with Dorothea) that the Englishman "boldly accepted."[21]

Britain's ambassador at Brussels, Lord Howard de Walden, confirmed that

---

* *Tsarist autocracy strangled free enterprise, causing Russia to lag behind Western Europe in building the infrastructure that Great Power status demanded. No railways connected St. Petersburg and Moscow to the south, so Russia could not move men and materiel efficiently to the Crimea. Communications and roads were poor, and finances so chaotic that Nicholas could not even equip his army with modern weapons.*

"Lansdowne's opinion had prevailed in the English cabinet ... Sevastopol finishes all."[22]★

Sevastopol defied the Allied siege. So Palmerston descended on Paris to stiffen the apathetic French. Lord Howard met him; "he came to see me one hour after his return to give me all the details." The "taking of Sevastopol is an idea fixed in the mind of every Englishman." The country preferred peace, but thought Russia's tepid attitude made it impossible. Napoleon, "annoyed (the word Lord Howard used)" at Russia's fierce resistance, nonetheless agreed to continue the siege. Time, the Allies felt, favored them; hence, "they are resolved to continue to bomb, to ruin as much as they can, but not to mount an assault until later, and that could take a long time. While waiting they will fortify Balaclava and a French camp that is the program" Palmerston, Cowley (ambassador to France), and Howard discussed "the day before yesterday,"[23] and intended the princess to convey to her court without delay.

"I write to Your Imperial Majesty very ill, for the past ten days I spit blood, that worries me, above all in contemplating from my window Brussels's gloomy misty and cold sky and my even more miserable shelter. I do not even dare go out in my carriage."[24]

Dorothea counted the days until November 20th.

Frantic to return to Paris, she had enlisted Morny's aid while they were at Ems. Morny immediately spoke to Napoleon. Perfectly pleased at the prospect of Princess Lieven's return (had she not been one of his earliest supporters?), the emperor agreed to issue a passport and residence permit. Morny promised them by November 20th.

The date came and went. No documents.

"I am always ill and I spit blood, and it kills to keep me here! I do not go out at all. I am even forbidden the carriage."[25]

"My evil cough continues, and my isolation too. When will the door of my prison be open?" Dorothea asked François. "I beg you go to Morny. I beg you go to him at once."[26]

> I spent three quarters of an hour with M.... They are desperate to keep the alliance and to remove those who want to rupture it. Intentions are the same. But a little patience is needed.... [Morny] assured me it would be done. He will use every [opening].... I said all that could be said to support, to exhort, to press. But evidently for now one must wait.[27]

Palmerston had been perfectly plain. Were the princess allowed back in Paris, she would work day and night to break the Anglo-French alliance. Nonetheless, Napoleon promised Morny that he would let Princess Lieven return, but did not commit to a date. So Morny counseled Dorothea to write him a letter which he could show only to the emperor.

"Thank you thousands and thousands of times for your good advice. Useful, excellent, you give the tone, I sing the song."[28]

Princess Lieven's letter[29] elicited much sympathy, but no documents. So Morny suggested an appeal to her English friends. Dorothea demurred; how absurd for them to assign her such importance that she must dispel their doubts. Duty made her leave Paris, decorum, to set an example she could no longer sustain. Napoleon should take pity on the poorly princess's suffering, and let her live in Paris.

★*The princess told her court that Russia must be resigned to the fall of Sevastopol. Once landed in the Crimea Britain could not leave without a major victory; Napoleon needed victory to appease his army.*

Meanwhile, military reversals forced Tsar Nicholas to accept the Four Points. Yet Palmerston, now predominant in Aberdeen's cabinet, doubted Russian sincerity. No one wanted peace more than Russia, the princess told Lord Howard, but Russia suspected Allied sincerity; Britain and Russia must "decide to believe in each other."[30]

Soon after the princess reported this to Russia, Lord Howard received a letter from his chief, Lord Clarendon, and immediately sought a tête-à-tête. The cabinet would consider the Four Points only on condition that England add "comments whose nature is vague."

If "there is desire for peace" Russia's concession "must be taken with both hands," the princess countered, and above all England must "believe in our good faith."[31]

Would Russia's acceptance of the Four Points satisfy England? she asked Greville that day.

> You never believe me when I speak about us, I think myself truly honest and I can really swear to my private certainty that my Tsar has no ulterior motive in what he says today. Thus do not let fall, do not repel his acceptance.... I have great trouble writing these few lines, my present routine need not last much longer, I shall succumb.... [If] I am not got out of this quickly you will have no more green letters.[32]

₧☍₨

At the same time a Russian lady passing through Berlin told Dorothea's diplomat nephew Constantine Benckendorff how, in St. Petersburg, rumors were rife that the French government soon would announce Princess Lieven's return to Paris. This, Constantine exploded to his aunt, would mean a break with him as well as with her sons. And she could expect the Russian treasury to stop paying her pension.

That frightened Dorothea. Before, when she went to Paris against the tsar's will she had reason on her side; now, a return to the enemy capital would justify Nicholas's anger. So Dorothea told Guizot to say that *if* she came to Paris, it would be only "to consult her doctor and then to go south to Nice★ if he allows it and if she still has the strength."[33]

Two hours later Dorothea urged Guizot to write instantly. He must stress

> how my state worries you, how everyone is talking about it. You have spoken with [Dr.] Andral, he knows I spit blood. Nothing will perhaps be needed, but he must see me to judge, that in any case the Brussels climate is too harsh for me & then you will beg me to leave quickly & not wait until it is too late. Be very worried and very pressing, I need that and I count on it. For the rest your usual letter, only no disobliging sentences for us and enough interest to motivate me to forward it. I am really most miserable.[34]

Having omitted to mention a possible return to Paris to her court so as to be able to present it with a fait accompli, Dorothea then wrote Empress Alexandra and Meyendorff about Nice—as a "type of lightning-rod against the lightning."[35]

Lord Howard de Walden called again. "I feel very ill today and will only give a condensed version," Dorothea wrote Alexandra. Despite "the bellicose tone of the Queen's speech, the preparations, the huge sacrifices they have made for war," a true

---

★*Nice belonged to the kingdom of Sardinia.*

desire for peace united Aberdeen's cabinet. Still, the government must show surface sincerity for war, so that the public would be all the more willing to end it. And what about the public mood in Russia? The princess affirmed its pugnacity. Would that prevent the tsar from making peace? Prevent? The tsar's voice had roused his subjects; it "would make them accept peace with the same enthusiasm if he wished it."[36] Lord Howard listened closely.

He then said the sticking point would be naval parity in the Black Sea. Preliminaries would omit Sevastopol; "all discretion is being sought and will be sought, linguistic artifices to give all proposals respect and a lofty tone. I repeat exactly what was told me."[37] Of course Howard's demands were "the height of English perversity. Negotiation would greatly modify it. He agreed." Again the princess commended Howard's message to her court. "I am suffering so much, Madame, that I cannot continue this letter."[38]

Dorothea felt as if she would surely "succumb. The electric wire will tell you in time, for I do not want to die without seeing you again," she confided to François. "Another whole night without sleep. Oh what frightful images occupy my thought! And my helplessness! For how to rise up against this obstacle when I am so ill."[39]

"I am going to tell you rather in haste about my conversation" with Morny, Guizot replied. "Three quarters of an hour. Still the Emperor Nap's goodwill; but goodwill mixed with sadness and strain. They have new strong insistences from London."[40]

> I got your letter. I did not sleep all night & am too sad to write. The shortest would be to die; that would remove embarrassment for everyone. I only pity you, for you really love me. But I, to have you so close and not be with you? Do you see that this destroys my heart, and my health cannot take it. I have so little health left.
>
> I have no more strength to write. I spent the whole day in bed.... I had a violent attack of bile, inevitable result of all this emotion.[41]

After another night of nagging worry the princess struggled to a sitting position in bed, and carefully draped a fine cashmere shawl around her shoulders against the ubiquitous draught. As the black Brussels sky slowly turned into a nasty gray dawn Dorothea reached a difficult decision: she must swallow her pride.

"To whom can I turn in my current state, if not to you my friend of forty years," the princess wrote Lady Palmerston. "Absence or silence cannot efface a trust of such long-standing."

> I am dying here. I wrote you that 6 weeks ago. I say it more certainly today. I spit blood. I have acute liver attacks, my strength is ebbing. I no longer leave my room at all, on occasion not even my bed. The King's doctor ... [has] exhausted his resources, and blames my condition on the harsh and humid Brussels climate. He wants to be rid of me (and I of him).
>
> If I placed myself at Paris in the hands of my enemy, how on earth could I be a target of mistrust? Would it not be to my maximum benefit to make myself invisible? To live there, if I do live, retired, isolated, focused only on caring for my health and for my friends?
>
> Implore your husband to help me. The question concerns pure humanity.... [Let] me believe that the memory, the memory of so many years of friendship, of this very time of year [Christmas and Dorothea's birthday] that we always spent together in such pleasant and tender happiness, that all these reminders will motivate you to help me. This is all I ask of you: tell them at Paris that you are not a barrier, and do not let me die.[42]

A week later Princess Lieven's maid drew back the curtains to reveal all too frequent rain drops crawling jerkily down the window pane. Several promising letters lay in a pile on Dorothea's breakfast tray, the top one addressed in Lady Palmerston's familiar hand-writing.

> I am distressed to know that you are sick and miserable—And to see that you think I can do anything about it—for in truth I can do nothing at all. Nor can my husband—I know there are a large number of people here and in Paris who seriously fear your return to Paris and the power of your Salon and who think that in the present situation the Emperor must exclude Russian ladies from Paris. But I know of no one who can have talked to him about this matter.
>
> Certainly the Salons of Paris have a really important influence, and of course those that belong to Russia cannot approve of the close alliance between our two constitutional countries.

To jeopardize the Anglo-French alliance would be as disastrous for Britain as for Europe. Hence, Dorothea "must forgive those who work for the good of their country, and who justifiably although perhaps mistakenly, fear the influence you might apply."[43]

If nothing else, Emily Palmerston's letter testified to Dorothea Lieven's power.

⁂C&#x3;

Late on the evening of December 30, 1854, the Brussels train puffed slowly into the main Paris railway station. When it had steamed to a full stop the conductor solicitously handed down from her carriage a tall, dignified old lady elegantly dressed in black. One day before Princess Lieven entered her seventieth year she received her "passport & residence & without limit."[44] Emperor Napoleon III had braved his British ally.

"I want my joy to be complete, it cannot be. I will always have the nightmare of Petersburg."[45] Dorothea had already told the Empress Alexandra about her plan of going to Nice to salvage her health; had asked Guizot to write a letter full of worry about her health but with enough political interest to forward to Alexandra. Now,

> after much indecision, struggles, my health miseries, the absolute concern it causes me, the positive counsel of the doctor made me decide to leave Brussels, and yesterday the means unexpectedly offered itself. My friends in Paris have long known, as is known in St. Petersburg, of my deplorable state, they are extremely worried; they organized a campaign and last evening the French minister ... [told me] that a telegraphic dispatch brought him the order to offer me a passport for France. This morning Morny's letter confirmed it most courteously. I am very troubled by this sudden news and a little eager to resist, but as I plan on going to Nice I accept, on reflection, this more direct way of getting myself there, the only practical one in this season. I shall consult Doctor Andral in Paris ... [and] leave as soon as my strength allows.[46]

"Very troubled." Dorothea Lieven again defied her tsar, but under different circumstances. Before, when she went to Paris against his wishes, her sycophantic husband and brother protected her at court; at this point, "dear Princess, count on the friendship of your appreciative Alexandra."[47] So the court confined itself to Meyendorff's counsel. "You are, even when ill, a personage"; thus, "I would wish that you could continue" to Nice at once. "Here one does not want you to give the impression of progress in our relations."[48]

Dr. Andral found damage to Princess Lieven's lung. "Fits of painful, choking coughing frighten me."[49] Since Andral insisted on keeping her under observation, the ailing princess lived the life of a semi-invalid, "retired, peaceful, and ignored"— her "duty and interest, and my letters are not censored."[50] Still, the princess scrawled on the letter she had dictated for Alexandra, although Andral forbad her to speak he did not forbid her to listen. So Dorothea saw a few close friends, "those who can inform me the best."[51] "I have the essence of the cream, you know the layer that gives such a good taste to the coffee?"[52]

ಬಿಎಜ

At the end of January Aberdeen's coalition collapsed, and Palmerston became prime minister. Concomitantly, Princess Lieven's old friend Lord John Russell arrived in Paris to prepare joint strategy for peace negotiations. Not so long before, Dorothea, despite debilitating illness, had written her friend Charles Greville from Brussels that England must believe in the sincerity of Russia's pacific intentions. Extremely close to foreign secretary Clarendon, Greville now asked Dorothea to convince Lord John of Russia's good faith.

In February Tsar Nicholas I, contrary to Romanov tradition, died in his bed— of a fever. "The country is showing great unity. It would like peace, but not a *humiliating* one. The four points are the agreed basis and more than suffice if peace is truly desired," Meyendorff wrote. Dorothea copied his barely legible handwriting to make sure Morny understood. Nicholas's death might be "a providential answer to the eastern question. Do they need to complain," to "fear his ambition, his pride, his prestige? All that vanishes in the presence of his tomb. Perhaps the new reign will begin with peace! That would be a joy for all, for Europe as for Russia and France."[53]

"For Russia and France." Meyendorff did not mention England. That glaring omission, his overall tone, and his confidence in Dorothea Lieven's friendship with Morny indicate that Meyendorff's letter meant to extend a peace feeler towards France.

Meanwhile the war raged on, but for Dorothea Tsar Nicholas's death brought peace of a sort. Meyendorff had seen "those whose sufferings you take to heart."* The "*master* read your letter with great interest, and his mother wants to tell you many loving things."[54]

By March British, French, and Russian diplomats prepared to meet in Vienna to discuss peace. "My mind feels very contentious, between all the news that each hour of the day brings me on the great question of peace or continuation of this horrible war. One cannot unravel what could come out of this conflict of interests, of influence."[55] After checking and re-checking her sources Dorothea daily sent Alexandra fact-filled analyses, adjuring Meyendorff to read them. Guizot, now president of the prestigious Académie Française, had another long tête-à-tête with Napoleon. The emperor asked the former foreign minister about "the various ways to interpret the third point,[56] showed himself even baffled." Guizot found it strange that the Allies had "not yet debated the capital point of the negotiations among themselves," but what "struck him in the whole talk was the Emp.'s evidently sincere penchant for peace."[57]

---

*Empress Alexandra had been extremely ill and deeply mourned her beloved husband. Her son Tsar Alexander II, formerly Prince Lieven's charge, had been very close to his father.

The diplomats reached agreement. Determined to destroy Russian naval power, prime minister Palmerston convinced Emperor Napoleon to reject it.

෯ාC৪

Sevastopol still stood in June. Princess Lieven's intimates fled Paris for the countryside. As a Russian residing in the enemy capital she, having moved heaven and earth for permission to live there, would hardly hazard leaving for German spas. Nor did Dorothea have great choice in French resorts. Her "enemy" status made many hesitate to socialize with her, Guizot explained. Fortunately this painful fact had so far escaped the princess, living, as she did, within her exclusive circle of friends. Elsewhere in France it would be obvious.

Depressed as much by being alone as by her doctor's dictum that she would never be rid of her racking cough, Dorothea craved a change of scene. So as the summer weeks slipped slowly by, the princess decided to join a few close friends in the delightful village of Maintenon, near Paris.

Lamenting her lot to "love a writer, a historian!"[58] Dorothea lured François away from his labors. They strolled through Maintenon's scenic park in the soft September sunshine, they admired the magnificent gothic castle, once residence of Louis XIV's secret wife the Marquise de Maintenon. A beautiful river wound all the way around the turreted castle, forming tranquil pools among flower-bedded islands linked by enchanting small bridges. Stately trees stood everywhere, and

> the serpentine river on the other side under an avenue of formal swaying poplars. The pretty gondolas navigating under their shade. A varied vegetation of every color green, superb lawns and to crown all a fine aqueduct that Louis XIV began facing the chateau and at the end of the pools and flower-beds.[59]

News of terrible butchery broke into this idyllic beauty. On September 8 France prevailed at Malakhov—losing 5,000 men. Sevastopol fell two days later.

Princess Lieven greeted the news with mixed feelings. Russia's defeat pierced her patriotic pride, yet stirred hope that the war would end. Instead, Dorothea "received a letter from Constantine." The "Tsar is sending him to the Crimea, to undertake the autumn campaign. He asks my forgiveness"—for his anger at Dorothea's return to Paris. "He entrusts his wife and children to me. His words are affecting, simple, sad. I am touched.

"Constantine promises to be in Berlin by winter if.—Oh this miserable war."[60]

෯ාC৪

Meanwhile, startling news from London. "Present difficulties put *the allies among themselves* at odds when it comes to peace,"[61] the princess informed her tsaritsa. Palmerston wanted to continue the war despite Sevastopol's fall, but French victories had satisfied Napoleon's need for glory.

Thus the emperor sent a message to Russia or, in other words, Morny responded to Meyendorff's earlier peace feeler. "I dare to affirm that goals would be less difficult and less demanding after the success than before," Morny wrote the princess. "But when one is two and even four,* it is hard to predict if one will encourage or curb

---

The kingdom of Sardinia had joined Britain and France; Austria threatened to follow.

the other." Since France could "only lose by continuing," and had "all the honors of the campaign my opinion is to hold to that, for our position will be immense."[62]

And Rothschild called on the princess immediately after having spent a congenial day hunting wild boar with Napoleon. Troubled about financing more fighting, the banker to governments and power brokers wanted peace.

> In two months the situation could be much changed. I will not burden myself by reiterating all his explanations about numbers, lacking today, and which could flood in then. Briefly, today they need it, today at least the money men* would weigh in with all their might to achieve it,

the princess promptly wrote Meyendorff.

> The need, the proclivity for peace here, now, the real possibility of change in two months, making it too late, thus the urgency if we want peace, to make it now. Thiers also visited and chattered to me although he never comes. Same text, same reasons.... [The Allies were] preparing gigantic means against us.... [As the] general word *for* war meant *Sevastopol*—today the *neutrality* of the Black Sea is *for* peace. They will not budge from that. We must agree or the war will be endless. And they cannot understand why we do not give in.... [Neutrality] strikes everyone, there is no disgrace. We only need warships for aggression, what they found at Sevastopol fully justifies past suspicions and precautions about the future.
>
> I tell you everything, faithfully without exaggeration. We ignored more than one warning, three, four times, we could have had peace, we did not want it ... [and] each stage has worsened our position. That is the truth. Is it allowed in our country?
>
> Morny fully confirms what Thiers and Rothschild say. They are preparing to attack Kronstadt[63] with hellish inventions on a huge scale in the spring.[64]

Princess Lieven suggested that Rothschild send such important news directly to St. Petersburg. But because Russia had ignored his advice in the past, Rothschild preferred to convey his message through a more certain medium.

The frail old lady pounded on differences between Britain and France. Her "London correspondent" Charles Greville sent

> quite favorable news. Your Imp. Maj. will see from the latest ... [letter that] Palmerston's resistance seems a little shaken. The work meanwhile is difficult; but if the Emp. Nap. persists, I think him a good man who will reach his goal by gentle means, but he must be persuaded that he runs no risk of falling out with England.[65]

"The game is good for us, let us try to play it," the princess urged Meyendorff.

> To speak to you with this [assurance] ... I must feel myself strongly enough convinced to do it; my conscience must truly agree with my motive. My words have been granted interest and attention for 25 years. I perhaps have more right to that today. Always give my seasoned experience and devotion the trust they merit.[66]

To her intense gratification Meyendorff's letters made the princess "think mine have a certain value where you are, and that you and others place some confidence in me."[67]

֍

Austria opened 1856 with a threat. She would join the Allies unless Russia negotiated for peace based on the Four Points plus two new ones. Tsar Alexander II agreed.

---

*Napoleon's trusted financial advisor, the Jewish financier Achille Fuld (sometimes spelled Fould), had already impressed on Princess Lieven the need for peace and Franco-Russian friendship.

Napoleon's prestige stood so high that the Powers chose to hold Europe's first peace conference in forty years at Paris rather then Vienna, traditional center of diplomacy.

Foreign secretary Clarendon urged Greville to propose to the princess that the tsar tell his envoys not to haggle over concessions, to accede to all British and French demands, relying on them not to ask for anything contrary to Russia's honor. Greville thought "it most likely Madame de Lieven will se moquer de moi,[68] and think me very extravagant gravely to propose that" her tsar "voluntarily offer to give us all we want merely to enable us to gratify the English public with a greater show of triumph over Russia."[69]

So a different letter left London. Princess Lieven copied the most pertinent part for the empress, so that she could "see the good intentions with which Lord Clarendon arrives here, he evidently wished that I should know about them."[70]

Clarendon and ambassador Cowley wanted to reach agreement. The British foreign secretary greatly respected Orlov,[*] trusted they would "settle all knotty points in a very short time," and relied "entirely on his and Brunnow's sincere & correct desire to make peace." Dorothea marked Greville's next paragraph for her court's special notice:

> "The state of opinion here is curious. There is an unusual acquiescence in the attempt to make peace, & not a single public meeting or petition for going on with the war, but in spite of these pacific appearances nothing would be so universally popular as the return of Clarendon with an announcement that he had failed, and that the war must go on, with or without France, tho' of course the concurrence of France would be greatly preferred."[71]

೮೦౧೪

The end of hostilities restored Princess Lieven's salon as a diplomatic force. There, the day after his arrival to represent Russia at the peace conference, Baron Brunnow met Count Morny. Morny explained that Napoleon wanted overtly to show the importance of his English alliance, but secretly to forge closer ties to Russia. Skillful diplomacy would be needed to develop this policy, Morny impressed on Brunnow.

So France's tactful treatment of England resulted "in restraint that feels a little like weakness and makes cowards believe peace is not so certain."[72] Russia must remember that Napoleon wanted peace to emerge from Paris. Yes, Clarendon's language convinced Dorothea that Palmerston told him to make new demands. But "I am always assured that the Emp. Nap. will repel" them; yet, "he will not risk entangling himself with England."[73]

Princess Lieven lived in Talleyrand's former apartment. In the room that she used for her salon, Tsar Alexander I and the king of Prussia "decided the fate of France and of Europe (the Tsar stayed at M. de Talleyrand's) in this same salon where yesterday we discussed the events of this peace signature; of this peace[†] made under the auspices of the proscribed man's nephew."

---

[*]Count Orlov figured in Dorothea Lieven's story during the diplomatic crisis over Belgium, and when she resisted her husband's order not to return to Paris for the third time. Orlov now represented Russia at the peace conference together with Baron Brunnow, formerly ambassador to Britain.
[†]Peace of Paris, March 1856. Russia made concessions in the Balkans, ceded ancient rights in the Ottoman Empire, and agreed to the neutrality of the Black Sea.

"42 years ago today the Allies entered Paris; they hailed the fall of the conqueror who made the world quake, they forbad his race. What a parallel with today's events!"[74]

⊰⊱

After basking in the attentions of her sons Dorothea anticipated a soothing summer at spas. But she seemed always to feel nauseous, and Empress Alexandra's insistence on meeting her at either Stuttgart or a nearby resort threw Dorothea's plans into disorder. "I am tired to death of packing, of preparations." Guizot must forgive his princess "for being so low but it is a marvel I can write even one word."[75]

Alexandra decided on Wildbad. Dorothea hated it. The spa's location guaranteed maximum sunshine but torrential rain persisted throughout the princess's stay. At any rate, having already facilitated Morny's appointment as ambassador to Russia, Dorothea derived some satisfaction from smoothing his path with the tsaritsa* and Meyendorff.

Barely did Princess Lieven arrive at Schlangenbad when an intestinal disorder attacked. It so debilitated her that Dorothea considered breaking her twenty-year habit of writing Guizot daily. Besides, while horrible Wildbad had at least been mentally stimulating, in Schlangenbad she met no one to give her letters interest. So with apologies to François for boring content, Dorothea took up her pen. "If I fail you, I am lost."[76]

She could never bore him, Guizot replied. "There is not one of your feelings that I do not understand and that do not please me, in the most intimate and the most serious sense of this, so often profaned, word."[77]

Pleurisy, sufficiently serious at her age, soon assailed the princess's weak chest. Forbidden to strain her lungs with speech, Dorothea lightened her slow recovery by listening to her son Paul and her nephew Constantine discuss diplomacy.

Recurring illness demoralized Dorothea; nonetheless, she showed the world a cheerful face, complaining only to François that Schlangenbad, her doctors, and their medicines failed to do her good. Perhaps Baden-Baden would be better. Quite by chance an early supporter of her diplomatic career—her former chief—stayed at the same hotel. Count Nesselrode and Princess Lieven delighted in each other's company, but she did not understand how he could bear to retire, much less enjoy retirement. Nesselrode could not comprehend Princess Lieven's abiding passion for politics.

⊰⊱

In November, Lord Granville found his mother's old friend "as fresh as a four-year-old. She pumped me with the force of a steam engine."[78]

"Here is my humble New Year gift. I would wish to bring it to you myself & embrace both of you. But I am infected," Dorothea wrote her friends the Hollands. "Thousand thousand wishes, and stay for me what you are. I love you both very much."[79]

"After fifteen days of a cold and eight days of acuate bronchitis, without pain

Because of Alexander I's deference to his mother the Empress Maria, the empress-mother took precedence over the reigning tsar's wife.

and in full control of her faculties, frailty against the illness rather than its force, defeated her." Until Saturday evening the 24th, concern about her health and fear of death consumed Dorothea. On reaching her house at ten o'clock on Sunday, Guizot got "three lines from her written in pencil, in a firm hand: 'Write, I beg of you, to M. Cuvier to come to me after the service. I am sending him my carriage. I wish to take communion!'" Guizot entered

> her room; I found her perfectly tranquil, very weak, very changed, but with no spiritual distress. Evidently she had seen her fate and made her decision. M. Cuvier arrived at two-thirty. She wanted her son and me to stay in her room. He read the service, the liturgical prayers and gave her communion, she sat in her bed, composed, calm, plainly sad.
>
> Paul, acutely touched, turned away to cry; she caught sight of him, summoned him, embraced him; he turned away again, in tears; she made a sign to me, and drew my attention to him with a rather sudden flash of maternal pride, she said "He has a heart!" called him to her and taking my hand: "I ask you always to have friendship for him."
>
> In great weakness she spent Sunday 25th in mental peace that also turned into physical peace. In the evening Baron Meyendorff came into the drawing room; she wished to see him alone for one minute; he stayed in her room for ten minutes. She said to him: "I thought I would die this evening, that has not happened." The night from Sunday to Monday was difficult; no strength to expectorate. All the symptoms were present.
>
> On Monday morning she said to her son: "No funerals; some prayers in my room and immediately the train to Courland." She always wanted to be buried at the family estate next to her two sons who died at Petersburg in 1835.
>
> I found her much more feeble, again much changed, but always calm, speaking very little, but occupying herself with the smallest things, including the dinner menu for her recently arrived Benckendorff nephew and wife. At noon she said: "If I do not die this time it would be a pity, I feel myself so ready!" In the evening, towards ten o'clock, she beckoned to me: "I am suffocating! ... my fan!" I gave it to her, she tried to fan herself. A mustard plaster was put on her chest.
>
> When it began to take effect she gestured that she wanted to write. She was given pencil and paper. She wrote very legibly: "How long must this go on?" and a few minutes later, she said: "Go away, all of you go away. I want to sleep." We left her room, her son, her nephew, and I. After an hour, they looked for me. She was no more. I am convinced she saw herself at the point of death and did not wish us to see her dying.[80]

Like her mother, Dorothea Lieven died with dignity, "serenity, and exemplary resignation."

"Her son gave me a letter," Guizot concluded, that "she had written in pencil and sealed the evening before: 'I thank you for twenty years of love and happiness. Do not forget me.'"[81]

Epilogue

"Last night, one of the personalities who, for a half century, ranked as the most notable in the diplomatic world and on the great European scene, disappeared from it." Princess Dorothea Lieven had witnessed "the eighteenth century, had been the last representative of a great epoch and the last reservoir of strong traditions." The Austrian ambassador felt he had "lost a friend and Paris loses its last salon."[1]

Indeed, her death created "a void that can never be filled. Without being in total intimacy with Princess Lieven, I had a great deal of liking for her society," wrote another ambassador, "I agreed with her in mind and in judgment; she was a person of the greatest intelligence and of a noble and trustworthy character."[2] Her friend's death could "not leave me without a certain emotion," the duchess of Dino confided to a diplomat. "You will feel, you too, the space she has left, I do not say precisely the person, but Mme. de Lieven's salon."[3] She "makes a great blank," asserted a future foreign secretary, "both as regards herself and her salon, which is unreplaceable and unreplaced."[4]

London, Paris, and St. Petersburg seethed with speculation over the disposal of Princess Lieven's papers. She "had known everyone in the Courts and cabinets for thirty or forty years." Dorothea participated, directly or indirectly, in every significant diplomatic development. She "knew all the secret annals of diplomacy."[5]

Fully aware that posterity would treasure her papers, the princess, shortly before her death and with her son Paul's consent, entrusted them to her French executor "for fear of any claim being made on them by the Russian Embassy."[6] After a prudent interval, his co-executor transferred the papers to Paul Lieven, who left them to his brother. Alexander Lieven died in 1886. His will specified that the entire collection stay sealed for fifty years.

Shortly before World War One Alexander's heir deposited the papers for safekeeping in the archives of the Livonian nobility. Those archives disappeared during the Bolshevik revolution. Sometime between 1917 and 1919, however, several sizeable cardboard boxes were smuggled into Germany. When the archivists at Berlin's State Library opened them, they were surprised to see Princess Lieven's papers. The Lieven family resumed possession. They subsequently sold the collection to the British Museum Library.

"You know, dear Princess, my feelings towards you. Like yours, they are sheltered from the influences of space and time," Tsar Alexander II wrote Princess Lieven

251

towards the end of the Crimean War. "If your family has a hereditary devotion to us, the attachment we bear them, also passes from one generation to" another.

"I will never forget the days when, at my entry into the World, you gave me so many proofs of affection."

"I gratefully accept your good wishes. I agree with yours in favor of peace, and I shall certainly not refuse the benefit to Russia as to Europe."[7]

Dorothea Lieven's last tsar had written a fitting epitaph.

Appendix

Princess Lieven's Medical Testimonial

"The Uterine Irregularities and Variations that have been attended by more or less profuse Hemorrhages even on moderate bodily exertion, or mental excitement together with excessive sensibility of the Nervous System generally; the frequent Disorders of the Digestive Organs and resultant Debility; disturbed and unrefreshing sleep, and laterally the Emaciation without any obvious sources of fatigue beyond those above enumerated and under which Her Highness, The Princess Lieven, at present labors, are decided marks of the presence of that Climacteric Epoch or Crisis which demands the greatest care and attention, both generally and particularly, in order to avert the invasion of certain serious diseases peculiar to this period of life.

"From some knowledge of Her Highness's constitution, acquired in the three years I have had the honor to be Princess Lieven's medical advisor, but, more especially, since witnessing the symptoms that followed Her Highness's recent journey to England, although short, and not productive of much fatigue, in going and returning, I am definitely of the opinion that a state of complete mental and bodily repose are at this moment, and for some time to come will be, essential to Her Highness's health, which has, laterally, been much affected and impaired by change of place and bodily fatigue.

"Robert Alexander Chermside, M. D. K. H. Fellow of the Royal College of Physicians, London. M. D. of the University of Edinburgh V. C. Physician Extraordinary to Her Royal Highness the Duchess of Kent. Paris, 26th August, 1837" (British Library, Lieven Papers, ADD. 47416, # 57).

Princess Lieven's Letter of Resignation

"Monsieur le Comte [Nesselrode], a letter" from "the Imperial Ministry under Your Excellency's orders engaged me to come to St. Petersburg during the spring. It is with very sincere regret that today, I must constrain myself to renounce the execution of this duty. My health entirely obliges me to take the waters in Germany. Forced for a number of years to have recourse to this periodic remedy every summer

I cannot conceal from myself that this state of affairs is incompatible with the duties of service.

"In today rendering my decision I beg Your Excellency to believe it is with a deep sorrow that I retire from my career where your goodness accepted me and supported me during the first years with a tolerance I shall never forget. Accept ... my sincere words of respectful recognition of the consideration I receive" (British Library, Lieven Papers, ADD. 47356B, # 205, end of 1838, Lieven to Nesselrode).

Princess Lieven's Letter to Count Morny to Show Only to Emperor Napoleon III

"My health and my patience are at an end. Your friendship is not there. I am going to beg you to put it to work. I am tired of nine months of vagabondage, of every kind of privation, of the miseries of a hotel. I suffer always and for some time suffer exceedingly. (Miserable war! Do you always need a cannon ball for it to kill you?) I am perishing, this air is too harsh for me. The winter is coming, I cannot sustain it. I need my doctor, I need my nest and my bed, I need Paris. For all that I need your Master, and to get to him, I need you.

"The Emperor and you, you are going to determine my destiny for the rest of my life. I am seventy years old, that will not be long. Goodbye" (Morny, *Au Temps de la Guerre de Crimée*, p. 548, Nov. 15, 1854, Lieven to Morny).

Notes

Prologue

1. Princess Dorothea Lieven, *Letters of Princess Lieven to Lady Holland*, A.E. Smith, ed., Lady Holland's introduction, pp. 3–4.
2. Lieven, *Letters to Holland*, Lady Holland's introduction, pp. 3–4.
3. Baron de Barante, *Souvenirs, 1782–1866*, vol. viii, p. 155, Jan. 30, 1857, Barante to Anisson de Perron.
4. Princess Dorothea Lieven, *The Private Letters of Princess Lieven to Prince Metternich*, Peter Quennell, ed., p. 146, June 17, 1822.
5. Comte A. Nesselrode, ed., *Lettres et Papiers du Chancelier Comte de Nesselrode*, vol. ix, pp. 171–176, Feb. 1, 1831.
6. Count Joseph Hübner, *Neuf Ans des Souvenirs d'un Ambassadeur*, vol. 1, p. 37.

Chapter 1

1. François Guizot, *Mélanges Biographiques*, p. 190.
2. Marchioness of Londonderry, *Russian Journal of Lady Londonderry, 1836–1837*, p. 48.
3. Princess Dorothea Lieven, *Correspondence of Princess Lieven and Earl Grey*, Guy LeStrange, ed., vol. ii, p. 455, July 6, 1833, Lieven to Grey.
4. Baroness Georgiana Bloomfield, *Reminiscences of Court and Diplomatic Life*, pp. 166–167.
5. Bloomfield, *Reminiscences*, pp. 190–191, Apr. 18, 1847.
6. Bloomfield, *Reminiscences*, pp. 167–168.
7. Ivan Golovine, *La Russie sous Nicholas I*, vol. I, pp. 142–143.
8. The title "military governor of Riga" changed in 1801 to the equivalent "governor-general of Russia's Baltic provinces" (modern Estonia, Latvia and Lithuania).
9. Some sources cite Dorothea's mother as Charlotte, others as Juliana. I chose the latter to avoid confusion with her later mother-in-law, Charlotte Lieven.
10. Most sources, including the eminent French historian François Guizot, who knew Dorothea better than most, agree that she was born at Riga castle during the time her father served as Riga's military governor.

11. In Dorothea Lieven's day, the civilized world *was* Europe. Five "Great Powers" (Austria, France, Great Britain, Prussia, and Russia) predominated.
12. Less than two percent of all Russians were nobles. Less than ten out of one hundred nobles were aristocrats holding the titles (in descending order of importance) prince, count, and baron.
13. The Baltic Sea determined the Barons' wealth. Profiting from the thick pine forests that still carpet the Latvian landscape, they exported timber, vital to shipbuilding; they traded and distilled grain. Unlike the rest of Russia, their capital, bustling Hanseatic Riga, boasted a thriving middle class.
14. Benckendorff Papers, Estonian Historical Archives, 2249, I, 18, #50, Mar. 31, 1795, D. Lieven to C. Benckendorff (Juliana Benckendorff to her husband).
15. Lieven Papers, by permission of the British Library, ADD. 47379, #3, undated; unpublished Lieven memoirs.
16. As Russia became increasingly important in Europe's councils during the eighteenth century, the nobility felt themselves part of a primary European nation. Europe had adopted French culture as its standard, and Empress Catherine admired the Enlightenment. So Russian nobles used French as their first language.
17. Lieven Papers, British Library, ADD. 47379, #4, undated; unpublished Lieven memoirs.
18. Lieven Papers, British Library, ADD. 47379, #4–5, undated; unpublished Lieven memoirs.
19. Today Tallinn, the capital of Estonia, on the Gulf of Finland.
20. Benckendorff Papers, Estonian Historical Archives, 2249, I, 18, #50, Mar. 31, 1795, D. Lieven to C. Benckendorff.
21. Empress Maria Federovna, *Correspondence avec Mlle. de Nelidoff*, pp. 1–2, March 2, 1797.
22. Federovna, *Correspondence avec Nelidoff*, pp. 1–2, March 2, 1797.
23. François Guizot, *Lettres de François Guizot et de la Princesse de Lieven*, Jacques Naville, ed., vol. iii, p. 109, Mar. 4, 1844, Lieven to Guizot.
24. Lieven Papers, British Library, ADD. 47379, #6, undated, unpublished Lieven memoirs.
25. Lieven, *Correspondence of Lieven and Grey*, vol. I, pp. 191–192, Nov. 25, 1828.

26. Guizot, *Lettres de Guizot et de Lieven*, vol. 1, p. 121, Sept. 25, 1837, Lieven to Guizot.

27. Lieven Papers, British Library, ADD. 47379, #6, undated, unpublished Lieven memoirs.

28. Lieven, *Letters to Holland,* Holland Introduction, p. 1.

29. Benckendorff Papers, Estonian Historical Archives, 2249, I, 18, #31, 1794, D. Lieven to C. Benckendorff.

30. Benckendorff Papers, Estonian Historical Archives, 2249, I, 18, #31, 1794, D. Lieven to C. Benckendorff.

31. Guizot, *Lettres de Guizot et de Lieven*, vol. 1, p. 11, July 2, 1837, Lieven to Guizot.

32. Lieven, *Letters to Holland,* Holland Introduction, pp. 2–3.

33. Lieven Papers, British Library, ADD. 47379, #9, undated; unpublished Lieven memoirs.

34. A seventeenth century French noblewoman whose over fifteen hundred stylistically elegant, witty letters constitute an astute, classic chronicle of her times.

35. Charles Greville, *The Great World,* p. 321.

36. Lieven Papers, British Library, ADD. 47379, #5 & 7, undated, unpublished Lieven memoirs.

37. Lieven Papers, British Library, ADD. 47379, #5 & 7, undated, unpublished Lieven memoirs.

38. Lieven Papers, British Library, ADD. 47379, #5 & 7, undated, unpublished Lieven memoirs.

39. Lieven Papers, British Library, ADD. 47379 # 8, undated, unpublished Lieven memoirs.

40. Lieven, *Letters to Metternich*, p. 67, Oct. 25, 1820.

41. Quasi-prime minister Alexis Arakcheiev, sixteen years Dorothea's senior (a not unusual age difference at that time), universally dreaded for his cruelty, horrified young Dorothea. Fortunately, before he could begin seriously to court her, Arakcheiev fell from favor in one of Tsar Paul's frequent and erratic purges of his senior staff.

42. Governess to Russia's royal children meant taking charge of their upbringing and household.

43. The equivalent of about $15,000 today.

44. Lieven Papers, British Library, ADD. 47341, #2, summer 1799, Maria Federovna to Lieven.

45. Lieven Papers, British Library, ADD. 47341, #2, summer 1799, Maria Federovna to Lieven.

46. Dascha or Dachou was her family's nickname for Dorothea.

47. Lieven Papers, British Library, ADD. 47341, #2, summer 1799, Maria Federovna to Lieven.

48. Lieven Papers, British Library, ADD. 47395, #25, undated, probably November 1799, C. Lieven to D. Benckendorff.

49. Smolny headmistress.

50. Lieven Papers, British Library, ADD. 47395, #25, undated, probably November 1799, C. Lieven to D. Benckendorff.

51. Lieven Papers, British Library, ADD. 47395, #36, after November 1799 and before February 24, 1800, D. Benckendorff to C. Lieven.

52. Lieven Papers, British Library, ADD. 47395, #38, after November 1799 and before February 1800, D. Benckendorff to C. Lieven.

53. Lieven Papers, British Library, ADD. 47414, #2, written before February 24, 1800, D. Benckendorff to C. Benckendorff.

54. Lieven Papers, British Library, ADD. 47414, #2, written before February 24, 1800, D. Benckendorff to C. Benckendorff.

55. Lieven, *Letters to Metternich*, pp. 9–10, Feb. 24, 1820.

Chapter 2

1. Lieven, *The Unpublished Diary and Political Sketches of Princess Lieven*, H.W.V. Temperley, ed., p. 251.

2. Ernest Daudet, *Une Vie d'Ambassadrice au Siècle Dernier*, pp. 23–24.

3. Golovine, *La Russie sous Nicholas I*, vol. I, p. 135.

4. Golovine, *La Russie sous Nicholas I*, vol. I, pp. 131–132.

5. Lieven, *Unpublished Diary*, pp. 86–87.

6. Marquis de Custine, *Journey for our Time*, p. 115.

7. Custine, *Journey for our Time*, p. 115.

8. Imitation ornamental marble.

9. Londonderry, *Russian Journal*, p. 103.

10. "Idleness."

11. Lieven, *Unpublished Diary*, pp. 86–87.

12. Martha and Catherine Wilmot, *Russian Journals*, p. 234.

13. In sum, approximately $700,000 today.

14. Lieven Papers, British Library, ADD. 47415, #42, July 6, 1820, A. Benckendorff to Lieven.

15. Approximately $440,000 today.

16. Lieven, *Correspondence of Lieven and Grey*, vol. iii, p. 44, Nov. 1, 1834, Lieven to Grey.

17. Lieven, *Unpublished Diary*, pp. 244–245.

18. Lieven, *Unpublished Diary*, pp. 243–244.

19. Lieven, *Unpublished Diary*, pp. 244–245.

20. Lieven, *Unpublished Diary*, p. 246.

21. Lieven, *Unpublished Diary*, p. 245.

22. Lieven, *Unpublished Diary*, p. 247.

23. Lieven, *Unpublished Diary*, p. 247.

24. Lieven, *Unpublished Diary*, p. 248.

25. Lieven, *Unpublished Diary*, p. 249.

26. Lieven, *Unpublished Diary*, p. 249.

27. Lieven, *Unpublished Diary*, p. 254–255.

28. March 11, the old-style Julian calendar date, still used in Russia at the time, is sometimes given. The modern, Gregorian calendar date is March 23.

29. Lieven, *Unpublished Diary*, p. 250.

30. Lieven, *Unpublished Diary*, p. 251.

31. Lieven, *Unpublished Diary*, p. 251.

32. Lieven, *Unpublished Diary*, p. 251.

33. Lieven, *Unpublished Diary*, pp. 251–252.

34. Lieven, *Unpublished Diary*, p. 252.

35. Lieven, *Unpublished Diary*, p. 252.

36. Lieven, *Unpublished Diary*, p. 252.

37. Lieven, *Unpublished Diary*, p. 251.

38. Lieven, *Unpublished Diary*, p. 249.

39. Lieven, *Unpublished Diary*, p. 261–262.

40. Lieven, *Unpublished Diary*, p. 265.

41. Lieven, *Unpublished Diary*, p. 265.

42. Lieven, *Unpublished Diary*, pp. 264-265.

43. Lieven, *Unpublished Diary*, p. 263.

44. Guizot, *Lettres de Quizot et de Lieven*, vol. ii, p. 43, Mar. 24, 1840, Lieven to Guizot.

Chapter 3

1. Lieven Papers, British Library, ADD. 47379, #10, undated; unpublished Lieven memoirs.

2. Ernest Daudet, *Une Vie d'ambassadrrice au siècle dernier*, p. 44, Lieven to A. Benckendorff.

3. Lieven Papers, British Library, ADD. 47379, #9–10, undated; unpublished Lieven memoirs.

4. Charles-Maurice Talleyrand-Périgord, *Mémoires*, vol. iii, p. 405.

5. *Vie*, pp. 37–8, February 27, 1803, Lieven to A. Benckendorff.

6. Apponyi Archive, Bibliotheca Nationalis Hungariae, vol. 11/62, #1, April 18/30, 1804, A. Benckendorff to Lieven.

7. *Vie*, pp. 49–50, Lieven to A. Benckendorff.

8. Lieven Papers, British Library, ADD. 47400, #56–57, Oct. 14/26, 1835, D. Lieven to C. Lieven.

9. Lieven Papers, British Library, ADD. 47379, #10, undated; unpublished Lieven memoirs.

10. Apponyi Archive, Bibliotheca Nationalis Hungariae, vol. 11/62, #3, Nov. 6/18, 1804, A. Benckendorff to Lieven.

11. Apponyi Archive, Bibliotheca Nationalis Hungariae, vol. 11/62, #5, Jan. 2/14, 1805, A. Benckendorff to Lieven.

12. Lieven, *Unpublished Diary*, p. 23.

13. Lieven, *Unpublished Diary*, p. 23.

14. "Very attentive and courteous."

15. Lieven, *Unpublished Diary*, p. 27.

16. *Vie*, p. 53, Lieven to A. Benckendorff.

17. *Vie*, p. 53, Lieven to A. Benckendorff.

18. Lieven Papers, British Library, ADD. 47379, #11, undated; unpublished Lieven memoirs.

19. Lieven, *Letters to Holland*, Holland introduction, pp. 1–2.

20. Lieven Papers, British Library, ADD. 47379, #11, undated; unpublished Lieven memoirs.

21. *Vie*, pp. 56–57, Lieven to her sister Marie Schevitsch.

22. *Vie*, p. 56, Lieven to Schevitsch.

23. Lieven Papers, British Library, ADD. 47414, #42, June 24, 1810, C. Benckendorff to Lieven.

24. Lieven Papers, British Library, ADD. 47414, #63, October, 1810, C. Benckendorff to Lieven.

25. *Vie*, p. 56, Lieven to Schevitsch.

26. Lieven Papers, British Library, ADD. 47379, #11, undated; unpublished Lieven memoirs.

27. *Vie*, p. 58, May 24, 1812, Lieven to A. Benckendorff.

28. *Vie*, p. 60, C. Lieven to A. Benckendorff.

Chapter 4

1. Lieven Papers, British Library, ADD. 47371, #83–87, Oct. 4/10, 1855, Lieven to Meyendorff.

2. Lamb Papers, by permission of the British Library, ADD. 45556, #214, Aug. 12, 1841, Lieven to Cowper (later Palmerston).

3. Lieven Papers, British Library, ADD. 47379, #13, undated; unpublished Lieven memoirs.

4. Pink was the Tory color.

5. Metternich Family Archive, National Archive (Prague), Acta Clementina (AC) 6, #45–48, Mar. 19–24, 1820, Lieven to Metternich.

6. Robert Southey, *Letters from England*, pp. 49–50.

7. Frederick von Raumer, *England in 1835*, pp. 29–30, Mar. 24, 1835.

8. Southey, *Letters*, pp. 49–50.

9. Southey, *Letters*, pp. 153–154.

10. Dorothea Lieven and her contemporaries equated democracy with Jacobinism and mob rule.

11. *Letters of Dorothea, Princess Lieven during her Residence in London (1812–1834)*, Lionel G. Robinson, ed., pp. 18–19, Nov. 8, 1815, to A. Benckendorff.

12. Guizot, *Lettres de Guizot et de Lieven*, vol. ii, p. 59, April 2, 1840, Guizot to Lieven.

13. *Greville Memoirs*, vol. I, p. 15, Feb. 3, 1819.

14. "Attentiveness."

15. Harriet Granville, *A Second Self: The Letters of Harriet Granville*, V. Surtees, ed., p. 97, Feb. 14 or 15, 1816, to Lady Morpeth.

16. Guizot, *Lettres de Guizot et de Lieven*, vol. ii, p. 11, Mar. 3, 1840, Lieven to Guizot.

17. Lieven, *Letters ... London*, p. 22, Jan. 9, 1816, to A. Benckendorff.

18. Arthur Wellington, *Wellington and His Friends*, p. 302, Dec. 27, 1823, Wellington to Lieven.

19. Harriet Arbuthnot, *The Journals of Mrs. Arbuthnot, 1820–1832*, vol. ii, pp. 53–54, Nov. 1826.

20. Lieven, *Letters to Metternich*, p. 100, March 7, 1821.

21. Harriet Granville, *Letters of Harriet, Countess Granville 1810–1845*, F. Leveson-Gower, ed., vol. 1, p. 348, Nov. 23, 1827, to Lady Carlisle.

22. Granville, *Letters*, vol. I, p. 221, January, 1822, to Lady Morpeth.

23. Thomas Creevey, *Creevey's Life and Times, 1768–1838*, p. 248, Sept. 24, 1827.

24. R.H. Gronow, *Captain Gronow's Recollections and Anecdotes*, pp. 31–32.

25. Lieven, *Letters ... London*, p. 22, Jan. 9, 1816, to A. Benckendorff.

26. Lieven, *Letters ... London*, p. 26, May 16/28, 1816, to A. Benckendorff.

27. Earl of Aberdeen, *Correspondence of Lord Aberdeen and Princess Lieven*, E. Jones Parry, ed., vol. 1, p. 135, Mar. 7, 1840, Aberdeen to Lieven.

28. Lieven, *Letters to Metternich*, p. 251, Jan. 30, 1824.

29. "Brutal frankness."

30. Granville, *Letters*, vol. 1, p. 226, March 14, 1824.

31. Metternich Family Archive, National Archive (Prague), AC 6, #18–22, Feb. 12, 1820, Lieven to Metternich.

32. Granville, *Letters*, vol. I, pp. 55–56, July 14, 1815, to Morpeth.

33. "Self-sacrifice."

34. Granville, *A Second Self*, p. 89, Oct. 8, 1815, Granville to Morpeth.

35. Granville, *Letters*, vol. ii, pp. 279–280, Jan. 1839, Granville to Devonshire.

36. Pozzo later joined the Russian diplomatic service.

37. Lieven, *Letters to Metternich*, pp. 117–118, Dec. 29, 1821.

38. Lamb Papers, British Library, ADD. 45556, #213, Aug. 12, 1841, Lieven to Cowper.

39. Mme. de Boigne, *Memoirs of the Comtesse de Boigne*, vol. ii, p. 156.

40. "Grins and bears it."

41. Granville, *A Second Self*, p. 89, Oct. 8, 1815, Granville to Morpeth.

42. Betty Askwith, *Piety and Wit: A Biography of Harriet Granville*, p. 95, 1816.

43. Metternich Family Archive, National Archive (Prague), AC. 6, #18–22, Feb. 12, 1820, Lieven to Metternich.

44. About $1.4 million at present value.

45. Thomas Raikes, *A Portion of the Journal*, vol. I, pp. 233–235, May 25, 1834.

46. Boigne, *Memoirs*, vol. ii, pp. 154–155.

47. Arbuthnot, *Journals*, vol. ii, pp. 53–54, Nov. 1826.

48. Lieven, *Letters ... London*, p. 29, Oct. 30, 1816, to A. Benckendorff.

49. Lieven, *Letters to Metternich*, pp. 54–55, Aug. 6, 1820.

50. Lieven, *Letters to Metternich*, p. 207, April 16, 1823.

Chapter 5

1. Lieven, *Letters to Holland*, Holland introduction, pp. 3–4.

2. The monarch approved the choice of ministers, contributed to policy, and granted titles.

3. Lieven, *Unpublished Diary*, p. 34.

4. This episode took place while the Powers were re-drawing the map of Europe at the Congress of Vienna.

5. Lieven, *Unpublished Diary*, pp. 36–37.

6. Lieven, *Unpublished Diary*, p. 37.

7. Lieven, *Unpublished Diary*, p. 37.

8. Lieven, *Letters to Metternich*, pp. 303–305, May 14, 1826.

9. Lieven, *Letters to Metternich*, pp. 306–307, May 14, 1826.

10. Nicholas Mikhalovitch, Grand Duke, ed., *Scenes of Russian Court Life*; Excerpt from Princess Lieven's Memoirs, pp. 278–279.

11. Lieven, *Letters ... London*, pp. 2–3, April 6, 1813, to A. Benckendorff.

12. Mikhalovitch, *Scenes of Russian Court Life*; Lieven Memoirs, p. 265.

13. Russia's aristocracy had little sympathy for their Tsar's liberal ideas.

14. Barante, *Souvenirs*, vol. ii, pp. 30–31.

15. Mikhalovitch, *Scenes of Russian Court Life*; Lieven Memoirs, pp. 267–268.

16. Mikhalovitch, *Scenes of Russian Court Life*; Lieven Memoirs, p. 268.

17. Mikhalovitch, *Scenes of Russian Court Life*; Lieven Memoirs, pp. 271–272.

18. Mikhalovitch, *Scenes of Russian Court Life*; Lieven Memoirs, p. 282.

19. Mikhalovitch, *Scenes of Russian Court Lif*; Lieven Memoirs, p. 286.

20. Mikhalovitch, *Scenes of Russian Court Life*; Lieven Memoirs, p. 286.

21. Wellington, *Wellington and His Friends*, p. 295, June 10, 1821, Wellington to Lieven.

22. Lieven, *Letters ... London*, p. 47, February 8, 1820, to A. Benckendorff.

23. Granville, *Letters* vol. I, p. 148, Jan. 19, 1820.

24. Boigne, *Memoirs*, vol. ii, p. 155.

25. To Streatham Park near London, an estate that the Lievens leased.

26. Lieven Papers, British Library, ADD. 47395, #245, Aug. 13, 1815, C. Lieven to D. Lieven.

27. "Really."

28. Boigne, *Memoirs*, vol. ii, pp. 155–156.

29. Boigne, *Memoirs*, vol. ii, p. 156.

30. Lieven, *Letters to Holland*, Holland introduction, pp. 1–2.

31. Lieven, *Letters to Metternich*, pp. 132–133, Mar. 14, 1822.

Chapter 6

1. Lieven, *Letters to Metternich*, p. 146, June 17, 1822.

2. Lieven, *Letters to Metternich*, pp. 132–133, Mar. 14, 1822.

3. Lieven Papers, British Library, ADD. 47417, #142, Sept. 11/27, 1818, Constantine Benckendorff to Lieven.

4. Lieven Papers, British Library, ADD. 47414, #103, Oct. 19, 1818, C. Benckendorff to Lieven.

5. Lieven, *Letters ... London*, pp. 37–8, Jan. 3/15, 1819, to A. Benckendorff.

6. Metternich Family Archive, National Archive (Prague), AC C-19–1, #26, Tues. the 28th (probably May 1849), Lieven to Metternich.

7. The militarily strong Austrian Empire stretched across middle Europe from the Baltic Sea to the Mediterranean.

8. Clemens Lothar Metternich-Winneburg, *Lettres de Prince Metternich à la Comtesse de Lieven*, Jean Hanoteau, ed., pp. 179–180, Oct. 18, 1819.

9. Metternich Family Archive, National Archive (Prague), AC 8, Aug. 2, 1824, Metternich to Lieven.

10. Metternich Family Archive, National Archive (Prague), AC 8, Aug. 13, 1824, Metternich to Lieven.

11. Metternich, *Lettres de Metternich à Lieven*, p. 340, Mar. 15, 1819.

12. Metternich, *Lettres de Metternich à Lieven*, pp. lxiii–lxiv, Mar. 24, 1820.

13. Lieven, *Letters to Metternich*, p. 237, Oct. 4, 1823.

14. Lieven, *Letters to Metternich*, p. 232, Aug. 29, 1823.

15. Metternich, *Lettres de Metternich à Lieven*, p. 204, Feb. 18, 1819.

16. Lieven, *Letters to Metternich*, p. 117, Dec. 26, 1821.

17. Lieven, *Letters to Metternich*, pp. 35–36, July 1, 1820.

18. A Roman Emperor who wallowed in egregious debauchery.

19. Lieven, *Letters to Metternich*, p. 121, Jan. 26, 1822.

20. Metternich, *Lettres de Metternich à Lieven*, pp. 149–150, Jan. 29, 1819.

21. Metternich, *Lettres de Metternich à Lieven*, pp. 183–184, Oct. 20, 1819.

22. Lieven, *Letters to Metternich*, p. 98, Feb. 28, 1821.

23. Metternich, *Lettres de Metternich à Lieven*, p. 171, Feb. 1, 1819.

24. Metternich, *Lettres de Metternich à Lieven*, pp. 337–338, Mar. 9, 1819.

25. Metternich, *Lettres de Metternich à Lieven*, p. lxv, Nov. 28, 1818.

26. Ernest Daudet, *À Travers Trois Siècles*, p. 203, Sept. 5, 1819, Lieven to Metternich.

27. Metternich Family Archive, National Archive (Prague), AC 6, #26, June 27, 1820, Lieven to Metternich.

28. Metternich, *Lettres de Metternich à Lieven*, pp. 164–165, Jan. 30, 1819.

29. Lieven, *Letters to Metternich*, p. 211, April 26, 1823.

30. Metternich, *Lettres de Metternich à Lieven*, p. 84, Dec. 25, 1818.

31. Metternich, *Lettres de Metternich à Lieven*, pp. 1–2, probably Nov. 4, 1818.

32. Metternich, *Lettres de Metternich à Lieven*, pp. 4–5, Nov. 16, 1818.

33. Metternich Family Archive, National Archive (Prague), AC 6, #26, June 27, 1820, Lieven to Metternich.

34. Metternich, *Lettres de Metternich à Lieven*, pp. 29–31, Nov. 28, 1818.

35. Metternich, *Lettres de Metternich à Lieven*, p. 18, Nov. 20, 1818.

36. Metternich, *Lettres de Metternich à Lieven*, pp. 20–21, Nov. 24, 1818.

37. Daudet, *À Travers Trois Siècles*, pp. 204, Sept. 6, 1819, Lieven to Metternich.

38. Daudet, *À Travers Trois Siècles*, pp. 201–202, Sept. 3 & 4, 1819, Lieven to Metternich.

39. Metternich, *Lettres de Metternich à Lieven*, p. 179, Feb. 3, 1819.

40. Metternich, *Lettres de Metternich à Lieven*, pp. 67–68, Dec. 18, 1818.

41. Metternich, *Lettres de Metternich à Lieven*, p. 14, Nov. 18, 1818.

42. Metternich, *Lettres de Metternich à Lieven*, pp. 195–196, Dec. 27, 1819.

43. Metternich, *Lettres de Metternich à Lieven*, pp. 195–196, Dec. 27, 1819.

44. Metternich, *Lettres de Metternich à Lieven*, p. 197, Dec. 28, 1819.

45. Lieven, *Letters to Metternich*, pp. 215–216, May 15, 1823.

46. Metternich Family Archive, National Archive (Prague), AC 6, #40, Apr. 9, 1820, Lieven to Metternich.

47. Daudet, *À Travers Trois Siècles*, p. 203, Sept. 5, 1819, Lieven to Metternich.

48. Metternich, *Lettres de Metternich à Lieven*, pp. 29–30, Nov. 28, 1818.

49. Metternich, *Lettres de Metternich à Lieven*, pp. 164–165, Jan. 30, 1819.

50. Metternich, *Lettres de Metternich à Lieven*, pp. 61–62, Dec. 14, 1818.

51. Daudet, *À Travers Trois Siècles*, pp. 200–202, Sept. 3, 1819, Lieven to Metternich.

Chapter 7

1. Metternich Family Archive, National Archive (Prague), AC 6, #40–41, Apr. 12, 1820, Lieven to Metternich.

2. Lieven, *Letters ... London*, pp. 37–38, Jan. 3/15, 1819, to A. Benckendorff.

3. Daudet, *À Travers Trois Siècles*, p. 184, Oct. 22, 1819, Metternich to Lieven.

4. Lieven, *Letters ... London*, pp. 24–46, Feb. 8, 1820, to A. Benckendorff.

5. Lieven, *Letters to Metternich*, p. 177, Jan. 7, 1823.

6. Metternich Family Archive, National Archive (Prague), AC 6, #29–32, Apr. 15–19, 1820, Lieven to Metternich.

7. Metternich Family Archive, National Archive (Prague), AC 6, #37–43, Apr. 15–19, 1820, Lieven to Metternich.

8. The Austrian embassy's first secretary Neumann knew the nature of Metternich and Dorothea's relationship; he facilitated their correspondence.

9. Metternich Family Archive, National Archive (Prague), AC 6, #38, Apr. 8, 1820, Lieven to Metternich.

10. Metternich Family Archive, National Archive (Prague), AC 6, #18–22, Feb. 12–17, 1820, Lieven to Metternich.

11. Metternich, *Lettres de Metternich à Lieven*, p. 154, Jan. 22, 1819.

12. Count Pozzo di Borgo, Russian ambassador to France.

13. Metternich, *Lettres de Metternich à Lieven*, pp. 154–155, Jan. 28, 1819.

14. Daudet, *À Travers Trois Siècles*, p. 204, Sept. 5, 1819, Lieven to Metternich.

15. Grand Duke Nicholas Mikhailovitch, *Rapports Diplomatiques de Lebzeltern*, p. 228, June 5, 1820, Metternich to Lebzeltern.

16. Metternich Family Archive, National Archive (Prague), AC 6, #42–43, Apr. 14, 1820, Lieven to Metternich.

17. Metternich Family Archive, National Archive (Prague), AC 6, #18–20, Feb. 15, 1820, Lieven to Metternich.

18. Metternich Family Archive, National Archive (Prague), AC 6, #22, Feb. 17, 1820, Lieven to Metternich.

19. Metternich Family Archive, National Archive (Prague), AC 6, #129–32, Apr. 15–19, 1820, Lieven to Metternich.

20. Metternich Family Archive, National Archive (Prague), AC 6, #32, Apr. 19, 1820, Lieven to Metternich.

21. Metternich Family Archive, National Archive (Prague), AC 6, #43, Apr. 12, 1820, Lieven to Metternich.

22. Lieven, *Letters to Metternich*, p. 137, May 8, 1822.

23. Metternich Family Archive, National Archive (Prague), AC 6, #25–28, June 27, 1820, Lieven to Metternich.

24. Lieven, *Letters to Metternich*, p. 36, July 8, 1820.

25. Lieven, *Letters to Metternich*, pp. 42–43, July 22, 1820.

26. Lieven, *Letters to Metternich*, p. 46, Aug. 12, 1820.

27. Lieven, *Letters to Metternich*, p. 48, Aug. 19, 1820.

28. Parliament voted Caroline an annuity but forbade her coronation. She died soon afterwards.

29. Lieven, *Letters to Metternich*, pp. 41–42, July 21, 1820.

30. Lieven, *Letters to Metternich*, p. 44, July 31, 1820.

31. Mikhailovitch, *Rapports Diplomatiques de Lebzeltern*, p. 96, Aug. 13, 1825, Metternich to Lebzeltern.

32. The Greek national revolt against Ottoman rule.

33. Lieven, *Letters to Metternich*, pp. 128–129, Mar. 4, 1822.

34. Lieven, *Letters to Metternich*, p. 41, July 29, 1820.

35. Clemens Lothar Metternich-Winneborg, *Mémoires, Documents, et Écrits divers*, Richard Metternich, ed., vol. iii, p. 403, Nov. 20, 1820, Metternich probably to Lieven.

36. Metternich, *Mémoires*, vol. iii, p. 488, Feb. 23, 1821, Metternich probably to Lieven.

37. Metternich Family Archive, National Archive (Prague), AC 8, July 14, 1824, Metternich to Lieven.

Chapter 8

1. Lieven, *Letters to Metternich*, pp. 19–20, April 5, 1820.

2. Metternich Family Archive, National Archives (Prague), AC 6, #33–35, Sept. 23–29, 1820, Lieven to Metternich.

3. Metternich owned an estate on the Rhine.

4. Metternich Family Archive, National Archive (Prague), AC 6, #34, Sept. 26, 1820, Lieven to Metternich.

5. Wellington, *Wellington and His Friends*, pp. 297–298, July 1, 1821, Wellington to Lieven.

6. Metternich Family Archive, National Archive (Prague), AC 6, #34, Sept. 26, 1820, Lieven to Metternich.

7. Lieven, *Letters to Metternich*, p. 276, Nov. 24, 1824.

8. Lieven, *Letters to Metternich*, p. 108, June 3, 1821.

9. Lieven, *Letters to Metternich*, p. 109, June 6, 1821.

10. Lieven Papers, British Library, ADD. 47396, #21, July 15, 1821, D. Lieven to C. Lieven.

11. Lieven Papers, British Library, ADD. 47396, #41, Aug. 20, 1821, D. Lieven to C. Lieven.

12. Lieven Papers, British Library, ADD. 47396, #26, Oct. 3, 1821, D. Lieven to C. Lieven.

13. Lieven Papers, British Library, ADD. 47396, #20, Aug. 15, 1821, D. Lieven to C. Lieven.

14. Lieven Papers, British Library, ADD. 47418, #53, Sept. 28, 1821, Lieven to Constantine Benckendorff.

15. Banker to Europe's royalty and aristocracy, Rothschild had his headquarters at Frankfurt.

16. Lieven Papers, British Library, ADD. 47396, #26, Oct. 3, 1821, D. Lieven to C. Lieven.

17. The insular British distrusted continental entanglements. Castlereagh relied on the Concert of Europe to keep peace; his Tory colleagues agreed to some extent. The Whigs opposed.

18. Lieven, *Letters to Metternich*, p. 116, Dec. 23, 1821.

19. Lieven, *Letters to Metternich*, p. 147, June 17, 1822.

20. Lieven, *Letters to Metternich*, pp 149–150, June 24, 1822.

21. Lieven, *Letters to Metternich*, p. 140, May 21, 1822.

22. Lieven, *Letters to Metternich*, p 127, Feb. 23, 1822.

23. Lieven, *Letters to Metternich*, p. 134, Apr. 28, 1822.

24. Lieven, *Letters to Metternich*, pp. 160–161, Aug. 16, 1822.

25. Lieven, *Letters to Metternich*, p. 168, Sept. 10, 1822.

26. Lieven, *Letters to Metternich*, p. 79, Dec. 22, 1820.

27. Lieven, *Letters to Metternich*, p. 168, Sept. 10, 1822.

28. Nesselrode, *Lettres et Papiers*, vol. vii, p. 142, Dec. 9, 1822, Countess Nesselrode to Nesselrode.

29. Lieven, *Letters ... London*, pp. 59–60, Dec. 1, 1822, to A. Benckendorff.

30. Lieven, *Letters ... London*, pp. 59–60, Dec. 1, 1822, to A. Benckendorff.

31. Lieven, *Letters to Metternich*, p. 273, Oct. 8, 1824.

32. Lieven, *Letters to Metternich*, p. 273, Oct. 8, 1824.

Chapter 9

1. Metternich Family Archive, National Archive (Prague), AC 8, Aug. 4, 1824, Metternich to Lieven.

2. Lieven, *Letters to Metternich*, pp. 228–229, Aug. 14, 1823.

3. Lieven, *Letters to Metternich*, pp. 185–186, Jan. 28, 1823.

4. Lieven, *Letters to Metternich*, p. 188, Jan. 28, 1823.

5. Lieven, *Letters to Metternich*, pp. 190–191, Feb. 1, 1823.

6. Lieven, *Letters ... London*, pp. 66–67, Aug. 6, 1823, to A. Benckendorff.

7. Lieven Papers, British Library, ADD. 47414, #82, Jan. 15, 1817, C. Benckendorff to Lieven.

8. Lieven Papers, British Library, ADD. 47414, #84, May 20, 1817, C. Benckendorff to Lieven.

9. Lieven Papers, British Library, ADD. 47414, #149, Summer, 1823, C. Benckendorff to Lieven.

10. Lieven Papers, British Library, ADD. 47418, #117–118, Feb. 9, 1823, Lieven to Constantine Benckendorff.

11. Lieven Papers, British Library, ADD. 47414, #149, Summer, 1823, C. Benckendorff to Lieven.

12. Lieven, *Letters ... London*, p. 66, Aug. 6, 1823, to A. Benckendorff.

13. Lieven, *Letters to Metternich*, pp. 224–225, July 27, 1823.

14. T. Schiemann, *Geschichte Russlands*, vol. I, p. 587, Sept 11/23, 1823, C. Lieven to Nesselrode.

15. Lieven Papers, British Library, ADD. 47396, #100, Sept. 29, 1823, D. Lieven to C. Lieven

16. Lieven, *Letters to Metternich*, p. 175, Jan. 5, 1823.

17. Lieven, *Letters to Metternich*, p. 239, Oct. 13, 1823.

18. Lieven, *Letters to Metternich*, pp. 239–240, Oct. 20, 1823.

19. Lieven, *Letters to Metternich*, p. 239, Oct. 14, 1823.

20. Lieven, *Letters to Metternich*, p. 251, Jan. 21, 1824.

21. Lieven, *Letters to Metternich*, p. 250, Jan. 21, 1824.

22. Lieven, *Letters to Metternich*, p. 252, Feb. 12, 1824.

23. Lieven, *Letters to Metternich*, p. 245, Nov. 21, 1823.

24. Lieven, *Letters to Metternich*, pp. 231–232, Aug. 24, 1823.

25. Metternich, *Mémoires*, vol. iv, p. 99, Feb. 5, 1824, Metternich probably to Lieven.

26. Lieven Papers, British Library, ADD. 47397, #11, Jan. 13, 1824, D. Lieven to C. Lieven.

27. Lieven Papers, British Library, ADD. 47397, #11, Jan. 13, 1824, D. Lieven to C. Lieven.

28. Metternich, *Mémoires*, vol. iv, p. 101, Mar. 11, 1824, Metternich probably to Lieven.

29. Lieven, *Letters to Metternich*, p. 257, Apr. 20, 1824.

30. "Nothing more pressing."

31. "Crazy about him."

32. Arbuthnot, *Journals*, vol. I, pp. 319–320, June, 1824.

33. Metternich Family Archive, National Archive (Prague), AC 8, July 2, 1824, Metternich to Lieven.

34. Metternich Family Archive, National Archive (Prague), AC 8, Nov. 28, 1824, Metternich to Lieven.

35. Lieven, *Letters to Metternich*, pp. 273–274, Oct. 8, 1824.

36. George Canning, *Some Official Correspondence of George Canning*, E.J. Stapleton, ed., vol. I, pp. 256–257, Mar. 11, 1825, Canning to Granville.

37. Canning, *Some Official Correspondence*, vol. I, pp. 257–258, Mar. 11, 1825, Canning to Granville.

38. Canning, *Some Official Correspondence*, vol. I, pp. 257–258, Mar. 11, 1825, Canning to Granville.

39. Canning, *Some Official Correspondence*, vol. I, pp. 257–258, Mar. 11, 1825, Canning to Granville.

40. Metternich Family Archive, National Archive (Prague), AC 8, Aug. 10, 1824, Metternich to Lieven.

41. Metternich Family Archive, National Archive (Prague), AC 8, Sept. 23, 1824, Metternich to Lieven.

42. Lieven, *Letters to Metternich*, p. 275, Oct. 14, 1824.

43. Metternich, *Lettres de Metternich à Lieven*, p. 42, Dec. 1, 1818.

44. Metternich Family Archive, National Archive (Prague), AC 9, Mar. 29, 1825, Metternich to Lieven.

45. Metternich, *Lettres de Metternich à Lieven*, p. 180, Feb. 4, 1819.

46. Lieven, *Letters to Metternich*, p. 290, May 18, 1825.

Chapter 10

1. Nesselrode, *Lettres et Papiers*, vol. xi, p. 149, Oct. 25, 1825, Alexander I to Nesselrode.

2. Metternich Family Archive, National Archive (Prague), AC 8, Aug. 19, 1824, Metternich to Lieven.

3. Lieven, *Unpublished Diary*, p. 82.

4. Lieven, *Unpublished Diary*, p. 81.

5. Lieven, *Unpublished Diary*, p. 82.

6. Lieven, *Unpublished Diary*, p. 83.

7. Lieven, *Unpublished Diary*, p. 83.

8. Canning, *Some Official Correspondence*, vol. I, p. 256, Mar. 11, 1825, Canning to Granville.

9. Lieven, *Unpublished Diary*, p. 84.

10. Metternich Family Archive, National Archive (Prague), AC 8, Oct. 23, 1824, Metternich to Lieven.

11. Lieven, *Unpublished Diary*, p. 85.

12. Lieven Papers, British Library, ADD. 47418, #192, May 26, 1825, Lieven to Constantine Benckendorff.

13. Lieven Papers, British Library, ADD. 47397, #131, July 6/18, 1825, D. Lieven to C. Lieven.

14. Center of Baltic Baron scholarship; Lieven's brother served as rector.

15. Lieven Papers, British Library, ADD. 47397, #133–134, July 19/31, 1825, D. Lieven to C. Lieven.

16. Lieven, *Unpublished Diary*, p. 86.

17. Lieven, *Unpublished Diary*, p. 86.

18. Lieven Papers, British Library, ADD. 47397, #157, Aug. 5/19, 1825, D. Lieven to C. Lieven.

19. Lieven, *Unpublished Diary*, p. 88.

20. Lieven, *Unpublished Diary*, p. 88.

21. Lieven, *Unpublished Diary*, p. 88.

22. Lieven, *Unpublished Diary*, pp. 88–89.

23. Lieven, *Unpublished Diary*, p. 90.

24. Mikhailovitch, *Rapports Diplomatiques de Lebzeltern*, p. 96, Aug. 13, 1825, Metternich to Lebzeltern.

25. Lieven, *Unpublished Diary*, p. 91.

26. Lieven, *Letters to Metternich*, pp. 292–293, Oct. 22, 1825.

27. Lieven, *Diary*, p. 92.

28. Lieven, *Diary*, p. 95.

29. Lieven Papers, British Library, ADD. 47375, #16, Aug. 30, 1825, Nesselrode to Lieven.

30. Lieven, *Unpublished Diary*, pp. 95–96.

31. Lieven, *Unpublished Diary*, pp. 96–97.

32. Lieven, *Unpublished Diary*, p. 97.

33. Lieven, *Unpublished Diary*, p. 97.

34. Lieven, *Unpublished Diary*, p. 98.

35. Lieven, *Unpublished Diary*, p. 98.

36. "Household peace."

37. "Giving it birth."

38. Lieven, *Unpublished Diary*, pp. 98–99.

39. Lieven, *Unpublished Diary*, pp. 99.

40. Lieven, *Letters to Metternich*, p. 292, Oct. 23, 1825.

41. Lieven, *Unpublished Diary*, p. 100.

42. Lieven Papers, British Library, ADD. 47355, #41, Sept. 22/Oct 4, 1825, Lieven to Nesselrode.

43. Schiemann, *Geschichte Russlands*, vol. I, p. 613, Sept. 23/Oct. 5, 1826, C. Lieven to Nesselrode.

44. Nesselrode, *Lettres et Papiers*, vol. xi, p. 149, Oct. 25, 1825, Alexander I to Nesselrode.

45. Lieven, *Unpublished Diary*, pp. 103–104.

46. Lieven, *Unpublished Diary*, p. 108.

47. H. Temperley, "Princess Lieven and the protocol of 4 April, 1826," *English Historical Review*, vol. 39, Jan. 1924, pp. 66–67.

48. Schiemann, *Geschichte Russlands*, vol. I, p. 348 (note), Oct. 18/30, C. Lieven to Nesselrode, private letter.

Chapter 11

1. Wellington, *Wellington and His Friends*, pp. 68–69, Sept. 4, 1826, Wellington to Mrs. Arbuthnot.

2. Constantine's renunciation of the throne, a condition of his morganatic marriage to a minor Polish noble, had been kept secret.

3. Dowager Duchess of Argyll, *George Douglas, eighth Duke of Argyll*, vol. 1, p. 347.

4. Lieven, *Letters ... London*, pp. 85–86, Feb. 18/Mar. 2, 1826, to A. Benckendorff.

5. Arbuthnot, *Journals*, vol. ii, p. 50, Oct. 1826.

6. Lieven, *Unpublished Diary*, pp. 107–108.

7. Lieven, *Unpublished Diary*, pp. 106–107.

8. Lieven, *Unpublished Diary*, pp. 107–108.

9. Lieven, *Unpublished Diary*, p. 111.

10. Lieven, *Unpublished Diary*, p. 112.

11. A.G. Stapleton, *George Canning and His Times*, pp. 471–472, Canning to Granville, January 13, 1826.

12. Wellington, *Wellington and His Friends*, pp. 56–57, Mar. 5, 1826, Wellington to Mrs. Arbuthnot.

13. Lieven, *Letters to Metternich*, pp. 297–298, Mar. 10, 1826.

14. The National Archives of the UK (formerly Public Record Office): Foreign Office 360, Howard de Walden papers, 1817–1834, 53861, May 25, 1826, D. Lieven to C Lieven.

15. The National Archives of the UK: Foreign Office 360, Howard de Walden Papers, 1817–1834, 53861, Apr. 15/27, 1826, D. Lieven to C Lieven.

16. Lieven Papers, British Library, ADD. 47397, #199, February 28/Mar. 12, 1826, D. Lieven to C. Lieven.

17. Lieven Papers, British Library, ADD. 47397, #230, Mar. 26/Apr. 6, 1826, D. Lieven to C. Lieven.

18. Lieven, *Unpublished Diary*, pp. 112–113.

19. The National Archives of the UK: Foreign Office 360, Howard de Walden Papers, 1817–1834, 53861, Apr 23/ May 6, 1826, D. Lieven to C. Lieven.

20. Lieven, *Diary*, p. 112–113.

21. Lieven, *Unpublished Diary*, p. 113.

22. Lieven, *Letters to Metternich*, pp. 299–301, Mar. 20, 1826.

23. Lieven, *Letters to Metternich*, pp. 305–306, May 16, 1826.

24. Lieven, *Letters to Metternich*, p. 308, June 14, 1826.

25. The National Archives of the UK: Foreign Office 360, Howard de Walden Papers, 1817–1834, 53861, Jun 13/25, 1826, Nesselrode to Lieven.

26. Lieven Papers, British Library, ADD. 47397, #304–305, June 27, 1826, D. Lieven to C. Lieven.

27. Lieven Papers, British Library, ADD. 47397, #300–301, June 23, 1826, D. Lieven to C. Lieven.

28. Lieven Papers, British Library, ADD. 47397, #304–305, June 27, 1826, D. Lieven to C. Lieven.

29. Lieven, *Letters to Metternich*, p. 312, Nov. 22, 1826.

30. Lieven, *Unpublished Diary*, p. 116.

31. Lieven, *Unpublished Diary*, p. 117.

32. Lieven, *Unpublished Diary*, p. 117.

33. Lieven, *Unpublished Diary*, pp. 117–118.

34. Lieven, *Unpublished Diary*, pp. 120–121.

35. Lieven, *Unpublished Diary*, pp. 122.

36. Lieven, *Unpublished Diary*, p. 125.

37. "Bitter public quarrel."

38. Lieven, *Unpublished Diary*, pp. 124–127.

39. Lieven, *Unpublished Diary*, pp. 129–130.

40. Lieven, *Unpublished Diary*, p. 128.

41. Lieven, *Letters ... London*, pp. 107–108, Oct. 8/20, 1827, to A. Benckendorff.

42. Lieven, *Unpublished Diary*, pp. 131–132.

Chapter 12

1. Lieven, *Letters to Metternich*, p. 164, Aug. 29, 1822.

2. Lieven Papers, British Library, ADD. 47398, #24, 1828, C. Lieven to D. Lieven.

3. Lieven Papers, British Library, ADD. 47398, #25–26, 1828, D. Lieven to C. Lieven.

4. Lieven Papers, British Library, ADD. 47398, #27–28, 1828, D. Lieven to C. Lieven.

5. Arthur Wellington, *Private Correspondence: A Selection*, the Seventh Duke, ed., pp. 195–196, Oct. 30, 1827, Lieven to Wellington.

6. Wellington, *Private Correspondence*, pp. 195–196, Oct. 30, 1827, Lieven to Wellington.

7. Wellington, *Private Correspondence*, pp. 195–196, Oct. 30, 1827, Lieven to Wellington.

8. Wellington, *Private Correspondence*, p. 198, Nov. 7, 1827, Lieven to Wellington.

9. The evidence does not specify their nature.

10. Wellington, *Private Correspondence*, pp. 202–203, Dec. 22, 1827, Cowper to Wellington.

11. Wellington, *Private Correspondence*, pp. 202–203, Dec. 22, 1827, Cowper to Wellington.

12. E. Ashley, ed., *Life and Correspondence of Palmerston*, vol. 1, p. 204, May 8, 1828, Palmerston to Temple.

13. Arthur Wellington, *The Eastern Question from His Correspondence*, pp. 31–32, Sept. 8, 1829, Wellington to Heytesbury.

14. Wellington, *Eastern Question*, pp. 31–32, Sept. 8, 1829, Wellington to Heytesbury.

15. Arthur Wellington, *Despatches, Correspondence & Memoranda*, vol. vi, p. 292, Nov. 8, 1829, Wellington to Aberdeen.

16. Lieven, *Letters ... London*, p. 132, May 7/19, 1828, to A. Benckendorff.

17. Today approximately $800,000 and $1,200,000, respectively.

18. Lieven, *Unpublished Diary*, p. 164.

19. Lieven, *Unpublished Diary*, pp. 163–164.

20. Lieven, *Unpublished Diary*, pp. 164–165.

21. Lieven, *Correspondence of Lieven and Grey*, vol. I, p. 267, Aug. 11, 1829, Lieven to Grey.

22. Lieven, *Letters ... London*, p. 255, Sept. 25/Oct. 6, 1830, Lieven to A. Benckendorff.

23. Lieven, *Letters ... London*, p. 136, June 18/30, 1828, Lieven to A. Benckendorff.

24. Lieven, *Letters ... London*, pp. 136–137, June 18/30, 1828, Lieven to A. Benckendorff.

25. Lieven, *Letters ... London*, pp. 175–178, Jan 3/15, 1829, to A. Benckendorff.

26. Lieven, *Letters ... London*, pp. 175–178, Jan 3/15, 1829, to A. Benckendorff.

27. Philip von Neumann, *Diary*, E.B. Chancellor, ed., vol. I, p. 198, Mar. 6, 1829.

28. Lieven, *Correspondence of Lieven and Grey*, vol. I, p. 366, Dec. 1, 1829, Lieven to Grey.

29. Lieven, *Letters to Metternich*, p. 37, July 8, 1820, and p. 114, May 13, 1823, respectively.

30. Lieven, *Correspondence of Lieven and Grey*, vol. ii, pp. 421–422, Nov. 28, 1832, Lieven to Grey.

31. Lieven, *Correspondence of Lieven and Grey*, vol. 1, pp. 90–91, Dec. 13, 1827, Lieven to Grey.

32. Lieven, *Correspondence of Lieven and Grey*, vol. 1, p. 20, Jan. 5, 1826, Grey to Lieven.

33. Lieven, *Correspondence of Lieven and Grey*, vol. 1, pp. 49–50, Aug. 7, 1827, Lieven to Grey.

34. Lieven, *Correspondence of Lieven and Grey*, preface, Princess Lieven to the Duke of Sutherland, Oct. 13, 1846.

35. Lieven, *Correspondence of Lieven and Grey*, vol. iii, p. 38, Nov. 4, 1834, Grey to Lieven.

36. Lieven, *Correspondence of Lieven and Grey*, vol. 1, pp. 57–58, Sept. 12, 1827, Lieven to Grey.

37. Lieven, *Correspondence of Lieven and Grey*, vol. 1, pp. 57–58, Sept. 12, 1827, Lieven to Grey.

38. Lieven, *Correspondence of Lieven and Grey*, vol. 1, p. 59, Sept. 17, 1827, Grey to Lieven.

39. Lieven, *Correspondence of Lieven and Grey*, vol. 1, p. 62, Oct. 1, 1827, Lieven to Grey.

40. Lieven, *Correspondence of Lieven and Grey*, vol. 1, p. 59, Sept. 17, 1827, Grey to Lieven.

41. Lieven, *Correspondence of Lieven and Grey*, vol. 1, p. 402, Jan. 1, 1830, Grey to Lieven.

42. Lieven, *Correspondence of Lieven and Grey*, vol. 1, p. 403, Jan. 4, 1830, Lieven to Grey.

43. Lieven, *Correspondence of Lieven and Grey*, vol. I, pp. 398–399, Dec. 28, 1828, Lieven to Grey.

44. "I am all yours heart and soul." Lieven, *Correspondence of Lieven and Grey*, vol. 1, pp. 416–417, Jan. 23, 1829, Grey to Lieven.

45. Lieven, *Correspondence of Lieven and Grey*, vol. 1, pp. 159–60, Oct. 8, 1828, Lieven to Grey.

46. Lieven, *Correspondence of Lieven and Grey*, vol. 1, pp. 168–170, Oct. 22, 1828, Lieven to Grey.

47. Lieven, *Correspondence of Lieven and Grey*, vol. 1, p. 242, Feb. 10, 1829, Lieven to Grey.

48. Lamb Papers, British Library, ADD, 45555, #57, Dec. 11, 1829, Lieven to Cowper.

49. Lieven Papers, British Library, ADD. 47418, #207, Apr. 18/30, 1828, Constantine Benckendorff to Lieven.

50. Lieven, *Letters ... London*, p. 154, Sept. 4/16, 1828, to A. Benckendorff.

51. Lieven, *Letters ... London*, pp. 154–155, Sept. 27/Oct. 9, 1828, to A. Benckendorff.

52. Lieven Papers, British Library, ADD. 47415, #63, Sept. 20/Oct. 2, 1828, A. Benckendorff to Lieven.

53. Lieven, *Letters ... London*, p. 155, Sept. 27/Oct. 9, 1828, to A. Benckendorff.

54. Lieven, *Letters ... London*, p. 184, Feb. 1/13, 1829, to A. Benckendorff.

55. Lieven, *Letters ... London*, p. 161, Nov. 12/24, 1828, to A. Benckendorff.

56. Lieven, *Letters ... London*, p. 169, Dec. 3/15, 1829, to A. Benckendorff.

57. Lieven, *Letters ... London*, p. 182, Feb. 1/13, 1829, to A. Benckendorff.

58. Lieven, *Letters ... London*, p. 194, Aug. 15/27, 1829, to A. Benckendorff.

59. Close to Constantinople on the Maritsa river, bordering modern Bulgaria and Turkey.

60. Earl of Malmesbury, *Memoirs of an Ex-Minister*, p. 375, Dec. 8, 1855, Sidney Herbert to Malmesbury.

61. Lieven, *Correspondence of Lieven and Grey*, vol. 1, pp. 361–362, Nov. 21, 1829, Lieven to Grey.

62. Lieven, *Letters ... London*, pp. 194–197, Aug. 15/17, 1829, to A. Benckendorff.

63. Greville, *Memoirs*, vol. ii, p. 325, Oct. 7, 1832.

64. Wellington, *Despatches*, vol. vi, p. 34, July 21, 1829, Wellington to Aberdeen.

Chapter 13

1. Lieven, *Letters ... London*, p. 215, Feb. 14/26, 1830, to A. Benckendorff.

2. Lieven, *Unpublished Diary*, p. 136.

3. Also spelled Capo d'Istria. This native Greek had entered Russia's foreign service; for four years he shared leadership of the foreign ministry with Nesselrode.

4. Lieven, *Unpublished Diary*, pp. 144–145.

5. Lieven, *Unpublished Diary*, p. 138.

6. Lieven, *Unpublished Diary*, p. 141.

7. Lieven, *Unpublished Diary*, pp. 141–142.

8. Lieven, *Unpublished Diary*, pp. 142–143.

9. Lieven, *Unpublished Diary*, p. 143.

10. Lieven, *Unpublished Diary*, pp. 145–146.

11. Lieven, *Unpublished Diary*, p. 146.

12. Lieven, *Unpublished Diary*, p. 147.

13. Lieven, *Unpublished Diary*, p. 148.

14. Lieven, *Unpublished Diary*, p. 148.

15. Lieven, *Unpublished Diary*, p. 149.

16. Lieven, *Unpublished Diary*, pp. 149–150.

17. Lieven, *Unpublished Diary*, pp. 149–150.

18. Lieven, *Unpublished Diary*, p. 151.

19. "Hand to hand."

20. Lieven, *Unpublished Diary*, p. 151.

21. Lieven, *Unpublished Diary*, pp. 151–152.

22. Lieven, *Correspondence of Lieven and Grey*, vol. I, p. 440, Feb. 13, 1830, Lieven to Grey.

23. Lieven, *Correspondence of Lieven and Grey*, vol. I, pp. 433–434, Feb. 9, 1830, Lieven to Grey.

24. Granville, *Letters*, vol. ii, p. 57, Feb. 8, 1830, Granville to Carlisle.

25. Lieven, *Unpublished Diary*, p. 152.

26. Lieven, *Unpublished Diary*, pp. 153–154.

27. Lieven, *Unpublished Diary*, pp. 153–154.

28. Lieven, *Unpublished Diary*, pp. 153–154.

29. Lieven, *Unpublished Diary*, pp. 153–154.

30. Lieven, *Correspondence of Lieven and Grey*, vol. I, pp. 290–291, Sept. 12, 1829, Lieven to Grey.

31. Lieven, *Correspondence of Lieven and Grey*, vol. I, pp. 291–292, Sept. 14, 1829, Grey to Lieven.

32. Wellington wanted to restrict Greece to the Morea (modern Greece's southern archipelago) and a few islands.

33. Lieven, *Correspondence of Lieven and Grey*, vol. I, p. 294, Sept. 16, 1829, Lieven to Grey.

34. Lieven Papers, British Library, ADD. 47397, #181, undated but probably late 1829, D. Lieven to C. Lieven.

35. Lieven Papers, British Library, ADD. 47397, #183, undated but probably late 1829, D. Lieven to C. Lieven.

36. Lieven, *Correspondence of Lieven and Grey*, vol. I, p. 316, Oct. 2, 1829, Lieven to Grey.

37. Lieven, *Correspondence of Lieven and Grey*, vol. I, pp. 325–326, Oct. 12, 1829, Lieven to Grey.

38. Lieven, *Correspondence of Lieven and Grey*, vol. I, pp. 325–326, Oct. 12, 1829, Lieven to Grey.

39. Lieven, *Correspondence of Lieven and Grey*, vol. I, p. 437, Feb. 12, 1830, Grey to Lieven.

40. Nesselrode had sent Count André Matuscewitz, a senior diplomat, to assist Lieven at the Conference on Greece.

41. Lieven, *Correspondence of Lieven and Grey*, vol. I, p. 440, Feb. 13, 1830, Lieven to Grey.

Chapter 14

1. Lieven, *Letters ... London*, p. 275, Nov. 8/20, 1830, Lieven to A. Benckendorff.

2. Lieven, *Letters ... London*, p. 130, Mar. 22/Apr. 3, 1828, Lieven to A. Benckendorff.

3. Lieven, *Letters ... London*, p. 221, June 23/July 5, 1830, Lieven to A. Benckendorff.

4. Lieven, *Correspondence of Lieven and Grey*, vol. ii, p. 27, July 21, 1830, Grey to Lieven.

5. The former Duke of Clarence.

6. Lieven, *Letters ... London*, p. 258, Oct. 2/14, 1830, Lieven to A. Benckendorff.

7. Lieven, *Correspondence of Lieven and Grey*, vol. ii, pp. 71–72, Aug. 31, 1830, Lieven to Grey.

8. Lieven, *Correspondence of Lieven and Grey*, vol. ii, p. 113, Oct. 26, 1830, Lieven to Grey.

9. Lieven, *Letters ... London*, p. 289, Dec. 10/22, 1830, Lieven to Benckendorff.

10. Lieven, *Letters ... London*, p. 224, July 8/20, 1830, Lieven to A. Benckendorff.

11. Lieven, *Letters ... London*, pp. 248–249, Oct. 4, 1830, Lieven to A. Benckendorff.

12. Lieven, *Letters ... London*, pp. 248–249, Oct. 4, 1830, Lieven to A. Benckendorff.

13. Sir Robert Peel, Tory home secretary and leader in the House of Commons.

14. Palmerston Papers, University of Southampton, Hartley Library, GC/LI/27, Oct. 7, 1830, Lieven to Cowper (Palmerston).

15. Palmerston Papers, University of Southampton, Hartley Library, GC/LI/27, Oct. 7, 1830, Lieven to Palmerston.

16. Lieven, *Unpublished Diary*, pp. 166–167.

17. Lieven, *Unpublished Diary*, p. 165.

18. Lieven, *Unpublished Diary*, p. 165.

19. Lieven, *Unpublished Diary*, p. 165.

20. Lieven, *Unpublished Diary*, p. 167.

21. Lieven, *Letters ... London*, p. 275, Nov. 8/20, 1830, Lieven to A. Benckendorff.

22. "Some shit is a silk stocking."

23. The Duchess was a daughter of the last reigning Duke of Courland.

24. Talleyrand-Périgord, *Mémoires*, vol. iii, p. 280.

25. Lieven, *Correspondence of Lieven and Grey*, vol. ii, p. 82, Sept. 9, 1830, Grey to Lieven.

26. Lieven, *Letters ... London*, p. 252 Sept. 25/Oct. 6, 1830, to A. Benckendorff.

27. Lieven, *Letters ... London*, pp. 315–318, Nov. 3/15, 1831, to A. Benckendorff.

28. Lieven, *Correspondence of Lieven and Grey*, vol. ii, pp. 142, Jan. 23, 1831, Grey to Lieven.

29. Lieven, *Correspondence of Lieven and Grey*, vol. ii, p. 268, Aug. 25, 1831, Lieven to Grey.

30. Lieven, *Correspondence of Lieven and Grey*, vol. ii, pp. 142, Jan. 23, 1831, Grey to Lieven.

31. Prince William had married the Grand Duchess Anna, Tsar Nicholas's favorite sister.

32. Lieven Papers, British Library, ADD. 47379, #113, undated; unpublished Lieven memoirs.

33. Lieven Papers, British Library, ADD. 47379, #113, undated; unpublished Lieven memoirs.

34. Belgium's representative at the London Conference.

35. Lieven Papers, British Library, ADD. 47379, #113, undated; unpublished Lieven memoirs.

36. Talleyrand-Périgord, *Mémoires*, vol. iv, pp. 10–11, Jan. 12, 1831, Talleyrand to Mme. Adelaide.

37. Lieven Papers, British Library, ADD. 47379, #113, undated; unpublished Lieven memoirs.

38. The Grand Duchess Anna was extremely wealthy.

39. Lieven, *Unpublished Diary*, p. 174.

40. Lieven, *Unpublished Diary*, p. 175–176.

41. Count Matuscewitz had stayed in London to assist Lieven at the London conference on Belgium.

42. Lieven, *Unpublished Diary*, p. 175–176.

43. Lieven, *Unpublished Diary*, p. 176.

44. Lieven, *Unpublished Diary*, p. 177.

45. Lieven Papers, British Library, ADD. 47355, #110, Monday, probably January 1831, Grey to Lieven.

46. Lieven, *Correspondence of Lieven and Grey*, vol. ii, p. 139, Jan. 21, 1831, Grey to Lieven.

47. Lieven, *Unpublished Diary*, pp. 176–177.

48. Dorothea Lieven's diary does not tell why the Orange plot failed.

49. Lieven, *Unpublished Diary*, pp. 177–178.

50. Lieven, *Unpublished Diary*, p. 178.

51. Lieven, *Correspondence of Lieven and Grey*, vol. ii, pp. 152–153, Feb. 1, 1831, Lieven to Grey.

52. Lieven, *Correspondence of Lieven and Grey*, vol. ii, p. 156, Feb. 1, 1831, Lieven to Grey.

53. Lieven, *Correspondence of Lieven and Grey*, vol. ii, pp. 161–162, Feb. 9, 1831, Lieven to Grey.

54. A pastry, such as a cream-puff.

55. Lieven, *Correspondence of Lieven and Grey*, vol. ii, p. 164, Feb. 11, 1831, Lieven to Grey.

56. Lieven Papers, British Library, ADD. 47355, #151, July 3/15, 1831, Lieven to Nesselrode.

57. Lieven, *Letters ... London*, pp. 304–305, June 26, 1831 Lieven to A. Benckendorff.

Chapter 15

1. Nesselrode, *Lettres et Papiers*, vol. vii, p. 173, Feb. 1, 1831, Nesselrode to Lieven.

2. Metternich Family Archive, National Archive (Prague), AC 6, #45–48, March 19–24, 1820, Lieven to Metternich.

3. Lieven, *Correspondence of Lieven and Grey*, vol. ii, p. 73, Aug. 31, 1830, Lieven to Grey.

4. Lieven, *Correspondence of Lieven and Grey*, vol. ii, pp. 74–75, Sept. 3, 1830, Grey to Lieven.

5. Lieven, *Correspondence of Lieven and Grey*, vol. ii, p. 77, Sept. 6, 1830, Lieven to Grey.

6. Lieven, *Correspondence of Lieven and Grey*, vol. ii, p. 304, Dec. 14, 1831, Grey to Lieven.

7. Lieven, *Correspondence of Lieven and Grey*, vol. ii, p. 306, Dec. 15, 1831, Lieven to Grey.

8. Lieven, *Correspondence of Lieven and Grey*, vol. ii, p. 306, Dec. 15, 1831, Lieven to Grey.

9. Lieven, *Letters ... London*, pp. 323–324, Jan. 18/30, 1832, Lieven to Benckendorff.

10. Lieven Papers, British Library, ADD. 47356 A, #77, Jan. 15/27, 1832, Lieven to Nesselrode.

11. Lieven Papers, British Library, ADD. 47356 A, #80, Jan. 31/Feb. 11, 1832, Lieven to Nesselrode.

12. Lieven, *Correspondence of Lieven and Grey*, vol. ii, pp. 295–297, Dec. 3, 1831, Grey to Lieven.

13. Lieven, *Correspondence of Lieven and Grey*, vol. ii, p. 298, Dec. 5, 1831, Lieven to Grey.

14. Lieven, *Correspondence of Lieven and Grey Grey*, vol. ii, pp. 295–297, Dec. 3, 1831, Grey to Lieven.

15. Lieven, *Correspondence of Lieven and Grey*, vol. ii, p. 297, Dec. 5, 1831, Lieven to Grey.

16. Lieven, *Correspondence of Lieven and Grey*, vol. ii, p. 297, Dec. 5, 1831, Lieven to Grey.

17. Lamb Papers, British Library, ADD. 45555, #134–135, Jan. 4, 1832, Lieven to Cowper.

18. The tsar gave this ardent nationalist, assiduous courtier and able diplomat important missions (e.g., Orlov had negotiated the Treaty of Adrianople, which ended the 1828–9 Russo-Turkish War). A member of one of Russia's powerful court families, Orlov envied and opposed Baltic Baron influence; he led the "Russian" faction at the foreign ministry against Nesselrode and "the Germans."

19. Lieven, *Correspondence of Lieven and Grey*, vol. ii, pp. 329–30 Feb. 13, 1832, Lieven to Grey.

20. Lieven Papers, British Library, ADD. 47356 A, #106, Apr. 22/May 4, 1832, Lieven to Nesselrode.

21. Lieven, *Correspondence of Lieven and Grey*, vol. ii, pp. 340–341, May 4, 1832, Lieven to Grey.

22. Lieven, *Correspondence of Lieven and Grey*, vol. ii, pp. 340–341, May 4, 1832, Lieven to Grey.

23. Lieven, *Correspondence of Lieven and Grey*, vol. ii, pp. 341–342, May 4, 1832, Grey to Lieven.

24. Lieven, *Correspondence of Lieven and Grey*, vol. ii, pp. 342–343, May 4, 1832, Lieven to Grey.

25. Lieven, *Correspondence of Lieven and Grey*, vol. ii, p. 344, May 4, 1832, Grey to Lieven.

26. Lieven, *Correspondence of Lieven and Grey*, vol. ii, pp. 362–363, July 6, 1832, Grey to Lieven.

27. Lieven, *Letters ... London*, p. 327, May 3, 1832, Lieven to A. Benckendorff.

28. Lieven, *Correspondence of Lieven and Grey*, vol. ii, p. 289, Oct. 11, 1831, Lieven to Grey.

29. Lieven, *Correspondence of Lieven and Grey*, vol. ii, p. 387, Sept. 2, 1832, Lieven to Grey.

30. Lieven, *Correspondence of Lieven and Grey*, vol. ii, pp. 392–393, Sept. 10, 1832, Grey to Lieven.

31. Lieven, *Correspondence of Lieven and Grey*, vol. ii, pp. 394–396, Sept. 15, 1832, Lieven to Grey.

32. Lieven, *Correspondence of Lieven and Grey*, vol. ii, pp. 394–396, Sept. 15, 1832, Lieven to Grey.

33. The duke of Buckingham's country seat.

34. Lieven Papers, British Library, ADD. 47363, Sept. 24, 1832, Lieven to Grey.

35. Lieven Papers, British Library, ADD. .47363, Sept. 27, 1832, Grey to Lieven.

36. Nesselrode, *Lettres et Papiers*, vol. vii, pp. 234–236, Oct. 29, 1832, Lieven to Nesselrode.

Chapter 16

1. Dorothée de Talleyrand-Périgord, *Memoirs of the Duchess of Dino*, vol. I, pp. 59–60, May 22, 1834.
2. Prince Adam Czartoryski, *Memoirs*, vol. ii, p. 319.
3. A newspaper considered friendly to the government.
4. Lieven, *Correspondence of Lieven and Grey*, vol. ii, pp. 181–182, Mar. 8, 1831, Lieven to Grey.
5. Lieven, *Correspondence of Lieven and Grey*, vol. ii, pp. 182–183, Mar. 8, 1831, Grey to Lieven.
6. Lieven Papers, British Library, ADD. 47355, #187, Sept. 21, 1831, Palmerston to Cowper, included in Lieven to Nesselrode, Sept. 23, 1831.
7. Lamb Papers, British Library, ADD. 45555, # 83, Jan. 8, 1831, Lieven to Cowper.
8. Nesselrode, *Lettres et Papiers*, vol. ix, p. 173, Feb. 1, 1831, Nesselrode to Lieven.
9. Lieven, *Correspondence of Lieven and Grey*, vol. ii, pp. 184–185, Mar. 11, 1831, Lieven to Grey.
10. Nesselrode, *Lettres et Papiers*, vol. vii, p. 177, Mar. 12, 1831, Grey to Lieven, included in Lieven to Nesselrode.
11. Lieven, *Correspondence of Lieven and Grey*, vol. ii, p. 185, Mar. 12, 1831, Lieven to Grey.
12. Lieven, *Correspondence of Lieven and Grey*, vol. ii, pp. 243–245, June 18, 1831, Lieven to Grey.
13. Lieven, *Correspondence of Lieven and Grey*, vol. ii, pp. 243–245, June 18, 1831, Lieven to Grey.
14. Lieven, *Letters ... London*, p. 243–244, Sept. 8/20. 1830, Lieven to Benckendorff.
15. Lieven, *Letters ... London*, p. 322, Jan. 9, 1832, Lieven to Benckendorff.
16. Lamb Papers, British Library, ADD. 45555, # 97, Oct. 27, 1831, Lieven to Cowper.
17. Lieven Papers, British Library, ADD. 47356 A, #11, Oct. 16/28, 1831, Lieven to Nesselrode.
18. Lieven Papers, British Library, ADD. 47356 A, #23–26, Nov. 3/15, 1831, Lieven to Nesselrode.
19. Lieven Papers, British Library, ADD. 47356 A, #23–26, Nov. 3/15, 1831, Lieven to Nesselrode.
20. Talleyrand-Périgord, *Mémoires*, vol. iv, p. 164.
21. Aberdeen, *Correspondence*, vol. ii, p. 584, June 19, 1851, Lieven to Aberdeen.
22. Lieven, *Correspondence of Lieven and Grey*, vol. ii, p. 310, Jan. 1, 1832, Grey to Lieven.
23. Lieven, *Correspondence of Lieven and Grey*, vol. ii, pp. 311–312, Jan. 2, 1832, Lieven to Grey.
24. Lieven, *Correspondence of Lieven and Grey*, vol. ii, pp. 312–314, Jan. 4, 1832, Grey to Lieven.
25. Lieven, *Correspondence of Lieven and Grey*, vol. ii, pp. 312–314, Jan. 4, 1832, Grey to Lieven.
26. Lieven, *Correspondence of Lieven and Grey*, vol. ii, pp. 315–316, Jan. 5, 1832, Grey to Lieven.
27. Lieven, *Correspondence of Lieven and Grey*, vol. ii, p. 318, Jan. 5, 1832, Lieven to Grey.
28. Lieven, *Correspondence of Lieven and Grey*, vol. ii, p. 319–321, Jan. 6, 1832, Grey to Lieven.
29. Lieven, *Correspondence of Lieven and Grey*, vol. ii, p. 322, Jan. 7, 1832, Lieven to Grey.
30. Lieven Papers, British Library, ADD. 47356 B, #92, Aug. 26/Sept. 7, 1833, Lieven to Nesselrode.
31. Grey's government had sent cabinet member Lord Durham on a special diplomatic mission to Russia.
32. Lieven Papers, British Library, ADD. 47356 B, #92–94, Aug. 26/Sept. 7, 1833, Lieven to Nesselrode.
33. Lieven, *Correspondence of Lieven and Grey*, vol. ii, p. 466, Sept. 18, 1833, Lieven to Grey.
34. Lieven, *Correspondence of Lieven and Grey*, vol. ii, p. 467, Sept. 22, 1833, Grey to Lieven.
35. Lieven, *Correspondence of Lieven and Grey*, vol. ii, p. 484, Oct. 23, 1833, Lieven to Grey.
36. Lieven, *Correspondence of Lieven and Grey*, vol. ii, p. 486, Oct. 27, 1833, Grey to Lieven.

Chapter 17

1. Nesselrode, *Lettres et Papiers*, vol. vii, pp. 174–175, Feb. 1, 1831, Nesselrode to Lieven.
2. Nesselrode, *Lettres et Papiers*, vol. vii, pp. 174–175, Feb. 1, 1831, Nesselrode to Lieven.
3. Stanley Lane-Poole, *Life of Lord Stratford de Redcliffe*, vol. ii, p. 19, Nov. 17, 1832, Bligh to Palmerston.
4. Lieven, *Letters ... London*, p. 305, June 26, 1831, to A. Benckendorff.
5. Lieven, *Letters ... London*, pp. 327–329, June 17/29, 1832, to A. Benckendorff.
6. Lieven, *Correspondence of Lieven and Grey*, vol. ii, p. 395, Sept. 15, 1832, Lieven to Grey.
7. Lieven Papers, British Library, ADD. 47356A, #201, Oct. 6/18, 1832, Lieven to Nesselrode.
8. Lieven Papers, British Library, ADD. 47356A, #201, Oct. 6/18, 1832, Lieven to Nesselrode.
9. Lieven Papers, British Library, ADD. 47356A, #201, Oct. 6/18, 1832, Lieven to Nesselrode.
10. Nesselrode had officially informed Lieven that Russia refused to receive Stratford Canning.
11. Palmerston Papers, University of Southampton, Hartley Library, GC/LI/36, Jan. 26, 1833, Lieven to Palmerston.
12. Lieven, *Correspondence of Lieven and Grey*, vol. ii, p. 431, Dec. 31, 1832, Lieven to Grey.
13. Lieven, *Correspondence of Lieven and Grey*, vol. ii, pp. 433–434, Jan. 1, 1833, Grey to Lieven.
14. Lieven Papers, British Library, ADD. 47356B, #72, June 14, 1833, Lieven to Nesselrode.
15. Palmerston Papers, University of Southampton, Hartley Library, GC/LI/37, June 22, 1833, Lieven to Palmerston.
16. Lieven Papers, British Library, ADD. 47398, #212, July 5/14, 1833, D. Lieven to C. Lieven.
17. Lieven Papers, British Library, ADD. 47398, #224, July 17/29, 1833, D. Lieven to C. Lieven.
18. Lieven Papers, British Library, ADD. 47398, #233–237, 1832 or 1833, D. Lieven to C. Lieven.
19. Lieven Papers, British Library, ADD. 47398, #233–237, 1832 or 1833, D. Lieven to C. Lieven.
20. Lieven Papers, British Library, ADD. 47398, #233–237, 1832 or 1833, D. Lieven to C. Lieven.
21. Lieven Papers, British Library, ADD. 47398, #233–237, 1832 or 1833, D. Lieven to C. Lieven.
22. Lieven Papers, British Library, ADD. 47398, #233–237, 1832 or 1833, D. Lieven to C. Lieven.
23. Lieven Papers, British Library, ADD. 47398, #233–237, 1832 or 1833, D. Lieven to C. Lieven.
24. Lieven Papers, British Library, ADD. 47398, #233–237, 1832 or 1833, D. Lieven to C. Lieven.
25. Lieven Papers, British Library, ADD. 47398, #233–237, 1832 or 1833, D. Lieven to C. Lieven.
26. Lieven Papers, British Library, ADD. 47398, #233–237, 1832 or 1833, D. Lieven to C. Lieven.
27. Lieven Papers, British Library, ADD. 47379, #11, undated, unpublished Lieven memoirs.

28. Convention of Münchengrätz, September 1833.

29. *Greville Memoirs*, vol. ii, p. 358, Feb. 16, 1833.

30. *Greville Memoirs*, vol. ii, p. 358, Feb. 16, 1833.

31. Aberdeen, *Correspondence*, vol. 1, pp. 18–20, Oct. 11/13, 1834, Lieven to Aberdeen.

32. Guizot, *Lettres de Guizot et de Lieven*, vol. ii, p. 101, May 20, 1840.

Chapter 18

1. Lieven, *Correspondence of Lieven and Grey*, vol. iii, p. 109, Apr. 29, 1835, Lieven to Grey.

2. Lieven, *Letters ... London*, pp. 375–376, Apr. 29/May 11, 1834, to A. Benckendorff.

3. Lieven, *Letters ... London*, pp. 375–376, Apr. 29/May 11, 1834, to A. Benckendorff.

4. Lieven, *Correspondence of Lieven and Grey*, vol. ii, p. 499, May 23, 1834, Lieven to Grey.

5. State Archive of the Russian Federation, 728, 1, 2396, #20–21, May 15/27, 1834, Empress Alexandra to Lieven.

6. State Archive of the Russian Federation, 728, 1, 2396, #20–21, May 15/27, 1834, Empress Alexandra to Lieven.

7. Dorothée de Talleyrand-Périgord, *Memoirs*, vol. 1, pp. 79–80, June 8, 1834.

8. Dorothée de Talleyrand-Périgord, *Memoirs*, vol. 1, p. 62, May 24, 1834.

9. Lieven, *Correspondence of Lieven and Grey*, vol. ii, p. 509, Aug. 6, 1834, Lieven to Grey.

10. Lieven, *Correspondence of Lieven and Grey*, vol. iii, p. 20, Sept. 23, 1834, Grey to Lieven.

11. Lieven, *Correspondence of Lieven and Grey*, vol. iii, pp. 9–11, Aug. 6/18, 1834, Lieven to Grey.

12. Lieven, *Correspondence of Lieven and Grey*, vol. iii, pp. 9–11, Aug. 6/18, 1834, Lieven to Grey.

13. Lieven Papers, British Library, ADD. 47403, #182–184, 1835, Nov. 10, 1835, D. Lieven to C. Lieven.

14. Lieven Papers, British Library, ADD. 47403, #182–184, Nov. 10, 1836, D. Lieven to C. Lieven.

15. Lieven, *Correspondence of Lieven and Grey*, vol. iii, p. 12, Aug. 24/Sept. 5, 1834, Lieven to Grey.

16. Lieven, *Correspondence of Lieven and Grey*, vol. iii, p. 20, Sept. 23, 1834, Grey to Lieven.

17. Lieven, *Correspondence of Lieven and Grey*, vol. iii, pp. 12–14, Aug. 24/Sept. 5, 1834, Lieven to Grey.

18. Lamb Papers, British Library, ADD. 45555, #231, Oct. 7, 1834, Lieven to Cowper.

19. Lamb Papers, British Library, ADD. 45555, #234–235, Oct. 23 & 24, 1834, Lieven to Cowper.

20. Lieven, *Correspondence of Lieven and Grey*, vol. iii, pp. 20–22, Sept. 4/16, 1834, Lieven to Grey.

21. Lieven, *Correspondence of Lieven and Grey*, vol. iii, pp. 20–22, Sept. 4/16, 1834, Lieven to Grey.

22. August Theodor von Grimm, *Alexandra Federovna, Empress of Russia*, vol. ii, p. 111.

23. Grimm, *Alexandra Federovna*, vol. ii, pp. 110–111.

24. Lieven, *Correspondence of Lieven and Grey*, vol. iii, p. 44, Nov. 1, 1834, Lieven to Grey.

25. Lieven, *Correspondence of Lieven and Grey*, vol. iii, pp. 64–65, Dec. 4/16, 1834, Lieven to Grey.

26. Lieven Papers, British Library, ADD. 47379, #11, undated; unpublished section of the Lieven memoirs.

27. Lieven, *Correspondence of Lieven and Grey*, vol. iii, pp. 70–72, Jan. 4, 1835, Lieven to Grey.

28. Lieven, *Correspondence of Lieven and Grey*, vol. iii, pp. 70–72, Jan. 4, 1835, Lieven to Grey.

29. Lamb Papers, British Library, ADD. 45556, #3, Jan. 6, 1835, Lieven to Cowper.

30. Lamb Papers, British Library, ADD. 45556, #4, Jan. 6, 1835, Lieven to Cowper.

31. Lamb Papers, British Library, ADD. 45556, #2, Jan. 6, 1835, Lieven to Cowper.

32. Lamb Papers, British Library, ADD. 45556, #8, Jan. 12/24, 1835, Lieven to Cowper.

33. Lieven, *Correspondence of Lieven and Grey*, vol. iii, pp. 31–32, Oct. 6, 1834, Lieven to Grey.

34. Lamb Papers, British Library, ADD. 45556, #10, Feb. 6, 1835, Lieven to Cowper.

35. Lieven, *Correspondence of Lieven and Grey*, vol. iii, pp. 25–26, Sept. 12/24, 1834, Lieven to Grey.

36. Lamb Papers, British Library, ADD. 45556, #12, Feb. 8–20, 1835, Lieven to Cowper.

37. Lieven, *Correspondence of Lieven and Grey*, vol. iii, p. 96, Mar. 9, 1835, Lieven to Grey.

38. Lieven, *Correspondence of Lieven and Grey*, vol. iii, p. 94, Mar. 26, 1835, Grey to Lieven.

39. Lieven, *Correspondence of Lieven and Grey*, vol. iii, pp. 96–97, Mar. 18/30, 1835, Lieven to Grey.

40. Lieven, *Correspondence of Lieven and Grey*, vol. iii, p. 96, Mar. 18/30, 1835, Lieven to Grey.

41. Lieven, *Correspondence of Lieven and Grey*, vol. iii, p. 97, Mar. 18/30, 1835, Lieven to Grey.

42. Lieven, *Correspondence of Lieven and Grey*, vol. iii, pp. 98–99, Apr. 6, 1835, Grey to Lieven.

43. Lieven, *Correspondence of Lieven and Grey*, vol. iii, p. 106, Apr. 22, 1835, Lieven to Grey.

44. Metternich Family Archive, National Archive (Prague), AC 19–1, #6, May 29, 1835, Lieven to Metternich.

Chapter 19

1. Lieven, *Correspondence of Lieven and Grey*, vol. iii, p. 107, Apr. 22, 1835, Lieven to Grey.

2. Lieven Papers, British Library, ADD. 47399, #3, April 25, 1835, D. Lieven to C. Lieven.

3. Lieven Papers, British Library, ADD. 47399, #2, Apr. 25, 1835, C. Lieven to D. Lieven.

4. Lieven Papers, British Library, ADD. 47399, #3, April 25, 1835, D. Lieven to C. Lieven.

5. Lieven, *Correspondence of Lieven and Grey*, vol. iii, pp. 108–110, Apr. 29, 1835, Lieven to Grey.

6. Lamb Papers, British Library, ADD. 45556, #17, Apr. 17, 1835, Lieven to Cowper.

7. Lamb Papers, British Library, ADD. 45556, #17–18, Apr. 17, 1835, Lieven to Cowper.

8. Lieven, *Correspondence of Lieven and Grey*, vol. iii, pp. 108–110, Apr. 29, 1835, Lieven to Grey.

9. Lieven, *Correspondence of Lieven and Grey*, vol. iii, pp. 108–110, Apr. 29, 1835, Lieven to Grey.

10. Guizot, *Lettres de Guizot et de Lieven*, vol. iii, p. 209, Mar. 4, 1846, Lieven to Guizot.

11. Lieven, *Correspondence of Lieven and Grey*, vol. iii, pp. 106–107, Apr. 22, 1835, Lieven to Grey.

12. Lieven, *Correspondence of Lieven and Grey*, vol. iii, pp. 108–110, Apr. 29, 1835, Lieven to Grey.

13. Guizot, *Lettres de Guizot et de Lieven*, vol. iii, p. 109, Mar. 4, 1844, Lieven to Guizot.

14. Lieven Papers, British Library, ADD. 47374, #1, 1835 or after. D. Lieven's pocket diary.

15. Aberdeen, *Correspondence*, vol. 1, pp. 30–31, May 10, 1835, Lieven to Aberdeen.

16. Aberdeen, *Correspondence*, vol. 1, pp. 1–2, Sept. 3, 1832, Lieven to Aberdeen.

17. Aberdeen, *Correspondence*, vol. 1, pp. 30–31, May 10, 1835, Lieven to Aberdeen.

18. Aberdeen, *Correspondence*, vol. 1, pp. 28–29, May 5, 1835, Aberdeen to Lieven.

19. Aberdeen, *Correspondence*, vol. 1, p. 32, June 28, 1835, Lieven to Aberdeen.

20. Lieven, *Correspondence of Lieven and Grey*, vol. iii, p. 112, May 5, 1835, Grey to Lieven.

21. Lamb Papers, British Library, ADD. 45556, #20, May 11 & 13, 1835, Lieven to Cowper.

22. Lieven Papers, British Library, ADD. 47399, #62, June 1, 1835, D. Lieven to C. Lieven.

23. Lieven, *Correspondence of Lieven and Grey*, vol. iii, pp. 120–121, May 20, 1835, Lieven to Grey.

24. Lieven Papers, British Library, ADD. 47399 #62, June 1, 1835, D. Lieven to C. Lieven.

25. Lamb Papers, British Library, ADD. 45556, #21, May 11 & 13, 1835, Lieven to Cowper.

26. Lieven Papers, British Library, ADD. 47399, Aug. 1, 1835, D. Lieven to C. Lieven.

27. Dorothée de Talleyrand-Périgord, *Memoirs*, vol. 1, pp. 237–238, summer, 1835.

28. Lieven Papers, British Library, ADD. 47399, #102, July 5, 1835, D. Lieven to C. Lieven.

29. Lamb Papers, British Library, ADD. 45556, #34, July 8, 1835, Lieven to Cowper.

30. Lieven, *Correspondence of Lieven and Grey*, vol. iii, p. 139, July 30, 1835, Lieven to Grey.

31. Lamb Papers, British Library, ADD. 47368, #40, July 28, 1835, Cowper to Lieven.

32. Lamb Papers, British Library, ADD. 47368, #40, July 28, 1835, Cowper to Lieven.

33. Lamb Papers, British Library, ADD. 47368, #47, Aug. 14, 1835, Cowper to Lieven.

34. Lamb Papers, British Library, ADD. 45556, #36, Aug. 19, 1835, Lieven to Cowper.

35. Lamb Papers, British Library, ADD. 47368, #51, Aug. 27, 1835, Cowper to Lieven.

36. Lamb Papers, British Library, ADD. 45556, #42, Sept. 2, 1835, Lieven to Cowper.

37. Lamb Papers, British Library, ADD. 45556, #39, Aug. 22, 1835, Lieven to Cowper.

38. Lieven Papers, British Library, ADD. 47399, #143, July 29, 1835, D. Lieven to C. Lieven.

39. Lieven Papers, British Library, ADD. 47399, #147, Aug. 1, 1835, D. Lieven to C. Lieven.

40. Lieven Papers, British Library, ADD. 47399, #171, Aug. 18, 1835, D. Lieven to C. Lieven.

41. *Vie*, p. 167, autumn 1835, Lieven to A. Benckendorff.

42. *Vie*, p. 167, autumn 1835, Lieven to A. Benckendorff.

43. Lieven Papers, British Library, ADD. 47376, #55–56, Aug. 24, 1835, Devonshire to Lieven.

44. Lamb Papers, British Library, ADD. 45556, #320, July 19, 1842, Lieven to Palmerston (formerly Cowper).

Chapter 20

1. Lieven, *Unpublished Diary*, p. 198.

2. Guizot, *Lettres de Guizot et de Lieven*, vol. 1, pp. 47–49, July 23–25, 1837, Lieven to Guizot.

3. Lieven Papers, British Library, ADD. 47400, #12–13, Oct. 12, 1835, D. Lieven to C. Lieven.

4. Lieven Papers, British Library, ADD. 47400, #168–169, Dec. 2/14, 1835, C. Lieven to D. Lieven.

5. Lieven Papers, British Library, ADD. 47400, #35, Oct. 4/16, 1835, D. Lieven to C. Lieven.

6. Lieven Papers, British Library, ADD. 47401, #180, Mar. 12, 1836, D. Lieven to C. Lieven.

7. Lieven Papers, British Library, ADD. 47402, #2–7, Apr. 2–4, 1836, D. Lieven to C. Lieven.

8. Lieven Papers, British Library, ADD. 47404, #162–164, Feb. 9/21, 1837, D. Lieven to C. Lieven.

9. Lieven Papers, British Library, ADD. 47400, #56–57, Oct. 14/26, 1835, D. Lieven to C. Lieven.

10. Lieven Papers, British Library, ADD. 47400, #92–94, Oct. 30/Nov. 11, 1835, C. Lieven to D. Lieven.

11. Lieven Papers, British Library, ADD. 47403, #143, Oct. 10/30, 1836, C. Lieven to D. Lieven.

12. Charles Rémusat, *Mémoires de ma Vie*, vol. iv, p. 41.

13. Lieven Papers, British Library, ADD. 47400, #99, Nov. 1/13, 1835, D. Lieven to C. Lieven.

14. Granville, *Letters*, vol. ii, p. 236, June 30, 1838, Granville to Carlisle.

15. Granville, *Letters*, vol. ii, p. 236, June 30, 1838, Granville to Carlisle.

16. Lieven, *Correspondence of Lieven and Grey*, vol. iii, pp. 161–162, Oct. 23, 1835, Lieven to Grey.

17. Granville, *Letters*, vol. ii, p. 236, June 30, 1837, Lady Granville to Lady Carlisle.

18. Lieven Papers, British Library, ADD. 47401, #38–39, Jan. 1/13, 1836, D. Lieven to C. Lieven.

19. Lieven Papers, British Library, ADD. 47401, #117–118, Feb. 1/13, 1836, D. Lieven to C. Lieven.

20. Lieven Papers, British Library, ADD. 47401, #143–145, Feb. 12/24–14/26, 1836, D. Lieven to C. Lieven.

21. Lieven Papers, British Library, ADD. 47401, #143–145, Feb. 12/24–14/26, 1836, D. Lieven to C. Lieven.

22. Lieven Papers, British Library, ADD. 47401, #139–144, Feb. 12/24–14/26, 1836, D. Lieven to C. Lieven.

23. Lieven Papers, British Library, ADD. 47401, #139–144, Feb. 12/24–14/26, 1836, D. Lieven to C. Lieven.

24. Lieven Papers, British Library, ADD. 47401, #139–144, Feb. 12/24–14/26, 1836, D. Lieven to C. Lieven.

25. Lieven Papers, British Library, ADD. 47402, #57, Apr. 9/21, 1836, C. Lieven to D. Lieven.

26. Lieven Papers, British Library, ADD. 47402, #174 & 179, June 11 & 7/19, 1836, D. Lieven to C. Lieven.

27. Lieven Papers, British Library, ADD. 47402, #256–257, Aug. 7, 1836, D. Lieven to C. Lieven.

28. Lieven Papers, British Library, ADD. 47402, #256–257, Aug. 7, 1836, D. Lieven to C. Lieven.

29. Lieven Papers, British Library, ADD. 47402, #285–286, Aug. 12/24, 1836, C. Lieven to D. Lieven.

30. Lieven Papers, British Library, ADD. 47402, #287, Aug. 12/24, 1836, C. Lieven to D. Lieven.

31. Lieven Papers, British Library, ADD. 47402, #283, Aug. 12/24, 1836, C. Lieven to D. Lieven.

32. Lieven Papers, British Library, ADD. 47402, #283–284, Aug. 12/24, 1836, C. Lieven to D. Lieven.

33. Lieven Papers, British Library, ADD. 47402, #286, Aug. 12/24, 1836, C. Lieven to D. Lieven.

34. Lieven Papers, British Library, ADD. 47402, #287, Aug. 12/24, 1836, C. Lieven to D. Lieven.

35. Lieven Papers, British Library, ADD. 47402, #288, Aug. 12/24, 1836, C. Lieven to D. Lieven.

36. Lieven Papers, British Library, ADD. 47403, #59–60, Oct. 3, 1836, D. Lieven to C. Lieven.

37. Lieven Papers, British Library, ADD. 47403, #59–60, Oct. 3, 1836, D. Lieven to C. Lieven.

38. Lieven Papers, British Library, ADD. 47403, #182–184, Nov. 10,1836, D. Lieven to C. Lieven.

39. Lieven Papers, British Library, ADD. 47403, #10–11, Aug. 18/30, 1836, Lieven to Tsar Nicholas I.

40. Lieven Papers, British Library, ADD. 47403, #10–11, Aug. 18/30, 1836, Lieven to Tsar Nicholas I.

41. Lieven Papers, British Library, ADD. 47403, #10–11, Aug. 18/30, 1836, Lieven to Tsar Nicholas I.

42. Lieven Papers, British Library, ADD. 47403, #38–40, Sept. 5/17, 1836, D. Lieven to C. Lieven.

43. Lieven Papers, British Library, ADD. 47403, #38–40, Sept. 5/17, 1836, D. Lieven to C. Lieven.

44. Lieven Papers, British Library, ADD. 47403, #182–184, Nov. 10, 1836, D. Lieven to C. Lieven.

45. Lieven Papers, British Library, ADD. 47403, #182–184, Nov. 10,1836, D. Lieven to C. Lieven.

46. Lieven Papers, British Library, ADD. 47403, #186–188, Sept. 28/Oct. 10, 1836, A. Benckendorff to Lieven; D. Lieven to C. Lieven Nov. 10, 1836.

47. Lieven Papers, British Library, ADD. 47403, #186–188, Sept. 28/Oct. 10, 1836, A. Benckendorff to Lieven; D. Lieven to C. Lieven Nov. 10, 1836.

48. Lieven Papers, British Library, ADD. 47403, #182–184, Nov. 10,1836, D. Lieven to C. Lieven.

49. Lieven Papers, British Library, ADD. 47404, #27, Jan. 12, 1837, D. Lieven to C. Lieven.

50. Granville, *Letters*, vol. ii, p. 221, Jan. 1837, Granville to Carlisle.

51. Charles Greville, *Memoirs of the Reign of George IV and William IV*, vol. iii, pp. 379–380, Jan. 19, 1837.

52. "In a three-way conversation."

53. Granville, *Letters*, vol. ii, p. 221, Jan., 1837, Granville to Carlisle.

54. Lieven Papers, British Library, ADD. 47376, #21, *The Press*, Dec. 15, 1836.

55. Lieven Papers, British Library, ADD. 47405, #113, Apr. 27/May 7, 1837, C. Lieven to D. Lieven.

56. Lieven Papers, British Library, ADD. 47404, #221–223, Mar. 5/17, 1837, D. Lieven to C. Lieven.

57. Lieven Papers, British Library, ADD. 47405, #153, May 12/24, 1837, C. Lieven to D. Lieven.

58. Lieven Papers, British Library, ADD. 47405, $183, June 7, D. Lieven to C. Lieven.

Chapter 21

1. Guizot, *Lettres de Guizot et de Lieven*, vol. I, pp. 15–16, July 4, 1837, Lieven to Guizot.

2. Lieven Papers, British Library, ADD. 47405, #108, May 6, 1837, D. Lieven to C. Lieven.

3. Guizot, *Lettres de Guizot et de Lieven*, vol. I, p. 1, Feb. 16, 1837, Lieven to Guizot.

4. Guizot, *Lettres de Guizot et de Lieven*, vol. I, p. 4, Feb. 20, 1837, Lieven to Guizot.

5. Guizot, *Lettres de Guizot et de Lieven*, vol. I, p. 4, Feb. 20, 1837, Lieven to Guizot.

6. Guizot, *Lettres de Guizot et de Lieven*, vol. I, pp. 4–5, Mar. 19, 1837, Lieven to Guizot.

7. Guizot, *Lettres de Guizot et de Lieven*, vol. I, pp. 55–56, July 29, 1837, Guizot to Lieven.

8. Guizot, *Lettres de Guizot et de Lieven*, vol. I, p. 7, June 18, 1837, Lieven to Guizot.

9. Guizot, *Lettres de Guizot et de Lieven*, vol. 1, pp. 130–131, Sept. 30, 1837, Guizot to Lieven.

10. Guizot, *Lettres de Guizot et de Lieven*, vol. I, pp. 9–10, July 1, 1837, Lieven to Guizot.

11. Guizot, *Lettres de Guizot et de Lieven*, vol. I, p. 15, July 3, 1837, Lieven to Guizot.

12. Guizot, *Lettres de Guizot et de Lieven*, vol. I, p. 15, July 3, 1837, Lieven to Guizot.

13. Guizot, *Lettres de Guizot et de Lieven*, vol. I, pp. 15–16, July 4, 1837, Lieven to Guizot.

14. Guizot, *Lettres de Guizot et de Lieven*, vol. I, pp. 15–16, July 4, 1837, Lieven to Guizot.

15. Guizot, *Lettres de Guizot et de Lieven*, vol. I, pp. 20–21, July 7, 1837, Guizot to Lieven.

16. Guizot, *Lettres de Guizot et de Lieven*, vol. I, pp. 15–16, July 4, 1837, Lieven to Guizot.

17. Guizot, *Lettres de Guizot et de Lieven*, vol. I, pp. 27–28, July 14, 1837, Lieven to Guizot.

18. Guizot, *Lettres de Guizot et de Lieven*, vol. I, pp. 30–32, July 15–17, 1837, Lieven to Guizot.

19. Guizot, *Lettres de Guizot et de Lieven*, vol. I, pp. 29–32, July 15–17, 1837, Lieven to Guizot.

20. Guizot, *Lettres de Guizot·et de Lieven*, vol. I, pp. 29–32, July 15–17, 1837, Lieven to Guizot.

21. Guizot, *Lettres de Guizot et de Lieven*, vol. I, pp. 29–32, July 15–17, 1837, Lieven to Guizot.

22. Aberdeen, *Correspondence*, vol. I, pp. 77–79, Aug. 9, 1837, Aberdeen to Lieven.

23. Guizot, *Lettres de Guizot et de Lieven*, vol. I, p. 43, July 21, 1837, Lieven to Guizot.

24. Guizot, *Lettres de Guizot et de Lieven*, vol. I, p. 45–46, July 21, 1837, Guizot to Lieven.

25. Guizot, *Lettres de Guizot et de Lieven*, vol. I, p. 52, July 29, 1837, Lieven to Guizot.

26. Lieven Papers, British Library, ADD. 47406, #16, July 8/20, 1837, C. Lieven to D. Lieven.

27. Guizot, *Lettres de Guizot et de Lieven*, vol. I, pp. 47–49, July 23–25, 1837, Lieven to Guizot.

28. Guizot, *Lettres de Guizot et de Lieven*, vol. I, pp. 47–49, July 23–25, 1837, Lieven to Guizot.

29. Guizot, *Lettres de Guizot et de Lieven*, vol. I, pp. 47–49, July 23–25, 1837, Lieven to Guizot.

30. Lieven Papers, British Library, ADD. 47406, #20–22, July 22–25, D. Lieven to C. Lieven.

31. Lieven Papers, British Library, ADD. 47406, #20–22, July 22–25, 1837, D. Lieven to C. Lieven.

32. Lieven Papers, British Library, ADD. 47406, #20–22, July 22–25, 1837, D. Lieven to C. Lieven.

33. Guizot, *Lettres de Guizot et de Lieven*, vol. I, pp. 64–65, Aug. 6, 1837, Lieven to Guizot.

34. Guizot, *Lettres de Guizot et de Lieven*, vol. I, p. 89, Aug. 28, 1837, Lieven to Guizot.

35. Guizot, *Lettres de Guizot et de Lieven*, vol. I, p. 97, Sept. 14, 1837, Lieven to Guizot.

36. Guizot, *Lettres de Guizot et de Lieven*, vol. I, pp. 156–157, May 18, 1838, Guizot to Lieven.

37. Guizot, *Lettres de Guizot et de Lieven*, vol. I, p. 79, Aug. 13, 1837, Guizot to Lieven.

38. Guizot, *Lettres de Guizot et de Lieven*, vol. I, pp. 20–21, July 7, 1837, Guizot to Lieven.

Chapter 22

1. Guizot, *Lettres de Guizot et de Lieven*, vol. 1, pp. 133–134, Oct. 13, 1837, Guizot to Lieven.

2. Guizot, *Lettres de Guizot et de Lieven*, vol. 1, p. 135, Oct. 13, 1837, Lieven to Guizot.

3. Lieven Papers, British Library, ADD. 47416, #52–54, Aug. 14/26, 1837, D. Lieven to C. Lieven.

4. Please see appendix.

5. Guizot, *Lettres de Guizot et de Lieven*, vol. 1, pp. 130–131, Sept. 30, 1837, Guizot to Lieven.

6. Guizot, *Lettres de Guizot et de Lieven*, vol. 1, p. 109. Sept. 18, 1837.

7. Guizot, *Lettres de Guizot et de Lieven*, vol. 1, pp. 121–122, Sept. 25, 1837, Lieven to Guizot.

8. Guizot, *Lettres de Guizot et de Lieven*, vol. 1, pp. 119–120, Sept. 24 1837, Lieven to Guizot, verbatim quote from Prince Lieven's letter.

9. Guizot, *Lettres de Guizot et de Lieven*, vol. 1, p. 127, Sept. 27, 1837, Lieven to Guizot.

10. Guizot, *Lettres de Guizot et de Lieven*, vol. 1, p. 132, Oct. 1, 1837, Lieven to Guizot.

11. *Vie*, pp. 178–179.

12. *Vie*, pp. 178–179.

13. *Vie*, pp. 178–179.

14. *Vie*, p. 180, Dec. 23, 1837, Lieven to A. Benckendorff.

15. *Vie*, p. 180.

16. *Vie*, pp. 182–183.

17. *Vie*, pp. 182–183.

18. Lieven Papers, British Library, ADD. 47406, #83–84, Oct. 16, 1837, D. Lieven to C. Lieven.

19. Lieven Papers, British Library, ADD. 47406, #83–84, Oct. 16, 1837, D. Lieven to C. Lieven.

20. Lieven Papers, British Library, ADD. 47406, #81–82, Oct. 15, 1837, C. Lieven to D. Lieven.

21. Guizot, *Lettres de Guizot et de Lieven*, vol. 1, pp. 147–148, Oct. 21, 1837, Lieven to Guizot.

22. Guizot, *Lettres de Guizot et de Lieven*, vol. 1, pp. 147–148, Oct. 21, 1837, Lieven to Guizot.

23. Lieven Papers, British Library, ADD. 47406, #104–105, Jan. 20, 1838, C. Lieven to D. Lieven.

24. Dorothée de Talleyrand-Périgord, *Memoirs*, vol. ii, p. 76, Nov. 1, 1836.

25. Guizot, *Lettres de Guizot et de Lieven*, vol. 1, p. 158, June 28, 1838, Lieven to Guizot.

26. Guizot, *Lettres de Guizot et de Lieven*, vol. 1, pp. 184–185, Sept. 3, 1838, Lieven to Guizot.

27. Lieven Papers, British Library, ADD. 47402, #56, Apr. 2 & 3, 1838, D. Lieven to C. Lieven.

28. Guizot Papers, Archives Nationales, dossier 2, #435, Oct. 4, 1838, Lieven to Guizot.

29. Lieven, *Correspondence of Lieven and Grey*, vol. iii, p. 259, March 2, 1838, Lieven to Grey.

30. Guizot, *Lettres de Guizot et de Lieven*, vol. 1, p. 182, Aug. 26, 1838, Lieven to Guizot.

31. Guizot Papers, Archives Nationales, dossier 2, Sept. 27, 1838, Lieven to Guizot.

32. Guizot, *Lettres de Guizot et de Lieven*, vol. 1, p. 187, Sept. 5, 1838, Guizot to Lieven.

33. Guizot, *Lettres de Guizot et de Lieven*, vol. 1, pp. 188–189, Sept. 5, 1838, Lieven to Guizot.

34. Guizot, *Lettres de Guizot et de Lieven*, vol. 1, p. 191, Sept. 7, 1838, Guizot to Lieven.

35. Guizot, *Lettres de Guizot et de Lieven*, vol. 1, p. 191, Sept. 7, 1838, Guizot to Lieven.

36. Guizot, *Lettres de Guizot et de Lieven*, vol. 1, p. 191, Sept. 7, 1838, Guizot to Lieven.

37. There is no evidence as to the precise circumstances of Prince Constantine Lieven's death.

38. Lieven, *Correspondence of Lieven and Grey*, vol. iii, pp. 281–282, Nov. 13, 1838, Lieven to Grey.

39. Lieven, *Correspondence of Lieven and Grey*, vol. iii, pp. 281–282, Nov. 13, 1838, Lieven to Grey.

40. Lamb Papers, British Library, ADD. 45556, #155, Nov. 14, 1838, Lieven to Cowper.

41. Lieven, *Correspondence of Lieven and Grey*, vol. iii, pp. 281–282, Nov. 13, 1838, Lieven to Grey.

42. Lamb Papers, British Library, ADD. 45556, #155, Nov. 14, 1838, Lieven to Cowper.

43. Lieven Papers, British Library, ADD. 47416, #139, Jan. 9, 1839, D. Lieven to C. Lieven.

44. Lieven Papers, British Library, ADD. 47416, #120–122, Aug. 1, 1838, C. Lieven to D. Lieven.

45. His illness is not known.

46. Granville, *Letters*, vol. ii, pp. 279–280, Jan. 1839, Granville to Devonshire.

47. Aberdeen, *Correspondence*, vol. I, pp. 123–124, Feb. 25, 1839, Lieven to Aberdeen.

48. Lieven, *Correspondence of Lieven and Grey*, vol. iii, pp. 302–303, June 26, 1839, Lieven to Grey.

49. Lamb Papers, British Library, ADD. 45556, #170, Aug. 18, 1839, Lieven to Cowper.

50. Guizot, *Lettres de Guizot et de Lieven*, vol. 1, pp. 266–267, Aug. 5, 1839, Lieven to A. Benckendorff.

51. Lieven Papers, British Library, 47368, #265, Apr. 16, 1839, Cowper to Lieven.

52. Granville, *Letters*, vol. ii, p. 292, Granville to Carlisle, July 23, 1839.

53. The National Archives of the UK: Public Record Office 30/29, Leveson-Gower, 1st Earl Granville and predecessors and successors: Papers; Subseries within PRO 30/29 Henrietta Elizabeth, Countess Granville, correspondence from Princess Lieven, 195, Sept. 13, 1839.

54. Guizot, *Lettres de Guizot et de Lieven*, vol. 1, p. 290, Sept. 19, 1839, Guizot to Lieven.

Chapter 23

1. Guizot, *Lettres de Guizot et de Lieven*, vol. ii, p. 255, Oct. 10, 1840, Lieven to Guizot.

2. Guizot, *Lettres de Guizot et de Lieven*, vol. ii, p. 188, Aug. 18, 1840, Lieven to Guizot.

3. Guizot, *Lettres de Guizot et de Lieven*, vol. ii, p. 243, Oct. 4, 1840, Lieven to Guizot.

4. Daudet, *À Travers Trois Siècles*, pp. 210–211, Lieven to Guizot, probably September 1840.

5. Lieven, *Unpublished Diary*, pp. 196–197.

6. Lieven, *Unpublished Diary*, pp. 198–199.

7. Guizot, *Lettres de Guizot et de Lieven*, vol. ii, p. 70, Apr. 6, 1840, Lieven to Guizot.

8. Guizot Papers, Archives Nationales, dossier 4, Apr. 14, 1840, Guizot to Lieven.

9. Guizot, *Lettres de Guizot et de Lieven*, vol. ii, p. 11, Mar. 3, 1840, Lieven to Guizot.

10. Lamb Papers, British Library, ADD. #175, Dec. 13, 1839, Lieven to Palmerston.

11. Guizot, *Lettres de Guizot et de Lieven*, vol. ii, pp. 116–117, Mar. 6, 1840, Lieven to Guizot.

12. Guizot, *Lettres de Guizot et de Lieven*, vol. ii, pp. 120–121, Mar. 8–9, 1840, Lieven to Guizot.

13. Guizot, *Lettres de Guizot et de Lieven*, vol. ii, p. 221, Sept. 24, 1840, Lieven to Guizot.

14. Guizot, *Lettres de Guizot et de Lieven*, vol. ii, pp. 26–27, Mar. 13–14, 1840, Lieven to Guizot.

15. Guizot, *Lettres de Guizot et de Lieven*, vol. ii, p. 92, Apr. 23, 1840, Lieven to Guizot.

16. Guizot, *Lettres de Guizot et de Lieven*, vol. ii, pp. 62–63, Apr. 4, 1840, Lieven to Guizot.

17. Guizot, *Lettres de Guizot et de Lieven*, vol. ii, pp. 67–68, Apr. 5, 1840, Lieven to Guizot.

18. Guizot Papers, Archives Nationales, dossier 4, Apr. 14, 1840, Guizot to Lieven.

19. Guizot Papers, Archives Nationales, dossier 5, May 4, 1840, Lieven to Guizot.

20. Guizot, *Lettres de Guizot et de Lieven*, vol. ii, pp. 25–26, Mar. 14, 1840, Guizot to Lieven.

21. Guizot Papers, Archives Nationales, dossier 5, May 4, 1840, Lieven to Guizot.

22. Guizot, *Lettres de Guizot et de Lieven*, vol. ii, p. 60, Apr. 3, 1840, Guizot to Lieven.

23. Guizot Papers, Archives Nationales, dossier 4, Apr. 14, 1840, Guizot to Lieven.

24. Guizot, *Lettres de Guizot et de Lieven*, vol. ii, p. 128, May 16, 1840, Lieven to Guizot.

25. Guizot, *Lettres de Guizot et de Lieven*, vol. ii, p. 135, May 18, 1840, Lieven to Guizot.

26. Guizot, *Lettres de Guizot et de Lieven*, vol. ii, pp. 133–134, May 18, 1840, Guizot to Lieven.

27. Guizot, *Lettres de Guizot et de Lieven*, vol. ii, p. 142, May 20, 1840, Lieven to Guizot.

28. Lamb Papers, British Library, ADD. #194, May 7, 1840. Lieven to Palmerston.

29. Guizot, *Lettres de Guizot et de Lieven*, vol. ii, p. 137, May 18, 1840. In this letter to Guizot, Dorothea included a verbatim quote from Emily's letter.

30. Emily Palmerston, *Letters of Lady Palmerston*, Sir Tresham Lever, ed., p. 229, July 17, 1840, E. Palmerston to her daughter.

31. Guizot, *Lettres de Guizot et de Lieven*, vol. ii, pp. 264–266, Oct. 20, 1840, Lieven to A. Benckendorff.

32. Palmerston, *Letters*, pp. 229–230, July 17, 1840, E. Palmerston to Mme. De Flahault.

33. Nesselrode, *Lettres et Papiers*, vol. viii, pp. 98–101, Dec. 26, 1840, Countess to Count Nesselrode.

34. Guizot Papers, Archives Nationales, dossier 4, Mar. 19, 1840, Guizot to Lieven.

35. Guizot, *Lettres de Guizot et de Lieven*, vol. ii, p. 261, Oct. 17, 1840, Lieven to Guizot.

36. Guizot, *Lettres de Guizot et de Lieven*, vol. ii, pp. 20–21, Mar. 8–9, 1840, Lieven to Guizot.

37. Guizot, *Lettres de Guizot et de Lieven*, vol. ii, pp. 270–271, Oct. 23, 1840, Lieven to Guizot.

38. Guizot, *Lettres de Guizot et de Lieven*, vol. ii, p. 272, Oct. 23, 1840, Lieven to Guizot .

39. *Selections from the Correspondence of the Earl of Aberdeen*, A. H. Gordon, ed., vol. xii, pp. 286–287, Feb. 25, 1857, Guizot to Aberdeen.

40. Guizot, *Lettres de Guizot et de Lieven*, vol. iii, pp. 65–66, Aug. 14, 1843, Guizot to Lieven.

41. Guizot, *Lettres de Guizot et de Lieven*, vol. ii, p. 243, Oct. 4, 1840, Lieven to Guizot.

42. Guizot, *Lettres de Guizot et de Lieven*, vol. ii, p. 216, Sept. 23, 1840, Guizot to Lieven.

43. Guizot, *Lettres de Guizot et de Lieven*, vol. ii, p. 238, Sept. 30, 1840, Lieven to Guizot.

44. Guizot, *Lettres de Guizot et de Lieven*, vol. ii, pp. 227–228, Sept. 27, 1840, Lieven to Guizot.

45. Guizot, *Lettres de Guizot et de Lieven*, vol. ii, p. 273, Oct. 24, 1840, Lieven to Guizot.

46. Guizot, *Lettres de Guizot et de Lieven*, vol. ii, p. 233, Sept. 29, 1840, Guizot to Lieven.

Chapter 24

1. Metternich, *Lettres de Metternich à Lieven*, p. 211, Feb. 21, 1819, Metternich to Lieven.

2. Aberdeen, *Correspondence*, vol. I, p. 194, Dec. 27, 1841, Lieven to Aberdeen.

3. Guizot, *Lettres de Guizot et de Lieven*, vol. iii, p. 167, May 13, 1845, Lieven to Guizot.

4. Guizot, *Lettres de Guizot et de Lieven*, vol. iii, p. 167, May 13, 1845, Guizot to Lieven.

5. "Comfortable with each other."

6. Guizot, *Lettres de Guizot et de Lieven*, vol. ii, p. 247, Oct. 5, 1840, Lieven to Guizot.

7. "Our place."

8. Guizot, *Lettres de Guizot et de Lieven*, vol. iii, p. 9, July 9, 1841, Lieven to Guizot.

9. Guizot, *Lettres de Guizot et de Lieven*, vol. iii, p. 17, Aug. 27, 1841, Lieven to Guizot.

10. Aberdeen, *Correspondence*, vol. 1, p. 199, Feb. 25, 1842, Lieven to Aberdeen.

11. Barante, *Souvenirs*, vol. vii, pp. 106–109, Aug. 26, 1844, Lieven to Barante.

12. Guizot Papers, Archives Nationales, dossier 6, Aug. 16, 1843, Lieven to Guizot.

13. Guizot, *Lettres de Guizot et de Lieven*, vol. iii, pp. 98–100, Sept. 5, 1843, Lieven to Guizot.

14. Guizot, *Lettres de Guizot et de Lieven*, vol. iii, pp. 98–100, Sept. 5, 1843, Lieven to Guizot.

15. Guizot Papers, Archives Nationales, dossier 6, Sept. 1, 1843, Lieven to Guizot.

16. Guizot, *Lettres de Guizot et de Lieven*, vol. iii, pp. 98–100, Sept. 5, 1843, Lieven to Guizot.

17. Aberdeen, *Correspondence*, vol. I, pp. 215–216, Oct. 1, 1843, Lieven to Aberdeen.

18. Princess Lieven's "resignation" letter is in the appendix.

19. Lieven Papers, British Library, ADD. 47415, #204, July 24, 1840, A. Benckendorff to Lieven.

20. Guizot, *Lettres de Guizot et de Lieven*, vol. ii, pp. 264–266, Oct. 20, 1840, Lieven to A. Benckendorff.

21. Lamb Papers, British Library, ADD. #257, Nov. 2, 1843, Lieven to Palmerston.

22. Lieven Papers, British Library, ADD. 47416A, #183–186, Oct. 1/13, 1843, Lieven to A. Benckendorff.

23. Lieven Papers, British Library, ADD. 47416A, #183–186, Oct. 1/13, 1843, Lieven to A. Benckendorff.

24. Guizot, *Lettres de Guizot et de Lieven*, vol. iii, p. 127, Aug. 3, 1844, Lieven to Guizot.

25. Guizot, *Lettres de Guizot et de Lieven*, vol. iii, p. 128, Aug. 5, 1844, Lieven to Guizot.

26. Guizot, *Lettres de Guizot et de Lieven*, vol. iii, p. 128, Aug. 5, 1844, Lieven to Guizot.

27. Guizot, *Lettres de Guizot et de Lieven*, vol. iii, p. 132, Aug. 6, 1844, Lieven to Guizot.

28. Guizot, *Lettres de Guizot et de Lieven*, vol. iii, p. 137, Aug. 11, 1844, Lieven to Guizot.

29. Guizot, *Lettres de Guizot et de Lieven*, vol. iii, pp. 125–126, Aug. 3, 1844, Guizot to Lieven.

30. Guizot, *Lettres de Guizot et de Lieven*, vol. 111, pp. 128–129, Aug. 5, 1844, Lieven to Guizot.

31. Guizot, *Lettres de Guizot et de Lieven*, vol. iii, p. 151, Oct. 10, 1844, Lieven to Guizot.

32. The National Archives of the UK: Public Record Office 30/29, Subseries Countess Granville, correspondence from Princess Lieven, 382, Oct 20, 1844.

33. Guizot, *Lettres de Guizot et de Lieven*, vol. iii, p. 156, Oct. 11, 1844, Lieven to Guizot.

34. Aberdeen, *Correspondence*, vol. 1, p. 234, Oct. 6, 1844, Lieven to Aberdeen.

35. Brougham Papers, University College London, Library Services, #40789, Oct. 24, 1842, Lieven to Brougham.

36. Guizot, *Lettres de Guizot et de Lieven*, vol. iii, p. 157, Oct. 11, 1844, Lieven to Guizot.

37. Guizot, *Lettres de Guizot et de Lieven*, vol. iii, p. 157, Oct. 13, 1844, Guizot to Lieven.

38. Guizot, *Lettres de Guizot et de Lieven*, vol. iii, pp. 126–127, Aug. 3, 1844, Lieven to Guizot.

39. Aberdeen, *Correspondence*, vol. 1, pp. 229–230, Sept. 1, 1844, Lieven to Aberdeen.

40. Nesselrode, *Lettres et Papiers*, vol. viii, p. 346, Sept. 20, 1846, Countess to Count Nesselrode.

41. Guizot, *Lettres de Guizot et de Lieven*, vol. iii, p. 171, July 30, 1845, Guizot to Lieven.

42. Guizot, *Lettres de Guizot et de Lieven*, vol. ii, p. 174, June 12, 1840, Guizot to Lieven.

43. Guizot, *Lettres de Guizot et de Lieven*, vol. iii, p. 182, Aug. 6, 1845, Guizot to Lieven.

44. Guizot, *Lettres de Guizot et de Lieven*, vol. iii, p. 195, Aug. 19, 1845, Lieven to Guizot.

45. Guizot, *Lettres de Guizot et de Lieven*, vol. ii, p. 192, Sept. 8, 1840, Guizot to Lieven.

46. Guizot, *Lettres de Guizot et de Lieven*, vol. iii, p. 209, Jan. 1, 1846, Guizot to Lieven.

47. Guizot, *Lettres de Guizot et de Lieven*, vol. iii, p. 209, Mar. 4, 1846, Lieven to Guizot.

48. Nesselrode, *Lettres et Papiers*, vol. viii, pp. 340–341, Aug. 30, 1846, Countess to Count Nesselrode.

49. Guizot, *Lettres de Guizot et de Lieven*, vol. iii, p. 67, Aug. 15, 1843, Guizot to Lieven.

50. The king promised that no son of his would marry the Spanish queen; if, however, she married and *had children*, Montpensier could marry the infanta. Victoria promised that England would not push Coburg.

51. Guizot, *Lettres de Guizot et de Lieven*, vol. iii, p. 230, July 27, 1846, Lieven to Guizot.

52. Guizot Papers, Archives Nationales, dossier 9, Aug. 8, 1846, Guizot to Lieven.

53. Boigne, *Memoirs*, vol. iv, p. 400.

Chapter 25

1. Lieven, *Letters to Holland*, Holland introduction, p. 1.

2. "Long live the Republic," "Down with the King," "Down with Guizot."

3. Guizot Papers, Archives Nationales, dossier 11, Feb. 2, 1848, Lieven to Guizot.

4. Lieven Papers, British Library, ADD. 47371, #238, Lieven to Meyendorff, undated but probably early 1848.

5. Lieven Papers, British Library, ADD. 47371, #238, Lieven to Meyendorff, undated but probably early 1848.

6. Guizot Papers, Archives Nationales, dossier 11, Feb. 29, 1848, Guizot to Lieven.

7. Guizot Papers, Archives Nationales, dossier 11, Feb. 29, 1848, Lieven to Guizot.

8. Thiers gave Princess Lieven's salon (also known as "the listening post of Europe") this nickname.

9. Metternich Family Archive, National Archive (Prague), AC-19-1, #9, April 26, 1848, Lieven to Metternich.

10. Princess Pauline Metternich, *The Days That Are No More*, p. 56.

11. Guizot Papers, Archives Nationales, dossier 12, Aug. 30, 1848, Lieven to Guizot.

12. Guizot Papers, Archives Nationales, dossier 12, Aug. 31, 1848, Guizot to Lieven.

13. Aberdeen, *Correspondence*, vol. ii, p. 327, Sept. 19, 1849, Lieven to Aberdeen.

14. Nephew of the Emperor Napoleon, he had been trying to orchestrate a return to the imperial throne for most of his adult life.

15. Guizot Papers, Archives Nationales, dossier 13, June 29, 1849, Lieven to Guizot.

16. Guizot Papers, Archives Nationales, dossier 13, Aug. 30, 1849, Lieven to Guizot.

17. Lieven, *Letters to Holland*, p. 47, Aug. 17, 1849, Lieven to Holland.

18. Lieven, *Letters to Holland*, pp. 37–38, May 23, 1849, Lieven to Holland.

19. Barante, *Souvenirs*, vol. vii, p. 440, Apr. 20, 1849, Sainte-Aulaire to Barante.

20. Dorothée de Talleyrand-Périgord, *Memoirs*, vol. iii, p. 283, Dec. 14, 1849.

21. Count Rudolph Apponyi, *Vingt-cinq ans à Paris*, vol. iv, pp. 447–448, April 5, 1852.

22. State Archive of the Russian Federation, 728, 1, 2396, #42–43, Apr. 15/19, 1850, Empress Alexandra to Lieven.

23. State Archive of the Russian Federation, 728, 1, 2396, #42–43, Apr. 15/19, 1850, Empress Alexandra to Lieven.

24. State Archive of the Russian Federation, 728, 1, 2396, #46–47, May 24/Jun. 5, 1851, Empress Alexandra to Lieven.

25. State Archive of the Russian Federation, 728, 1, 2396, #48–49, Dec. 5/17, 1851, Empress Alexandra to Lieven.

26. Aberdeen, *Correspondence*, vol. ii, pp. 373–374, Feb. 6, 1850, Aberdeen to Lieven.

27. Aberdeen, *Correspondence*, vol. ii, p. 376, Feb. 8, 1850, Lieven to Aberdeen.

28. Aberdeen, *Correspondence*, vol. ii, pp. 389–390, Feb. 10, 1850, Aberdeen to Lieven.

29. Aberdeen, *Correspondence*, vol. ii, pp. 402–403, Feb. 26, 1850, Lieven to Aberdeen.

30. Aberdeen, *Correspondence*, vol. ii, p. 494, June 20, 1850, Lieven to Aberdeen.

31. *Hansard's Parliamentary Debates*, 3rd series, cxii, p. 719, 38, vol. ii, p. 499, June 28, 1850.

32. Ashley, *Life and Correspondence of Palmerston*, vol. ii, pp. 149–151, May 24, 1850, Palmerston to Bloomfield.

33. Guizot Papers, Archives Nationales, dossier 15, June 11, 1850, copy of Emily Palmerston's letter in Lieven to Guizot.

34. Guizot Papers, Archives Nationales, dossier 15, June 11, 1850, Lieven to Guizot.

35. Guizot Papers, Archives Nationales, dossier 15, June 11, 1850, Guizot to Lieven.

36. Guizot Papers, Archives Nationales, dossier 15, July 6, 1850, Lieven to Guizot.

37. Guizot Papers, Archives Nationales, dossier 15, July 6, 1850, Lieven to Guizot.

38. Guizot Papers, Archives Nationales, dossier 15, July 6, 1850, Lieven to Guizot.

39. Lieven Papers, British Library, ADD. 47370, #8, Nov. 10, 1845, Meyendorff to Lieven.

40. State Archive of the Russian Federation, 2396, #52–53, Jun. 20/Jul. 2, 1853, Empress Alexandra to Lieven.

41. Guizot Papers, Archives Nationales, dossier 17, June 29 1852, Lieven to Guizot.

42. Guizot Papers, Archives Nationales, dossier 17, July 26, 1852, Lieven to Guizot.

43. Guizot Papers, Archives Nationales, dossier 17, June 7, 1852, Lieven to Guizot.

44. Guizot Papers, Archives Nationales, dossier 17, June 6, 1852, Lieven to Guizot.

45. Guizot Papers, Archives Nationales, dossier 17, July 29, 1852, Lieven to Guizot.

46. State Archive of the Russian Federation, 728, 1, 2396 #52–53, Aug. 14/26, 1852, Empress Alexandra to Lieven.

47. Guizot Papers, Archives Nationales, dossier 17, June 29 1852, Lieven to Guizot.

Chapter 26

1. Hübner, *Neuf Ans des Souvenirs d'un Ambassadeur*, vol. 1, p. 37.

2. Aberdeen, *Correspondence*, vol. ii, p. 642, Mar. 1, 1853, Lieven to Aberdeen.

3. Aberdeen, *Correspondence*, vol., ii, pp. 646–647, Sept. 8, 1853, Aberdeen to Lieven.

4. Lieven Papers, British Library, ADD. 47370, #165, Oct. 4, 1853, Lieven to Meyendorff.

5. Aberdeen, *Correspondence*, vol. ii, p. 654, Jan. 7, 1854, Lieven to Aberdeen.

6. Guizot Papers, Archives Nationales, dossier 20, Feb. 24, 1854, Lieven to Guizot.

7. Guizot Papers, Archives Nationales, dossier 20, Feb. 27, 1854, Lieven to Guizot.

8. Guizot Papers, Archives Nationales, dossier 20, Apr. 10, 1854, Lieven to Guizot.

9. Aberdeen, *Selections from the Correspondence*, vol. xii, pp. 286–287, Feb. 25, 1857, Guizot to Aberdeen.

10. Lieven Papers, British Library, ADD. 47342, #125, Mar. 1/13, 1854, Lieven to the Empress Alexandra.

11. Lieven Papers, British Library, ADD. 47344, #60, Feb. 3/16, 1855, Lieven to the Empress Alexandra.

12. Guizot Papers, Archives Nationales, dossier 20, June 11, 1854, Lieven to Guizot.

13. Charles Auguste Morny, *Au Temps de la Guerre de Crimée: Correspondance inédite du Comte de Morny et de la Princesse de Lieven*, Geneviève Gille, ed., *La Revue des Deux Mondes*, Feb. 1966, p. 340, Lieven to Morny, Aug. 10, 1854.

14. Lieven Papers, British Library, ADD. 47343, #46, July 12/24, 1854, Lieven to the Empress Alexandra.

15. Guizot Papers, Archives Nationales, dossier 21, Aug. 28, 1854, Lieven to Guizot.

16. Guizot Papers, Archives Nationales, dossier 21, Aug. 8, 1854, Lieven to Guizot.

17. Morny, *Au Temps de la Guerre de Crimée*, p. 343, Sept. 24, 1854, Lieven to Morny.

18. Guizot Papers, Archives Nationales, dossier 21, Sept. 28, 1854, Lieven to Guizot.

19. Lieven Papers, British Library, ADD. 47370, #118–190, Sept. 18, 1854, Lieven to Meyendorff.

20. In addition to the tsar, his Crown Council had only six other members.

21. Lieven Papers, British Library, ADD. 47370, #192–193, Oct. 3–14, 1854, Lieven to Meyendorff.

22. Guizot Papers, Archives Nationales, dossier 21, Nov. 7, 1854, Lieven to Guizot.

23. Lieven Papers, British Library, ADD. 47343, #183–187, Nov. 8/20, 1854, Lieven to the Empress Alexandra.

24. Lieven Papers, British Library, ADD. 47343, #183–187, Nov. 8/20, 1854, Lieven to the Empress Alexandra.

25. Guizot Papers, Archives Nationales, dossier 21, Nov. 19, 1854, Lieven to Guizot.

26. Guizot Papers, Archives Nationales, dossier 21, Nov. 20, 1854, Lieven to Guizot.

27. Guizot Papers, Archives Nationales, dossier 21, Nov. 23, 1854, Guizot to Lieven.

28. Morny, *Au Temps de la Guerre de Crimée*, p. 547, Nov. 13, 1854, Lieven to Morny.

29. Please see the appendix.

30. Lieven Papers, British Library, ADD. 47343, #191–193, Nov. 12/24, 1854, Lieven to the Empress Alexandra.

31. Lieven Papers, British Library, ADD. 47343, #195–198, Nov. 15/27, 1854, Lieven to the Empress Alexandra.

32. Lieven Papers, British Library, ADD. 47377, #224, Nov. 27, 1854, Lieven to Greville.

33. Guizot Papers, Archives Nationales, dossier 21, Dec. 7, 1854, Lieven to Guizot.

34. Guizot Papers, Archives Nationales, dossier 21, Dec. 7, 1854, Lieven to Guizot.

35. Guizot Papers, Archives Nationales, dossier 21, Dec. 9, 1854, Lieven to Guizot.

36. Lieven Papers, British Library, ADD. 47343, #223–226, Dec. 3/15, 1854, Lieven to the Empress Alexandra.

37. Lieven Papers, British Library, ADD. 47343, #223–226, Dec. 3/15, 1854, Lieven to the Empress Alexandra.

38. Lieven Papers, British Library, ADD. 47343, #223–226, Dec. 3/15, 1854, Lieven to the Empress Alexandra.

39. Guizot Papers, Archives Nationales, dossier 21, Nov. 29, 1854, Lieven to Guizot.

40. Guizot Papers, Archives Nationales, dossier 21, Dec. 16, 1854, Guizot to Lieven.

41. Guizot Papers, Archives Nationales, dossier 21, Dec. 17, 1854, Lieven to Guizot.

42. Lamb Papers, British Library, ADD. 45556, #318, 319, & 320, Dec. 21, 1854, Lieven to Palmerston.

43. Lamb Papers, British Library. ADD. 47369, #301, 302, & 303, Dec. 28, 1854, Palmerston to Lieven.

44. Guizot Papers, Archives Nationales, dossier 21, Dec. 27, 1854, Lieven to Guizot.

45. Guizot Papers, Archives Nationales, dossier 21, Dec. 28, 1854, Lieven to Guizot.

46. Lieven Papers, British Library, ADD. 47343, #234, Dec. 16/28, 1854, Lieven to Empress Alexandra.

47. State Archive of the Russian Federation, 728,1,2396, #52–53, Jun. 20/Jul. 2, 1853, Empress Alexandra to Lieven.

48. Lieven Papers, British Library, ADD. 47371, #6, Jan. 8/20, 1855, Meyendorff to Lieven.

49. Lieven Papers, British Library, ADD. 47344, #7–11, Dec. 29/Jan. 10, 1855, Lieven to the Empress Alexandra.

50. Lieven Papers, British Library, ADD. 47371, #3–5, Jan. 2/16, Lieven to Meyendorff.

51. Lieven Papers, British Library, ADD. 47344, #7–11, Dec. 29/Jan. 10, 1855, Lieven to the Empress Alexandra.

52. Lieven Papers, British Library, ADD. 47371, #11, Feb. 1, 1855, Lieven to Meyendorff.

53. Morny, *Au Temps de la Guerre de Crimée*, p. 555, Mar. 12, 1855, Lieven to Morny.

54. Guizot Papers, Archives Nationales, dossier 22, May 15, 1855, Meyendorff to Lieven, sent to Guizot May 25, 1855.

55. Lieven Papers, British Library, ADD. 47344, #116–121, Mar. 17/29, 1855, Lieven to the Empress Alexandra.

56. Neutrality of the Black Sea.

57. Lieven Papers, British Library, ADD. 47344, #116–121, Mar. 17/29, 1855, Lieven to the Empress Alexandra.

58. Guizot Papers, Archives Nationales, dossier 23, Oct. 4, 1855, Lieven to Guizot.

59. Lieven Papers, British Library, ADD. 47344, #226–227, Aug. 24/Sept. 5, 1855, Lieven to the Empress Alexandra.

60. Guizot Papers, Archives Nationales, dossier 23, Oct. 20, 1855, Lieven to Guizot.

61. Lieven Papers, British Library, ADD. 47375, #23–24, Oct. 16/28, 1855, Lieven to the Empress Alexandra.

62. Morny, *Au Temps de la Guerre de Crimée*, p. 559, Sept. 14, 1855, Morny to Lieven.

63. Kronstadt is the island fortress guarding the approach to St. Petersburg.

64. Lieven Papers, British Library, ADD. 47371, #104–106, Nov. 9, 1855, Lieven to Meyendorff.

65. Lieven Papers, British Library, ADD. 47345, #54–56, Nov. 14/26, 1855, Lieven to the Empress Alexandra. .

66. Lieven Papers, British Library, ADD. 47371, #121–122, Dec. 12, 1855, Lieven to Meyendorff.

67. Lieven Papers, British Library, ADD. 47371, #178, Mar. 3, 1856, Lieven to Meyendorff.

68. "Make fun of me."

69. *Greville Diary*, vol. ii, p. 528, Feb. 21, 1856.

70. Lieven Papers, British Library, ADD. 47345, #111, Feb. 2/14, 1856, Lieven to the Empress Alexandra.

71. Lieven Papers, British Library, ADD. 47378, #113–115, Feb. 15, 1856, Greville to Lieven.

72. Lieven Papers, British Library, ADD. 47375, #117–119, Feb. 9/21, 1856, Lieven to the Empress Alexandra.

73. Lieven Papers, British Library, ADD. 47375, #121, Feb. 13/25, 1856, Lieven to the Empress Alexandra.

74. Lieven Papers, British Library, ADD. 47375, #151–153, Mar. 19/31, 1856, Lieven to the Empress Alexandra.

75. Guizot Papers, Archives Nationales, dossier 24, #4504, Jun. 12, 1856, Lieven to Guizot.

76. Guizot Papers, Archives Nationales, dossier 24, #4539, Jul. 8, 1856, Lieven to Guizot.

77. Guizot, *Lettres de Guizot et de Lieven*, vol. I, pp. 67–68, Aug. 8, 1837, Guizot to Lieven.

78. Lord Edmund Fitzmaurice, *The Second Earl of Granville*, vol. I, p. 219, Nov. 24, 1856, Granville to Canning.

79. Lieven, *Letters to Holland*, p. 82, Jan. 1, 1857, Lieven to Holland.

80. Barante, *Souvenirs*, vol. viii, p. 155–156, Feb. 3 and 9, 1857, Guizot to Barante.

81. Barante, *Souvenirs*, vol. viii, p. 155–156, Feb. 3 and 9, 1857, Guizot to Barante.

Epilogue

1. Hübner, *Neuf Ans de Souvenirs d'un Ambassadeur*, vol. ii, pp. 6–7, Jan. 27, 1857.

2. Barante, *Souvenirs*, vol. iii, p. 155, Jan. 30, 1857, Barante to Mme. Anisson du Perron.

3. *Vie*, pp. 313–314.

4. Lord Edmond Fitzmaurice, *The Second Earl of Granville*, vol. I, p. 228, Apr. 8, 1857, Granville to Canning.

5. Rémusat, *Mémoires*, vol. iv, p. 41.

6. Viscountess Enfield, *Leaves from the Diary of Henry Greville*, vol. iii, p. 21, Mar. 20, 1857.

7. Lieven Papers, British Library, ADD. 47341, #78, Mar. 8, 1855, Tsar Alexander II to Lieven.

Select Bibliography

Archives

Papers of Princess Dorothea Lieven. The British Library, London.

Lieven-Brougham Correspondence. University College London.

Lieven-Granville Correspondence. The National Archives of the UK.

Lieven-Guizot Correspondence. Archives Nationales, Paris.

Lieven-Morny Correspondence. Archives Nationales, Paris.

Lieven-Palmerston Correspondence. Hartley Library, University of Southampton, UK.

Benckendorff Papers. Bibliotheca Nationalis Hungariae, Budapest.

Benckendorff Papers. Estonian Historical Archives.

Empress Alexandra Federovna's Letters to Princess Lieven. State Archive of the Russian Federation, Moscow.

Howard de Walden Private Papers. The National Archives of the UK.

Lamb Papers. The British Library, London.

Metternich Family Archive. National Archive (Prague).

Primary Sources

Aberdeen, Earl of. *Correspondence of Lord Aberdeen and Princess Lieven*. E. Jones Parry, ed. London: Camden Society, 1938–9.

Aberdeen, George Hamilton Gordon. *Selections from the Correspondence of the Earl of Aberdeen*. A. H. Gordon, ed. London: Privately printed, 1854–1858.

Apponyi, Count Rudolph. *Vingt-cinq ans à Paris*. Paris: Librairie Plon, 1913–1936.

Arbuthnot, Harriet. *The Journals of Mrs. Arbuthnot, 1820–1832*. London: Macmillan, 1950.

Barante, Baron de. *Souvenirs 1782–1866*. Paris: Calmann Lévy, 1897–1901.

Bloomfield, Georgiana, Baroness. *Reminiscences of Court and Diplomatic Life*. New York: G.P. Putnam's Sons, 1883.

Boigne, Mme. D. *Memoirs of the Comtesse de Boigne*. New York: Scribner's Sons, 1907.

Canning, George. *Some Official Correspondence*. E.J. Stapleton, ed. London: Longmans, Green, 1887.

Chateaubriand, Comte de. *Mémoires d'outre tombe*. Paris: Garnier Frères, 1850.

Creevey, Thomas. *Creevey's Life and Times, 1768–1838*. London: John Murray, 1934.

_____. *The Creevey Papers*. H. Maxwell, ed. London: John Murray, 1903.

Croker, J.W. *The Croker Papers*. London: John Murray, 1884.

Custine, Marquis de. *Journey for Our Time*. New York: Pellegrini and Cudahy, 1951.

Czartoryski, Prince Adam. *Memoirs*. London: Remington, 1888.

Ellenborough, Earl of. *A Political Diary 1828–1830*. London: Richard Bentley and Son, 1881.

Enfield, Viscountess. *Leaves from the Diary of Henry Greville*. London: Smith, Elder, 1883.

Golovine, Countess. *Memoirs*. G.M. Fox-Davies, trans. and ed. London: D. Nutt, 1910.

Golovine, Ivan. *La Russie sous Nicholas I*. Paris: Comptoir des Imprimateurs-Unis, 1845.

Granville, Harriet. *Letters of Harriet Countess Granville 1810–1845*. F. Leveson-Gower, ed. London: Longmans, Green and Co., 1894.

_____. *A Second Self: Harriet Granville Letters*. V. Surtees, ed. England: Michael Russell, 1990.

Greville, Charles. *Greville Diary*. New York: Doubleday, Page, 1927.

_____. *The Greville Memoirs: A Journal of the Reign of Queen Victoria*. London: Longmans, Green, 1885.

_____. *Memoirs*. London: MacMillan, 1938.

_____. *The Great World*. New York: Doubleday, 1963.

Grimm, August Theodor von. *Alexandra Federovna, Empress of Russia*. Edinburgh: Edmonston and Douglas, 1870.

Gronow, R.H. Capt. *Gronow's Recollections and Anecdotes*. London: Smith, Elder, 1864.

_____. *Celebrities of London and Paris*. London: Smith, Elder, 1865.

_____. *Last Recollections*. London: Smith, Elder, 1866

_____. *Reminiscences and Recollections 1810–1860*. London: J.C. Nimro, 1892.

Guizot, François. *Lettres de François Guizot et de la Princesse de Lieven*. Jacques Naville, ed. Paris: Mercure de France, 1963–4.

_____. *Mélanges Biographiques et Littéraires*. Paris: Michel Lévy, 1868.

Hansard's Parliamentary Debates. London: Baldwin and Craddock, 1829–1891.

Hodgetts, E.A.B. *The Court of Russia in the Nineteenth Century*. London: Methuen, 1908.

Holland, Lady. *Letters of Lady Holland to Her Son*. London: John Murray, 1946.

Holland, Lord and Lady. *The Holland House Diaries*. A.D. Kriegel, ed. London: Routledge and Paul, 1977.

Hübner, Count Joseph. *Neuf Ans des Souvenirs d'un Ambassadeur*. Paris: Librairie Plon, 1904.

Lieven, Princess Dorothea. *Correspondence of Princess Lieven and Earl Grey*. G. LeStrange, ed. London: Richard Bentley, 1890.

_____. *Letters of Dorothea, Princess Lieven During Her Residence in London (1812–1834)*. L.G. Robinson, ed. London: Longmans, Green, 1902.

_____. *Letters of Princess Lieven to Lady Holland*. A.E. Smith, ed. Oxford: Roxburgh Club, 1956.

_____. *Lettres de Princesse Lieven à M. Bacourt*. Comtesse Mirabeau, ed. *Correspondent*, Aug. 10, 1893.

_____. *The Private Letters of Princess Lieven to Prince Metternich 1820–26*, P. Quennell, ed. and trans.; D. Powell, co-trans. London: John Murray, 1948.

_____. *Unpublished Diary and Political Sketches of Princess Lieven*. H.W.V. Temperley, ed. London: Jonathan Cape, 1925.

Londonderry, Marchioness of. *Russian Journal of Lady Londonderry, 1836–7*. London: John Murray, 1973.

Malmesbury, Earl of. *Memoirs of an Ex-Minister*. London: Longmans, Green, 1885.

Maria Federovna. *Correspondence de l'Impératrice Maria Federovna avec Mlle. De Nelidoff*. Paris: Ernest Leroux, 1896.

Metternich, Princess Pauline. *The Days That Are No More*. London: Eveleigh, Nash and Grayson, 1921.

Metternich-Winneburg, Clemens Lothar. *Lettres de Prince Metternich à la Comtesse de Lieven*. J. Hanoteau, ed. Paris: Plon-Nourrit and Cie, 1909.

_____. *Mémoires, documents, et écrits, divers*. Richard Metternich, ed. Paris: n.p., 1880–84.

Meyendorff, Peter von. *Politischer and Privater Briefwechsel*. Berlin: Walter de Gruyter, 1923.

Morny, Charles Auguste. *Au Temps de la Guerre de Crimée*: Correspondence inédite du Comte de Morny et de la Princesse de Lieven. Geneviève Gille, ed. *La Revue des Deux Mondes*, Feb. 1966.

Nesselrode, Comte, ed. *Lettres et Papiers du Chancelier de Nesselrode*. Paris: Lahure, 1908.

Neumann, Philip von. *Diary*. E.B. Chancellor, ed. London: Philip Allen and Co., 1928.

Nicholas Mikhailovitch, Grand Duke, ed. *Scenes of Russian Court Life*. H. Havelock, trans. London: Jarrolds, 1919.

_____. *Rapports Diplomatiques de Lebzeltern*. St. Petersburg: Printer of State Papers, 1913.

_____. *Russian Portraits of the 18 and 19 Centuries*. St. Petersburg: Printer of State Papers, 1905.

Palmerston, Emily. *The Letters of Lady Palmerston*. Sir Tresham Lever, ed. London: John Murray, 1957.

Raikes, Thomas. *A Portion of the Journal*. London: Longman, Brown, Green, 1856.

_____. *A Visit to St. Petersburg*. London: Richard Bentley, 1836.

Raikes, Thomas, and Knight, Cornelia. *Personal Reminiscences*. New York: Scribner, Armstrong and Co., 1876.

Raumer, Frederick von. *England in 1835*. Philadelphia: Carey, Lea and Blanchard, 1836.

Rémusat, Charles. *Mémoires de ma Vie*. Paris: Librairie Plon, 1960.

Russell, Lord John. *Later Correspondence*. G.P. Gooch, ed. London: Longmans, Green, 1925.

Southey, Robert. *Letters from England*. London: Cresset Press, 1951.

Talleyrand-Périgord, Charles-Maurice. *Mémoires*. New York: G.P. Putnam's Sons, 1892.

Talleyrand-Périgord, Dorothée de. *Memoirs of the Duchesse de Dino*. Princess Radziwill, ed. London: Heineman, 1909.

Urquart, David. *Materials for the True History of Lord Palmerston*. London: Hartwicke, 1866.

Wellesley, Henry, Earl Cowley. *The Paris Embassy during the Second Empire*. London: Butterworth, 1928.

Wellington, Arthur. *Despatches, Correspondence and Memoranda*. London: John Murray, 1877–80.

_____. *The Eastern Question from His Correspondence*. London: John Murray, 1877.

_____. *Private Correspondence: A Selection.* The 7th Duke, ed. London: Dropmore Press, 1952.

_____. *Wellington and His Friends.* The 7th Duke, ed. London: Macmillan, 1965.

Westmoreland, Priscilla, Countess of. *Correspondence, 1813–1870.* London: J. Murray, 1909.

Wilmot, Martha and Catherine. *Russian Journals.* London: Macmillan and Co., 1934.

Secondary Sources

Airlie, Mabel, Countess of. *In Whig Society, 1775–1818.* London: Hodder and Stoughton, 1921.

_____. *Lady Palmerston and Her Times.* London: Hodder and Stoughton, 1922.

Alison, A. *The Lives of Lord Castlereagh and Sir Charles Stewart.* London: Blackwood, 1861.

Allison, J.M.S. *Monsieur Thiers.* New York: W.W. Norton and Co., 1936.

Argyll, Dowager Duchess of. *George Douglas, Eighth Duke of Argyll.* London: n.p., 1906.

Artz, F.B. *Reaction and Revolution, 1814–1832.* New York: Harper and Row, 1934.

Ashley, E., ed. *Life and Correspondence of Palmerston.* London: R. Bentley & Son, 1879.

Askwith, Betty. *Piety and Wit: A Biography of Harriet Granville.* London: Collins, 1982.

Aspinall, Arthur, ed. *The Letters of Princess Charlotte.* London: Home and Van Thal, 1949.

Aurenheimer, R. *Prince Metternich.* New York: Alliance Book Corp., 1940.

Bagot, J. *George Canning and His Friends.* London: John Murray, 1909.

Balfour, Lady Frances. *George, 4th Earl of Aberdeen.* London: Hodder and Stoughton, 1923.

Banac, Ivo and Bushkovitch, Paul. *The Nobility in Russia and Eastern Europe.* Columbus, Ohio: Slavica, 1983.

Bartlett, C.J. *Castlereagh.* London: Macmillan, 1966.

_____. *Europe's Balance of Power.* London: Macmillan, 1979.

Baumgart, Winfried. *The Peace of Paris, 1856.* Oxford, England: Clio Press, 1981.

Beik, Paul. *Louis Philippe and the July Monarchy.* Princeton, N.J.: D. Van Nostrand, 1965.

Bell, Robert. *The Life of George Canning.* New York: Harper and Brothers, 1846.

Benson, A.C. and Esher, Viscount. *The Letters of Queen Victoria.* London: John Murray, 1908.

Bernard, J.F. *Talleyrand.* New York: G.P. Putnam's Sons, 1973.

Billy, George. *Palmerston's Foreign Policy, 1848.* New York: Peter Lang, 1993.

Bingham, Madeleine. *Princess Lieven: Russian Intriguer.* London: Hamish Hamilton, 1982.

Bourke, Hon. Algernon, ed. *Correspondence of Mr. Joseph Jekyll.* London: John Murray, 1894.

Bourne, Kenneth. *The Foreign Policy of Victorian England 1830–1902.* London: Oxford University Press, 1970.

_____. *Palmerston, the Early Years, 1784–1841.* London: Allen Lane, 1982.

Brinton, C. Crane. *The Lives of Talleyrand.* New York: W.W. Norton and Co., 1963.

Broglie, Duc de. *Le Dernier Bienfait de la Monarchie.* Paris: Calmann Lévy, 1902.

Broglie, Gabriel de. *Guizot.* Paris: Perrin, 1990.

Broughton, Lord. *Recollections of a Long Life.* New York: AMS Press, 1910.

Bryant, Arthur. *The Great Duke.* London: Collins, 1971.

Buckingham and Chandos, Duke of. *Memoirs of the Court of England: The Regency.* London: Hurst and Blackett, 1856.

_____. *Memoirs of the Court of England: The Reign of George IV.* London: Hurst and Blackett, 1859.

Bullen, Roger. *Palmerston, Guizot and the Collapse of the Entente Cordiale.* London: Athlone Press, 1974.

Bulwer, Henry Lytton, Lord Dalling. *Historical Characters.* London: R. Bentley & Son, 1876.

Bulwer, Henry Lytton, Lord Dalling and Ashley. *Life of H.J. Temple, Viscount Palmerston.* Philadelphia: Lippincott, 1871.

Cavendish, F.W.H. *Society, Politics, and Diplomacy.* London: T. Fisher Unwin, 1913.

Cecil, Algernon. *British Foreign Secretaries.* London: G. Bell and Sons, 1927.

_____. *Metternich.* London: Eyre and Spottiswoode, 1933.

Chamberlain, Muriel. *Lord Aberdeen.* London: Longman, Green, 1983.

Cooper, A. Duff. *Talleyrand.* London: Harper and Brothers, 1932.

Corti, Egon. *Metternich und die Frauen.* Zurich: Europe-Verlag, 1948–9.

Crawley. *The Question of Greek Independence.* England: Cambridge University Press, 1930.

Crozals, J. de. *Guizot.* Paris: Société Française, 1890.

Cunningham, A.B. *Peel, Aberdeen, and the Entente Cordiale.* Bulletin of the Institute of Historical Research: University of London, 1957.

Daudet, Ernest. *Une Vie d'ambassadrrice au siècle dernier.* Paris: Librairie Plon, 1903.

_____. *À Travers Trois Siècles.* Paris: Librairie Hachette, 1911.

Delaforce, Patrick. *Wellington the Beau.* Gloucestershire: Windrush Press, 1990.

Derry, John W. *Castlereagh.* London: A. Lane, 1976.

_____. *Charles, Second Earl Grey.* Cambridge, Mass.: Blackwell, 1992.

Deutsch-Lettischen Beziehungen Baltisch. Leipzig: E. Hirzel, 1916.

Dixon, Peter. *Canning.* London: Weidenfeld and Nicholson, 1976.

Dolgorouky, Prince Pierre. *Notice sur Principales Familles Russe.* Osnabruck: Zeller Verlag, 1988.

Dupuy, Micheline. *La Duchesse de Dino.* Paris: Perrin, 2002.

Edgcombe, R., ed. *Diary of Frances, Lady Shelley.* London: John Murray, 1912–3.

Ellesmere, Lord Francis. *Personal Reminiscences: Wellington.* London: John Murray, 1904.

Elnett, Elaine. *Historic Origins and Social Development of Family Life in Russia.* New York: Columbia University Press, 1926.

Ferrero, G. *The Reconstruction of Europe.* New York: G.P. Putnam's Sons, 1941.

Fishman, J.S. *Diplomacy and Revolution: The London Conference of 1830 and the Belgian Revolt.* Amsterdam: CHEV, 1988.

Fitzmaurice, Lord Edmond. *The Second Earl of Granville.* London: Longmans, Green, 1905.

Florinsky, Michael. *Russia.* New York: Macmillan Company, 1955.

Fueter, E. *World History 1815–1920.* New York: Chautauqua Press, 1924.

Fulford, R.T.B. *George IV.* London: Gerald Duckworth, 1935.

Gash, Norman. *Mr. Secretary Peel.* Boston: Harvard University Press, 1961.

Gleig, G.R. *Personal Reminiscences of the First Duke of Wellington.* New York: Scribner's, 1904.

Goldfrank, David. *Origins of the Crimean War.* England: Longman Group, 1994.

Golovkin, Fedor G. *La cour et la règne de Paul I.* Paris: Plon-Nourrit, 1905.

Grimsted, Patricia K. *The Foreign Ministers of Alexander I.* Berkeley: University of California Press, 1969.

Grunwald, Constantin de. *Tsar Nicholas I.* London: Douglas Saunders, 1964.

Guedella, Philip. *The Duke.* London: Hodder and Stoughton, 1931.

_____. *Palmerston.* London: Ernest Benn, 1936.

Guizot, Guillaume. "Princess Lieven; biographic notice." *Biographie Universelle* v. 25, 1955.

Guyot, Raymond. *La Première Entente Cordiale.* Paris: F. Rieder et Cie., 1926.

Hayes, Paul. *Modern British Foreign Policy in the 19th Century.* New York: St. Martin's Press, 1975.

Hayward, Abraham. *Autobiography, Letters, Literary Remains of Mrs. Piozzi.* London: Longman, Green, 1861.

Hazen, C.D. *Europe Since 1815.* New York: Henry Holt, 1924.

Hibbert, Christopher. *Wellington.* London: Harper Collins, 1997.

Hinde, Wendy. *Castlereagh.* London: Collins, 1981.

_____. *George Canning.* New York: St. Martin's Press, 1974.

Hosking, Geoffrey. *Russia.* Cambridge, Mass.: Harvard University Press, 1996.

Hyde, H. Montgomery. *Princess Lieven.* Boston: Little, Brown, 1938.

Ilchester, Earl of. *Chronicles of Holland House.* London: J. Murray, 1937.

Ingle, H.N. *Nesselrode and Russia's Rapprochement with Britain.* Berkeley: University of California Press, 1976.

Iremonger, Lucille. *Lord Aberdeen.* London: Collins, 1978.

Jackson, J.H. *Estonia.* London: George Allen and Unwin, 1941.

Jelavich, Barbara. *A Century of Russian Foreign Policy.* Philadelphia: Lippincott, 1963.

Jennings, Lawrence C. *France and Europe in 1848.* Oxford: Clarendon Press, 1973.

Johnson, Douglas W. *Guizot.* London: Routledge and Paul, 1963.

Karpovich, M. *Imperial Russia 1810–1817.* New York: Henry Holt, 1932.

Knapp, John M. *Behind the Diplomatic Curtain.* Ohio: University of Akron Press, 2001.

Kornilov, Aleksandr. *Modern Russian History.* New York: Knopf, 1943.

Kuester, M.F. *Reminiscences of Baltic Germans.* Edmonton, Canada: Cent. and E. European Studies of Alberta, 1985.

Kukiel, *Czartoryski and European Unity.* Princeton, NJ: Princeton University Press, 1955.

Lane-Poole, Stanley. *The Life of Lord Stratford de Redcliffe.* London: Longmans, Green, 1888.

Leigh, Ione. *Castlereagh.* London: Collins, 1951.

Lenz, W. *Deutschbaltisches Biographisches Lexicon.* Köln: Bohlau Verlag, 1970.

Lobanov-Rostovsky, A.A. *Russia and Europe 1789–1825.* New York: Greenwood Press, 1968.

_____. *Russia and Europe 1825–1878.* Michigan: George Wahr, 1954.

Longford, Elizabeth. *Wellington.* London: Weidenfeld and Nicholson, 1972.

Malcolm-Smith, E. Benn *The Life of Stratford Canning.* London: n.p., 1933.

Marriott, J.A.R. *The Eastern Question.* Oxford: Clarendon Press, 1924.

_____. *England Since Waterloo.* London: Methuen, 1954.

_____. *George Canning and His Times.* London: John Murray, 1903.

Martin, Sir T. *Life of the Prince Consort.* London: Smith, Elder, 1877.

Marx, Karl. *The Story of the Life of Lord Palmerston.* New York: International Publishers, 1969.

Masson, C.P.F. *The Court of St. Petersburg.* Philadelphia: George Barrie and Sons, 1898.

May, A.J. *The Age of Metternich*. New York: Holt and Co., 1933.

Mazour Anatole. *The First Russian Revolution, 1825*. Stanford, Calif.: Stanford University Press, 1937.

Mirsky, Prince D.S. *Russia: A Social History*. London: Cresset Press, 1931.

Molloy, J.F. *The Russian Court in the 18th Century*. London: Hutchinson and Co., 1906.

Monas, Sidney. *The Third Section*. Cambridge, Mass.: Harvard University Press, 1961.

Monypenny, W.F. and Buckle, G.E. *The Life of Benjamin Disraeli*. New York: Macmillan Company, 1929.

Morton, Edw. *Travels in Russia and Residence in St. Petersburg 1827–9*. London: Longmans, 1830.

Mosely, P.E. *Russian Diplomacy and the Opening of the Eastern Question*. Cambridge, Mass.: Harvard University Press, 1934.

Murray, Venetia. *An Elegant Madness*. New York: Penguin Putnam, 1999.

Namier, Lewis. *Vanished Supremacies*. London: Hamish Hamilton, 1958.

Naryshkina, Elizaveta. *Under Three Tsars*. New York: E.P. Dutton and Co., 1931.

Nechkina, M.V., ed. *Russia in the 19th Century*. Ann Arbor, Michigan: Edwards Bros., 1953.

Neuschaffer, Hubertus. *Beitrage zur Baltischen Geschichte*. Hannover: Harro v. Hirshheydt, 1975.

Olins, Peter Z. *The Teutonic Knights in Latvia*. Riga: B. Lamey Edition, 1928.

Pallain, G., ed. *Ambassade de Talleyrand à Londres*. Paris: Flon, Nourrix, 1891.

Palmer, Alan. *Metternich, Councilor of Europe*. London: Harper and Row, 1972.

_____. *The Banner of Battle*. London: Weidenfeld and Nicholson, 1987.

Palmer, F.H.E. *Russian Life in Town and Country*. New York: G.P. Putnam's Sons, 1901.

Palmer, R.R. *A History of the Modern World*. New York: Alfred A. Knopf, 1956.

Pares, B. *A History of Russia*. New York: A.A. Knopf, 1953.

Parming, M.R. and T. *The Bibliography of English Language Sources on Estonia*. New York: Estonian Learned Society in America, 1974.

Parry, E. Jones. *The Spanish Marriages*. London: Macmillan and Co., 1936.

Parturier, Maurice. *Morny et son Temps*. Paris: Librairie Hachette, 1969.

Peel, George, ed. *The Private Letters of Sir Robert Peel*. London: John Murray, 1920.

Potiemkin, Victor. *Histoire de la Diplomatie*. Paris: Librairie des Medicis, 1946.

Prothero, G.W., ed. *Courland, Livonia and Estonia*. London: H.M. Stationery Office, 1920.

Purves, J.G. and West, D.A. *War and Society in the 19th Century Russian Empire*. Toronto: New Review Books, 1972.

Puryear, V.J. *England, Russia and the Straits Question*. Berkeley: n.p., 1931.

Pushkarev, S. *The Emergence of Modern Russia*. New York: Holt, Rhinehart and Winston, 1963.

Ridley, Jaspar. *Lord Palmerston*. USA: E.P. Dutton, 1971.

Rigby, Elizabeth (Lady Eastlake). *Letters from the Baltic*. London: John Murray, 1942.

Rollo, O.J.V. *George Canning*. London: MacMillan and Co., 1965.

Roosevelt, Priscilla. *Life on a Russian Country Estate*, New Haven: Yale University Press, 1995.

Russell, Rollo. *The Early Correspondence of Lord John Russell*. London: T. Fisher Unwin, 1913.

Sanders, L.C. *Lord Melbourne's Papers*. London: Longmans, Green and Co., 1889.

Sauvigny, Berthier de. *Metternich*. Paris: Fayard, 1986.

Schiemann, T. *Geschichte Russlands*. Berlin: Georg Reimer, 1913.

Schremmer, Berndt. *Metternich, Kavalier and Kanzler*. Halle: Mitteldeutscher Verlag, 1990.

Schroeder, Paul W. *The Transformation of European Politics*. New York: Clarendon Press, 1994.

Scott, A. MacCallum. *Beyond the Baltic*. New York: George H. Doran Co., 1926.

Seton-Watson, Hugh. *The Russian Empire*. Oxford: Clarendon Press, 1967.

Shumigorski, E.S. *Imperatritsa Mariia Feodorovna*. St. Petersburg: Tip. I.N. Skorokhodova, 1892.

Smith, E.A. *Lord Grey*. New York: Oxford University Press, 1990.

_____. *Wellington and the Arbuthnots*. London: Far Thrupp, 1994.

Smucker, S.M. *Life and Reign of Nicholas I*. Auburn, N.Y.: J.W. Bradley, 1956.

Sneyd, Ralph. "Notice of the Late Princess Lieven." *Philbiblion Society* v. 13, no. 4 (1871–72).

Soloveytchik, G. *Potemkin: A Picture of Catherine's Russia*. London: Butterworth, 1938.

Southgate, D. *The Most English Minister*. New York: St. Martin's Press, 1966.

Squire, P.S. "Metternich and Benckendorff." *Slavonic and E. European Review* XLV, no. 104.

Stanhope, Fifth Earl. *Notes of Conversations with Wellington*. London: Oxford University Press, 1938.

Stapleton, A.G. *The Political Life of George Canning*. London: Longman and Green, 1831.

_____. *George Canning and His Times*. London: J.W. Parker, 1850.

Stockmar, Baron. *Memoirs*. London: Longmans, Green and Co., 1872.

Strachey, Lytton. *Portraits in Miniature*. London: Chatto & Windus, 1931.

Sumner, B.H. *A Short History of Russia*. New York: Harcourt Brace, 1943.

Temperley, H.W.V. "Princess Lieven and the Protocol of 4 April, 1826." *English Historical Review* v. 39, London (1924).

Trevelyan, G.M. *British History in the 19th Century*. New York: Harper and Row, 1937.

_____. *Lord Grey of the Reform Bill*. London: Longmans, Green and Co., 1920.

Urban, William L. *The Baltic Crusade*. DeKalb: Northern Illinois University Press, 1975.

Urquart, David. *Materials for the True History of Lord Palmerston*. London: R. Hartwicke, 1866.

Uustalu, Evald. *The History of the Estonian People*. London: Boreas Publishing, 1952.

Uxkull, Boris. *Arms and the Woman*. London: Secker & Warburg, 1966.

Vane, Charles, ed. *Memoirs and Correspondence of Castlereagh*. London: Wm. Shorberl, 1853.

Waliszewski, K. *Paul the First of Russia*. London: Wm. Heinemann, 1913.

Walpole, Spencer. *Essays Political and Biographical*. New York: E.P. Dutton and Co., 1908.

_____. *History of England*. London: Longmans Green and Co., 1886.

_____. *Life of Earl Russell*. New York: Longmans Green and Co., 1889.

Ward A.W. and Gooch, G.P. *The Cambridge History of British Foreign Policy*. New York: Cambridge University Press, 1923.

Webster, Sir Charles. *The Foreign Policy of Castlereagh*. London: G. Bell and Sons, 1963.

_____. *The Foreign Policy of Palmerston*. New York: Humanities Press, 1969.

Willis, G.M. *Ernest, Duke of Cumberland, King of Hanover*. London: Arthur Barker, 1954.

Woodhouse, C.M. *A Short History of Modern Greece*. New York: Frederick A. Praeger, 1968.

Woodward, E.L. *Three Studies in European Conservatism*. London: Constable and Co., 1929.

Wortman, Richard S. *Scenarios of Power*. Princeton, NJ: Princeton University Press, 1995.

Wright, Gordon. *France in Modern Times*. Chicago: Rand McNally and Co., 1960.

Zamoyska, Priscilla. *Arch Intriguer*. London: Heinemann, 1857.

Ziegler, Philip. *The Duchess of Dino*. London: Collins, 1962.

Index

Princess Lieven's name is abbreviated to DL, Prince Lieven's to L

281